Marx Beyond Marx

Antonio Negri

MARX BEYOND MARX

Lessons on the Grundrisse

Translated by Harry Cleaver,
Michael Ryan and Maurizio Viano

Edited by Jim Fleming

AUTONOMEDIA / PLUTO

Published in the United States by
Autonomedia
55 South Eleventh Street
POB 568 Williamsburgh Station
Brooklyn, New York 11211-0568 USA

Published in the United Kingdom by
Pluto Press
345 Archway Road
London N6 5AA England

Printed in the United States of America

Library of Congress Cataloging in Publication Data

Negri, Antonio, 1933–
　Marx Beyond Marx.

　Translation of Marx oltre Marx.
　Bibliography: p.
　Includes index.
　1. Marx, Karl, 1818–1883. Grundrisse der Kritik der politischen Ökonomie. 2.
Marxian economics. I. Fleming, Jim. II. Title.
HB97.5 M3319 N4313　　1984　　335.4'12　　84-302
ISBN 00-89789-018-3
ISBN -936756-25-X pbk

British Library Cataloguing in Publication Data

Negri, Antonio
　Marx Beyond Marx: Lessons on the Grundrisse. I. Title. II. Fleming, Jim.
335.401
ISBN 0-7453-0575-X
ISBN 0-7453-0576-8 pbk

Originally published in French by Christian Bourgois, Editeur, Paris, France and
in Italian by Feltrinelli, Milan, Italy. Hardcover English edition published 1984
　　by Bergin & Garvey Publishers, Inc., South Hadley, Massachusetts.

Contents

Editor's Preface

This is an English translation of one of the most crucial documents in European Marxism since . . . well, since maybe ever. The work of Antonio Negri, as part of the variegated movement on the Italian left known most easily as *Autonomia,* brings to realization an overwhelming new set of possibilities in the theory and practice of class struggle. No political movement in the world in the 1970's opened up more revolutionary potential for liberation than the Italian *Autonomia,* and no expressions of its history exceed Negri's in transformative power and conceptual brilliance. This book, as nearly all of Negri's works, is intellectually demanding and often feels, to the casual reader, hermetic, precious and obscure. Partly, this is due to a set of counter-terms—precise and exact, but novel—that the "experienced" Marxist reader will find transgressive but revelatory. Partly, too, the difficulty of the book can be located in Negri's understanding of and respect for the political efficacy of language itself, an insight and attitude which may be the most common heritage of the post-war waves of structuralism, semiotics, and their antecedents. But partly this struggle-to-read induced by Negri is something like a process that might be called—in a metaphor of simultaneous separation and coherence—"conversion." The change—overturning, reversal, supersession, inversion—makes all the difference. But according to Negri, what's "beyond" is still, or finally, just Marx.

This book is the product of a series of seminars given by Negri in the spring of 1978 at the École Normale Supérieure at the invitation of Louis Althusser. More about this can be read in the author's own Preface to the original edition, which follows this Preface, along with Negri's later note (written from prison) to the American reader. The translation into English from the 1979 French and Italian editions was accomplished by Harry Cleaver, Michael Ryan, and Maurizio Viano. Each of them has written something for the reader of this volume. Harry Cleaver has aimed primarily at the militant and activist audience, and helps to point out the immediate and direct political consequences of Negri's work for present currents in the U.S. movement. Michael Ryan, in a broad summary of Negri's other work, offers a theoretical and historical context for *Autonomia,* particularly for readers previously unexposed to this tendency. Maurizio Viano provides a suggestive gloss on politics as creating, or imagining, or "fict"ing, with some hints about the redundancy, or monotony, or co-optive "centrality" of "scientific" texts, "socialist" above all others. Readers inclined to move toward these pieces first should do so at once, and read in any direction they choose. I will continue here with a brief glossary of some key terms, acknowledgements, and a note about texts cited in this book. But, owing to its absence elsewhere in English, and its usefulness for the events in the life of Negri subsequent to the composition of *Marx Beyond Marx*, a brief biography may be in order.

Antonio Negri was born in 1933 in Padua, Italy. At age 23 he graduated with a degree in philosophy and with a dissertation on German historicism. For the two years following, 1957–58, he studied with Chabod at the Benedetto Croce Institute for Historical Studies in Naples. In 1959—quite young, by Italian standards at that time—he won a professorship in Philosophy of Law. Until 1967, he was an assistant teaching at Padua, and in that year he won the professorship in Doctrine of the State. Married to Paola Meo, Negri became father in 1964 to a daughter and in 1967 to a son.

At Padua, beginning in the late 1960's, a group of reputable scholars began to form, coming to include Sergio Bologna, Luciano Ferrari Bravo, Ferruccio Gambino, Guido Bianchini, Sandro Serafini, Alisa del Re, and MariaRosa Dalla Costa (whose writings on feminist theory sparked an international debate). Their presence made the Institute for Political Sciences a national and international crossroads for radical thought.

In addition to his academic life, Negri maintained an intense political and journalistic commitment. By 1956 he was already the director of *Il Bo,* the journal of student representation at Padua University. In 1959, elected a municipal councilman for the Italian Socialist Party, he directed the journal of the Padua section of the Party, *Il Progresso Veneto.* He held this post until 1963, the year of the first center-left coalition (the alliance of the Christian Democrats and the Socialist Party in the Italian government), when he also left the Socialists. The summer of 1963 had been "hot." Veneto had undergone a rapid transformation from sleepy rural village into an urban, industrial center. In a period in Italy in which the Communist Party had turned towards external objectives (e.g., getting Italy out of NATO), the Italian working class was barely unionized and hardly organized. But it was among these workers that Negri had begun to move. In August, 1963, a supplement to *Il Progresso Veneto* was issued entitled *Potere Operaio* ("Workers' Power"). Also in that month, Negri, Paola Meo and Massimo Cacciari (a well-known philosopher and later parliamentarian for the Communist Party) organized a course to read Marx's *Capital* among the workers of the Porto Marghera petro-chemical center. In the same period, *Quaderni Rossi* ("Red Notebooks") was started in Turin, but with editorial boards also in Milan, Rome, and Padua. *Quaderni Rossi* was the magazine that, under the direction of Rainiero

Panzieri and Romano Alquati, first gave voice to the theory of working class autonomy. Negri, Sergio Bologna, Mario Tronti, Alberto Asor Rosa, and many other of the best Italian left intellectuals participated in its publication, and out of (usually friendly) splits in *Quaderni Rossi* there later appeared, in order, *Classe Operaia* ("Working Class"), *Contropiano* ("Counter-Planning"), and other journals addressing the same conceptual fields. By 1967, *Potere Operaio* had become the journal of the workers at the large Marghera petrochemical plant. Negri's collaboration there led to later collaborations on a regular basis with many other publications, like *Aut-Aut,* the philosophy journal edited by Enzo Paci, and *Critica del Diritto,* the journal of the democratic magistrates, which publishes essays on the philosophy of law.

The tumultuous year 1968, which brought near-revolution to France, began in Italy in 1967 and stayed for nearly a decade. Contrary to the experience elsewhere in Europe, where students and workers flirted but parted ways, in Italy the student and workers struggles merged. By the "hot autumn" of 1969, Negri had focused his political activities around the massified factory and around issues seldom adequately addressed by the unions: safety, reduction of speed on the assembly lines, worker discipline. The fall season of 1969 brought the formation of a number of groups to the left of the Italian Communist Party, with names like Lotta Continua ("Struggle Continues"), Avanguardia Operaia ("Workers' Vanguard"), Movimento Studentesco ("Student Movement," later "Workers and Students Movement"), and Potere Operaio. This political formation, after its journal, claimed Negri as its most famous theoretician. This group would survive until 1973, when—under the impetus of the Communist Party's "Historic Compromise" strategy of alliance with the ruling Christian Democrats—it led a number of similar but less developed groups into auto-dissolution.

By 1973, many of Negri's basic concepts had been formed, and it is from this period that the birth of *Autonomia* can be fixed, beginning with the "autonomous committees" inside the factories, which were now in large measure filled with a younger and more militant generation of workers, restless and hostile to all codified ideologies and parties, left or right. The refusal of the organizational forms born out of the sixties, now widely held to be sterile and repetitive, and the definition of new needs and objectives for liberating everyday life from labor time, were the themes that united disparate autonomous groups, groups otherwise very different in their practices. Women's groups, students, workers, radical youth, cultural figures, ecologists and environmentalists, "autonomous" collectives proliferated at the margins which remained invisible to traditional "working class" analyses. Free radio stations like "Radio Alice" in Bologna played a large role in the so-called Spring Rebellion, which brought many of these autonomists into the streets in protest of the politics of "austerity" and "sacrifice" that everybody—including the unions and the Communist Party—demanded of the "working class."

This protest touched Negri close to home. Demonstrations and rallies at the university in Padua brought disorder and much destruction, including materials housed in the Institute for Political Sciences. When the protests spread to other areas of the city, Negri was charged with inciting to riot and accused of being the fomentor of violence even up to the national scale. It was precisely at this time that Negri, in the face of intense political pressure and criminal charges, fled to Paris and the École Normale. Though in the later months of 1977 he was cleared of these charges, and by the year's end had returned to teach at Padua, Negri spent much of 1978–79 living and teaching in France.

Marx Beyond Marx shows all the signs of this period of tumult, but the subsequent months would have much, much more in store. Returning to Milan from France in April of 1979, Negri was arrested on unspecified charges in the context of the investigation of the death of Aldo Moro at the hand of the Red Brigades, another of the new groups formed in Italy in the 1970's, but one with which Negri had had no visible association. While many of the members of the Red Brigades could be identified in previous formations like Potere Operaio, the elite-style tactics and perspectives of the "armed commando" organization apparently had little in common with the participatory, autonomous "movement" groups. By the time *Marx Beyond Marx* was published (and moved onto Italian non-fiction "bestseller" lists!), its author was in prison, charged (finally) with "subversive association," although a number of other more grievous charges occupied the headlines of Italian newspapers. Nearly two dozen professors, writers, journalists, and other people identified with the *Autonomia* movement were arrested the same day Negri was, and soon found themselves being heralded as the "secret brains" behind the Red Brigades and virtually all "terrorist" actions which had occurred in Italy in the previous decade. In Negri's case, an early prosecution effort sought to claim that Negri's voice could be heard on a tape recording of a phone call made by the Red Brigades to Mrs. Moro while her husband, the former Prime Minister of Italy, was a kidnapping hostage.

The "April 7th" arrests, and particularly Negri's, were a media sensation and soon a "cause célèbre." Italy has, as a remnant of fascist legislation, never successfully or completely replaced provisions allowing for pre-trial detention in "normal" procedures lasting as long as twelve years. As the weeks and months awaiting trial stretched on, speculation increased that the penal system in Italy was being subjected to abuses of a political nature. There was little question in anyone's mind that Negri was a supporter of politics far to the left of the Italian mainstream, and even of the Communist Party (which had become one of the most vigorous sources of Negri's denigration), as any of Negri's writings would show. But the evidence, judicial and legal, of criminality was not forthcoming.

Negri remained in prison until the summer of 1983, when, in a campaign organized by the Radical Party, he received sufficient votes in a national election to lead the Radical Party list in the Italian Parliament. Another provision in Italian law, largely untested, allowed prosecutorial immunity to members of the parliament, and following contentious debate Negri was freed. He addressed public meetings in Italy in the late summer of 1983, while further parliamentary discussions took place over whether or not he would actually be seated. Finally, in September of 1983, as debate turned against him and he feared being returned to prison, Negri disappeared. Throughout the fall of 1983 and early 1984, it was widely believed that he had returned to Paris. Depending upon how one views political exile, the Antonio Negri of 1984 is either, or both, the Prisoner or Free Man of his Preface to the American edition of *Marx Beyond Marx*.

✱ ✱ ✱

A number of terms may be of use to readers unfamiliar with the general vocabulary of the *Autonomia* Movement. Owing to the distinct political traditions by region in Italy, and the workers' offensives resulting in the early 1960's from southern migration, the *Quaderni Rossi* quite early began attending to the *new composition* of the working class. Against the term "hegemony," which implied a static and passive working class determined by its relations to capital, *class composition* (and its *political recomposition*) refers to the process of socialization of the working class, and the extension, unification, and generalization of its *antagonistic tendency against capital*, in struggle, and *from below*. This search for a new, collective, working class subject, or agent of historical change, led to an attention to *cycles*, or progressively "higher," more socialized terrains of struggle, marked by different compositions of the class, different relations to organizational forms—like parties or unions—as well as new strategic contents or goals of "the revolution." Since many of the organizational forms addressed to the "mass worker" in the 1960's were seen as fully within the Keynesian strategy of planned development, "socialist" productivism, and the "value of labor," *autonomy* from the mediating forms of parties and unions was seen to correspond to the present cycle, one based on struggles against the extension or full socialization of capitalist relations beyond the factory, or struggles against the *social factory* or *social capital*. If socialism was the "realization of productive labor," in the Soviet phase, that led only to the "planned development of productive forces," or *capitalist socialism*. The latest cycle, however, would take as its goal the "realization of needs," and this would come through the *refusal of work*. If work by the worker was the source of surplus value for the capitalist—for Marx, labor has no value "outside" of capital—working class autonomy indicated the present path of departure or *separation* for the anti-capitalist struggle, one based not on the "general social interest" of need subordinated to labor, but *antagonistic* to and against the social whole. This *tendency,* through the refusal of work, was the overall orientation toward the strategy of *immanent communism.* In the absence of this strategy at this cycle of the struggle, communism could be indefinitely deferred. The movement toward communism would be a *class self-valorization,* one occurring as a struggle for *re-appropriation* of the class' material self-interest. Capital's response is, through the managed crisis, to revalorize work through *social command,* i.e., to enforce the wage-work nexus and unpaid surplus work over society by means of the State. This involves the "social worker," the extension of the "mass worker" into the sphere of the social reproduction of capital, or into *reproduction.* Battles here take place over "unpaid labor," housework, schooling, capitalist forms of sociality, anything which bears the work relation without the wage. In the productive sphere or in the factory, the struggle is for the "political wage," or away from hierarchical or divisive forms of qualification or renumeration. The way in which capital "manages" the crisis as a means to forcibly re-impose the wage-work relation is referred to as the *crisis-State.* This is a cursory introduction to a number of difficult and exacting concepts, and while it may help the reader through some passages of the present volume, it can hardly substitute for serious reading in the larger literature of *Autonomia.*

A bibliography of Antonio Negri's major work and of English-language work on *Autonomia* is found at the back of the book. Most readers might be best served by consulting first, for further reading or for assistance with this book, the fine anthologies edited by the Conference of Socialist Economists and Red Notes in Britain and by Semiotext(e) in New York.

The citations to the *Grundrisse* in this translation are to the Penguin Books edition, translated and with a foreword by Martin Nicolaus, published in Middlesex, England and New York, as well as Australia, Canada, and New Zealand. Citations occur in the form (*Grundrisse,* p. 543;441–43); the second page citation in each case is to the German edition of 1953 published by the Dietz Verlag, Berlin. Citations to *Capital* are to Volume One, introduced by Ernest Mandel and translated by Ben Fowkes, Vintage Books edition, New York. Where it has been published in English, the Marx/Engels correspondence cited in the text is from Saul K. Padover, *The Letters of Karl Marx* (Englewood Cliffs, N.J.: Prentice Hall), 1979. Where unavailable elsewhere, we have provided our own translation. Citations to Rosdolsky are to Roman Rosdolsky, *The Making of Marx's Capital,* translated by Pete Burgess (London: Pluto Press), 1977. Other citations from the Italian edition remain as cited by Negri himself: Vitalij Vygodskij, *Introduzione ai "Grundrisse" di Marx,* La Nuova Italia, Firenze, 1974; Sergio Bologna, *Moneta e crisi: Marx corrispondente della New York Daily Tribune,* in Bologna-Carpignano-Negri, *Crisi e organizzazione operaia,* Feltrinelli, Milano, 1974. The circumstances of the writing of the original perhaps necessitated a casual attitude toward some lesser references, and we have not sought to document further what the author felt no obligation to do himself. In this judgement, and in other matters generally about the merit of this edition, I bear the primary responsibility.

I would like to acknowledge here a number of people who were crucial to the work on this book. The greatest debt is owed the three translators, Harry Cleaver, Michael Ryan, and Maurizio Viano. Harry Cleaver also produced the index and did most of the proofreading. Sylvie Coyaud helped with innumerable matters related to publication rights and agreements. Jim Bergin of Bergin & Garvey Publishers was a prime mover in seeing the book to completion, as well as being committed to the subject itself. Ferruccio Gambino, Silvia Federici, George Caffentzis, and John Downing helped with translations problems, interpretations, gave advice or commiserated. Peter Bell produced a draft on which much of the Bibliography could be based. Peter Linebaugh helped conduct relations with Red Notes and the Conference of Socialist Economists in London, and Ed Emory and Les Levidow were better correspondents concerning this volume than was I. I also owe to Red Notes and CSE much help with material. The edition of *Semiotext(e)* edited by Sylvere Lotringer and Christian Marazzi was instrumental in getting the project off the ground. And Lewanne Jones made the project possible from the outset.

Note for the Paperback Edition

The bibliography of works in the Autonomist Marxist tradition has been revised, extended and updated for the Autonomedia / Pluto paperback edition.

The author remains in exile in Paris, where he continues writing, teaching, and organizing.

Additional thanks for assisting with this new edition go to Ann Beach, Roger Van Zwanenberg, Michael Hardt, Brian Massumi and Gayatri Spivak.

Author's Preface(s)

I

In these lessons I collect all the materials that I used for nine seminars on the *Grundrisse* at the École Normale Supérieure (Rue d'Ulm) in the Spring of 1978. First of all, I must thank Louis Althusser for inviting me to teach this seminar, which wouldn't have been possible without the fraternal help of Roxanne Silberman, Yann Moulier, Daniel Cohen, Pierre Ewenzyk, Danielle and Alain Guillerm. Whether my suggestions have been more important than their critical interventions, I don't know. It is certainly true that I have fused everything together into the text. Other discussions have been useful to me during my stay in Paris. On the one hand I would like to thank Felix Guattari for all that he gave me (and it is a lot), and on the other hand the comrades for whom I worked at the Université Paris Septième (Jussieu). Last but not least I want to thank those blockheads who, forcing me to emigrate, have also forced me to gather together my ideas better than I had the chance to do before.

A.N.
Milan, 1978

II

Author's Preface to the English language edition

Dear English language Readers,
You ask me to rethink for a moment *Marx Beyond Marx*. These are notebooks for lessons that I taught in the Spring of 1978 at the École Normale in Paris. It seems to me as though a century has passed since then. Looking back at

the book, I like it. But it is as though another person had written it, not I. A free person, while I've been in jail for centuries. I must then engage in a supreme act of abstraction in order to talk with the author of that book. The author is free; I'm a prisoner. I will try anyway, with great effort, to provide a dialogue between a free man, the author of *Marx Beyond Marx,* and a prisoner.

Free Man: "These lessons are just lessons, and they must be taken as a moment of reflection and of passage."
Prisoner: "This seems to me to be the case. It looks to me that when you were considering this passage and experience, it is as though they were very near, as though communism were already a living substance."
Free Man: "Certainly. I still think that. These lessons have many limits, but also a fundamental advantage: that of being fresh, non-polluted. This freshness might have led to an important development in the analysis, to a lush ripeness."
Prisoner: "A transitional work, then. But where did you want to go? Where would your revisited Marx have led you?"
Free Man: "Beyond the disfiguration of Marxism operated by Marxists. Marxism shows Marx as a professor and not as a militant. Moreover, Marxism shows us Marx as the author of the old competitive capitalism, incapable of coping with the social capitalism of the present stage. I hate this betrayal as much as I hate the mummification."
Prisoner: "I agree with you, and with your motives. But is it possible?"
Free Man: "Marx takes up the classic theory of value, but above all we find in him the critique of the law of surplus value. But Marx is not a classic, he is beyond all that."
Prisoner: "But the critique of the law of value, insofar as it presents itself as the law of surplus value, leads to catastrophism. Isn't yours just one extremist variant of Marxism?"
Free Man: "The critique of the law of value and/or surplus value has undoubtedly had catastrophist connotations, but these catastrophist connotations are kept at bay in *Marx Beyond Marx,* where what is insisted upon is the definition of the subjectivity of the passage to communism, as a process that develops concomitantly with the crisis of the law of value."
Prisoner: "I am probably in jail because I haven't understood this very well. Do you want to try to explain it to me a little better?"
Free Man: "Certainly. Marx's *Grundrisse* founds and undoes the law of value. In the *Grundrisse,* Marx appears as a communist militant who forces the theoretical limits of the classical analysis of value, and who justifies communist hope. He does not deceive himself as to the immediacy of the process, but he does clarify its subjective necessity. And you, my prisoner friend, are being a smart ass. If you didn't agree with this, why would you then endure prison?"

Prisoner: "I don't like argument *ad hominem,* always easy for those who are on the outside. In reality, here in jail, I am certainly subjected to both the law of value and the law of surplus value. Concretized in an immense system of domination, they weight on me in an unbearable way."

Free Man: "That of course is just what's said in *Marx Beyond Marx,* and I don't understand how you fail to realize that. The capitalist supersession of the law of value—what Marx calls the process of real subsumption—dislocates the relations of exploitation as a whole. It transforms exploitation into a global social relation. Jail equals factory."

Prisoner: "I don't need to be persuaded that the world is a prison, but how to get out of it?"

Free Man: "The great problem that is posed in *Marx Beyond Marx* is that of the definition of antagonism in this real subsumption. What does it mean to struggle against capital when capital has subjugated all of lived time, not only that of the working day, but all, all of it. Reproduction is like production, life is like work. At this level, to break with capital is to make a prison break."

Prisoner: "It seems to me that these so-called post-modernist theories disclose the social potency of capital, but by recognizing that capital occupies the whole of society, they deny the possibility of class struggle at this level."

Free Man: "Sure, the post-modernists mystify. In reality, the operation of real subsumption does not eliminate the antagonism, but rather displaces it to the social level. Class struggle does not disappear; it is transformed into all the moments of everyday life. The daily life of a proletarian is posited as a whole against the domination of capital. The real subsumption, far from eliminating the antagonism, immensely enriches it."

Prisoner: "Okay, critique of the law of value, its effectiveness only at the social level, the simultaneous displacement of domination and class struggle . . . Look, practically, how does all of this work?"

Free Man: "It works on the totality of everyday life: 'My life against yours, you dog of the social Master! My time against yours!' All the problems of exploitation are by now immediate political problems. Only when we keep in mind the critique of surplus value within the framework of the real subsumption, only then do we have the capacity for submitting to a communist critique the present fundamental plans for domination."

Prisoner: "Class antagonism in the post-modern world. Maybe you're right. Then it means, at this point, filling with a material content the struggle against power."

Free Man: "Precisely. In the conviction that the struggle against the capitalist organization of production, of the job market, of the working day, of the restructuration of energy, of family life, etc., all of this involves the people, the community, the choice of lifestyle. To be communist today means *to live as* a communist."

Prisoner: "This, I think, is possible even in prison. But not outside, at least until you free us all."
Free Man: "You're right. *Marx Beyond Marx* says this, too. But don't pretend to total impatience when you know very well that theory allows you to cope."

End of dialogue. Those who feel they remain alone naturally hope. Hope of having said the truth, and that the truth is revolutionary. An embrace for you all.

A.N.
Rebibbia Prison

Introduction

I

First and foremost, Antonio Negri's *Marx Beyond Marx* is a book for revolutionary militants. Formally, the book is a reading of Marx's *Grundrisse*— a sweeping reinterpretation of the central thrust and particular developments of Marx's 1857 notebooks. But it is more than that. *Marx Beyond Marx* is above all a passionately political work designed to present an alternative to orthodox interpretations of Marx by demonstrating how the *Grundrisse* contains a Marxist science of class struggle and revolution in action. To accomplish this demonstration, Negri weaves together a fierce polemic and a detailed examination and reinterpretation of the text itself. *Marx Beyond Marx* is a difficult book, and its difficulty creates the danger that its study will be limited to academic Marxists. This would be tragic. We have edited and translated this book, not to contribute another volume to the shelves of English-speaking Marxists, but to put a new and exciting weapon into the hands of working-class militants. However difficult *Marx Beyond Marx* may be—and its difficulty stems both from the raw complexities of the *Grundrisse* itself and from Negri's own theoretical language—its study is more than worth the effort to any militant seeking new ways to understand and use Marxism to come to grips with working class struggle in the present crisis.

For Negri, the *Grundrisse* represents the "summit of Marx's revolutionary thought"—a summit that can provide a powerful foundation for revolutionary political practice. He contrasts the *Grundrisse* to *Capital,* which, he correctly points out, has often been interpreted in an objectivist and determinist fashion to justify reactionary politics. Negri argues that it is harder to do this with the *Grundrisse.* In these notebooks, we discover a less polished but more passionate Marx, writing feverishly far into the nights of the crisis of 1857. The *Grundrisse* is no prelude to *Capital,* no rough draft of a later, more mature work.

Rather it is the *Grundrisse* that is the broader, more sweeping work, and it is here that we can find the richest, most complete working through of

Marx's understanding of the class struggle that both constitutes and ultimately explodes capitalism. In this, Negri differs from many previous interpreters of the *Grundrisse,* such as E. Hobsbaum or Roman Rosdolsky, many of whose positions he takes to task in the course of the book.

Negri begins his commentary on the *Grundrisse* noting how Marx's dissection of Alfred Darimon's theory of money was partly a pretext for Marx to explore the relationship between money and crisis, between money and the class struggle. Many who will read Negri on Marx may object that his interpretation of the *Grundrisse* is, sometimes, also a pretext to lay out his own analysis of the class struggle. He has, they may protest, taken from Marx only what suits him. As he works through Marx's notebooks, spurning a bit of analysis here (of productive labor), lamenting the absence of analysis there (the lack of a special chapter on the wage and working class subjectivity), dismissing other pieces as philosophical lapses (the general law of historical development) and marking many instances of ambiguity and of limitations to the analysis, it does become obvious that Negri has pieced together an interpretation of the major lines of Marx's argument through his own selective process. But we should not be afraid to pick and choose among Marx's ideas. This is what Marxists have always done, whether they are honest about it or not. Traditional Marxists have always focused on the objectivist elements of Marx because that fit their political proclivities. Critical theory seems to have ignored Marx's theory of the working class as subject because of a deep-seated pessimism acquired in a period of crisis. For those of us who share Negri's commitment to the constant renewal of revolutionary practice, we can focus on those elements of Marx that inform the analysis of our own struggles. Several generations of Marxists have given us the habit of perceiving the mechanisms of domination. What we need now is to use Marx to help us discover the mechanisms of liberation. We can leave to Marxologists the debate as to whether Negri is right about what Marx *really* meant. We can read Negri for Negri, and judge the insightfulness of his comments on their own merits. When, at the end of chapter 5, Negri questions the correctness of his interpretation, we are tempted to say it doesn't matter. If Marx did not mean what Negri says he did, so much the worse for Marx. This, it seems to me, is the only spirit that can take us along Marx's path in such a way that we can indeed go "beyond Marx."

Negri's reading of the *Grundrisse* is what I call a *political* reading in the sense that his work tries to show how each category and relationship examined by Marx, "relates to and clarifies the antagonistic nature of the class struggle." At the same time—and here is the domain of his polemic—he examines the meaning of the analysis for the political strategy of the working class. From the earliest chapters of *Marx Beyond Marx,* in his examination of Marx's analysis of money as a critique of power, we recognize that for Negri there is no separate "political" sphere in Marx. Understood as the domain of class struggle, politics is omnipresent; all of the categories are political. There is no need to riffle *Marx Beyond Marx* looking for the "political" passages. Every line is a political moment. There is a political excitement here that carries the reader forward, through the more difficult passages, toward ever more concrete analyses of the class struggle.

This approach is radically different from traditional Marxism, which has always treated politics as one subject among others, especially distinct from economics, and often carefully tucked away in the attic of the superstructure. Over the years Marxism has been all but sterilized by being reduced to a critique of capitalist hegemony and its "laws of motion." The fascination of Marxists with capitalist mechanisms of despotism in the factory, of cultural domination and of the instrumentalization of working-class struggle has blinded them to the presence of a truly antagonistic subject. The capitalist class is the only subject they recognize. When they do see working-class struggle, it is almost always treated as a derivative of capital's own development. The true dynamic of capitalist development is invariably located in such "internal" contradictions among capitalists as competition.

Negri's reading of the *Grundrisse* is designed to teach—or to remind— that there have always been not one, but *two* subjects in the history of capitalism. His political reading follows the chronological development of the notebooks on two interconnected levels; he simultaneously carries out an analysis of the political content of the categories and examines Marx's method at work in their development. On both levels he argues that what we observe is a growing tension between capital's dialectic and an antagonistic working-class logic of separation. The dialectic is not some metaphysical law of cosmological development. It is rather the form within which capital seeks to bind working-class struggle. In other words, when capital succeeds in harnessing working-class subjectivity to the yoke of capitalist development, it has imposed the contradictory unity of a dialectical relation. But to bind working-class struggle, to impose a unity, means that capital must overcome this other subject—the working class—that moves and develops with its own separate logic. This logic, Negri argues, is a non-dialectical one. It is a logic of antagonism, of separation, that characterizes a class seeking not to control another, but to destroy it in order to free itself. Two different logics for two different and opposed classes.

Negri shows that Marx saw clearly how the historical development of capitalist society has always involved the development of the working class as a separate and antagonistic subject—a subject which develops the power to throw the system into crisis and to destroy it. He points out how, in the *Grundrisse*, Marx is able to trace the simultaneous development of both subjects. At the same time that Marx tracks capital from its formal domination of production via money, through its direct domination of both production and circulation, to the level of the world market and crisis, he also simultaneously brings to light the growth of the working class from dominated living labor power, through its stage as industrial proletariat, to its full development as revolutionary class at the level of social reproduction. Two subjects, locked together by the power of the one to dominate the other, but never the less *two historical subjects,* each with the power to act, to seize the initiative in the class struggle.

What has happened to capitalist hegemony? To the objectivity of capital's laws of motion? To the location of the sources of capitalist growth in the competitive interaction of capitalists? From the point of view of the developing working-class subject, capitalist hegemony is at best a tenuous, momentary control that is broken again and again by workers' struggle. We should not confuse the fact that capitalists have, so far, been able to regain control with the concept of an unchallengeable hegemony. In a world of two antagonistic subjects, the only objectivity is the outcome of their conflicts. As in physics, where two vector forces create a resultant force whose direction and magnitude is distinct from either of the two, so too in the class struggle that constitutes the development of capital the "laws of motion" are the unplanned outcomes of confrontation. However, in the development of this clash of subjectivities the continual development of the working class from dominated labor power to revolutionary class (a growth in the relative strength of the working class vector) increasingly undermines capitalist control and imposes its own directions on social development. Because of this, competition among capitalists is less a driving force and more what Negri calls "sordid family quarrels" over which managers are at best imposing discipline on the working class.

It is this analysis of working-class subjectivity that infuses Negri's work with immediate relevance to those in struggle. In this period when capital is trying to wield fiscal and monetary policy as weapons against the working class, Negri's analysis helps us see that capitalist crisis is always a crisis in its ability to control the working class. A global crisis, such as the present one, Negri argues, can only be produced by the combined and complementary struggles of the world's working classes operating simultaneously in production and reproduction—at the highest level of socialization. In Negri's reading we discover all of this at that abstract and general level Marx could reach writing in the midst of crisis in 1857. But we can also examine these abstractions within the concrete determinations of our own situation and struggles within capitalism. Negri's work is clearly conceived with such a project in mind. And isn't this, always, the most exciting aspect of Marxism: its usefulness for exploring our own transformative power as living subjects?

The reading begins with Marx's own first notes: on money, money in the crisis, and ultimately money as power. Within and behind money Marx discovers value, and the social relations of production. At the social level money is (above all) capitalist power over labor. But capitalist power over labor is the ability to force people into the labor market, to force people to work for capital in production, and to coerce surplus labor in the labor process. What could be more relevant today, when capital is using monetary policy at both the national and international levels as a weapon against working-class consumption? Moreover, that monetary attack on consumption is aimed directly at forcing people to work, and at controlling the exchange between labor and capital so that profits (surplus labor) are increased.

Even at this stage Marx's arguments—and Negri's analysis of Marx—surprise us with their topicality, their ability to inform the present. Yet if Marx had stopped here, he would have been just one more Marxist peering deeply into the nature of capitalist exploitation. He doesn't.

As Negri points out, Marx is keenly aware that capital's power to extort surplus labor is a power exerted over an "other" whose own active subjectivity must be harnessed to capital's designs. Marx explored this subjectivity and saw that it fought the primitive accumulation of the classes: the forced creation of the labor market and the forced submission of people to the lives of workers. He explored this subjectivity and saw that *it struggles against being forced to work.*

Although he paints a true horror story of living labor being dominated by capitalist-controlled dead labor, Marx also makes clear that living labor cannot be killed off totally or capital itself would die. The irony of capitalist reproduction is that it must assure the continued reproduction of the living subject. The antagonism is recreated on higher and higher levels as capital develops. What begins as the horror of zombie-like dead labor being summoned against living labor, becomes, over time, an increasingly desperate attempt by capital to protect its own existence against an ever-more-powerful-and-hostile working class. Capital can never win, totally, once and for ever. It must tolerate the continued existence of an alien subjectivity which constantly threatens to destroy it. What a vision: capital, living in everlasting fear of losing control over the hostile class it has brought into existence! This is the peacefully placid capitalist hegemony of traditional Marxism turned inside out, become a nightmare for the ruling class.

When surplus labor (value) takes on its monetary form of profit, it becomes a socialized surplus value at the level of social capital. It becomes both a pole and a measure of the antagonistic development of capital. At this point the law of capitalist crisis emerges in the *Grundrisse* as the continuing contradiction between the working class as necessary labor and capital as surplus labor. The most fundamental dynamic of that law produces the tendency of the rate of profit to fall. This tendency, which has been for so long mystified by Marxists, becomes in Negri's interpretation of Marx an easily understood manifestation of the way working-class struggle blocks capitalist development. Although we can critique part of Negri's formulation (it is not necessary to argue that working-class struggle raises necessary labor as long as that struggle forces capital to raise the organic composition of capital through its relative surplus-value strategy), the basic thrust is keen and revealing. It is the continued working-class pressure on capital that accentuates the contradictions and creates crisis. Every time capital responds to workers' demands by expanding fixed capital and reorganizing the labor process, the working class politically recomposes itself in a new cycle of struggle. The full implications of this process become clear in Negri's reading of Marx's fragment on machines. We see how the frantic accumulation of fixed capital leaves less and less scope for capital to impose work and to extract surplus work, thus undermining the very basis of capitalist command. The more value capital sets in motion, the smaller the proportion of surplus value it is able to extort. Today, as capital proceeds to substitute ever more robot machines for increasingly threatened and threatening industrial workers, it faces the very problem Marx forsaw in the *Grundrisse:* a growing difficulty in finding new ways of putting people to work in order to control them socially.

This analysis of the working-class subject at the point of production is then displaced in Marx's analysis to the sphere of circulation. Here Negri carefully brings out Marx's argument that circulation is the sinew which organizes and ties together not only all of the separate moments of production, but also all of the social conditions of reproduction. Circulation involves the socialization of capital—its emergence as social capital. But again, we are not left with simply an ode to the comprehensiveness of capitalist hegemony. By exploring Marx's analysis of the two-sided character of the wage, Negri is able to bring out how the wage functions for the working class. This is the domain of small-scale circulation: of the exchange of labor power for the wage and the subsequent exchange of the wage for use-values—those products of necessary labor which satisfy working-class needs. The wage here appears as working-class power to impose its needs, and the extent of that power is only determined by the class struggle itself.

Once more we can study that unusual but inspiring vision of capital striving desperately to contain an autonomously developing working-class subject, hell-bent on the continuous extension and diversification of its own projects and needs at the same time that it increasingly refuses capitalist control via the imposition of surplus labor. Are we not, once again, at a most contemporary moment of the analysis? What were the 1960s and 1970s, if not a simultaneous explosion of both autonomous needs and of the refusal of capitalist work? What are the 1980s, if not a renewed capitalist offensive to contain the explosion of needs, to roll them back through a vicious attack on consumption, on the wage?

Negri argues that the analysis reaches its highest development in Marx at the level of the world market, where capitalist imperialism, fleeing the obstacles created by class struggle at home, spreads its class antagonisms across the globe. This is the moment of the world market, but also of the global factory and the international working class. From this point on, capital can only respond to working-class attack by reorganizing its modern industrial apparatus internationally and by attempting to reorganize the global reproduction of labor and the labor market. Is this not the present project of capital in the crisis? Is not what is called "reindustrialization" actually capitalist restructuration designed to decompose that working-class power which created the crisis, and to create new conditions for development? Certainly it is trying to do this, in many ways, in many countries.

But the crisis continues because so far capital has failed to achieve this decomposition. And that failure is simultaneously a measure of the power of the working class to protect the ground it has gained, and even, in places, to push forward its offensive. To listen to the droning litanies of traditional Marxist hymns to capitalist power is to be overwhelmed and exhausted by doomsaying. To read Negri—and through him, Marx—is to be invigorated with the sense of working-class movement and dynamism. It is to see the tenuousness of capitalist control and the real, tangible possibilities of its destruction!

At the end of this book Negri takes up directly the central issue raised by the emergence of working-class subjectivity: *revolution,* the end of capitalism, and the creation of a new society. The bulk of his discussion of these issues is reminicent of the *Communist Manifesto,* as he outlines the implications of his reading of the *Grundrisse* for the emergence of the new society— Communism (he retains Marx's word for it)—and rejects other contemporary positions.

In the language of traditional Marxism, revolution and the emergence of a new society has always been addressed as the question of the "transition": of the passage through socialism to communism. Negri argues forcibly that this is totally inconsistent with Marx's analysis in the *Grundrisse.* The only "transition" in that work is the reversal and overthrow of all of capital's determinations by the revolutionary subject. Because capital's central means of social domination is the imposition of work and surplus work, the subordination of necessary labor to surplus labor, Negri sees that one of the two most fundamental aspects of working-class struggle is the struggle *against work.* Where profit is the measure of capitalist development and control, Negri argues that the refusal of work measures the transition out of capital. The refusal of work appears as a constituting praxis that produces a new mode of production, in which the capitalist relation is reversed and surplus labor is totally subordinated to working-class need.

The second, positive side to revolutionary struggle is the elaboration of the self-determined multiple projects of the working class in the time set free from work and in the transformation of work itself. This self-determined project Negri calls *self-valorization.* Communism is thus constituted both by the refusal of work that destroys capital's imposed unity and by the self-valorization that builds diversity and "rich, independent multilaterality."

By this time it should be clear that Negri rejects "socialism" as, at best, an advanced form of capitalism. His major objection is that while socialism is understood as the planned redistribution of income and property, it invariably retains the planned imposition of work, and thus fails to escape the dynamic of capitalist extortion of surplus work and the subordination of needs to accumulation. Any existing socialist regime or socialist party program could be taken as an example. But the point is more than a critique of the Italian Communist Party's participation in the imposition of austerity, or of the Soviet labor camps. It is an affirmation that the concept of socialism has never grasped the real issue: the abolition of work or the liberation of society from narrow production fetishism. Socialism can only constitute a repressive alternative to the collapse of market capitalism—a more advanced level of capitalist planning at the level of the state. Today, when there is a growing "socialist" movement in the United States calling for national planning, the nationalization of industry, and "more jobs," Negri's arguments deserve the closest attention.

Negri also rejects all *utopian* approaches to the conceptualization of the end of capitalism. Very much in the tradition of Marx's own denunciation of utopianism, Negri refuses to think of the transition in terms of the achievement of some preconceived goal, however laudable. At this point scientific Marxism not only demands that the present movement be followed forward into the future, but, Negri argues, we must also recognize that this movement occurs without determinacy or teleology. In this interpretation of Marx we are simultaneously freed from the blinding romanticism of utopia and the paralysing weight of determinism. The central present movement that will constitute the future is that of the revolutionary subject as it reverses capital's determinations and constitutes its own self-valorization. The antagonistic logic of working-class separation reaches its conclusion as it explodes and destroys capital's dialectic. It explodes all binary formulae, as Negri says, bursting the dialectical integument and liberating a multidimensional and ever-changing set of human needs and projects.

As we discover the revolutionary subject to be both self-constituting and rich in multilaterality, we are also implicitly freed of the traditional organizational formula of the party. There is no place here for any narrow formulation of "class interest" to be interpreted by a revolutionary elite. There is only the multiplicity of autonomously-determined needs and projects. Although Negri does not take up the issue of revolutionary organization here—it is not his project at this point—he does strongly reject one variant on the party theme: a voluntarist violence that only negates capitalist violence, which by not being organized on the material basis of revolutionary self-valorization falls into *terrorism*. This is one of the many points in his work that shows his distance from and antagonism toward those armed "vanguards" with which the Italian state has sought to associate him as an excuse for imprisoning him.

To sum up Negri's exposition of Marx's line of argument in the *Grundrisse:* capitalism is a social system with *two subjectivities,* in which one subject (capital) controls the other subject (working class) through the *imposition of work* and surplus work. The logic of this control is the *dialectic* which constrains human development within the limits of capitalist valorization. Therefore, the central struggle of the working class as independent subject is to break capitalist control through the *refusal of work.* The logic of this refusal is the logic of antagonistic *separation* and its realization undermines and destroys capital's dialectic. In the space gained by this destruction the revolutionary class builds its own independent projects—its own *self-valorization. Revolution* then is the simultaneous overthrow of capital and the *constitution of a new society: Communism.* The refusal of work becomes the planned abolition of work as the basis of the constitution of a new mode of producing a new multidimensional society.

What are the implications of learning to read the categories of Marx's analysis politically? For one thing we can now readdress the question of *Capital.* Negri is absolutely correct when he points out that *Capital* has often been interpreted in an objectivist fashion. But it should now be clear that there is an alternative. Once we have learned to recognize and avoid the traps of objectivism and to carry out a political or class analysis of Marx's categories, we can read *Capital* (or any of Marx's writings) in this manner. There are many aspects of Marx's analysis in the *Grundrisse* which are more carefully and fully explored in *Capital.* Certainly we can gain from the study of this material. When we do read *Capital* politically, as I have tried to do elsewhere, we generate an interpretation that is not only largely consistent with the main lines of Negri's book, but which sharpens and enriches the analysis—the fruit of the ten years of Marx's work from 1857 to 1867, when the first volume of *Capital* appeared.

We follow Marx's path "beyond Marx" when we read Marx politically, from within the class struggle, and when we critique Marx from the vantage point of our own needs. It is precisely this kind of reading and critique that Negri has carried out. It is this that makes his work valuable and exciting.

Harry Cleaver

II

Marx Beyond Marx cannot be fully understood apart from its historical and its theoretical context. In the conclusion which follows the translation, I will describe those other writings of Negri's that provide a theoretical context for the book. Here, I will give a very brief description of the historical context as well as a short definition of the notion of "autonomy."

The "extra-parliamentary" life in Italy (as opposed to the communist and socialist parties, which engage in parliamentary activity) took off in the early 60s with the publication of the journal *Quaderni Rossi* and of the newspaper *Classe operaia;* the theoreticians were Mario Tronti, Raniero Panzieri, Sergio Bologna, and Antonio Negri. (In 1967, Tronti joined the Communist Party.) At this time also, a new militancy began to emerge in the factories, after a lengthy period of labor peace in the 50s. The extra-parliamentary or leftist critique in the 60s was directed against the "State-as-Planner," because with the center-left coalition government of 1965, a first attempt was made in Italy to introduce Keynesian planning. The leftist critics opposed the notion that capitalism was a form of mis-planning which could be corrected by planning; the focus of their analyses was the mass worker. The student movement of the late 60s, combined with an explosion of independent workers' uprisings in the factories (especially the automobile plants), led to the formation of *Potere operaia* (workers' power), as well as other groups such as *Lotta continua* (continuous struggle) and *il Manifesto.* The slogans of *Potere operaia* were the "refusal of work" (empirically, as absenteeism and sabotage, and in principle, as the denial of the law of value which establishes a false equivalence between hours worked and wages paid, while operating a real disequivalence of wages paid and value produced), and the "political" or "social" wage, a call for greater wages independent of productivity. It called itself "the party of insurrection." In 1970, an economic as well as a police crackdown against the movement began. By 1973, there was a great deal of repression in the factories. In 1974, the oil crisis began to be used against the workers, creating a large amount of unemployment for the first time in post-war Italy. In 1973, *Potere operaia* dissolved, and the Autonomy Movement as such came into being. (See the journal *Potere operaia,* anno v, no. 50 (November 1973). for an account of the break-up.)

At this time, theoreticians like Negri began to speak of the end of the law of value, of the replacement of capitalist exploitation by capitalist domination. The struggle was now purely political. The capital-labor nexus was no longer defined by the democratic model of exchange, but instead by a direct relation of force. At this point as well, Negri began to formulate the concept of the "social worker," made up not only of industrial workers, but also of youth, students, under- and unemployed. (Women as houseworkers were also included in this category, but they were never seen in any broader sense than simply as unemployed or non-waged. For a discussion of this issue, see *"le operaie della casa," rivista dell'autonomia femminista,* bimestriale no. 4 (Jan-Apr 1977).) The political or social wage became the hinge for bringing together factory workers and unemployed. This formulation of a different revolutionary subject was seen as necessary because the emphasis on industrial workers' wage struggles during the 60s was made ineffective by the capitalists' use of inflation, the raising of the costs of reproducing labor-power. Hence, the struggles had to be broadened to include the self-reduction of energy costs, political shopping (the direct appropriation of wealth), public spending, services. The sphere of reproduction became a terrain of struggle. (This shift explains the importance at this time of Jim O'Connor's *Fiscal Crisis of the State* for the Italian movement.) In addition, the new strategy was meant to counter the CPI ideology of "productive labor" which meant that the party supported capitalist development because it eventually led to the betterment of productive workers. The sector of under- and unemployed were ignored by the party, which accepted austerity programs (cuts in public spending that negatively affected the unemployed) for the sake of greater efficiency for more capitalist development.

There were no major developments until 1975, a watershed year which marked the defeat of Autonomy's old slogans. The call for more money for less work no longer succeeded because the level of power of the workers had diminished. Inflation and escalating unemployment were taking their toll. In addition, new levels of repression were reached, and an attempted coup made fascism seem a real alternative. A new social subject emerged, epitomized by the neo-hippie metropolitan Indians. This subject was characterized by an emphasis on drugs, communes, needs, and alternate forms of survival. It rejected discipline, leadership, and theory. Along with the women's movement, it marked a major departure from the traditional leftist model of organization. These developments provoked a change of line in the Autonomy Movement.

The faction led by Negri was less Leninist; the one led by Franco Piperno more Leninist. Negri argued that it was no longer possible to bargain in the factory; one could only resort to force because the relation with the state was now a pure relation of force. He called for the direct takeover of the state. One should not bargain around work, he argued, but instead take over the factories, exercise counter-power by creating liberated zones that would free the productive forces and prefigure communism. The call to refuse work was muted because the law of value, the regulator of work, no longer held. Capital no longer needed workers because technology made workers dispensable. The importance of the strike was neutralized by the ability of machines to replace workers. Negri's new strategic formula was "self-valorization," that is, working for oneself as a class, asserting one's own needs as primary to capital's need for value. In many ways, self-valorization gives theoretical expression to the programs of the newly emergent social subjects of the late 70s. The last great wave of militancy on the part of the Autonomy Movement occurred in 1977; the direct repression of the movement through the imprisonment of its leaders came in 1979.

The extra-parliamentary movement, of which the Autonomy Movement is a part, is situated within the larger communist tradition, but it also marks a denial of that tradition. The important concept for understanding that denial is the refusal of work, which is directed in part against Leninism (which represents the Taylorization and non-liberation of work) and Third International socialism, which merely represents capitalist development in a different form. Autonomy, as a movement and as a theory, opposes the notion that capitalism is an irrational system which can be made rational through planning. Instead, it assumes the workers' viewpoint, privileging their activity as the lever of revolutionary passage and as that which alone can construct a communist society. Economics is seen as being entirely political; economic relations are direct political relations of force between class subjects. And it is in the economic category of the social worker, not in an alienated political form like the party, that the initiative for political change resides. The word "autonomy" must be understood in light of this historical and theoretical context. It names a combination of rank-and-file radicalism with sphere-of-reproduction activism. The word "autonomy" at first named the independence and separation of the working class from capitalist development. By privileging itself, by valorizing its own needs, the class could subvert the valorization of capital, which is dependent on the subordination of workers. The word has acquired the additional meaning of that area of proletarian concerns, struggles, and organizations which is independent of the sanctioned institutions of the "productive" working class—the unions and the political parties. And, finally, autonomy names the chief characteristic of the subject in the communist society which it constitutes from its own multilateral productive potential.

Michael Ryan

III

After Harry Cleaver has shown the militant weight of these nine lessons, and after Michael Ryan has outlined the historical and textual growth of Negri's writings, both in his introduction and Epilogue, I feel that my introductory task is less that of prescriptive information than of informal provocation. Astride an imaginary border between the U.S. and Italy, I'll call forth (pro-vocare) the voices, or, better, *some* voices I hear coming from both directions. Therefore this will be neither the offer of the most appropriate political reading, nor the offer of the connections between *Marx Beyond Marx* and other cultural objects in the attempt to materialize a context, in the illusion of exhausting the totality of the determinations of the text. What is, in fact, the purpose of a context if not that of encircling a space where the pieces will all fit as if the articulations—at least the ones that matter in academic studies—could at some point be all present, all there, to allow the "correct" reading which reifies a text against any subjective appropriation? Not a context, then, but a pretext, not information but provocation; the motion of my words won't be that of a linear, consequential exposition, but it will be that of an apparently erratic wandering.

To wander is the activity of those who turn away from accepted beliefs and extend in an irregular course; to wander is the activity of those who do not have a fixed destination, and yet despise immobility. It seems that Spinoza, too, wandered against the grain of contemporary institutions, until he envisaged the illegitimate union of a negative throught ("pars destruens") with a constituting praxis. And it can be said that even Marx was wandering, in search of "Man," when he visualized the multidirectionality of communism. It is thus crucial to understand that Negri is also wandering, beyond the margins of an orthodox philosophizing, in an uneasy balance between the stillness of a satisfied ontology and the teleology of those who move as if they possessed the correct coordinates.

To wander then: blind to the glamorous colors of the party lines which, like neon banners, polarize and deceive the eyes, I'll try to record the sounds which can better accompany, as a soundtrack, the images that my words bead together. And my ears, cocked to catch the voices coming from both countries, are immediately attracted by the relentless humming of the institutionalized media in Italy which—by virtue of the monopoly of the channels—can conceive themselves as the "vox populi" and really constitute the totality of the information upon which the public opinion is formed.

A typical example of this media effect comes to us in these very days I'm writing this introduction: newspapers and T.V. stations emphasize the arrest of Franco Piperno in Canada and report "impartially" the charges against him, while defining him as the leader, or one of the leaders, of *Autonomia*. Again, then, terrorism and *Autonomia* are linked by the news-makers; again the collective imaginary of the nation is shaped in the direction of an association between *Autonomia* and Red Brigades; again the public opinion is brought to problematize *Autonomia,* to perceive it as a front-page threat. The press from Right to Left insists in visualizing and talking about an attack on the institutions that terrorists have allegedly announced for the fall, after a summer break: "The Red Brigades, what are they preparing? Who'll defend us?" says the front-page cover of the widely read, "progressive" magazine *Espresso.* Aside from the ridiculous notion that even terrorists would take a summer vacation (a notion that reinforces the supposed "naturalness" of the Italian rhythm of life), the practical result of all this is the preparation of the terrain for a series of "preventative" police operations aimed at "defending" the people against all the militants who aren't in jail yet. Countless exponents of *Autonomia* are in jail, to the general indifference of the so-called "democratic forces," precisely as a consequence of terroristic operations like this; where terrorism—let it be clear—means the practice of throwing the population into the irrational claws of terror; a terror which demonizes exclusively and loudly certain political fractions and ignores the wider social determinants that call for a radical militancy (and within such a militancy the existence of a violent, "infantile" wing is rather unavoidable) in this country. A country where people die daily of mafia executions, where scandals and corruption find the people so used to them that they are no longer news, where indifferent, metropolitan violence is slowly changing social life, where, as Bifo puts it, "the law turns into a combination of emergency and mass media, exists in the form of emergency as it becomes identified with the mass media, is the one in virtue of being the other." And it does not make any difference if the Autonomists and the later movements such as the powerful Neapolitan C.D.O. (Committee of Organized Unemployed Workers) reject openly the strategy of the armed groups and define them as "armed reformists," thus indicating a connivance between the Red Brigades and the State, both a centralized power deciding from above what people's needs are. It does not make any difference, because the target is not the armed struggle but the social antagonism.

In the flat, inquisitorial chorus with which the media punctuate the Italian tragedy we discern distinct, cyclical references to Toni Negri. And they have been so insistent, so presumptuous in *the* reconstruction of events that echoes have bounced beyond the Atlantic and a counterpoint can be heard in the U.S., even though the American ideology has shaped it according to the needed strategy. Negri, too, is referred to as the leader of *Autonomia* and in this—as with the aforementioned Piperno—there is already a fundamental distortion; that is, an example of that incomprehension between the groups belonging to the area of *Autonomia* and the official press/ideology. It is, in fact, difficult for the latter's "verticist" mentality to understand that *Autonomia* has—yes—prominent figures who might have left significant traces, but in no way has *a leader,* a central spokesman. The pointillism of its militancy, the refusal of party lines and of any hierarchical codification of needs, are the peculiar trait of this heterogeneous movement, and Toni Negri's writings are no exception to this, with all his allusions to the multilaterality of a recomposed proletariat and the exaltation of the concept of difference. The adoption of categories bespeaking the tendency towards a radical *separation* from a traditional anthropology creates a barrier of understanding, but such an incommunicability will be better seen when we come to report the voices from *Autonomia's* corner.

The commentary imposed by the prevailing information industry on Negri's work, on the academic department where he and his colleagues were doing social research and on *Autonomia* itself, as the de-centered point around which all sorts of alternative experiences gravitated, is also heavily marked by the "reflux" (*riflusso*) line. For the last few years, in fact, the word "reflux" has been a pivotal term, coined to describe in defeatist terms the state of the political struggles of the "social workers." After the "social workers" (new social subjects) have brought forth, throughout the seventies, political and cultural struggles, the password drummed in by the united media is that the Movement as a whole is in a state of "reflux," a receding tide; which is to say that once the "mistakes" leading to terrorism and idealism have been discerned, there is no other way out for all the new social subjects but that of an abjuring retreat. Needless to say, this point of view can be imposed because of the more basic belief in life as the consistent repetition of the same: the traditional belief that something is alive and well only if it develops identical to itself, the traditional belief that the absence of repetition means death, waning, and that only an immutable self-identity qualifies the life of a unitary organism. Perhaps such an immutability naturalizes one's life and constitutes a secure ontological space, but this interpretive grid applied to the Movement deforms unequivocally its essence. The Movement is no unitary organism: its reality is *also* in the effort *not* to adhere to one particular pattern of struggle, of existence; its reality is above all in the attempt to raise its antennae wherever needs and openings are, where a separation from capital logic is possible. And the demonstrations against the so-called Euromissiles (Perugia, Naples, Frankfurt), for the constitution of social centers for youth (Zurich), for a recognition of the occupation of buildings and apartments (Berlin, Amsterdam, Southern Italy after the earthquake) and of the organized unemployed workers (Naples) are a proof that the Movement is not where its alleged identity wants it to be.

It is no accident that "repentance" is the other recurrent word in Italy these days, and that the cultural atmosphere is that of a repenting confession: one repents of having been a communist (in the ultra-leftist connotation), since the acceptance of communist principles entails faith in the possibilities of inversion/reversal. One has to repent of that particular communism which meant a certain optimism, as well as a demystification of the traditional concept of *transition* as the passage to a paradise regained. Of communism as the optimism of a self-valorizing will that tries to structure and give reality to proletarian needs while, in the wake of a pessimistic view, only a retreating "repentance" of youthful dreams is offered as a cultural model for the collective imaginary of a generation, of an epoch. The desparate urge of communism loudly proclaimed by several voices of *Autonomia* was the expression of a need which configured itself not in terms of the seizure of a hypothetical power, but in the development—here, in the interstices of a capitalist world—of the potency that has been frozen by the rigidity of a "naturalized" existence in the realm of in-difference, in the realm of the equivalence (equi-violence) of exchange values.

"Reflux" of a homogeneous flow of marginal voices, and "repentance" of having desired a change, having sought the conceptual weapons to make this change possible. If these are the key notes around which the dominant self-representation of this country revolves, a perhaps deeper level of mystification can be detected within these voices which, as we have seen, would like to be considered those of the Italian people. It is the adoption of these voices' part of a "natural", common-sensical logic which is paradoxically common to Right, Left and Center. This "natural" logic, which somehow plays the role tonality has played in music, is so in-grown in our mode of thought that it can easily go unnoticed, it can easily disguise its being the result of a precise categorical choice. Binary in its inner mechanisms (the forced reduction of the complexity of the languages spoken by the social antagonisms to the informatic model of yes/no), a peculair trait of this "natural" logic has been the deployment of a linear causality in the interpretation of how new social subjects have risen to the level of multipolar struggles. A linear causality which seeks leaders and led ones, and describes Negri as the brain of a terrifying organization: the brain—that is, the highest part of a unitary organism, the part of a body where responsibilities can be sought and washing purifications can be exerted.

I'm not judging here as to the real directional participation of Negri in the armed struggle; I'm not issuing any verdict. What interests me is the need of projecting on a definable cause the responsibility for perturbing effects, however complex they might be, as if a causal genealogy could account for the molecular antagonisms that have constituted an opposition at all levels to the relation of capital. The need to project a causal link, forgetting that the principle of causality is their own cultural creation. The need to consider everything as a sign, an effect of something else, and thus the implicit affirmation of identity in these very causal relations; in this way self-identities are preserved, while the opposite notion that something is nothing but the sign of itself would ominously imply the constitutive non-identity with itself, its contradictory essence. As parents tend to seek the cause of a supposed misbehavior of their children in some bad, external influence (and in so doing leave the fundamental, reproductive mechanism of the family as unquestioned as possible), here the collective imaginary has been carefully shaped into one idea: the idea that the protest (and, in the large spectrum of this protest, terrorism, too) and the alternative valorizations of time and body have been directed from above by a central, malignant force—the typical projection of a teleological model ("God who creates everything") on the workings of history. If in the U.S. the imaginary is brought to establish a connection between the network of terror and the "international communist conspiracy", here in Italy things are different only on the surface, in that the genealogy of the social struggles has been traced back to some leaders, to some carcinogenic cells. And among these corrupting cells are Negri's writings, as though one could ignore the massive literature that for more than a decade has explored the broaching of potential spaces within the closure of a rigidly prescriptive social text: a massive output whose voice is not just the academic and rather esoteric flow of Negri's works, but also that of "street-talk" expressions of antagonism—the output of a mass of "social workers" who were enriching the communist, militant tradition with autonomous voices.

It is, however, clear to my wandering ears that the Italian Communist Party is far from considering itself enriched by works like this *Marx Beyond Marx*. The voices I hear coming from the site of orthodox communism, in fact, are among the most intransigent prosecutors of the autonomous line, and even though the traditional communists like to think of themselves as being the opposition, it is rather evident that their wave length is well-located within the area of that "natural" logic I tried to record above: a logic that is tied to the repetition (reproduction) of well-defined models of animality for women and men, so that traditional communists insist on the liberation *of* labor, while *Autonomia*'s line aims more at the liberation *from* labor (labor has ceased to be the ontological essence capable of realizing the human animal). A recent example of this clash comes from Rome, where *Autonomia* has maintained a certain strength, especially in some neighborhoods. In the S. Lorenzo/University area, where in the last years the Autonomists have successfully opposed the hegemony of the Italian Communist Party, the latter has not hesitated to unleash against the former the dogs of slandering mystification, mainly through the columns of their daily newspaper *L'Unità*. In the summer of 1981 the Autonomists of the neighborhood occupied Villa Mercede (a rather rundown building, with a surrounding garden, that is owned by an adjacent bank) and they are struggling to involve the people in the construction of a social center. A center in which the united proletarians can better struggle against the present enemies of the class, that is, against the culture of guilt/repentance and against heroin (two parallel strategies to suffocate and disperse the potential of the "social workers"; while the price of everything is rising sky high, that of heroin has basically remained the same as ten years ago!). A center in which a *free* kindergarten for the kids of that area can be started, a first step towards the creation of those *separate* proletarian institutions of which Negri speaks so often. Well, the Autonomists have to fight also against the envious diffidence and the open provocations of the party communists, who have traditionally dominated the area and made it into a vote reservoir. The *Unità* has repeated once more the farce of calling the Autonomists fascists, and has accused them of immorality, as is customary whenever one is short of rational, political arguments.

Besides these neglected examples of active, local resistance, however, there is a sign which reassures us statistically that the voices so far heard are not after all the "vox populi," do not represent the totality of the population, and this sign comes to us precisely from Rome. Rome, a traditional vote reservoir for the party feuds. Rome, a vast metropolitan territory where all the social events are turned into instruments for the reproduction of the existing political geography. During June 1981 elections the percentage of non-voters ("DO NOT VOTE" has been the "electoral campaign" of the Movement, careful not to play the game, not to be instrumental for a discourse whose logic cannot be accepted) has risen to the exceptional figure of 15%—and if we keep in mind that in Italy, unlike the U.S., voter turnout has always been around 92–95%, we come to realize how a new party that is not a party has been recently formed, even though its tacit constitution has been carefully silenced by the party-oriented press.

With this we have come to lend our ears to the dissonant voices evoked from the area that we loosely define as *Autonomia*'s. They are dissonant, and their dissonance is an anthropological declaration in praise of difference and multilaterality, a declaration bespeaking the dissociation from the system of needs as codified by the logic which, as we have seen, is common to most of the voices which mold and express, express while molding, the collective imaginary. It's time here to better define the incommunicability we talked about before. What is striking, in fact, whenever we listen to some of these autonomous voices is the language gap that separates them from the majority of the other representational sources. "Il linguaggio duro degli autonomi" ("the tough language of the Autonomists"): this is how the discursive form common to the various wings of the Movement has been described by the most attentive observers of Italian social life. And "tough" stands for "not soft", "harsh", "occasionally violent", but also for "difficult". Is it really difficult? It seems to us that the difficulty lies ultimately in the different conceptual categories mobilized by the autonomous discourse, a discourse which, observant of its own etymology, defines its rules *separately* from any a-priori, transcendent principle. It is, for instance, a careful consideration of the new class composition and of the emerging needs in this particular historical conjuncture (the passage from the Planning-State to the Crisis-State) that induces Negri to read the *Grundrisse* in that particular light, against any fetishism of a theory of reading a text. In the autonomous discourse, then, the potency of subjectivity is invoked against the power of objectified relations, so that attention is devoted not only to the quantifiable labor time but to the qualitatively important time of global life. The result is the "savage," "anomalous" exploration of the potential of a subject that can be so potent as to fecundate with the richness of its differences an otherwise indifferent reality. Fecundation, subjective appropriation: a *self-valorization* whose practice stems from the recognition that under the *real subsumption* of society by capital, everything that is produced-circulated-consumed is a mere cog in the wheel of the reproduction of the already existent. A *self-valorization* that announces the refusal of separating use value and desire value from the equivalence of exchange values. A *self-valorization* which attempts to wrench the libidinal economy away from an omnivorous State. Furthermore, the autonomous discourse proclaims itself to be affiliated with Marxism, and says that its ultimate goal is communism. But it is no surprise that a real curtain of incomprehension arises between the Autonomists and the occupants of traditional positions, who cannot translate the analyses and the behaviors of the Movement into their own system. Communism, in fact, here does not mean a direct assault on the institutions but the "scientific" organization of new social subjects engaged in the effort to surround a power that had surrounded them. And Marxism, too, is given in an anomalous way, beyond Marx, far from the Marx that has been frozen into the arteriosclerotic prophet of a messianic transition. It is rather a Marxism that has repudiated the Hegelian and positivist readings seeking an anomalous connection with Spinoza; a Marxism where the word "dialectics" is a term indicating something ultimately negative, to be itself superseded; a Marxism where dialectics means, yes, the recomposition of the oppositions into some kind of synthetic unity, but only in the name of the absorption of the proletarian body into the spirit of the social factory.

Common to the dissonant voices of the Movement is a terminology in which words such as "difference", "displacement", "leap forward", "imaginary" are pivots in the project of decomposing the traditional grid logic makes of continuity, unity, causality and identity. The magazine that perhaps better exemplifies this state of things was, and is *Metropoli,* although it is far from being the unilateral spokesman of the Movement. It is, however,

the most popular publication because of the negative publicity made for it
by the perpetual storm blowing around it—a judiciary repressive storm that
signals the attempts of the institutions to silence it. Negri writes several
articles for it, as other, still-imprisoned militants do. In *Metropoli* the orthodox communist perspective has completely disappeared: Russian socialism
has become the highest stage of State capitalism; the U.S.—a customary
target of the Italian left—is not always subjected to a unilateral critique.
On the contrary, an interest is shown for the "autonomous" experiences that
have taken place within the vast territory of the most advanced capitalist
country of the world. If this attention for the U.S. is peculiar to *Metropoli*
only, the terminology adopted by this magazine positions them unequivocally as voices coming from the area of *Autonomia;* a terminology which is
the expression of a precise effort to perfect the adequation of the symbolic
order to reality, that is, an effort to diminish the gap between theory and
a multifaceted reality that can no longer be straitjacketed in impotent formulae.

It is at this point that I think I can hear an objection raised by readers
of this book in the U.S. One might very well have the impression that the
autonomous language—as contingently exemplified by *Marx Beyond Marx*—
is extremely abstracted from that reality proclaimed as being the main target.
I can hear a common-sensical, reasonable protest, saying that Negri's book
is rather removed from any possible appropriation by an average proletarian
reader. While I hope that this won't deter the reader from pursuing his/her
interests in this area, I would like to anticipate a two-fold answer to this
objection. In the first place, one must remember that the analysis of the
new class composition has probed the concept of "social worker", and that
students and intellectuals are facets of this protei-form concept. It is then
conceivable that Negri's voice—the voice that uttered these very lessons in
Paris and organized them in Italy—is addressed to that particular sector of
the recomposed class. This is openly admitted, without any recrimination,
by the non-intellectual elements of the Movement, such as the Neapolitan
unemployed workers who have a high respect for Negri's work without
having had the opportunity to follow his intellectual gymnastics. It would
be an idealist mistake, rooted in the bourgeois notion of universal man, to
assume that a book can be consumed and appropriated indifferently by the
whole spectrum of the social subjects. It is moreover possible to find, in
Italian bookstores, "translated" (that is, "brought beyond"), parallel instances of the same discourse: non-academic voices can be heard all throughout the communication arteries of the Movement, and Negri's elaborated
language is nothing but an homage to *difference,* to the invaluable existence
of autonomous, separated bodies within the forces that oppose the State and
its leveling, homologizing strategies.

Secondly, the difficulty of a text must also be related to the workings of
its socio-cultural context, that is, to the direction imparted by cultural

politics. Our having listened to the language of the "normal", "natural" voices makes it clear that their discourse is like tonal music: easier to listen to than a music whose order and units are not repeated and hence not given the market monopoly which puts them within everybody's reach, which makes them catchy. The process of vocabulary (and category) acquisition is far from being a neutral one, and we cannot say that *Autonomia*'s terminology is something we are often exposed to. *Autonomia*'s language in general and Negri's in particular (Negri adds, after all, only a supplementary, academic difficulty to an already "tough" language) are then positioned at the margins by the existing system of symbolic reproduction. Better, they are positioned and *they posit themselves* at the margins, as a political project of dissociation—practical and discursive—from the centralized ideology of the State. And it is upon a careful consideration of the ramifications of this two-fold answer that I can hear the American readers soften their criticism when faced with the "tough" problems that *Marx Beyond Marx* poses. Soften their diffidence and spurring themselves to aim at a "savage" appropriation of anything in these lessons that might enrich their own subjectivity (subject-activity), their own potency. Perhaps it will not seem so different.

Maurizio Viano

Lesson One
The *Grundrisse*,
an Open Work

The subjective birth of a text: "the imminence of crisis," the starting points of the analysis. ☐ A formal description of the text. ☐ The *Grundrisse* and the outline of *Capital*: "the ensorcelling of the method, the blockage of research?" ☐ From the terrain of philology to a more substantial terrain: the two paths; the discovery of surplus value, the links of circulation: social capital—subjectivity—communism. ☐ The *Grundrisse*, an open work: some other hypotheses for reading. ☐ The "plural" universe of the Marxian method: *Forschung, Darstellung, neue Darstellung.* ☐ The traditional interpretations: (a) the *Grundrisse* as a delirium? (b) the renewal of *Diamat?* (c) homologous with *Capital?* (d) "a revolution from above"? ☐ No delegation in the theory. ☐ The *Grundrisse* as the dynamic center of Marxian thought, in its internal history as in its revolutionary project. ☐ An outline of the reading. ☐ Marx beyond Marx?

Eric Hobsbawm has said of the *Grundrisse* notebooks that they are a "kind of intellectual, personal and often indecipherable shorthand." The pertinence of this judgement is reaffirmed by Enzo Grillo in the introduction to his remarkable Italian translation. There is no doubt that in so far as their reading and their translation are concerned, we are led to this judgement: the *Grundrisse* constitutes a very difficult work. But we must not exaggerate the esoteric character of this work of Marx by drawing on certain passages. In fact, the difficulty comes more from the form of the manuscript, from the troubled character of its elaboration, than from the actual substance of the reasoning. If we examine Marx's project in all of its scope and density, the guiding line appears very clearly and is only partially confused by the difficulties of an impatient writing, the conjunctural character of some polemics, and the experimental side of some developments. There was an extreme urgency that led to the birth of this first great political synthesis

1

of Marx's thought: "The American crisis—which we foresaw, in the November 1850 issue of the review, would break out in New York—is fan-
tastic," Marx wrote to Engels on November 13, 1857, "even though my
financial situation is disasterous; I have never felt so 'cosy' since 1849 than
with this outbreak." "I am working like a madman for whole nights in order
to coordinate my work on economics, and to get together the *Grundrisse*
before the deluge." (To Engels, December 12, 1857.) "I am working like
a condemned man. Sometimes until 4 o'clock in the morning. It is a double
work: 1) the elaboration of some fundamental aspects of the economy . . .2)
the current crisis." (To Engels, December 18, 1857.) Ryazanov, the editors
of the *Grundrisse*, Rosdolsky, Vygodskij, and, last, no one better than Sergio
Bologna have each amply clarified the birth of the *Grundrisse*, its relation
to the work being done by Marx for the *New York Daily Tribune*, the links
to subsequent work, the political situation born out of the crisis of 1857–58,
and the expectations and hopes of Marx and Engels. I can do no better than
refer the reader to these discussions.

What I want to insist on is another element: it is a question of the basis
of the *synthesis* on the theoretico-practical level in Marx's project. The imminence of the crisis is not simply the occasion for an historical forecast; it
becomes a practico-political synthesis. The imminence of catastrophe is only
catastrophic for capital in so far as it is the *possibility of the party,* the possibility
to establish the party. The description of the imminent crisis is, at the same
time, a polemic against "true socialism," against all the mystifications and
travesties of communism. The "work of the condemned" in the area of theory
is an impatient refusal of eclipses in practice: if this practice is not given—
the *Correspondence* retraces fully its painful birth—analysis must discover it
as it occurs, in so far as analysis brings out the revolutionary subjectivity
implicated in the crisis. The synthetic character of Marx's work is to be
found within this relation between forecast and deluge: the catastrophies for
capital are the party, the deployment of communist subjectivity, and revolutionary will and organization. The crisis reactivates subjectivity and makes
it appear in all of its revolutionary potentiality at a level determined by the
development of the productive forces. The synthesis signifies the linkages
among the punctual and catastrophic character of the crisis, the rules of
development, and the dynamic of subjectivity. Where these different terms
are linked, the dialectic rules. And it is no accident if, alongside the activity
of the chronicler and polemicist aimed at an American newspaper, alongside
the critical exploration of the categories of political economy, we find Hegel
presiding over the birth of the *Grundrisse:* "For the rest, I am making great
progress. For example, I have thrown overboard all the theory of profit that
has existed until now. As far as the *method* goes, the fact of having leafed
through, once again, by mere accident, Hegel's *Logic* rendered me a great
service." (To Engels, Jan 14, 1858.) "By mere accident" but not "occasionally"; so much so that Marx continues, "If I ever find the time for a

work of this type, I would greatly desire to make accessible to the intellect of the common man . . . . . how much there is in Hegel's method of rationality and of mystification." The rational-methodical that Marx seeks here is the theoretico-practical of revolutionary insurrection. The imminence of the crisis demands this rationality. Marx's score with Hegel was settled long before; here it is only a question of going back to him in a critical and scientific manner. From Hegel it is a question of taking practically that which constitutes the irreducible contribution: the spirit of theorectico-practical synthesis.

Let us begin to examine the text, or rather the texts, published by the Marx-Engels Institute in Moscow in 1939–41, under the title of *Grundrisse der Kritik der politishen Oekonomie*. Here are the parts and the dates, taken from Grillo (*Prefazione* ai *Lineamenti* I, p.x-xi):

1) The *Einleitung* contained in a single notebook M, written between August 23 and mid-September 1857.

2) The manuscript of 7 notebooks (the *Grundrisse*) numbered and often dated by Marx himself, except for the first one, in the following order:

Notebook   I: October 1857
            II: around November 1857
           III: November 29–mid-December 1857, more or less
          IV: around mid-December 1857, February 1858
           V: January 22, 1858–around the beginning of February 1858
          VI: around February 1858
         VII: end of February-March, end of May, beginning of June 1858

The secondary texts, which make up the *Anhang,* and which are directly linked to the preceding texts, are:

3) The sketch of *Bastiat und Carey,* written in July 1857, before the *Einleitung*. Originally this text took up the first seven pages of the third notebook of the *Grundrisse.*

4) The *Index zu den 7 Heften,* written in June 1858, and inserted into the same notebook M which contains the *Einleitung.*

5) The *Urtext,* written between August and November 1858. It occupies two undated notebooks of which the first is marked B′, and the second divided into two parts B″ and B″II.

6) The *Referate,* related to the content of notebooks M (*Einleitung*), II-VIII (*Grundrisse*), (*Urtext*); written around February 1859 and found at the end of notebook B″.

7) The *Planentwurf,* of 1859.

8) A short series of extracts concerning Ricardo's theory of money, which is found in the fourth of the 24 notebooks between 1850–53, and dated: London, November 1850-December 1850.

9) A much longer series of systematic extracts of the third edition of Ricardo's *On The Principles of Political Economy,* which is found in the eighth notebook of the above series, written between April and May 1851. They are preceded by two very brief texts: a list of import categories that is found in Ricardo and a table of contents of the *Principles.* It is part of a notebook dated 1851 by Engels, which also contains the last part of the manuscript called *Das vollendete Geldsystem,* still unpublished.

My attention here will be focused essentially on the notebook M and the seven notebooks written between October 1857 and the spring of 1858. The sketch on *Bastiat and Carey* is also very important because it links the polemic against Proudhon to the "American" work of Marx. As we will see, the *Index* and the *Referate* have been generally taken up in the text, in those cited and in the summary.

Now, if we leave aside for the moment *Einleitung,* the *Grundrisse* appears at first sight to be a largely incomplete and fragmented work; but this doesn't mean that the notebooks do not have a center and a very strong dynamic. The argument runs through the following moments: from the analysis of money to the definition of the form of exchange (value) in notebook I; the second notebook emphasizes the passage money–capital; from surplus value to social capital is the object of notebook III; surplus value and profit begin to be taken into consideration in notebook IV, of which the most fundamental part is consecrated to the critical process of capital in circulation; in notebook V, after a long parenthesis on precapitalist forms (we will see later the justification for the insertion of this material) the analysis again takes up the question of the process of circulation and the conditions of reproduction of social capital; the sixth chapter poses, explicitly, the theme of capital as a collective force and the collective antagonism of workers–capitalists; in the seventh notebook the crisis of the law of value and its transformations (once again the theme of profit) leads us to a more precise definition of the crisis of the objective and subjective conditions of the production of capital. We thus see, throughout the *Grundrisse,* a *forward movement in the theory,* a more and more constraining movement which permits us to perceive the fundamental moment constituted by the *antagonism between the collective worker and the collective capitalist,* an antagonism which appears in the form of the crisis. There are two fundamental theoretical passages: in the first part of the *Grundrisse* there is the definition of *the law of value in the form of surplus value,* in other words the first developed formulation of the law of surplus value; in the second part, there is the *extension of the theory of exploitation* (the law of surplus value) *within the mechanisms of the reproduction and circulation of capital,* and thus the translation of the law of exploitation into the law of crisis and the class struggle for communism.

We could pause at this point to begin to measure the exceptional importance of the *Grundrisse.* But this importance is also underlined by the fact that in the *Grundrisse* we can read the outline of Marx's future development of his work, the outline of *Capital*. We will borrow here from Rosdolsky the list of outlines foreseen by Marx and the sketch of the most important modifications that occurred between the outline in the *Grundrisse* (which Rosdolsky calls "the original structure") and that of *Capital* (or the "modified structure") (see Table 1).

But is this philological approach correct? I have some doubts. But for the moment I will leave it at that; we will see, as we proceed with this research, whether these doubts will lead to something positive. Let us simply say at this point that one doubt is of a philological order: I ask myself if it is correct to consider the completed work of Marx, *Capital,* as the book which exhaustively recapitulates all of Marx's research. The genesis of *Capital*, which our very illustrious and knowledgeable camrades tell us about, is, according to me, invalidated by the fact that it supposes that *Capital* constitutes the most developed point in Marx's analysis. To see that they believe this, we have only to look, for example, at the explanation given by Rosdolsky (pp. 61–62) for Marx's "renouncing" of a specific volume on wage labor. Certainly this book, which is announced in the *Grundrisse,* does not exist, and part of the material put together for this chapter was finally incorporated in Volume I of *Capital*. But is this sufficient evidence for concluding that Marx "renounced" it? If to this philological doubt we add other, more substantial doubts, the question becomes even more problematical. The wage, such as it appears in the first volume of *Capital,* is on the one side a dimension of capital, on the other side it plays the role of motor in the production-reproduction of capital. The pages on the struggle over the reduction of the working day are fundamental for this question, and from three points of view: the dialectic between necessary labor and surplus labor, the reformist function of the wage, the role of the state in the modification/regulation of the working day. These three perspectives, as we find them in the *Grundrisse,* determine later on a concept of the wage in which antagonism rebounds on the concept of working class—which, in the *Grundrisse,* is always a concept of crisis and of catastrophe for capital, leaving aside the way in which it is also a very powerful allusion to communism. This specific volume on the wage, which is formally foreseen in the outline of the *Grundrisse,* this concept of the wage which in the *Grundrisse* is closely linked to that of the working class and to that of revolutionary subjectivity, can we really find these links in the first volume of *Capital?* We must respond to this question. Let us say right off that the usual path followed by the most famous interpreters does not seem to us to be the right one. Could it not be, as suggested in the preparatory outlines, that *Capital* is only one part, and a non-fundamental part at that, in the totality of the Marxian thematic? A part which has been overevaluated because it is the only one fully developed, and for less noble reasons, one that can, because of its partial nature, be limited and be led back within a field of interpretations fundamentally inadequate to the spirit of the total work of Marx? Kautsky, who had in his

Table 1   Outlines and Modifications of *Capital*

(1) September	1857	*Grundrisse*, p. 108
(2) October	1857	*Grundrisse*, pp. 227–228
(3) November	1857	*Grundrisse*, p. 264
(4) November	1857	*Grundrisse*, p. 275
(5) February	1858	Letter to Lassalle 22 February 1858, *Selected Correspondence*, p. 96.
(6) April	1858	Letter to Engels 2 April 1858, *ibid*. pp. 97–98
(7) June	1858	*Grundrisse*, German edn., pp. 855–859
(8) January	1859	*Contribution*, p. 19
(9) February–March	1859	*Grundrisse*, German edn., pp. 969–978
(10) December	1862	Letter to Kugelmann 28 December 1862, *MEW* Vol. 30
(11) January	1863	*Theories* I, pp. 414–416
(12) July	1865	Letter to Engels 31 July 1865, *MEW* Vol. 31
(13) October	1866	Letter to Kugelmann 13 October 1866, *ibid*.
(14) April	1868	Letter to Engels 30 April 1868, *Selected Correspondence*, pp. 191–195

The Original Plan
(6 Books)

The Changed Plan

I. ON CAPITAL

a) Capital in general

1) Production process

'CAPITAL' (3 Volumes):

I. Production process of capital (Sections):

    1) Commodity and money

    2) Transformation of money into capital

    3–5) Absolute and relative surplus-value

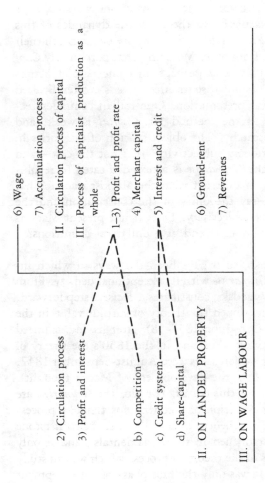

6) *Wage*
7) Accumulation process
II. Circulation process of capital
III. Process of capitalist production as a whole
1–3) Profit and profit rate
4) Merchant capital
5) Interest and credit
6) Ground-rent
7) Revenues

2) Circulation process
3) Profit and interest
b) Competition
c) Credit system
d) Share-capital
II. ON LANDED PROPERTY
III. ON WAGE LABOUR
IV. STATE
V. FOREIGN TRADE
VI. WORLD MARKET

SOURCE: Rosdolsky 55–56, English ed. Also see pp. 129–39 of Vygodskij, which are very important.

NOTE: Unbroken lines: changes within the first three books. Dotted lines: changes within the *Book on Capital*.

possession all of Marx's manuscripts, published (with vulgar errors) *Einleitung* in 1903 (*Neue Zeit*, XXI, 1) but did not publish the rest of the *Grundrisse*. Was this an accident? Maybe. The vicissitudes of the revolutionary movement rather prove the contrary. The fact is that the *Grundrisse* is not a text that can be used only for studying philologically the constitution of *Capital*; it is also a *political text* that conjugates an appreciation of the revolutionary possibilities created by the "imminent crisis" together with the theoretical will to adequately synthesize the communist actions of the working class faced with this crisis; the *Grundrisse* is the theory of the dynamics of this relationship. Reading the *Grundrisse* forces us to recognize not so much their homogeneity as their differences from other Marxian texts, particularly *Capital*. Inversely, *Capital* is quite seriously perhaps only one part of Marx's analysis. More or less important. In any case its effectiveness is often limited and transformed by its categorial presentation. Our Italian comrades recognized that "the ensorcelling of the method" in *Capital* is weak, and concluded that this "blocked research." The objectification of categories in *Capital* blocks action by revolutionary subjectivity. Is it not the case—and we will see this shortly—that the *Grundrisse* is a text dedicated to revolutionary subjectivity? Does it not reconstruct what the Marxist tradition has too often torn apart, that is to say the unity of the constitution and the strategic project of working class subjectivity? Does it not present Marx as a whole, where other texts cut him apart and give unilateral definitions?

Whisperings, loose talk, winks, such have been the ways in which interpreters have approached the *Grundrisse* with its exceptional density. From this point of view, the thesis of Vygodskij constitutes a decisive step forward. His thesis is that Marx finally developed the theory of surplus value in the *Grundrisse* (in the notebooks of Oct.-June 1857-58), after having acquired in the 1840's the classical theory of value, and in the 1850's the theory of historical materialism (*Einleitung*, which dates from August-September 1847, should be attached to this period in the development of Marx's thought). Rosdolsky, for example, doesn't see this (p. 2). For him the *Grundrisse* are only an important phase in the evolution of a continuous thought process that leads to *Capital* ("by 1848, 'his theory of surplus value, the cornerstone of his economic system, was established in its fundamentals', and it only remained to work out the details of the theory, a process which we can study in detail in the *Rough Draft*."). It was only the first phase of a development that occurred through adjustments, corrections, and successive parings. But even this theoretical step forward by Vygodskij—because grasping the movement forward by breaks and leaps constitutes a deepening of a theoretical element in Marx's thought—does not lead to determinant results. This is not simply because Vygodskij fails to go beyond the discovery of surplus value, but also because he does not fully grasp the importance of this discovery. To develop the theory of value as a theory of surplus-value, to recognize that the historical form of value is surplus value, signifies the development of "an immediately revolutionary project." (Letter to Lassalle, Sept. 15, 1860.) That would mean to find a lever of an antagonistic theory of capital, of a theory of social exploitation, in order to tip it toward *class composition as subjectivity of the struggle*. The theory of surplus value—as Isaac Rubin has already shown—thus becomes the dynamic center, the dynamic synthesis of Marx's thought, the point where the objective analysis of capital and the subjective analysis of class behavior come together, where class hatred permeates his science. But even this is insufficient. So far we have only the significance of the discovery of the law of exploitation. We must still discover the full implications, follow the effects and the repercussions in their fullness. We must thus go from the discovery of surplus value and its theoretical perfecting to the analysis of the linkages production–reproduction, circulation–crisis, social capital–working class subjectivity, and again development–crisis–communism. We must see how the totality of this process is permanently shaped by the fundamental antagonism and carries the mark of exploitation. In other words, the *dynamic unity of the process of surplus-value does not, in any way, eliminate the separation of the subjects* (wage labor and capital), but rather continually pushes each mediation (value form, money, forms of work or exchange, etc.) to its point of contradiction and its supercession. Crisis and class struggle are articulated so profoundly that the first takes on, within this anatagonistic dialectic, the form of catastrophe, while the second takes on the form of communism—the real, physical pole of an implacable will, necessary to eliminate the adversary. Historical materialism—the specified analysis of the class composition—is given new content here, within the abstraction of the critique of political economy, and the laws of crisis are mediated by the concrete emergence of the class struggle. Is there any place left for any ambiguity? Any of the ambiguities produced by the interpretation of *Capital*? I don't think so. Because here there is no possibility, even in the form of a paradox, of destroying the dynamism of this process by hypostatizing it, by rigidifying it into a totality with its own laws of development that one might be able to possess, or dominate, or reverse. No, here domination and reversal can only be accomplished by those who participate in an antagonistic relation. Outside of antagonism, not only is there no movement, but the categories do not even exist. The originality, the happiness, the freshness of the *Grundrisse* rest entirely with its incredible openness. The paradoxical *non-conclusive character* of the science is derived necessarily from the fact that it contains a subjective determination. Why then do we find such timidity in the reading and interpretation of the *Grundrisse*? The guiding line of the possibility and will to revolution is to be found in the movement from surplus value to the articulation social capital–crisis–subjectivity–communism, and thus the function of antagonism in the reproduction of the capitalist relation. The *Grundrisse* constitutes the subjective approach ("the imminent crisis") to the analysis of the revolutionary subjectivity in the process of capital. The note-books represent the strongest point of analysis and of imagination in the revolutionary will of Marx. All of the formal dualism about which so much debate occurs (theoretical analysis of capital as opposed to political analysis, dialectics as opposed to materialism, objectivity as opposed to subjectivity) is burned up and melted in the reality of that dualism which constitutes, antagonistically, the capitalist process.

All of the foregoing will be demonstrated. But it seems to me opportune and honest to lay out right away my theses, given the flatness, the ambiguous evaluations and narrations to which the *Grundrisse* has been subject. To this point, in order to characterize the reading I want to undertake, I have mainly underlined the points of rupture; I now want to underline some other points which seem to me to be particularly important, and around which my analysis will be developed:

(1) *From the form of money to the form of value.* In the Marx of the *Grundrisse* this relation is fundamental: the analysis of money is precisely what allows us to analyse the form of value. From this point of view, as we will see, the reality of mystification appears here in a more tangible form than in other passages of Marx where the commodity form is the central protagonist. On the contrary, use value, when it is juxtaposed to a value form derived from money, regains importance and a large space of development. Thus, to begin the *Grundrisse* with "II. Money"—which seems to refer to a "I. Value"—is not an accident. (The first chapter on value was never written, but we can find a beginning in notebook VII (*Grundrisse*, p. 881; 763) under the title "Value".) We must weigh all the consequences of this: it seems to me that on the one hand this leads to a radical critique of money and on the other hand it leads immediately to defining value in mystified terms.

(2) *The definition of work.* In the *Grundrisse,* work appears as immediately abstract labor. We can only understand it and integrate it within theory at this level. Work is abstract in so far as it is only immediately perceptible at the level of the social relations of production. Thus we can only define work on the basis of the relations of exchange and of the capitalist structure of production. We can find no concept of work in Marx that is not that of waged work, of work that is socially necessary to the reproduction of capital, thus no concept of any work to restore, to liberate, to sublimate, only a concept and a reality to suppress.

(3) As Cristina Pennavaja (in her presentation of Vygodskij) has under-lined, the analysis is conducted at a level where antagonism is such that we can in no case consider the theory of value as a closed theory, nor can we base upon it any theory of reproduction and circulation in equilibrium. "In the *Grundrisse, Marxism is an anti-economic theory,* criticism does not lead back to political economy, but, on the contrary, science is an antagonistic move-ment." All of so-called socialist economics is put into question by this

understanding of the law of value. Marxism has nothing in common with a socialist economy, be it utopian or already realized.

(4) The "system," a dynamic and open system, is completely dominated by the question of the relation between the crisis and the emergence of revolutionary subjectivity. This relationship is so fundamental that Marxism could well be entitled *the science of the crisis and of subversion.* To want to consider the crisis as a sickness to treat and to cure is not only to betray the revolutionary movement, it is also to fall into a banter that has nothing in common with Marxian categories. To want to reduce subjectivity to exploitation is to avoid the definition of subjectivity in Marx which is presented as subversion and transition. The *Grundrisse* are, from this point of view, perhaps the most important—even if not the only—Marxian texts on the *transition.* Let us take note how strange it is that none of the thousands of commentaries on the transition takes account of this.

(5) The Marxist definition of *communism* that we find in the *Grundrisse* takes an extremely radical form, which goes far beyond the features that normally characterize it. Notably, the articulation communism–class composition plays a fundamental role. We have here a conception of power that has nothing in common with those of traditional political science, Marxism included. Class composition–power, class composition–transition, the articulation of these relations are based on the materiality of the behaviors, the needs, and the structure of self-valorization. The theme of power in Marxism must be subjected to the fire of critique; we can only give it a new base by exploring these kinds of articulations. This is a problem that today we can no longer underestimate.

(6) The last particular point refers to the dynamic of concepts in the *Grundrisse* that define the working class. We have already begun to examine some of the negative effects of the facts that the book on wage labor (or on the wage) was not written and that some of its important elements were reduced to objective exposition in Volume I of *Capital.* But this does not resolve the problem positively. It is a question of following the text, of retracing the links which conceptually unite the critical definition of the wage and the revolutionary definitions of communism and of communist subjectivity. It is a question of at least perceiving the outline of the book foreseen by Marx on the wage and grasping the main articulations.

Here then are some of the fundamental problems that we will keep in view during this reading and definition of the two great moments of the analysis in the *Grundrisse* (surplus value and realization).

The exceptional importance of the *Grundrisse* in the configuration of Marxian thought is also based on the method. With *Einleitung* and its creative application to the project of the *Grundrisse,* Marx achieved, on the methodological level, a synthesis of his earlier impulses in this area. We will dwell at length on the *Einleitung*; now is not the moment to lay out a thorough analysis. I will content myself for the time being with saying that

Notebook M elaborates explicitly the method of *determinant abstraction,* the method of the *tendency,* the method of historical materialism; the research embodied in the *Grundrisse* is the first application which grafts the materialist method onto a refined dialectical practice. The synthesis of the two dialectical forces is open in every sense. On the one hand, dialectical reason intervenes in the relation between determination and tendency, it subjectifies the abstraction, the logical-heuristic mediation, and imposes on it a qualification and historical dynamic. On the other hand, the materialist method, in so far as it is completely subjectivized, totally open toward the future, and creative, cannot be enclosed within any dialectical totality or logical unity. The determination is always the basis of all significance, of all tension, of all tendencies. As for the method, it is the violent breath that infuses the totality of the research and constantly determines new foundations on which it can move forward. In this sense we can say again that the *Grundrisse* is an essentially open work, we can repeat that this is what characterizes it, even if this is still an hypothesis to be verified more thoroughly in the area of method. We can also insist equally that this phase is for Marx a moment of total happiness, a moment situated at a halfway point which is neither eclectic nor mediating: the wealth of forces is not reduced to an average indifferent term, the categories are not flattened out, the imagination does not stagnate.

These general considerations, although they are important, are not yet sufficiently concrete. They can only begin to indicate how what I like to call the "plural universe" of Marx's method actually emerges. They can only give some examples. They cannot show it at work in the Marxian laboratory. In the "Afterword" to the second edition of Volume I of *Capital* Marx distinguishes between the *Forschung* and the *Darstellung,* between the moment of research and the moment of scientific presentation: "Of course the method of presentation must differ in form from that of inquiry. The latter has to appropriate the material in detail, to analyse its different forms of development and to track down their inner connection. Only after this work has been done can the real movement be appropriately presented" (*Capital,* Volume I, Vintage edition, p. 102). In the *Grundrisse,* we can follow in all its stages the logical process that takes place between the *Forschung* and the *Darstellung.* Now, if we take account of the preceding indications, we realize very quickly that this process is neither linear nor, even less, unilateral. The dialectic research—presentation is, on the contrary, open on all sides: every conclusion that takes the form of a presentation of the research opens spaces to new research and new presentation. This occurs, not simply by some horizontal exhaustion of successive areas of research, but mainly through an historical and tendential movement where each determination of a new subject immediately reveals a new antagonism and sets in motion, through this, a process in which the determination of new subjects emerges. Thus the *Darstellung* is followed dialectically by a *neue Darstellung*: it is a question of a process that constitutes the totality of the real movement, that is

understood scientifically, that is renewed scientifically. Thus there is no
linear continuity, but only a plurality of points of view which are endlessly
solicited at each determinant moment of the antagonism, at each leap in the
presentation, in the rhythm of the investigation, always looking for new
presentations. In this sense, the *Grundrisse* constitutes, from the point of
view of method (of a method which, in a materialist way, always considers
the historical and concrete determination as fundamental and which, in a
dialectical way, always finds the dynamic and tendency of each determination
in the same movement where the antagonism of each constitutes itself,
resolves itself and reproposes itself)—the *Grundrisse* constitutes a "plural"
universe. Each research result, in the presentation, attempts to characterize
the content of the antagonism and to see it, tendentially, in its own dynamism; when this dynamism takes off, we observe a veritable conceptual
explosion. Further on we will take time to restate these things less formally
and to give some examples, among others examples of this way of always
being placed at the forefront of the debate, in constituting a *neue Darstellung*—
in such a way that the previous mode of presentation must, itself, be subjected
to research and must constitute in turn the material of a new presentation.
Holding to the mere presentation of my hypotheses, I only mention this
power of the *Grundrisse*'s method, this capacity to grasp a concept in order
to explode it, to displace the analysis each time onto a new indeterminate
terrain constituted such that it can be redefined, characterized. And so on.

Thus it is not by methodological fetishism that we have presented the
method of the *Grundrisse,* the method of Marx, in a polemical and didactic
manner! We can see in it the passion for totality, but only in the form of
a multiplicity of sequences and leaps, never in a monolithic sense; we can
find in it, above all, a dynamic which has the plurality and the same diversity
of subjectivity, and is nowhere closed. Sometimes, in the polemics on blind
objectivism of a certain Marxist tradition, some have attributed this mobility
of the method to the political discourse of Marxism, in order to liberate its
so-called "realism" from the shackles of a materialism degenerated into
determinism. But this does not resolve this grave problem; it is rather a
question of characterizing the mobility of the content studied by Marx, the
wealth of the subjective specifications he expresses and sometimes dominates.
The Marxist method constitutes the reality of science, in so far as it is an
adequate instrument to grasp the multiplicity and the plural dynamism of
reality. The Marxist method is a constituting one in so far as the class
struggle constitutes explosive antagonisms. Research must find its moment
of presentation—there is a qualitative leap in the presentation, which does
not correspond simply to the unique fact of its determinate synthesis, but
corresponds rather to the fact that this determinate synthesis defines for the
antagonism and its possibilities—potentialities of explosion, a new level of
diffusion, a new terrain of constitution. When we study the passage from
the theory of surplus value to that of realization, it will not be a question
of applying the first theory to the second; certainly not! The problem will

be to see how the constitution of the whole capitalist power reproduces the dynamic of surplus value on a social level—in new forms, as much from the point of view of capital as from the point of view of the class. When we study the constitution of the world market and the modification of its relations with national markets, here again we must reread our research (in its two forms: research and presentation) to gain new levels of generality. *Determinate abstraction, the method of the tendency, the new presentation and clarification of the field of research:* this dynamism of the method determines a "plural" universe in which it is risky to move, difficult to understand, and exciting to make progress.

One last element of our starting hypotheses on the method in the *Grundrisse:* it is a question of the crisis of the law of value, that is to say of the summit of Marx's research. The hypothesis is that we have already entered into an advanced phase of the crisis of the law of value. Our Marxist method, materialist and dialectical, must take into account the resulting modifications and must change accordingly. It will not be enough to pose the question. We must also offer a response. Nothing is more central than this question.

A brief parenthesis—to give us a moment to catch our breath. Very often today, we are told to relate the question of the methodology of the human sciences to a problem of the plurality of moments of self-valorization, of dynamism and of recomposition. This methodological sensibility is often equally opposed to Marxian methodology. It is enough to speak of the multiplicity of instances of recomposition, of transversality of the method of recomposition, in order to say: beyond Marx? But beyond which Marx? The Marx taught by the schools of the Party? Or the Marx that we discover in the practico-theoretical moment of the working class and proletarian struggle? When we reread the *Grundrisse*, one feeling dominates: that here we are truly "beyond Marx," but also beyond all possible methodologies of pluralism or of transversality. The field of research is determined by the continual tension between the plurality of real instances and the explosive duality of antagonism. What gives unity to this systematic (or anti-systematic) framework is antagonism, not as the basis of this totality but as the source of ever more powerful and plural expansion of this same antagonism. In methodology, the class struggle is even more antagonistic and destructive in so far as it melds with the liberty of the subjects. Marx beyond Marx? The *Grundrisse* beyond *Capital?* Maybe. What is certain is that the central character of the theory of surplus value puts an end to every scientific pretension to derive any centralization and domination from the theory of value. The theory of surplus value breaks down the antagonism into a microphysics of power. The theory of class composition restates the problem of power in a perspective where recomposition is not that of a unity, but that of a multiplicity of needs, and of liberty. Marx beyond Marx, this too is an important, urgent hypothesis.

The most celebrated interpreters of the *Grundrisse* have been seduced by it, unable to move freely within it. This is why, with a few exceptions, they have not read the text for itself, they have tried instead to force and reduce it to something else. The titles alone tell this story: *La storia di una grande scoperta* ("The history of a great discovery") or, more explicitly, *Bevor "das Kapital" entstand* ("Before the concept of *Capital*") or *Zur Entstehungsgeschichte des Marxschen "Kapital"* ("A contribution to the history of the elaboration of *Capital* of Marx"): what is said about the *Grundrisse* is often quite good, but it is always a question of making it into the genesis of another text and not of taking it for itself. What is being applied is a non-Marxian historiographic methodology, which is satisfied with the continuity of the genesis, the development of ideas, and is not attentive—or at least not sufficiently so—to the leaps, to the breaks, to the plurality of horizons, to the urgencies of practice.

The tragedy is that, when this materiality is taken into account, we are left with another error, which consists of classifying and systematizing. Yes, some will say, the *Grundrisse* is, effectively, an original work, but it is so much of one that we must take literally Marx's words in his letters: the *Grundrisse* notebooks were written in the delirium of a powerful inspiration, in the despair of extreme isolation, in a moment when practice had been checked. They were written feverishly, after midnight. So much for the form ("in charity we won't even look at the details: the mathematical calculations are all wrong, the dialectical method confuses concepts and multiplies definitions").

> As far as the content goes, the *Grundrisse* must be located before the rigorously materialist methodological rupture that characterizes Marxist "theory": they are the last work of the young Marx, the articulation of concepts and the progression of the analysis are still, in part, hazardous and fanciful—if the development of the theory of surplus value is valid, that of the theory of realization, with its explosions of subjectivity and its catastrophism, is a total failure; the material articulation gives way to almost metaphysical influences, at least organicist (as in *Die Formen*) or humanist (as in the "Fragment on Machines"). The text is thus characterized by a formidable innovative effort, but it can only reaffirm, repeat, and exhalt all that is still propedeutic in Marx's youthful humanism. The *Grundrisse* are thus only a draft that stinks of idealism and of individual ethics; the sketch of a definition of communism that we find in the "Fragment" is a synthesis of the scientific idealism of the 18th century and an individualist and libertarian attitude.

I must say that, faced with all these critiques, I often don't know what to say. I am tempted to show, with a "Germanic" meticulousness, how, in fact, faced with the concrete reading of the text, these critiques are false:

but why do it? How can we show that one cannot attribute to the delirium of Marx the delirium of the material in which he worked and forged his critical instruments? That it is there, in this material which appears, and in the most extreme determinations it takes on, that we find the exceptional character of the *Grundrisse*, the exaltation by Marxian science of contradiction pushed to the point where antagonism becomes unresolvable? "We propose to bring to light the contradictions [contained in capital]" (*Grundrisse*, p. 351; 257): in this science where contradiction becomes antagonism, there is no place for humanism, even if there is a place for the delirium of the material.

Let us return now to the most recent interpretations, those which we have said make particularly important use of the idea of genesis. They pay much attention—too much in my view—to the continuity of theoretical development in Marx. Of all these interpretations, that of Vitalij S. Vygodskij is without a doubt the most striking. It is unreproachable when it underlines the importance of the path traced by the *Grundrisse*. It is important for its definition and thematic reconstruction. Nevertheless, the work of Vygodskij is part of the "new look" of *Diamat*. When it comes to the class struggle against the operation of the law of value (an operation which is now only pure command, empty of any appearance, even minimal, of "economic rationality"), when it comes to the mounting revolt against valorization, Soviet Marxism is thrown on the defensive; it becomes necessary to give a new face to the old *Diamat*. What better, then, what more functional than to try and attenuate, using the dialectic of the *Grundrisse*, the rigorous but too rigid and inadequate apparatus of the Soviet ideological system? The importance of the reading undertaken by Vygodskij is beyond question; its role, its political line, the fact that it is *ad usum delphini*, are also beyond question. To conjugate together the *Grundrisse* and the vulgar Soviet interpretation of *Capital*, this is what gives a "new look" to *Diamat*, a new look imposed by the class struggle in the USSR—and what allows the power structure to make a better dialectical and conflictual usage of the potential for domination expressed by the theory of value and the economistic and/or Stalinist reading of *Capital*—and this in a part of the world where this reading exerts a real function of domination. The interpretation of Vygodskij is thus malignant and crafty: the fact that it is often correct takes away none of its negative characteristics, no more than the strong scientific realism of the 16th century authors of the "raison d'État" took away their ambiguities. Moreover, if we look closely we can see that the interpretation of Vygodskij— whatever its merits—produces no rupture in so far as content is concerned: although he emphasizes in the *Grundrisse* the antagonistic dimension of the dialectic, and the material and central character of the theory of surplus value, Vygodskij does not generalize this analysis to the totality of Marxian categories. On the contrary, as Pennavaja has already emphasized, he ultimately affirms that Marxian theory is "a closed economic theory"—an affirmation where we don't know whether it is more absurd to call Marxism "economic theory" or to define it as *"geschlossen"* ("closed"). A closed economic theory, therefore a theory of equilibrium: well, yes, Vygodskij would respond, and he would add: with a little conflictuality, with a little liberty, even.

We now arrive at Roman Rosdolsky. To criticize the pioneering work of this author is a task that is not only difficult but also unjust. The more so, given that Rosdolsky, while linking the *Grundrisse* and *Capital,* always sought an intermediary terrain; he never tried to linearly reduce the first to the second; he rather atempted a revolutionary interpretation and gave to *Capital* a reading that was often original and innovative. The *Grundrisse* and *Capital* are thus, for Rosdolsky, inside of each other and the system they form—because it still consists of a system—is entirely traversed by a strong conflictuality—to the point where Marx and/or Grossman come close to obstinancy, to exaltation and to catastrophism. The limits of Rosdolsky (beyond certain confusions and errors: we have already mentioned his position on the "Book on the Wage"; further on we will see and discuss other points) result, in my opinion, from the ideology of *the communist left* in the inter-war period that surrounded him: on one side an extreme objectivism, on the other the necessity to found that objectivism by recuperating Marxist orthodoxy. One element served the other: objectivism allowed the existence of a largely minority left communism; orthodoxy legitimized it. Grossman is, from this point of view, one of the clearest examples of this necessity. Rosdolsky moved with great flexibility between these objective limits. He was capable of a reading that was often extraordinary. But in the end he was faced with these limitations. In his reading of the *Grundrisse* he sought to find a mediation between the extraordinary novelty of the text—that Rosdolsky often confronted with the ingenuity of a true intellectual—and the continuity of orthodoxy. This does not satisfy us. Our lack of satisfaction is evident from a theoretical point of view, from the point of view of a reading of the text. We will see this in depth shortly. But it also fails to satisfy us from a political point of view.

We find ourselves in a phase where the revolutionary movement is seeking new foundations, and in a way that will not be that of a minority. We have nothing to do with orthodoxy. And we would be delighted to be able to ignore Marx himself. A break has been made, there is no denying it. The theory of value is worn to threads, as far as our struggles are concerned. Now the discovery of the *Grundrisse* restores Marx to us. Because of its power, not because of our fidelity. We no longer can take the pleasure or have the duty to argue with orthodoxy; our languages separate us, they are contradictory. Yet the *Grundrisse* restores Marx to us in more than one sense. Above all he is restored to us as the theoretician of the great upheavals of capital from the point of view of the crisis of the law of value. The analysis, even though partial, that Sergio Bologna develops on this subject is, we have already said, very important: Sergio Bologna analyses the historical context of the *Grundrisse* and especially the links among the polemic on money, the analysis of the American and world crisis (such as it was developed in Marx's articles of this period for the *New York Daily Tribune*), and theoretical research. Even if the synthesis of these moments cannot be conducted within a literary image of the "doubled" revolution, or within a theoretical response to the "revolution from above" carried out by the capitalist power structure. The Marx of the *Grundrisse* well knows that there is no theoretical alternative, that this alternative is either a function of the mass movement or it is not, that there is no delegation in theory. The synthesis of the different elements of Marx's analysis is based on the definition of the crisis as the moment where the revolutionary movement seeks new foundations. It is based on this continuity of the practico-theoretical fabric that the theory must attain and embrace. Reversing and paraphrasing Hobsbawm, we should say that the *Grundrisse* is for Marx a kind of collective theoretical shorthand: it is this ferocious obstinacy of theory for and within practice. The synthesis attained in the *Grundrisse* thus takes on all its meaning: the *Grundrisse* is the center of the theoretical development of Marx because it represents the moment where the system in its formation, far from closing, opens up on the totality of practice. The method of the *Grundrisse* constitutes the antagonism, the totality of the categories forms a grid of concepts which alone allow the deepening and the enlargement of class antagonism. The catastrophism of the *Grundrisse,* about which many have spoken, must in reality be related to this politico-practical articulation, to this moment that the power of the working class must impose against the system of value.

In so far as the *Grundrisse* flows through *Capital,* we can be happy. The concepts of *Capital* are, in this case, adequate for understanding the development of the antagonism. Nevertheless, there are several cases where the categories of *Capital* do not function in this way: as a result we can sometimes think that a certain exacerbated objectivism can be legitimated by a strict reading of *Capital.* Thus the movement of the *Grundrisse* toward *Capital* is a happy process; we cannot say the same of a reverse movement. The *Grundrisse* represents the summit of Marx's revolutionary thought; with these notebooks comes the theoretical-practical break which founds revolutionary behavior and its difference from both ideology and objectivism. In the *Grundrisse* theoretical analysis founds revolutionary practice. Let us render homage here to the reading undertaken by a young comrade, Hans Jürgen Krahl, to the sharp intelligence with which he was able (for his time) to perceive in the categorical development of the *Grundrisse* the constituting moments of the class struggle. Let us be clear: it is not a question of an abstract polemic against *Capital:* each of us was born in the reflection and the theoretical consciousness of the class hate which we experience in studying *Capital.* But *Capital* is also this text which served to reduce critique to economic theory, to annihilate subjectivity in objectivity, to subject the subversive capacity of the proletariat to the reorganizing and repressive intelligence of capitalist power. We can only reconquer a correct reading of *Capital* (not for the painstaking conscience of the intellectual, but for the revolutionary conscience of the masses) if we subject it to the critique of the *Grundrisse,* if we reread it through the categorical apparatus of the *Grundrisse,* which is traversed throughout by an absolutely insurmountable antagonism led by the capacity of the proletariat. From this point of view, the *Grundrisse* represents the critique of the capitalist "revolution from above" in the real movement. It is the confidence in the "revolution from below": it bears the strongest potential for the destruction of every kind of theoretical or political autonomy detached from the real movement. This is what the *Grundrisse* understands (through its categories) as the only possible foundation.

Except for Lesson 3, in which we will reread *Einleitung* and propose a series of methodological problems, we will follow in the other lessons the substance of the text of the *Grundrisse.* Lessons 2, 4, and 5 will describe the process that leads from the critique of money to the definition of the theory of value, and thus to the definition of the crisis and of catastrophe which forms the theoretical conclusion of this first milling of the analysis. In Lessons 6 and 7 we will see, through the analysis of realization and of circulation, how social capital is formed, the collective form of capital and its antithetical form: it is a question at this stage of tracing the outline of a possible "Book on the Wage." Lessons 8 and 9 draw the conclusions of this second stage: from subjectivity and the first definition of communism to a first general clarification of the analysis, which advances it along with the modification of a series of conditions which founds the antagonism. It is then a question of reconstituting the Marxian terms of the theme of communism between catastrophe and proletarian self-valorization.

What more can I say in this lesson than to propose these hypotheses and to suggest an interpretation? It seems to me I have already said too much! Nevertheless, I cannot refrain from adding how much I like to imagine what Lenin or Mao would have done if they had the *Grundrisse* in their hands, just as Marx had, at a certain moment, the *Logic* of Hegel. I am certain that they would have drawn from the *Grundrisse,* with considerable relish, exceptional food for practice. Just like bees with flowers. This is the path "beyond Marx" that I love.

Lesson Two
Money & Value

Why begin with the chapter on money? □ General plan of the chapter. □ Money and value: money as immediacy of value. Money as historic immediacy of crisis. □ The critique of the money form and of its mystification by Proudhon. □ The extreme radicality of Marx's approach. □ The tendency as the point of departure for the investigation. □ Analysis of the text: (a) Money and crisis. The meaning of "average labor" and of "socially necessary labor." The inversion of Proudhonism. And then, conversely, money as symbol; (b) Money and inequality: political excursus; (c) Systematic analysis of money: money as measure and general equivalent (and the refusal of labor?); money as a means of circulation; money as money and as capital; (d) Money-value-capital. □ A project for the further progress of the analysis. □ From the critique of money to the critique of power: an anticipation.

We begin the internal analysis of the *Grundrisse* in Notebook I and, in very small part, Notebook II ("Money") rather than in Notebook M ("Introduction") which precedes it chronologically and thematically, because we prefer to enter immediately into the heart of the matter. In Lesson 3, we will treat Notebook M and the theme of method, with the advantage of having already seen it function and of being able therefore to confront the systematization of this method with the transformations which it undergoes in contact with things. In this way, the nature, the quality of being a "passageway" which characterizes Notebook M, in Marx's definition of his method from the summer of '57, will thus appear more clearly, and it will perhaps be possible to identify the special productiveness of this approach.

For another reason, which has already been mentioned and which will only be recalled here, it is worthwhile to begin with the notebooks on money: it is in fact in the polemic on money that the lines which constitute the axes of the *Grundrisse* are tied, that is, the critique of "true socialism," the delay of the "imminent crisis," and the extraordinary effort at theoretical

21

investigation. It is on the basis of these notebooks that Marx's investigation makes a qualitative leap.

Therefore, the notebooks on money. Everything begins with a reference to "Alfred Darimon: On the Reform of Banks. Paris 1856." (p. 115). It seems to be the usual notebook of remarks and critical reflections of which there are so many in Marx. But that is not the case: this reference to Darimon, to the insufficiencies of his thesis (but, implicitly, to the entire polemic against Proudhon—this indeed is, as we shall see, an important basis), appears immediately to be a pretext. In fact:

A. (*Grundrisse,* pp. 115–151; 356-9). Marx begins by analyzing and criticizing point by point Darimon's book, but right away the problem becomes general, the admonitions against Darimon become jeering parentheses within the theory that is being developed. Practically speaking, we have here a *first part* of the manuscript which we can entitle "Money and Crisis." The immediacy of the problem of the crisis becomes the fundamental element of the investigation and at the same time its phenomenology becomes the motor of the analysis.

B. (*Grundrisse,* pp. 153–65; 71–82). Then, after a brief note on *The Economist* (pp. 151–53; 70–1), a second return to Darimon and the polemic on "time chits" and against the scandalous utopia of the Saint-Simonian Bank; but again immediately the problem is generalized. The *second part* of the manuscript, with a first large theoretical excursus ("money as a social relation") which, repeating indications from the "Introduction," leads to the heart of Marx's critique and to the theoretical starting point in the proper sense of the term. We can entitle this part "Money and Inequality."

C. (*Grundrisse,* pp. 166–213; 84–137). Another short parenthesis of a punctual character (pp. 165–6; 82–84). One is finished with Darimon: the passage from polemic to exposition which takes place here from A to B has produced the object which now can be analyzed in the systematic complexity of its characteristics. We can entitle this *third part*: "systematic analysis of money." Now, this third part divides in three systematic chapters:

C1. Money *as measure* (*Grundrisse,* pp. 166–72; 84–9) with a parenthesis on metal (pp. 172–86; 89–101).

C2. Money *as a means of circulation* (pp. 186–203; 101–17).

C3. Money *as money and as capital* (pp. 203–13; 117–37).

D. At this point (*fourth part*), the analysis returns to the relation "*Value–Money,*" that is, to the general level of the theory already touched upon in point B. This applies to *Grundrisse,* (pp. 213–18; 137–48), but even more the pages immediately following which constitute the premise of the new book: "III. *Capital*" (Grundrisse, 221; 151–62). In this frame the initial sketch of the chapter on value, already noticed in the first lesson, must be kept in mind.

We note first of all that the chapter on money is given the numeral II by Marx. Presumably it could be preceded by a chapter I on value. In fact, already in *Contribution to a Critique,* the first chapter on value becomes a chapter on commodities, thus preparing by this passage the definitive systematization of the material of *Capital.* But here there is no chapter on commodities, and we must ask ourselves whether this absence does or does not produce useful effects for Marx's procedure.

Now, in Notebooks I and II, *the route leads immediately from money to value*: value is presented there under the form of money. Value is thus the same shit as money. It is not philosophic *"taumasestein"*; the wonder, the stupor, and the desire of knowledge does not lead to ideal cognitive syntheses, to imaginary hypostases, but to the practical immediacy of the critique, the denunciation, and the refusal. In addition, we are not before value; we are in it: we are in that world made of money. Money represents the form of social relations; it represents, sanctions, and organizes them. Perhaps this immediacy of the approach, not to value, but to value under the form of money, as if money exhausted all possible value, is too naive? Yet the world represents itself thus, as a world of commodities which money represents completely, determining, through itself, the valorization of commodities. Darimon represents a useful, imbecilic, but comprehensive approach for the "ingenuous" Marx. In addition, what can a theory of value signify which would not be immediately subordinated and intimately and necessarily linked to a theory of money, to the form in which the capitalist organization of the social relation is presented in the everyday process of social exchange? If a theory of value is given, can it be given outside of an immediate reduction to the theory of money, of the capitalist organization of exchange, and, within exchange, of exploitation? I begin to appreciate the ingeniousness of (Marx's) approach. There is so much class hatred contained in this way of approaching the material! Money has the advantage of presenting me immediately the lurid face of the social relation of value; it shows me value right away as exchange, commanded and organized for exploitation. I do not need to plunge into Hegelianism in order to discover the double face of the commodity, of value: money has only one face, that of the boss.

This approach is typical of the *Grundrisse,* and we see it everywhere: it makes stand out *the primary practical antagonism within whatever categorial foundation.* The theory of value, as a theory of categorial synthesis, is a legacy of the classics and of the bourgeois mystification which we can easily do without in order to enter the field of revolution. That was true yesterday for the classics, as the attack of the *Grundrisse* demonstrates; today, one can show in the theory that is still applicable that it is in this way that we must begin, against all the repeaters of the theory of value, from *Diamat* to Sraffa.

It is vain, therefore, to try to find analogies with other versions (they are four, including those of the *Grundrisse,* according to Rosdolsky) of Marx's theory of money. Here the analysis is immediately under the form of value and thus, at least for the points we have numbered A, B, and D, the analysis will be displaced onto this theme. It is only the material which we gathered under point C which can be confronted with other versions of Marx's theory of money: we will see nevertheless with what extraordinary attentions and differences that cannot be reduced, as Rosdolsky on the contrary underlines, to simple literary variants. It is vain, therefore, also to seek subtle continuity, this time not only literary but substantial. The difference between the *Grundrisse* and the later works of Marx resides in the fact that in the first, *the law of value is presented not only mediatedly, but also immediately as the law of exploitation.* There is no logical way which leads from the analysis of commodities to that of value, to that of surplus value: the middle term does not exist; it is—that, yes—a literary fiction, a mystification pure and simple which contains not an ounce of truth. To make money the representative of the form of value signifies recognizing that money is the exclusive form of the functioning of the law of value. It is to recognize that it delimits the immediate terrain of the critique. Critique within immediacy.

The exceptional importance of this attack of the *Grundrisse* on money, considered as an eminent form of the expression of the law of value, is not nevertheless bound only to the immediate character of the critique. There is another point to be considered right away; it is that the social relation underlying this making extreme of the relation of value is not envisaged from the point of view of synthesis, but from the point of view of antagonism. Antagonism can only exist if the capitalist relation does not resolve itself in a synthesis. If therefore the relation of value is immediately related to the immediate dualism/pluralism of social antagonisms, if it does not constitute a mediating other, in that case the analysis must decide to take into account the actors who interpret the different roles of this play: the relation of value will always and only be the fiction which extends over the socio-political overdetermination of class conflict. One cannot speak of value without speaking of exploitation, but above all, without determining the function of valorization as overdetermination of the concrete contents of class struggle, as command and domination of one class over another—determining the composition of each one.

It is necessary, finally, to consider a third element in order to completely understand the extraordinary importance of this opening of the *Grundrisse* on money. *Money as the crisis* of the law of value (and its preventive demystification) was the first element. *Money as overdetermination* and as the tension toward command on the basis of the composition of the two classes in struggle: that is the second element. The third is the importance Marx attributes to the level of analysis which is immediately that of the socialization of capital. It would be impossible to start with money as an eminent/exclusive form of the manifestation of value—without taking the *process of socialization of capital as a premise.*

We will return at greater length further on to these arguments. For the moment, it seems to me opportune to respond to the question posed at the outset, that is, whether the fact that a chapter on commodities is missing and that the analysis begins with value as it appears immediately in money engenders in the *Grundrisse* useful effects. It seems to me necessary to give a positive response to this question. Under the form of money, the law of value is presented (1) in crisis, (2) in an antagonistic manner, and (3) with a social dimension. From the outset. Beginning from this assumption, one must add that *Capital* seems almost to be a propaedeutic for the *Grundrisse:* it minutely presents, through the concepts which resume the history of capitalism, the conclusion of this history which the *Grundrisse* takes as its object of critique.

This is the theoretical attack of the *Grundrisse.* But the fact is added, and it is not inessential, that money—in its historical presence—is offered for analysis as crisis. Therefore, what the theoretical approach contains implicitly in itself the historical analysis reveals explicitly. Sergio Bologna has brought a series of important elements of demonstration in this regard. Describing, on the basis of materials used by Marx in his journalistic work, the crisis taking place around 1857–58, the monetary aspect of the crisis appears as the central element. Therefore it is not an accident that Darimon is the initial object of Marx's polemic: throughout his work—as is the case in much more important terms through Proudhon's *Gratuité du Credit*—the *historic passage which the bourgeois state operates in taking the form of the extraction of surplus value* is mystified. Marx finds himself before "the first complete form of the modern state, the government of social capital; the first complete form of a modern monetary system, the centralized government of liquidity." All of this is presented under the form of crisis: Marx's route is that which descends from an adherence to the monetary imagel of the crisis (crises will always present themselves from now on under the monetary form) to an analysis of the crisis of social relations, from the crisis of circulation to the crisis of the relation between necessary labor and surplus labor. As if in an enormous effort of anticipation, the crisis comes to figure the historic tendency of capitalist development. And it is in this historical projection that the crisis becomes a crisis of the law of value. Within the historical projection of a form of production which becomes increasingly more social, in which the modern function of value is transformed into a function of command, of domination, and of intervention on the social fractions of necessary labor and accumulation. The State is here the "synthesis of civil society" (p. 109; 29): this definition, formulated in the *Introduction,* finds continuous confirmation in the *Grundrisse* (pp. 228, 265; 139, 175), already maturing into the more complete definitions which see in the State the direct representative of collective capital, which is itself—to use Engels' term—"collective capitalist." The passage is real, signalled by a crisis which defines its necessity while, at the same time, indicating the directions of a solution. On this result of the historic development of capitalism criticism should therefore be exercised and within these passages the consciousness of the tendential movement, that is, of the antagonism, should impose. Keeping in mind that the strong synthesis which capitalism tries to effectuate, in the form of the command, through its socialization and its institutionalization, requires an adequate categorial response. The theory cannot be detached from its adherence to history. Money, that leap forward of the monetary form of value, represents thus the historical immediacy of the crisis—but also of the tendency.

The Proudhonians cultivated this passage in order to mystify it. How do Proudhon and Darimon in fact respond to the question posed by the crisis? They respond by explaining that money is an equivalent and, insisting on this peculiar nature of it, they develop a polemic which aims at a revalorization of a pure, deployed, and abundant circulation. But, Marx notes, if money is an equivalent, if it has the nature of an equivalent, it is above all *the equivalence of a social inequality*. Crisis, then, does not come from the imperfection of circulation in a regime of equivalence, and it cannot be corrected by a reform of circulation in a regime of equivalence. Crisis derives from the inequality of the relations of production and can only be *suppressed* by suppressing that inequality. Money hides a content which is eminently a content of inequality, a content of exploitation. *The relation of exploitation is the content of the monetary equivalent:* better, this content could not be exhibited. And Marx demonstrates this. But the demonstration does not stop there: it is still necessary to underline the *form* under which money hides the content, something which is, ultimately, more important than the content itself. Because this form is that of the contradiction, of the antagonism which monetary circulation tries to terminate and to resolve. The reformism of "true socialism," at the very moment when it seeks to perfect—beyond the limits and the sequences of the crisis—the mechanism of circulation and of equivalence, comes thus to annul those concrete reflections which form takes from the antagonism of those contents which it hides. Capital seeks the development of reformism, which provides it with protections against critiques from the workers' side; capital restructures itself in relation to the necessity of displacing always further forward the limit of the contradiction which the form of circulation accumulates from the antagonism of the fundamental relation of production. To demystify "true socialism" means therefore to demonstrate this confluence of reformism and of the interest of capital in development. It means to insist on the centrality of form for the function of exploitation. It means carrying the analysis to the point where revolution appears as the liberation from the content of exploitation in the sense that is is the *liberation from the entire form of the circulation of value*, of value *tout court*—which is nothing but the form of the calculation of exploitation. But this is not enough. If the form and content of value are thus linked in exploitation, if all re-form is a deepening of the content of exploitation, the antagonism is placed at that level of totality

and radicality: there is no revolution without a destruction of bourgeois
society, and of wage labor, as a producer of value, and of money as an
instrument of the circulation of value and of command. All progress in the
socialization of the form of circulation accentuates the content of exploitation:
it is thus the progression of that nexus that should be destroyed, along with
all the ideological and institutional forms that represent and dynamize it—
all the more if they are "socialist." Money, the reformist's exercises in relation
to it: there is all the shit. On the other hand: *"Der Klassenkampf als Schluss,
worin die Bewegung und Auflösung der ganzen Scheisse auflöst"* (To Engels, April
30, 1868, *Correspondence.*) It is on this deep tissue that the diverse parts of
the notebooks on money are joined and articulated.

But the analysis must be still more attentively taken up. The polemic
against the Proudhonians thus contains three points. Which is to say that on
one side Marx concentrates, as we have seen, his theoretical and political
critique against the specific "socialist" mystification of the period, that is,
intervenes in a destructive manner in the polemic on banks and the general
equivalent. On the other hand, and in the second place, Marx places this
polemic on the margin of a tendency which is, in his eyes, and which
becomes, in the eyes of everyone, more and more fundamental: that is the
tendency to reform the State in terms of the complete representation of
bourgeois society, and to restructure the State in financial terms. With the
crisis of the '50s, that period opens which finally leads to Hilferding's and
Lenin's representation of the State and of finance capital: it is this tendential
element which Marx, with his insistence on money, also follows. Once again
the result is the presupposition. Now, through these two polemical movements,
the definitive figure of the theory of value in the writings of this period on
money is determined—as a third fundamental element: value as a social and
equivalent mediation of inequality, theory of value as part of the theory of
surplus value, theory of surplus value as social rule of social exploitation.
It is ultimately the level at which develops the polemic (money, the synthesis
of civil society in the form of the State, the deepening of the social form
of exploitation) to call for the characterization of the theory of value and its
definition *(together)* in terms exclusively of *surplus value* and of the *socialization*
of exploitation—terms which we find namely in the *Grundrisse.* One can
thus paradoxically say, while in *Capital* the categories are generally modelled
on private and competitive capital, in the *Grundrisse* they are modelled on
a tendential scheme of *social capital.* This is the meaning of the attack against
money, as defined by the polemic against the Proudhonians.

Let us now take up once again the point-by-point reading of the text of
Notebooks I and II on money. The first part, which we have entitled *"Money
and Crisis,"* is an entirely tormented movement at the intersection between
these two terms: crisis shows what money is. As for Darimon, his discourse—
if one follows the text—is nothing more than a succession of errors at the
statistical and calculatory level. (*Grundrisse,* pp. 108–22, 126, 130; 28–42,

46, 50). But one cannot only hold to the text; it is the political finality of the general discourse of the Proudhonians which must be considered—and immediately condemned.

> We have reached the fundamental question, which is no longer related to the point of departure. The general question would be this: Can the existing relations of production and the relations of distribution which correspond to them be revolutionized by a change in the instrument of circulation, in the organization of circulation? Further question: Can such a transformation of circulation be undertaken without touching the existing relations of production and the social relations which rest on them? If every such transformation of circulation presupposes changes in other conditions of production and social upheavals, there would naturally follow from this the collapse of the doctrine which proposes tricks of circulation as a way of, on the one hand, avoiding the violent character of these social changes, and, on the other, making these changes appear to be not a presupposition but a gradual result of the transformations in circulation. An error in this fundamental premise would suffice to prove that a similar misunderstanding has occurred in relation to the inner connections between the relations of production, of distribution and of circulation [*Grundrisse*, p. 122; 42].

In short, these gentlemen want to improve capitalism, the circulation of money "without abolishing and sublating the very relation of production which is expressed in the category money" (*Grundrisse*, p. 123; 42). But this is a "self-contradictory demand": it is not possible, in fact,

> to get around essential determinants of a relation by means of formal modifications. Various forms of money may correspond better to social production in various stages; one form may remedy evils against which another is powerless; but none of them, as long as they remain forms of money, and as long as money remains an essential relation of production, is capable of overcoming the contradictions inherent in the money relation, and can instead only hope to reproduce these contradictions in one or another form. One form of wage labor may correct the abuses of another, but no form of wage labor can correct the abuse of wage labor itself. [*Grundrisse*, p. 123; 42–3].

Certainly, the work of these Proudhonian gentlemen tries to mystify the reality of things: but how is that still possible, when something as preponderant as crisis re-proposes the very theorectical terms of the discourse? Money is a mediating category of the social antagonism: the definition stabilizes the *possibility* of crisis, the effectuation demonstrates it *in action*.

At this point, however, enough of the polemic: if the intersection of money and of crisis destroys the Proudhonian mystification, it also produces much more important effects. In particular, it demonstrates what value is. The definition of value is entirely brought back to the generality of money, in the middle of a crisis which demonstrates the exclusively tendential function of money to hide and to represent antagonistic social relations. It is thus in its character as money and under the tendency demonstrated through crisis that the theory of value must be reformulated. *The characteristics of money must be assumed into those of value.* The theory of value, as it has existed so far, is simply an allusion to money as a concrete representation of the social mediation of the antagonism. Value will be defined through average labor, through *socially necessary labor* in the sense in which money is defined in this framework. "What determines value is not the amount of labor time incorporated in products, but rather the amount of labor time necessary at a given moment" (*Grundrisse*, p. 135; 55). But, if one looks more closely, the definition of necessary labor is a definition which is already social. Consequently, "the *market value* is always different, is always below or above this average value of a commodity" (*Grundrisse*, p. 137; 56). "Considered as values, all commodities are qualitatively equal and differ only quantitatively" (*Grundrisse*, p. 141; 59). Here once again the Proudhonian hypothesis is inverted: that which the reformists see as a solution to the antagonism constitutes its basis. It is at this level of social mediation that money, as the eminent form of value, constitutes the terrain on which, against which, the theory will develop. Anything but a metaphysics of value! Marx leaves that to his predecessors, and too often as well to those who follow him. Value is money, is this shit, to which there is no alternative but destruction: the suppression of money. Let us study it then in order to destroy it.

And now we see the equation value-money-crisis. As a continual oscillation:

> The *market value* is always different, is always below or above this average value of a commodity. Market value equates itself with real value by means of its constant oscillations, never by means of an equation with real value as if the latter were a third party, but rather by means of constant non-equation of itself (Hegel would say, not by way of abstract identity, but by constant negation of the negation, i.e., of itself as negation of real value) [*Grundrisse*, p. 137; 56].

This oscillation is at once a law of movement and the possibility of crisis. This oscillation is the form of existence of value, the continuous commutation and the essential duality of value. This oscillation is the revelation of the social relation which in reality extends itself, the mode in which is consolidated exchangeability as an exclusive social relation. This oscillation is thus, still and always, the possibility of crisis. But what crisis? The crisis which constitutes the *concept* refers to the definition of the *real* as antagonism and crisis.

> To the degree that production is shaped in such a way that every producer becomes dependent on the exchange value of his commodity, i.e. as the product increasingly becomes the immediate object of production—to the same degree must *money relations* develop, together with the contradictions immanent in the *money relation,* in the relation of the product to itself as money. The need for exchange and for the transformation of the product into a pure exchange value progresses in step with the division of labor, i.e., with the increasingly social character of production. But as the latter grows, so grows the power of *money,* i.e., the exchange relation establishes itself as a power external to and independent of the producers. What originally appeared as a means to promote production becomes a relation alien to the producers. As the producers become more dependent on exchange, exchange appears to become more independent of them, and the gap between the product as product and the product as exchange value appears to widen. Money does not create these antitheses and contradictions; it is, rather, the development of these contradictions and antitheses which creates the seemingly transcendental power of money [*Grundrisse,* p. 146; 65].

To recapitulate. Value, in the figure of money, is given as contradiction, as "the possibility that these two separated forms in which the commodity exists are not convertible into one another" (*Grundrisse,* p. 147; 65). This antagonistic nature ("while the equation itself becomes dependent on external conditions, hence a matter of chance"—*Grundrisse,* p. 148; 66) is revealed spatially (commercial crisis) and temporally (cyclical crisis); but *the basis* of this is *the social relation* which founds the necessity of the form of exchangeability, of value and of money. It is here that the *possibility* of crisis is transformed into its *actuality:*

> It is absolutely necessary that forcibly separated elements which essentially belong together manifest themselves by way of forcible eruption as the *separation* of things which belong together in essence. The unity is brought about *by force.* As soon as the antagonistic split leads to eruptions, the economists point to the *essential unity* and abstract from the alienation [*Grundrisse,* p. 150; 68].

The discourse on "money and crisis" thus prepares a passage to an analysis of the real. On the one hand, Marx utilizes the Proudhonian hypothesis (reading it as a mystification of a definite passage, which is developed within the crisis, from the form of value to the form of money), and on the other, inverts this hypothesis, showing it to be a falsification and an attempt to hypothesize a real antagonism. *The critique must therefore make itself political, must assault the social conditions of the antagonism.* And this is in fact the road Marx follows. The second passage of the "Notebook on Money" begins on this terrain. As for the first passage, what we've examined up to here, it seems almost a run to prepare the leap, the entry into the middle of the things that materialist criticism should consider.

But before also entering ourselves onto this terrain, let us look for a moment at an element—often implicit, at times explicit—in the pages we have just considered, which we have not however taken into consideration. It is the attention paid to *money as a symbol*. This amounts to saying that Marx, at the very moment in which he considers the possibility of crisis, namely, the necessity of the function of money (value) to break from the antagonism which constitutes it, he considers also the ambiguous effect of this detachment. Break, scission, equal the deepening of the contrast of class which lies below the monetary relation. But the elements of the contrast, when they are not mediated, re-emerge in all their power of opposition. Further on in the *Grundrisse* Marx will insist more attentively on the composition of the working class at this level of scission. Here he insists instead on the political function of money as a symbol, as a function of command. *Money as a "mere symbol,"* as a "social symbol," as an "a priori idea"—in short "the money-subject" (*Grundrisse,* p. 141, 144, 167; 60, 63, 84)—can be the result of the moment of crisis, can be one solution of crisis. Let us look closely at this point: here Marx explains his dialectic, that it is not a Hegelian one of necessary mediation, that it is not a Proudhonian one of the law of value, but it is the logic of antagonism, of risk, of opening. *The symbol can become subject,* value can become command, overdetermination can break the dialectic and be in force with power and command. Fascism, barbarism, and regression are not impossible. The symbol can be stronger than reality because it is born from the conscious scission of reality. We will see further on the extraordinary importance of this Marxist intuition. (Too dry is the reading of Rosdolsky, pp. 145–47. While he justifiably insists on the possibility of attaining the theory of surplus value on the basis of this intrinsic element of Marx's theory of money, Rosdolsky undervalues the possibility of a *neue Darstellung* on this subject. Rosdolsky does not realize that this logical and theoretical passage can also be a historical and political passage.)

"Money and inequality." Once again a pedantic beginning: critique of Gray and of the Saint-Simonian bank. Marx repeats himself: general conditions of production, from money to exchange to the social conditions of the one and of the other: "The biggest exchange process is not that between commodities, but that between commodities and labor" (*Grundrisse,* p. 155; 73). But here, boom! The first big leap, *the first of the political excursuses of the **Grundrisse**.*

Let us begin with a more simple point: money, the form of value, is a relation of inequality, generically representative of the property relation, substantively representative of the power relation.

> The reciprocal and all-sided dependence of individuals who are indifferent to one another forms their social connection. This social bond is expressed in *exchange value,* by means of which alone each individual's own activity or his product becomes an activity and a product for him; he must produce a general product—*exchange value,* or, the latter isolated for itself and individualized, *money.* On the other side, the power which each individual exercises over the activity of others or over social wealth exists in him as the owner of *exchange values,* of *money.* The individual carries his social power, as well as his bond with society, in his pocket [*Grundrisse,* p. 156–7; 74–5].

Now, the less is the force of exchange, that much more is the force of the community that links individuals together: that is the form of ancient society.

> Personal independence founded on objective [*sachlicher*] dependence is the second great form, in which a system of general social metabolism, of universal relations, of all-round needs and universal capacities is formed for the first time. Free individuality, based on the universal development of individuals and on their social wealth, is the third stage. The second stage creates the conditions for the third [*Grundrisse,* p. 158; 75].

This a philosophy of history? One cannot properly say so: because in fact the history described is immediately inverted into an active and constructive relation, and at the same time into a dialectic so extreme that it can in no way be resolved. On the one hand, therefore, "exchange and division of labor reciprocally condition one another" (*Grundrisse,* p. 158; 77). Already in the body of labor is therefore implanted that duplicity of exchange and of money which totally absorbs it. This is thus "reification, reified relation, reified exchange value" (*Grundrisse,* p. 160; 78). But on the other hand, *destruction* of all this, conscious, voluntary, rational, creative destruction: "Universally developed individuals, whose social relations, as their own communal {*gemeinschaftlich*} relations, are hence also subordinated to their own communal control, are no product of nature, but of history" (*Grundrisse,* p. 162; 79). (If one looks closely: this development is struggle, break, creation. In no sense a restoration of an original essence. Here, humanism has no place. "It is as ridiculous to yearn for a return to that original fullness as it is to believe that with this complete emptiness history has come to a standstill. The bourgeois viewpoint has never advanced beyond this antithesis between itself and this romantic viewpoint, and therefore the latter will accompany it as legitimate antithesis up to its blessed end" (*Grundrisse*, p. 162; 80). Certainly, the dialectic of these two moments is necessary: "Universal prostitution appears as a necessary phase in the development of the social character of personal talents, capacities, abilities, activities" (*Grundrisse*, p. 163; 80): but even more necessary—and historical and conscious— is the collapse of this prostitution.

This theoretical and political explosion does not have content. It will be taken up once again further on; for now, it is an anticipation that awaits the maturation of seeds planted in order to represent themselves as protagonists. Let us therefore grow these seeds, turning to the analysis of money.

"Money as measure and as general equivalent." We know the problem and its solution. "Money is the physical medium into which exchange values are dipped, and in which they obtain the form corresponding to their general character" (*Grundrisse*, p. 167; 84). But it is only labor time which makes this generality: "Money is labor time in the form of a general object" (*Grundrisse*, p. 168; 85). What follows is the critique of Adam Smith, which assumes two determinations of labor—that which produces and that which produces for money—as juxtaposed. Now, producing for money is *at the same time* a moment of exploitation and a moment of socialization. Capitalist socialization exalts the sociality of money as exploitation, while communist socialization destroys money, affirming the immediate sociality of labor. "In the second case, the *presupposition is itself mediated;* i.e. a communal production, communality, is presupposed as the basis of production. The labor of the individual is posited from the outset as social labor" (*Grundrisse*, p. 172; 88). "His product is *not an exchange value."* Marx continues like this for a while.

Now, here it is worth the trouble to reconsider certain elements of the reasoning, elements which—moreover—we have already encountered. It continually strikes me that Marx's inversion of the reified generality of money (of value) into the *productive generality of associated labor* is fundamental. The inversion implies *no homology:* the antagonistic character of the categories and of Marx's method excludes it. The more fundamental the representation of value in the figure of money, the more fundamental is the *refutation of value,* the *radicality of its inversion.* Communism is not the realization of the interchangeability of value, the being in force of money as a real measure. Communism is the negation of all measure, the affirmation of the most exasperated plurality—creativity.

> Thus, economy of time, along with the planned distribution of labor time among the various branches of production, remains the first economic law on the basis of communal production. It becomes law, there, to an even higher degree. However, this is essentially different from a measurement of exchange values (labor or products) by labor time [*Grundrisse*, p. 173; 89].

Economy of time and free planned activity: let us keep in mind these two elements which here characterize communism. *Refusal of labor?* It will probably not be entirely useless to take up once again (as we shall do) this problematic.

"Money as a measure of circulation." We are in the middle of the "magnificent side" of money, of that aspect and that movement which creates at once socialization and crises. A long parenthesis on metals has anticipated this new theoretical attack. Now "the first task is firmly to establish the *general concept of circulation*" (*Grundrisse,* p. 187; 102). It is another of the central points of the *Grundrisse:* on this basis in fact will be developed the second great strand of the analysis, that which has to do with problems of social capital and of the antagonism at this level. And here, as always occurs in the extremely dense structure of this work, already some *anticipations* of this rich development are included. But let us look at the passages one by one. In the first place, money is presented as a universal in movement, as a *"perpetuum mobile,"* as "a circle of exchange, a totality of the same, in constant flux, proceeding more or less over the entire surface of society; a system of acts of exchange" (*Grundrisse,* p. 188; 103). But, in the second place, in this role as the motor of circulation, the deep actor of the unity of the market, money is also the fixation of the reification and *autonomization of the general equivalent.* "The precondition of commodity circulation is that they be produced as *exchange values,* not as *immediate use values,* but as mediated through exchange value. Appropriation through and by means of divestiture *{Entaüsserung}* and alienation *{Veraüsserung}* is the fundamental condition" (*Grundrisse,* p. 196; 111). And again: "Circulation is the movement in which the general alienation appears as general appropriation and general appropriation as general alienation" (*Grundrisse,* p. 196; 111). Money is represented as "a power over the individuals which has become autonomous." From this derive certain fundamental *consequences:* namely, that the antagonism inherent in this conceptual duplication of money in circulation produces circulation as a "false" process to infinity. In reality, the process is contradictory from all points of view; the acts presented in it are reciprocally "indifferent," distant in space and time. *The possibility of crisis,* already individuated at the level of the analysis of the general equivalent in itself, is represented *at the level of circulation.*

> In so far as purchase and sale, the two essential moments of circulation, are indifferent to one another and separated in place and time, they by no means need to coincide. Their indifference can develop into the fortification and apparent independence of the one against the other. But in so far as they are both essential moments of a single whole, there must come a moment when the independent form is violently broken and when the inner unity is established externally through a violent explosion. Thus already in the quality of money as a medium, in the splitting of exchange

into two acts, there lies the germ of crises, or at least their possibility, which cannot be realized, except where the fundamental preconditions of classically developed, conceptually adequate circulation are present [*Grundrisse,* p. 198; 112–13].

But, again, this is not enough. In the *Grundrisse,* all the turns the discourse makes around the antagonism of circulation, its spatial and temporal determinations, are immediately transferred to the *division of labor,* to the social conditions of the antagonism. It is also what happens here. And the corresponding passage also occurs, that of the inversion, that which gathers the richness of the process of capital within circulation in order to negate it, not toward a successive development, but in terms of destruction and of *communist appropriation.* This series of passages is fundamental because while it illustrates the possibility of crisis inherent in the concept of money, it also demonstrates the nature of Marx's categorial procedure. It is not in fact the dialectical possibility of crisis but the antagonistic violence of inversion which continually gives meaning to the argumentative process. It is evident that the very usage of the categories is modified: the categories return ceaselessly to the subjectivity of the antagonism; they can only be definitively read in this light; they can only function in this way.

But let us proceed. At this point money "appears here *firstly* as an end in itself, whose sole realization is served by commodity trade and exchange" (*Grundrisse,* p. 203; 117). "We must then observe money in its third quality, in which both of the former are included, i.e. that of serving as measure as well as the general medium of exchange and hence the realization of commodity prices." The dialectical scheme of the exposition is concluded: the synthesis demonstrates *"money as money and capital,"* as realized totality of the process. Here there is something like a pause in Marx's procedure: the antagonistic inversion is not in fact placed on the primary level. The analysis almost amuses itself in a long *phenomenology of the monetary synthesis.* This phenomenology is in fact intended to demonstrate all the potency, all the subjectivity on the part of capital. The potency of money as a representative of circulation, of its totality and general dominion over realization comes to be extremely accentuated. The dominion of money has the appearance and the indifference of mobility and fluidity; money exercises its dominion under the paradoxical form *of evanescence.* It is everywhere and it dilutes itself in persistence, but at the same time it recovers itself as a sign of the totality. Its intermediation is as supple as it is rigid. But that is how this paradox is materialized: the evanescent power of money attacks things and transforms them in its own image and resemblance. It is a *demiurgic power* which through a sign modifies reality. It is clear that in this Marx, money is a *tautology for power.* A power that extends everywhere. And in fact: money is represented as a *relation of production* ("the money relation is

itself a relation of production if production is looked at in its totality"—
Grundrisse, p. 214; 128), as *instrument of production* ("since circulation no
longer appears in its primitive simplicity, as quantitative exchange, but as
a process of production, as a real metabolism. And thus money is itself
stamped as a particular moment of this process of production"—*Grundrisse*,
p. 217; 130); as *power* (in its capacity of "diffusion and fragmentation in the
world of commodities"—(*Grundrisse*, p. 218; 132); money *"as the individual*
of general wealth" exercises "a general power over society, over the whole
world of gratifications, labors, etc."—*Grundrisse*, p. 222; 133), as—specifically—*power over wage labor* ("It is inherent in the simple character of
money itself that it can exist as a developed moment of production only
where and when *wage labor* exists; that in this case, far from subverting the
social formation, it is rather a condition for its development and a driving-
wheel for the development of all forces of production, material and mental"—
Grundrisse, p. 223; 134–35); *"As material representative of general wealth,* as
individualized exchange value, money must be the *direct* object, aim and product
of general labor, the labor of all individuals. Labor must directly produce
exchange value, i.e. money. It must therefore be *wage labor"*—(*Grundrisse*,
p. 224; 135), as a *productive power* ("Money as aim here becomes the means
of general industriousness": "It is clear, therefore, that when wage labor is
the foundation, money does not have a dissolving effect, but acts productively"—*Grundrisse*, p. 224; 135), as a *universal power* ("which produces new
needs," "a means for expanding the universality of wealth," "for creating
the true generality"—*Grundrisse*, p. 225; 136). And finally, money is presented as "the *real common substance* of wage labor and of capital."

It is not by chance that money represents the "real substance of wage
labor and of capital" in the passage we have just analyzed. While in fact in
the other passages of the analysis of money, the specific dialectical process
of the figure of capital contained, next to and in it, the process of inversion,
in the paragraphs devoted to *'"money as money"* this does not occur. It cannot
occur because that is the triumph of money, of its subjectivity: it is extreme
accentuation of the relation through the identification of one of its poles.
But the picture must be here immediately changed, inverted. All the contradictions which the categories have verified in their constitution and development are now going to be gathered into the operation of inversion. It
would be possible to reuse the theses which we gathered under point B,
since already in those pages the tension toward inversion is expressed. It
would be better nonetheless to concentrate on those new theses which constitute the end of Notebook I and the beginning of II. There is in these
pages a bit of weariness, but the movement of inversion is strongly launched
and is radical.

Marx insists on three themes: *money and world market, money and productive
circulation, the political and institutional form of social reproduction.* They are

three strictly related themes: in fact, on all three terrains, inversion can be given at a level of generality which is that produced by the development of the investigation finished at this point. One can say that, in distinction from what happens in point B, here the attention latches onto the extensive contradictions rather than onto the intensive contradiction.

The world market is the specific terrain on which crisis determines "the general intimation which points beyond the presupposition, and the urge which drives towards the adoption of a new historic form" (*Grundrisse*, p. 228; 139). The world market multiplies the contradictions of money in circulation, putting it all in movement. The relation attains the maximum of difference and accumulates in this immense area the totality of differences. The world market is the *tendency:* money in as much as it is universal potency moves preponderantly toward that dimension. But in so doing it carries to that signification the ensemble of contradictions which constitute it. The qualitative leap to the world market constitutes in antagonism the totality of contradictions. We will return to this point shortly—also to respond to the criticisms which Marx's presentation of the relation "world market-money-crisis" immediately gives rise to. It could be said in fact that the extensive dimension comes close to denying the intensive dimension and that the *relation* between the accumulation of contradictions and the resurgence of the antagonism is more *a logical leap* than a deduction. But we will come soon to this element. We pass then to the second proposed relation: that between money and circulation, and money and reproduction. Now, money as reproductive potency reproduces together itself and the world of production as its condition. Money lives "as relation to itself through the processs of circulation"; but this occurs because

> the process of circulation must also and equally appear as the process of the production of exchange values. It is thus, on one side, the regression of exchange value into labor, on the other side, that of money into exchange value, which is now posited, however, in a more profound character. With circulation, the determined price is presupposed, and circulation as money posits it only formally. The *determinateness* of exchange value itself, or the measure of price, must now itself appear as an act of circulation. Posited in this way, exchange value is *capital*, and circulation is posited at the same time as an act of production *{Grundrisse*, p. 235; 146].

"*Circulation as act of production.*" The inversion must therefore occur also inside circulation, inside productive circulation. That constitutes the synthesis of the complete process of capital; in it "money in its final, completed character now appears in all directions as a contradiction, a contradiction which dissolves itself, drives towards its own dissolution" (*Grundrisse*, p. 233; 144). And in this case as well (and in a much more convincing way than in the case of the world market) the tendency of money to constitute the synthesis of circulation and production determines the *explosion of the antagonism*. Finally, a third point to be considered, the relation money–institutional forms. Even here money is in possession of an extraordinary expansive force. In its light, "all inherent contradictions of bourgeois society appear extinguished in money relations as conceived in a simple form; and bourgeois democracy even more than the bourgeois economists takes refuge in this aspect (the latter are at least consistent enough to regress to even simpler aspects of exchange value and exchange) in order to construct apologetics for the existing economic relations" (*Grundrisse*, p. 240–1; 152). "The money system can indeed only be the realization of this system of freedom and equality" (*Grundrisse*, p. 246; 157). *The democracy of modern people is the total realization of exchange value.* All the institutional forms of democracy are only its representations. But here too the contradiction runs through the cumulation of effects of exchange value, of money in order to show the antagonistic conditions: "already the simple forms of exchange value and of money latently contain the opposition between labor and capital etc" (*Grundrisse*, p. 248; 159). The consequence, to the socialists,

> the proper reply . . . is: that exchange value or, more precisely, the money system is in fact the system of equality and freedom, and that the disturbances which they encounter in the further development of the system are disturbances inherent in it, are merely the realization of *equality and freedom*, which prove to be inequality and unfreedom. It is just as pious as it is stupid to wish that exchange value would not develop into capital, nor labor which produces exchange value into wage labor [*Grundrisse*, p. 248-49; 160].

It has been noted that the passage from money to the world market to crisis does not have the intensity and the same synoptic significance the other conclusive points of the chapter on money have. But, without denying the limits of Marx's argumentation, it is possible here to add certain annotations. The discourse on the *"world market"* appears in Marx, in the *Grundrisse*, as an indication of work to be done. Such is the case in Notebook M (*Grundrisse*, pp. 108–9; 28–29), such is the case, in many places, in the central notebooks (*Grundrisse*, pp. 228, 264; 139, 175). In every case the reference to the world market concludes Marx's project of work, a project of work through an articulation of books which should gather together the entire operation of the theoretical destruction of capitalist society. *World market versus crisis*. If one looks closely: when Marx projects the book on the world market and crisis he does not confuse it generically with the dimensions of the internationalization and of the consonant and concurrent processes of capital: he distinguishes them, on the contrary, explicitly. World market is then understood as a specific category. We will see further on—in Lesson 3 on method—how, in this case, a specificity of Marx's method matches clearly: it is worth saying that the cumulation of concrete elements determines a new categorial level; the analysis is displaced, *dislocated* forward. Well, one could demand that, at this new level, the intensity of the analysis of the antagonism correspond to its extension and density. It is an optical effect, the disproportion between the indication and the content of the analysis, which here, now, leaves us unsatisfied before Marx's proposition for analyzing the world market-crisis knot. But if only, in Marx's way, we fill that form with theoretical contents which centuries of class struggle on a world level have accumulated, then we will understand well how this indication is anything but disarmed. The other side is that which accentuates not so much the consideration of the category but its tendential formation on the basis of the antagonism of money. But of that we have already spoken.

We have thus come to the end of the reading of this chapter on money. It seems to me that the questions which were initially posed have found a first contribution to discussion and raised further reasons for being, at least approximately, developed. It seems to me, in particular, possible to confirm the judgment anticipated in regard to the utility of the attack, of the beginning of this chapter on money. Now, therefore, what are the theoretical advantages that this irruption of money contains? It seems to me possible to respond on several planes.

Above all on the plane of the simple reading. Here, it seems to me that *the value-money knot immediately proposed concretizes the theme of value as it never elsewhere occurs in Marx.* The passage from money-form to commodity-form, from the *Grundrisse* to *Capital,* only adds abstraction and confusion. Despite all the intentions and declarations to the contrary, that which the attack on the problem of commodities determines, it is a more idealist, Hegelian method. The insistence on money, in the second place, does not autonomize and separate the theory of value. We will see further on—in Lesson 4—how one can only speak of the theory of value as a part of the theory of surplus value: the reduction of value to money, while it also removes the temptation to autonomize the theory of value, introduces instead the sequel of the investigation; it initiates a good route. Money is a concrete thing which contains all the dynamism and the contradictions of value, as much from the formal as from the substantial point of view, without possessing the abstract void of the discourse on value.

From the formal point of view. Money can describe, and here it describes with great potency, *the dynamism of the tendency and that of the antagonism.* On the first plane, that of the tendency, it is indeed true what Marx underlines: Money "is itself the community [*Gemeinwesen*] and can tolerate none other standing above it. But this presupposes the full development of exchange values, hence a corresponding organization of society" (*Grundrisse,* p. 223; 134). And we recall as well that "when wage labor is the foundation, money does not have a dissolving effect, but acts productively" (*Grundrisse,* p. 224; 135). But with this, the basis of the antagonism is given directly. Money and division of labor, money and exploitation, constant relation of a *deepening of the scission as a result of its extension;* all of this is given in that perspective which introduces and develops the critique from within the immediacy of money. There's nothing, from the formal point of view, that the theory of value can give us and that the theory of money does not give us here in a more effective or colorful form.

All the more so in a substantial consideration. Here money, in its specific dynamism, shows us immediately *the law of value as crisis.* Money is the demonstration that the movement of value is pure precariousness, that its solidity is only tendential and can only determine itself within the continuous alternation between the social averaging of necessary labor and its compulsory overdetermination. It is necessary to insist on these motives which constitute the basis on which the theory of surplus value can and must be established. But that is constituted as a law of class struggle only in the sense in which the law of value becomes a horizon, not a self-sufficient category. And *money well represents this reduction of the law of value to a mere horizon.* Through the theory of money, in fact, on one side, we have the possibility of eliminating the *caput mortuum* of the theory of value: the relation *value–prices.* It is money which constitutes, immediately, this relation, interpreting the oscillation between the social averaging of values of social labor and the overdetermination of prices. Money represents this oscillation in itself; there is—outside this oscillation—no other reality: money is a constitutive oscillation, which mediates and demonstrates the complete value produced by social labor. On the other hand, it is also money which demonstrates, in its appearance as money, as "abstract sensuality," the route which *capitalist command* over society travels in order to overdetermine continually the oscillation of exploitation. Money will permit us to understand how surplus value is consolidated in social command; how to command crisis is the normal situation of capitalism. Centralizing the analysis of money permits Marx therefore *to radically innovate with respect to the theory of value of the classics,* in a double dimension: to reduce the theory of value to the figures of the averaging of social labor, and therefore to define it as oscillation, as conflictuality, as potentiality of antagonism.

But now it is necessary to determine this antagonism. It is not by chance that the analysis will proceed from the critique of money (of value) to that of power. The terrain has so far been prepared for the determination of the theory of surplus value as a fundamental element: but we will see how surplus value itself does not hold if it is not continually referred, as command, to the confrontations, oscillations, crises, the antagonism produced—at the same time as wealth—by social labor. A command attempting continuous political overdetermination. Thus, the attack on money in the *Grundrisse* opens and anticipates the general tone for the theoretical path which moves *from the critique of money to the critique of power.*

The Method of the
Antagonistic Tendency

Reading hypotheses for the *Introduction* (Notebook M). □ Materialist method and concept of production. □ Method and dialectic of the general concept of production. □ The synthesis-scission in production and the particular form of agglomeration in the method of the dialectic and of materialism. □ The three first elements of the critique of political economy: (a) determinate abstraction; (b) the tendency; (c) the criterion of practice. □ Self-critical pause in the development of the methodological research, and some problems. □ Some additional elements to deepen the theory of method: 1. The "sketch on value"; 2. Bastiat and Carey. □ Nevertheless, impossible to get out of it: the method caught between the "tendency" and the "projection." □ A fourth element of the methodic synthesis: (d) displacement and constitution. □ Critical conclusions and open problems.

Notebook M was written by Marx between the 23rd of August and mid-September 1857. Originally published by Kautsky, as noted above, it was republished—for philological reasons, in order to correct Kautsky's edition—in Moscow conjointly with the edition of the *Grundrisse*. It seems to me that putting the *Introduction* and the *Grundrisse* together in the same edition was not inopportune, not simply for philological reasons, but also from the point of view of their very content. Reading *the Introduction and the Grundrisse at the same time permits us to understand each one better.* That there exists a continuity between the two texts is demonstrated by the recurrence, the reappearance in both, of the same plan of work, whatever the modifications undergone (see Lesson 2). What is proposed here is that this continuity is not a simple temporal continuity, that it touches the very nature of the subject matter. There are those who deny all substantive continuity between the *Introduction* and the *Grundrisse*. Vygodskij, for example, who insists on the dialectical discoveries of the *Grundrisse,* entirely underestimates the methodological importance of the *Introduction:* according to him, the *Introduction* is only the resumé of Marx's studies and of the theory of historical materialism of the '40s and '50s; it does not yet bear the stamp of dialectical materialism (which leads to the theory of surplus value), which determines the originality, the true leap forward of the other notebooks. As for the French and Italian schools, which for decades have excessively dwelt on the method of the *Introduction,* they strike me as never having directly confronted the problem of its relation to the *Grundrisse.* In fact, given the "delirious" character of the latter, they have preferred to avoid the problem and to relate the *Introduction* directly to *Capital.* And to conclude: the methodology of 1857 is the materialist methodology of *Capital,* and therefore, the *Introduction* must yield to the latter. Neither of these points of view, which are in substantive agreement concerning the limiting of the methodology of 1857 to a strictly materialist horizon, satisfies me very much. It is no doubt true that Notebook M is not lit by that political and dialectical tension which runs through the other notebooks; it is equally true that there one senses strongly the limits of a slightly vulgar materialism: but, in regard to Vygodskij's thesis, I think that with the *Introduction* one is already fully within the *theoretical leap* which the *Grundrisse* operates, that the two texts derive from the same creative process, and that each one sheds light on the other; as for the theses of the Italian and French schools, it seems to me—in consequence—that one should deny them, and that the relationship that exists between the *Introduction* and *Capital* is identical to that which holds between the entire *Grundrisse* and *Capital.* Therefore, I propose to move on now to the reading of the text, where I will attempt to demonstrate to what extent my hypotheses are well-founded—I insist nevertheless on the usefulness of doing this reading only in Lesson 3, after already having penetrated to the heart of things with Lesson 2. I will continue to pull each text toward the other, in this lesson, but also from now on throughout the analysis.

"The object before us, to begin with, *material production*" (*Grundrisse,* p. 83; [5]). *But what is the concept of production?* There is no more classically philosophical a question than that: for centuries the philosophers have litigated over real and nominal definitions. But every name always possesses some sort of reality: the problem is that the referent not be mystified. In this search for a mediation between name and reality, the latest "philosophers," for example, seem to have fallen into the trap of the "merely aesthetic semblance, of the Robinsonades, great and small": in reality, they only mystify production by introducing an anticipation, "by inventing" production as a political function of bourgeois society in the process of becoming. How to harmonize name and reality correctly? Avoiding mystification does not imply avoiding a political project, but simply linking this political project to reality. Reality is political: but no less true because political.

Reality must thus serve as a target for politics: there is only one true and real politics. The 18th-century "philosophers" mystify reality because they plaster individualism over the concept of production, thus making themselves into an echo of the political project of bourgeois society: and it is false. One can only broach the concept of production by leaving behind the organic, general element which is its basis, by leaving behind the 18th century. But once that is done, once this general impulse is accomplished, this collective link which defines the human mode of producing, one still has not concluded anything: reality and name still remain distant from each other, and one runs the risk of making only a generic name of production. Of course, "all epochs of production have certain common traits, common characteristics." But this "characterization of historical processes of production" doesn't help us much. If *"production in general* is an abstraction," it is nevertheless

> a rational abstraction in so far as it really brings out and fixes the common element and thus saves us repetition. Still, this *general* category, this common element sifted out by comparison, is itself segmented many times over and splits into different determinations. Some determinations belong to all epochs, others only to a few. [Some] determinations will be shared by the most modern epoch and the most ancient. No production will be thinkable without them: however, even though the most developed languages have laws and characteristics in common with the least developed, nevertheless, just those things which determine their development, i.e. the elements which are not general and common, must be separated out from the determinations valid for production as such, so that in their unity—which arises already from the identity of the subject, humanity, and of the object, nature—their essential difference is not forgotten. The whole profundity of those modern economists who demonstrate the eternity and harmoniousness of the existing social relations lies in this forgetting [*Grundrisse*, p. 85; (7)].

This passage contains almost everything: the construction of general conceptual abstraction, its particular determination *on the basis of difference,* the polemic against all those conceptions which try to make the conceptual in general eternal by basing themselves on materialism (against the economists, as before, against the *philosophers* and their lucid ideology).

Up to this point, nonetheless, one cannot say that this constitutes great originality in terms of a definition of the concept. Any realist or materialist writer (even of the 18th century) could have said the same thing. It is necessary therefore to pursue the matter further. *Dialectically? But for there to be a dialectic, there have to be subjects.* Therefore, this is the question we must go into thoroughly.

If there is no production in general, then there is also no general production. Production is always a *particular* branch of production—e.g. agriculture, cattle-raising, manufactures, etc.—or it is a *totality*. But political economy is not technology. The relation of the general characteristics of production at a given stage of social development to the particular forms of production to be developed elsewhere (later). Lastly, production also is not only a particular production. Rather, it is always a certain social body, a social subject, which is active in a greater or sparser totality of branches of production [*Grundrisse*, p. 86; (7–8)].

Here emerges the concept of *totality as a relation and a unity of differences.* It would be necessary to open here a parenthesis (but we can only indicate it now) on the relationship *totality–subjectivity.* Too many writers gargle with this concept of totality, which they reduce to the intensity which would emanate from a knot of idealist determination, although, to the contrary, totality is here, very clearly, the subjective structure, the structure of a carrying subject. Within Marx's methodic horizon, the concept of totality is never intensive. It is extensive, organized, finalized, by the determination of abstraction. Marx's methodic horizon is never invested with the concept of totality; rather it is characterized by the *materialist discontinuity of real processes.* This passage too nevertheless resolves nothing. Certainly, subjectivity confers on the dialectic of the material structure an extremely important dynamism, and it enlarges its dimensions. The example which Marx gives (taking up one of his old but absolutely appropriate ideas) is that of the immediate reduction of property and of the juridical forms of social organization in general to that social structure. *In sum, materialism here subordinates the dialectic to itself,* makes use of it to characterize the subjective (capitalist) totality of the structure. But that is not enough: the dialectic is as impotent as simple materialism to define the revolutionary method. Materialism and dialectics have given us totality and difference, as well as the structural link which subjectively unites them. But that is not enough. It remains insufficient as long as this structure, this totality is *not internally split,* as long as we do not succeed in grasping *not* the structural (capitalist) subjectivity *but* the subjectivities which dialectically constitute the structure (the two classes in struggle). "Thus production, distribution, exchange and consumption form a regular syllogism; production is the generality, distribution and exchange the particularity, and consumption the singularity in which the whole is joined together" (*Grundrisse*, p. 89; [11]). But if these elements form a syllogism, it is necessary then to define the concreteness, the singularity, the difference of the elements of the syllogism. *The category of production,* in the essential terms which distinguish it, and with the totality which characterizes it—a veritable social articulation of reality—*can only be constituted as a category of difference,* as a totality of subjects, of differences, of antagonism. This is the path which we should follow. To accept the totality without insisting on the antagonisms which compose it is "to not conceive [these moments] in their unity. As if this rupture had made its way not from reality into the textbooks, but rather from the textbooks into reality, and as if the task were the dialectic balancing of concepts, and not the grasping of real relations" (*Grundrisse*, p. 90; [11]).

In this discussion of the formation of a category (that of production in this particular case), one has thus arrived at establishing its materialist (against 18th-century ideology) and its dialectical (against the economists) bases and insisted on the subjectivity of its determinate moments (against the reformists and the jurists). The base is solid, but still insufficient. Let us therefore deepen still further the differences of production by latching onto the production-consumption relation, which is the same thing as saying the relation of universality and individuality. This relation is formally circular: "No production without a need. But consumption reproduces the need"; "the object is not an object in general, but a specific object which must be consumed in a specific manner, to be mediated in its turn by production itself"; "Production not only supplies a material for the need, but it also supplies a need for the material" (*Grundrisse*, p. 92; [13–14]). But the circularity of the relation must be broken. "Nothing simpler for a Hegelian than to posit production and consumption as identical" (*Grundrisse*, p. 93; [15]). But one knows that Marx is not a Hegelian; he readily leaves this qualifier to the socialist literateur or to the vulgar economists. Marx is a Marxist: that is to say, a materialist and a dialectician (we have seen how), but, above all else, a revolutionary. *The relation must contain the possibility of scission;* there is no category which can be defined outside the possibility of scission. "In society, however, the producer's relation to the product, once the latter is finished, is an external one, and its return to the subject depends on his relations to other individuals" (*Grundrisse*, p. 94; [15].)

> The relations and modes of distribution thus appear merely as the obverse of the agents of production. An individual who participates in production in the form of wage labor shares in the products, in the results of production, in the form of wages. The structure of distribution is completely determined by the structure of production. Distribution is itself a product of production, not only in its object, in that only the results of production can be distributed, but also in its form, in that the specific kind of participation in production determines the specific forms of distribution, i.e., the pattern of participation in distribution. It is altogether an illusion to posit land in production, ground rent in distribution, etc. [*Grundrisse*, p. 95; (16–17)].

The "agents of production": here we are from all evidence at the central point of the analysis. The general concept of production breaks the limits of its materialist and dialectical definition in order to exalt *the subjectivity of its elements and their antagonistic relation.* This antagonistic relation invests the totality of the concept.

> But before distribution can be the distribution of products, it is: (1) the distribution of the instruments of production, and (2), which is a further specification of the same relation, the distribution of the members of the society among the different kinds of production. (Subsumption of the individuals under specific relations of production.) The distribution of products is evidently only a result of this distribution, which is comprised within the process of production itself and determines the structure of production. To examine production while disregarding this internal distribution within it is obviously an empty abstraction; while conversely, the distribution of products follows by itself from this distribution which forms an original moment of production [*Grundrisse,* p. 96; (17–18)].

Therefore: "The question of the relation between this production-determining distribution, and production, belongs evidently within production itself", which means inside "the general-historical relations in production, and their relation to the movement of history generally" (*Grundrisse,* p. 97; [18]). We obtain the same result to which the inquiry concerning production and consumption leads if we consider the other relation (of the economists' syllogism): the relation between production and circulation. In this case equally, identity is split into difference, and difference is acknowledged as antagonism. "The conclusion we reach is not that production, distribution, exchange and consumption are identical, but that they all form the members of a totality, distinctions within a unity" (*Grundrisse,* p. 99; {20}).

Difference, differences, antagonisms. We do not see how to read Marx's passages otherwise. *The category of production—like that of value—in its generality and its abstraction carries living within it the constitutive possibility of separation.* The dialectical approach is added to the materialist approach not in order to furnish the key to a totalitarian solution to determinacy, but in order to recognize the structural totality as the possibility of scission. The agglomeration of dialectics and of materialism is operated in the *Introduction,* from the outset, under the particular form of scission. One must not, among other things, underestimate the importance of the category chosen as an example of the method: the category of production. Is it possible to think that, no matter what the terminological precautions, Marx does not stand, when it has to do with production and the factory, on one side? The side of the workers? Can one not see production as scission, exploitation, and crisis? Unless one wants to accuse him of being Proudhonian!

The discourse here takes a further step forward: "the method of political economy," that is, the method of the critique of political economy. On this point, Marx establishes certain fundamental criteria. The first principle is that of *"determinate abstraction."* It consists in the methodic assertion that one cannot found the categories beginning naively with the "real" or the "concrete," but only on the basis of the development of a "process of synthesis" of the givens of intuition and of representation. The naive methodology begins with the concrete as a presupposition; Marx's methodology takes *the concrete as a result.* "The scientifically correct method [takes] the concrete as concrete because it is the concentration of many determinations, hence unity of the diverse (*Grundrisse,* p. 101; [21–22]). In this way, rather than make the concrete representation evaporate into an abstract determination, one succeeds, on the contrary, in constructing "abstract determinations [which] lead towards a reproduction of the concrete by way of thought". Therefore, from the abstraction to the concrete, to the determination. The cognitive process interrupts the vain avatars of a scientific behavior which fetishizes the object: it knows on the contrary that determination is the product of a theoretical approximation which utilizes general abstractions, polarities, and dimensions for this end. Truth is an objective. There is no epistemological skepticism in this: "The real subject retains its autonomous existence outside the head just as before; namely as long as the head's conduct is merely speculative, merely theoretical. Hence, in the theoretical method, too, the subject, society, must always be kept in mind as the presupposition" (*Grundrisse,* p. 102; [22]). No epistemological skepticism, but on the contrary, a destruction of every sort of fetishism of the concrete. The theoretical agglomeration of materialism and of dialectics here becomes *operative.* We are well within that reality whose concrete and multiple determinations we attempt, we try, we risk approximating through abstractions. There is will and intelligence, that is, a daily, human practice, in this first principle of the method. But that does not satisfy me: *There is as well the relation between the use value of abstract knowledge and the need for a transformation of knowledge.* In sum, this method of determinate abstraction and of determining abstractions, which throws me into the water in a very Cartesian manner, indicates to me "the path of abstract knowledge, rising from the simple to the combined," and in so doing helps us to discover, to invent reality. But, mind well—and I think that this element has not been sufficiently worked out in the history of the interpretation and methodology of Marxism: the process of determinate abstraction, of the approximation and of the abstract conquest of the concrete is a *collective process,* of collective knowledge. "In all forms of society there is one specific kind of production which predominates over the rest, whose relations thus assign rank and influence to the others. It is a general illumination which bathes all the other colors and modifies their particularity. It is a particular ether which determines the specific gravity of every being which has materialized within it" (*Grundrisse,* pp. 106–7); [27]). Well, the process of determinate abstraction is entirely given inside this collective proletarian illumination: it is therefore an element of critique and a form of struggle.

Determinate abstraction is a dynamic fact. It is in fact appropriate to its epistemological nature to establish a relation between the simple and the complex, between what is given and what is constructed, between a foundation and a project. The second constitutive element of Marx's methodology consists of an interpretation of this relation: it is *the method of the "tendency."* Marx considers the category of "exchange value": it is a rather concrete category in our society. Let us closely analyze it: "This very simple category, then, makes a historic appearance in its full intensity only in the most developed conditions of society," "Thus, although the simpler category may have existed historically before the more concrete, it can achieve its full (intensive and extensive) development precisely in a combined form of society, while the more concrete category was more fully developed in a less developed form of society" (*Grundrisse,* p. 103; [24]). What does all this mean? It means that the relation between the simple and the complex is *a relation* in the full sense of the term, and therefore *a dynamism,* animated by historical subjectivity, by the dynamic collective which is its mark. It means that there exist different degrees of abstraction: on the one hand, the abstraction which seeks the real in the concrete (determinate abstraction), and on the other hand, *the concrete which seeks in abstraction its determination* (the process of the tendency). It is an historical movement which is determined by production and class struggle: which goes from the first to the "second nature," from the first, immediate, concrete truth to the truth of the reversal and of the project. "As a rule, the most general abstractions arise only in the midst of the richest possible concrete development, where one thing appears as common to many, to all. Then it ceases to be thinkable in a particular form alone" (*Grundrisse,* p. 104; [25]).

This is *communism in methodology*; the theoretical method can also be defined as communist: the *Grundrisse* will show us how this methodological approach of the definition of the communist revolution can be concretized. How abstract it is, then, to want to separate the *Introduction* from the substance of the development of Marx's analysis!

> It would therefore be unfeasible and wrong to let the economic categories follow one another in the same sequence as that in which they were historically decisive. Their sequence is determined, rather, by their relation to one another in modern bourgeois society, which is precisely the opposite of that which seems to be their natural order or which corresponds to historical development [*Grundrisse,* p. 107; [28]).

And again: "Human anatomy contains a key to the anatomy of the ape" (*Grundrisse,* p. 105; [26]). It is therefore clear that the tendential method prevails in a decisive way, in Marx's work, from the point of view of its epistemology, over the genealogical method. We will return to this later. What is important to underscore for the moment is that, on this level as well, the method supposes an insertion in a real tissue of which the determination cannot be referred to the context of a simple individual. From this point of view as well, Marx's methodology is a *collective risk*. The tendency: it is not simply what permits a passive construction of the categories on the basis of a sum of historical acquisitions; it is above all what permits a reading of the present in light of the future, in order to make projects to illuminate the future. To take risks, to struggle. A science should adhere to that. And if occasionally one is an ape, it is only in order to be more agile.

The great meaning of the relation between abstraction and determination, between abstraction as verification and abstraction as a project, finds a moment of scientific verification: it is the third element of the methodology of the *Introduction,* it is the "true in practice." In order to define the third criterion of the method, Marx allies the method of determinate abstraction to that of the tendency, in regard to a category—that of "labor"—which constitutes the center of the ensemble of his research. Now, "labor seems a quite simple category." Nevertheless—and here is the method of determinate abstraction at work—when it is economically conceived in this simplicity, " 'labor' is as modern a category as are the relations which create this simple abstraction" (*Grundrisse,* p. 103; [24]). The analysis of the general relations which constitute this category makes evident that this unity, this unity and articulation of multiplicity, is a dynamic element, an intertwining and *a result of subjective forces.* The concept of labor moves in the historical reality of the economy toward ever higher forms of abstraction: it is the capitalist relations of production which determine this movement. In such a way that, slowly—and here again is the work of the tendency—the category broadens, labor becomes

> this abstraction of labor as such [which] is not merely the mental product of a concrete totality of labors. Indifference towards specific labors corresponds to a form of society in which individuals can with ease transfer from one labor to another, and where the specific kind is a matter of chance for them, hence of indifference. Not only the category, labor, but labor in reality has here become the means of creating wealth in general, and has ceased to be organically linked with particular individuals in any specific form [*Grundrisse,* p. 104; (25)].

Now, if one remarks well, "the point of departure of modern economics, namely the abstraction of the category 'labor,' 'labor as such,' labor pure and simple, becomes true in practice" (*Grundrisse,* p. 105; [25]). *The "true in practice" is thus the moment of the development of the category where the abstraction finds a point of focalization and attains the plenitude of its relation to historical reality.* Without this articulation of abstraction and of the tendency, without this moment where it opens onto the truth of practice, onto history in flesh and blood, it would be impossible to proceed scientifically. *"True in practice"* *is the science which becomes a concept of transformation, possibility and actuality of* *a force of transformation.* The Marxist categories are formed in this tangle, their mechanism of formation can only function when the material has been completely formed by these three criteria. "This example of labor shows strikingly how even the most abstract categories, despite their validity— precisely because of their abstractness—for all epochs, are nevertheless, in the specific character of this abstraction, themselves likewise a product of historic relations, and possess their full validity only for and within these relations" (*Grundrisse*, p. 105; [25]). The category is presented at this stage as "product and validity," that is, as real construction and scientific horizon. Let us take the exposition of the concept of "labor" as a concept of production, "as average socially necessary time." That this definition of the concept is produced by history is entirely clear: but it also defines the horizon within which the concept is developed, the keystone of all later development of the categories. We will see further on how the concept of labor, once the exposition has traced its contours in a definitive way, once the mechanism of the tendency has shown all the dialectical articulations that its movement puts into play, when, finally, it appears as true in practice, at the heart of struggles—we will see *how this concept saturated with subjectivity* is once again displaced and how this displacement determines further sequences. This series of methodological passages does not only concern the category "labor" (even if it appears particularly useful to take it as an example): it concerns all Marx's categories of analysis. It is thus not by chance if it is here, in these pages, that the first division of the material to be treated appears, a division to be related to the schematization of the method.

> The order obviously has to be (1) the general, abstract determinants which obtain in more or less all forms of society, but in the above-explained sense. (2) The categories which make up the inner structure of bourgeois society and on which the fundamental classes rest. Capital, wage labor, landed property. Their inter-relation. Town and country. The three great social classes. Exchange between them. Circulation. Credit system (private). (3) Concentration of bourgeois society in the form of the state. Viewed in relation to itself. The 'unproductive' classes. Taxes. State debt. Public credit. The population. The colonies. Emigration. (4) The international relation of production. International division of labor. International exchange. Export and import. Rate of exchange. (5) The world market and crises [*Grundrisse*, p. 108; (28–29)].

It is thus not difficult to see what the Marxist specificity of the articulation of the theoretical approach and the historical approach is: it is a process that goes from the abstract to the concrete, and *then,* in proportion to the historical extension of the horizon, of the tendency, goes again from the abstract to

the concrete, to the increasingly more complex. Thus, with the "world
market and crises" is reached the definitive point where the elementary
antagonism which is the motor of the whole ensemble is socialized in an
extreme way. *The criterion of the "true in practice,"* of the dynamism of the
practical relation, of the historical subjectivity of this movement, is here a
definitive and discriminating element. The criterion of the "true in practice"
restores to the materialist and dialectical methodology all of its dimension
of subjective, open, and constitutive sense which we have already underlined
in regard to the concept of "difference."

If we now consider the ensemble of the method proposed up to this point
in the *Introduction,* we should emphasize that the point of view which it
proposes has an enormous importance. To use other terms, the relation
between *Forschung* [research], *Darstellung* [presentation], and *neue Darstellung*
[new mode of presentation] is here perfectly delimited, and one must
recognize that *"die wirkliche Bewegung"* (the real movement) becomes in effect
the subject of the science. Still, something is lacking. It is quite true that
the materialist method which considers the object as foreign to the mind
belongs to science, is animated by the perspective which the tendency outlines, and is subjectivized by the criterion of the "true in practice." But,
that said, one must here acknowledge the irreducibility of the real to some
recomposition of idealism; the dynamism of the real, its laws and its articulations, are only assured by "difference," by the fundamental aspect of
historical materialism—in as much as the latter can be dynamized and
subjectivized. Inversely, in the *Grundrisse,* the movement is assured by
antagonism and by the direct importance it has in the formation of the
category: difference is made into antagonism, the frame of the method is
very much loosened, shattered in several dimensions. The *Introduction* therefore does not attain the ideological maturity of the *Grundrisse?* Probably not;
nevertheless, it prepares all the conditions for the passage toward the rule
of antagonism as the fundamental rule of *all* the categories. In addition, the
Introduction and the texts juxtaposed to it refer to this final passage and often
openly speak of it. We should see how this new perspective is presented.
Let us anticipate a little the response by noting that Marx himself, in the
conclusion to the *Introduction,* seems to warn of this difficulty. "Greek art
and modern society": these two pages (*Grundrisse,* pp. 109–10; [30–31])
form a pause and are linked to the preceding notes. They define the classical
problems of historical materialism and underscore on different levels the
difficulty of a solution. Thus, Marx, with this pause, in closing the *Introduction* on unresolved problems, seems to perceive *the limit of the proposition
of historical materialism* and to broach here a reflection which, with the *Grundrisse,* will lead him to give a creative conclusion to the presuppositions of
the *Introduction* and, in a general way, to arrive at the most advanced stage
of the method.

But in order for Marx's methodology to succeed in taking the form of a conclusion, it is necessary that certain elements of content can mature and that other conditions develop. Now, at the end of Notebook VII (*Grundrisse*, pp. 881–82; 763–4), we have the beginning of a "Section on Value," which (putting aside the philological polemic concerning the place where it should be inserted) seems to us to be particularly important. It appears to us opportune to take it into consideration because the theme of value has a direct influence on the articulation of the method and the fundamental categories, on the characterization of these fundamental categories, which is precisely our problem here. Marx, in order to engage the category of "value," thus puts the method to work: he insists on the dialectic of unity and difference which defines value. The difference of value is given as use-value. But "use value falls within the realm of political economy as soon as it becomes modified by the modern relations of production," when, therefore, it is reduced to the unity of the process. It is particularly interesting to repeat nevertheless this normal course of Marx's logic, as much as to see the form, the intensity, the force of the difference considered. It is precisely this potentiality which permits difference to be transmuted into antagonism. It is on this terrain that Marx now insists. "In fact, however, the use value of the commodity is a given presupposition—the material basis in which a specific economic relation presents itself." Therefore, Marx argues,

> Although directly united in the commodity, use value and exchange value just as directly split apart. Not only does the exchange value not appear as determined by the use value, but rather, furthermore, the commodity only becomes a commodity, only realizes itself as exchange value, in so far as its owner does not relate to it as use value. He appropriates use values only through their sale, their exchange for other commodities. Appropriation through sale is the fundamental form of the social system of production, of which exchange value appears as the simplest, most abstract expression" [*Grundrisse*, pp. 881–82; 763–4].

Objective premise—alienated presupposition: with this passage the difference becomes antagonism.

This is not the place to enter into the merits of the discussion on use-value in Marx's thought. (It is nevertheless a theme which we will address at greater length further on. For the moment, I suggest in this regard taking a look at the extremely balanced pages of Rosdolsky, pp. 112–40, as well as the works of Agnes Heller and of her comrades in Budapest). We are speaking here of methodology, and what interests us is the definition of how, by what formal mechanism, difference becomes antagonism. Well, it is the nature of the social relation, its capitalist dimension, which transforms the objective premise into an alienated presupposition, that is, which gives it a dynamic character that incessantly returns upon it to define it. Use value only becomes a category of the critique of political economy as an "alienated presupposition"—that is, when the dialectic of unity and difference, putting itself in motion, relaunches continually the movement, the infinite emergence, of value. Use value becomes the "true in practice" when it reconquers its independence of presupposition through alienation, through the incessantly changing phases—but which are not less real—of appropriation through alienation.

We will take equally into consideration here, within the frame of this line of reasoning, the text which is entitled "Bastiat and Carey," which occupies the beginning of Notebook III (*Grundrisse*, pp. 883–93; 843–53), and which was written in July 1857—thus before the *Introduction* but within the framework of the polemics which constitute the horizon of the *Introduction* and the *Grundrisse*. It concerns a review of Bastiat's *Economic Harmonies* (second edition, Paris, 1851): a typical review by Marx, that is to say, a pretext for elaborating certain themes of which we have already found some in the Notebooks on Money (cf. articularly *Grundrisse*, pp. 248–49; 160 and *passim*). By closely confronting the situation of bourgeois political economy in France (Bastiat) and in the United States (Carey), Marx has the means here of illustrating certain laws of the critique—of which I am interested in underscoring the formal and methodological characteristics. The first law which Marx tries to work out is that which concerns the tendency of a bourgeois society (like that of the United States) which developed autonomously, leaving behind the limits of the movement of the preceding century. Here, then, "even the antitheses of bourgeois society itself appear only as vanishing moments" (*Grundrisse*, p. 884; 844), and the State is the immediate synthesis of civil society: *capital is immediately social capital*. The second law which Marx thinks he can disengage is that which establishes a parallelism between *the centralization of capital and the centralization of the State*. Which means that capitalist socialization and concentration determine—as much in an open society like the United States, as in a closed society like that of the European continent—the necessity of a progressive expansion and centralization of the power of the State. This process is directly induced by the antagonism between production and circulation which arises from capitalist concentration. With the result that "the state, which was at first branded the sole disturber of these 'economic harmonies', is now these harmonies' last refuge" (*Grundrisse*, p. 886; 846). The third law described is that of the *deepening*, always necessary, *of contradictions and antagonisms at the level of the world market* in proportion as the figure of the (national) State becomes the (mediated or immediate) centralization of capital. The general relations of bourgeois society "become discordant when they put on their most developed form: the form of the world market:" "these world market disharmonies,"

Marx concludes, "are merely the ultimate adequate expressions of the disharmonies which have become fixed as abstract relations within the economic categories" (*Grundrisse*, p. 887; 847).

It suffices to hold on to this in order to see that the categories of Marx's method, at this happy moment which is the foundation of the system, are at their point of maturity: maturity above all in the sense of a dynamized and antagonistic foundation, where *antagonism is the motor of development of the system*, the foundation of a continuous resurgence of antagonism each time that the project, the history of capital, progresses. All materialist objectivism disappears as well: the relation is open to the extent that it is founded on antagonism. One could justifiably object that here nonetheless the development of the contradiction—and the deepening of its antagonism—remains at the level of capital, at the level of the categories of capital and of development, and that in consequence the subjective component of the process is underestimated. But Marx's review continues in regard to Bastiat's theory of wages. Here one has an inkling of what the chapter or the "Book on Wages" could have been. Contrary to Bastiat and his stupidity, Marx insists on the wage (wage labor, the working class) as an immediately revolutionary force, as the motor of all possibility of development. "In all these real historic transitions, wage labor appears as the dissolution, the annihilation of relations in which labor was fixed on all sides, in its income, its content, its location, its scope etc. *Hence as negation of the stability of labor and of its remuneration*" (*Grundrisse*, p. 891; 851). This immersion in subjectivity (dissolution, destruction, mobility, independence) gives a new base to the meaning of the antagonism of the categories of capital, shows it in a new way, leads it to a level of tension which the *Grundrisse* will definitively fix in the theory of surplus-value. *Even the method is at this point waiting for a final formulation of the theory of value;* it is thus not that up until this point its formulation has not greatly advanced: it is simply that it is necessary to wait until all the collected elements are assembled in a systematic fashion.

The formulation of Marx's method in the *Grundrisse* is a process which not only *is not linear* from the *Introduction* to the *Grundrisse*, but which also is not so within the *Grundrisse*. If in fact one returns a moment to certain passages—which we already looked at in Lesson 2—of the Chapter on Money, one can see in advance some delay and confusion concerning method. It is especially clear in the passages where—see in the Chapter on Money the texts assembled under points B and D—the force that tends to define the antagonism is at its extreme point. What in fact is going on in these texts? What is happening is that the deepening of the antagonism in the categories makes visible a link between capitalist development and capitalist crisis, a link that serves as the basis of the passage to communism (*Grundrisse*, pp. 159–64, 172–3, 173–4, 289; 77–82, 88–9, 89–90, 148). Now, this link that operates a reversal has not yet crossed the critical threshold where the process becomes subjective. The *antagonism,* we have said, is very strong: but *we still see it as the result of a projection instead of as a figure of an innovative leap,* as a figure of revolutionary liberty. In the discourse on communism, the *tendency is found flattened at the level of the "projection."* We would not insist on this flattening, which is the sign of an insufficiently extended analysis, if it were not that this mechanist attempt in the method arises often in the *Grundrisse,* reappears when one least expects it. Above all when it has to do with defining the ultimate and decisive antagonism and prefiguring communism. And yet it does not seem, in this case as well, that one can rest content there. The theme of the tendency can undergo mechanical flattening in an ideological "projection": in that case the problem of communism risks becoming a discourse of fantasy. But conversely, it is important to underscore that one can displace the theme of the tendency toward the "true in practice," toward subjective verification. If a play on words is permitted, one should therefore say that the tendency of the *Grundrisse* is to exalt, as one goes along, the tendency as the true in practice, as the imputation of subjectivity rather than as projection. Once again, it is necessary to add that *the theory of surplus-value, in being elaborated, will recuperate the greatest tensions of Marx's method;* and it is necessary: communism cannot be the correction of the disharmonies of capital.

Whatever the limits of its theoretical development, the *Introduction* remains nonetheless an exceptional text on method. This is what emerges once again when one examines *the fourth criterion of the method* which, after those of determinate abstraction, the tendency, and practice, appears in order to prepare and to organize the passage of the method to a level which is adequate to the theory of surplus-value (of exploitation). We will call this fourth element the criterion of the *"displacement" of the research* and of the theoretical domain, or of the *displacement of the subject,* or yet again the *principle of "constitution" (of the structure).* The process that generates this criterion appears at the crossroads of the three criteria already elaborated in the *Introduction,* and of the elements which we began to see in the passage on value and the text on Bastiat and Carey: an intensive deepening of the "difference" in the first case, which grows hollow to the point of lending it independence; the dynamic insistence on the use of alternation, over the methodological use of antagonism, in the second case. It is certainly true that the movement of the categories seems, at first glance to produce only "projections," mechanical tensions in the analysis. But in my opinion, all the conditions are given for a real overcoming of these limits—it is in the lesson on surplus-value that we will be able to follow this enriching of the methodological domain and at the same time verify its tremendous effects. It will be thus useful, however, to verify here these presuppositions and to see how one can formalize them. Now, if the systematic nature of the methodological principles of the *Introduction* is evident, their dynamism is no less evident:

determinate abstraction, tendency, and "the true in practice" are principles that generate categories in movement, principles that approximate not only the anatomy but also the physiology of reality, and not simply the structure, but also the revolution of reality. *But reality is not linear,* the dialectic is not totalitarian, the scientific course is not intuitive: on the contrary, reality is transformed continually and draws into its movement the antagonism of collective forces that knowingly exercise power. Thus: *the criteria which one has seen up to this point must be recomposed inside a last principle, which carries both the large alternatives of the course of history,* its qualitative changes, the jumps and turns of reality, and *the participation of subjects*—as causes and products— of that development. The historical horizon moves: the category defined by determinate abstraction is modified, the tendency is realized or is displaced, in any event is submitted to a strong variability; the subjects that move in this horizon and determine it in practical terms are themselves engaged, happily or not, in this process. The horizon is always plural, variated, mobile: the knowledge one has of it possesses the vivacity and the passion of the struggle. *The fourth criterion of Marx's methodology appears as the synthesis of the operative character of the methodological intervention:* this criterion considers before everything else, as a positive premise, the displacement of the theoretical frame consequent to the development of the struggles and the restructuring of the parameters of the conflict; it considers as negative the modification of the dynamic terms of the process, the dislocation of subjectivity, of its poles—within the newly stabilized theoretical framework; for synthesis it takes the constitution of a new structure, and thus of a new form of antagonism, of a new situation which must be resubmitted to the criterion of practice and to the principle of transformation. *It is thus the principle of constitution which defines the horizon at once central and radical of Marx's method.* If we consider how a principle is developed, if we follow its movement in all its directions, according to all the parameters which it contains, if we pay attention to all the levels that must be taken into consideration, in a symmetrical or a nonsymmetrical way, but in each case at least, in terms of a general modification of the frame, of its progression, then we see the development and the affirmation of the principle of constitution. It is a new world that has been constituted, it is a new cognitive reality that is being presented—*for transformation.* It is perfectly clear that the principle of constitution derives from other rules of Marx's method: but the novelty introduced by the principle is also clear, because it is the principle that makes it so that the tendency cannot be reduced to being a projection, the abstraction to a hypostasis of categorial objectivity, the criterion of practice to a realist fetish of historical continuity. The principle of constitution introduces into the methodology the dimension of the qualitative leap, a conception of history reduced to collective relations of force, thus a conception which is not skeptical, but dynamic and creative. Every constitution of a new structure is the constitution of a new antagonism. One can follow the different forms in the development and consider them in the light of the principle of constitution. *The principle of constitution carries crisis to the very heart of Marxist analysis, of its methodology, just as the principle of surplus value carries the subjectivity of antagonism to the heart of the theory.* It is thus not by chance that this principle is born straddling the *Introduction* and the *Grundrisse:* it is prepared in the first and developed in the second, because Marx's path, as we have seen, during this period, is completely axled on the problem of the constitution of the theory of crisis as a theory of capital, of the theory of surplus-value as a theory of revolution. The principle of constitution thus becomes the fundamental criterion for analyzing the *transformation*, the *transition:* the consciousness of the practical leap inside the continuity of the theory. Such is thus the horizon of Marx's theory: Marx beyond Marx? It would be necessary here again to pose the question and to laugh at all orthodoxy that would wish to present itself as Marxist science.

The old polemics over Marx's methodology and over the relations *Hegel–Marx* have never seemed to me to be very interesting. That Marx was Hegelian has never really seemed to me to be the case: on the sole condition of reading Marx and Hegel. It is in other respects self-evident that Marx's works are overflowing with references to Hegel; it is sufficient for that to read the *Grundrisse*. If one wanted to amuse oneself a little (and not in an absurd fashion by playing at philology in the manner of the editors of the *Grundrisse:* Enzo Grillo expresses very rightly his disagreement with that procedure in his preface), one could see that in the first pages that we have looked at up to this point there are at least thirty direct or indirect references to the works of Hegel, and that one finds there already entirely constituted that psychologically ambiguous attitude where Marx on the one hand broadly borrows from Hegel and elsewhere excuses himself of that Hegelian cargo. Here we can take two examples:

> The *market value* is always different, is always below or above this average value of a commodity. Market value equates itself with real value by means of its constant oscillations, never by means of an equation with real value as if the latter were a third party, but rather by means of constant non-equation of itself (as Hegel would say, not by way of abstract identity, but by constant negation of the negation, i.e. of itself as negation of real value) [*Grundrisse*, p. 137; 56].

Here (as always on this argument; see elsewhere, and in particular *Grundrisse*, pp. 211–12; 122–3) the reference to Hegel bears immediately on the content in the sense that it aids the research and permits its exposition. But in these same pages references to the works of Hegel multiply in the terminology, in the formation of concepts. In the second place, we find this other affirmation: "It will be necessary later, before this question is dropped, to correct the idealist manner of the presentation, which makes it seem as if it were merely a matter of conceptual determinations, and of the dialectic of these concepts. Above all in the case of the phrase: product (or activity) becomes commodity; commodity, exchange value; exchange value, money" (*Grundrisse*, p. 157; 69). To correct the idealist manner of the exposition: in this there is no sense of indulgence toward the profound forms of Hegelianism! And then? The polemic over Marx–Hegel is only a pretext: it is enough to have once put a hand on this Marx to realize immediately how they (Marx and Hegel) represent *each one the reverse face of the other*. Because Marx is revolutionary, materialist, and once again revolutionary, political, practical, in the methodology as in the more substantial part of his work. What we have just said does not constitute a kind of negation of the present limits of Marxist methodology, as far as the *Introduction* is concerned—as if we ourselves undergo the insinuations of orthodoxy which only see an absence of limits on Marxism when one denies Hegelian influences. It is not that. The limits of the methodology of the *Introduction* have nothing to do with Hegelianism; these limits are situated inside the passage to the theory of exploitation and the resolute subjectivisation of the antagonism, which Marx is in the process of doing. In other respects, they are very relative limits: perhaps inherent in the very status of the methodological approach, in its constitutive partiality and formality, rather than in the potential for creativity that the methodology contains. Whatever the case may be, it was necessary to operate this new passage. And we are getting ready to follow it.

Lesson Four
Surplus Value &
Exploitation

We are working on surplus value: plan of reading for Notebooks II and III. ☐ (a) From money to surplus value; the political approach. The tendency as the ground of the analysis and the projects of *Capital*. Parenthesis concerning a possible contradiction: the concept of productive labor. ☐ (b) The logical approach: M-C-M', the development of capital from money. ☐ (c) The materialist definition of the autonomization of capital and of labor. Labor as the source of value: subjectivity and abstraction. The possible chapter on wage: use value, necessary labor and "collective worker." The antagonistic character of capitalist appropriation. ☐ (d) The theory of surplus value as a theory of exploitation. Quantification of surplus value: constant capital and variable capital. "Collective capitalist" and valorization. ☐ (e) Definition of concepts and articulation of the theory of surplus value: surplus labor and surplus value, absolute surplus value and relative surplus value. ☐ (f) New problems. Surplus value and profit: towards an analysis of the crisis. ☐ Preliminaries on Marxism and socialism.

In Notebooks II and III (we consider in particular pages 293–341 of the *Grundrisse*) *the theory of surplus value* is developed. We should thus pick up the discourse at the point where we left it at the end of the second lesson, where money appeared to us as the common substance of wage labor and of capital. Its general domination is exercised within circulation and, on the one hand, appears as a totality of domination, as power over and in production, and on the other hand, appears as universality and indifference, as value in the proper sense (exchange value by antonomasia, that is, epithet or title). Between these two aspects of value-money, a dialectic develops that refers the qualitative differences of the process to a quantitative identity. Money is thus the common substance of wage labor and capital because it extends its power over this relation and imposes on this relation the rules of its own functioning. But here it is necessary to advance a step. "Notebook III, Capital": the Italian editors of the *Grundrisse* give this title. Marx in fact only entitled it "Money as Capital": it had to do in effect for him with a step, not a leap, in advance. The change of title, Rosdolsky notes, runs the risk of provoking confusion, since it would stress the difference between the categories (money and capital) and thus their static aspect, and not, as Marx wanted, the dynamic element of the problem (money as capital). Money represents in fact the mobility of capital, its liberty of command, and refers in a real way (that is to say, either as substance or as agency) to the whole process of the metamorphoses of capital. It is thus of a step in advance that one must speak—toward the theory of surplus value—without fetishizing the categories. All the more because the centrality of money in this passage is fundamental. It is to this role that the *first part* of the reading that I will undertake is devoted—and I will try to show here how the central role of money places in relief the "practical" and hence political characteristics of the theoretical approach. After that I will divide my exposé into five parts, treating in the *second* the passage from the political approach to that which is immediately theoretical; in the *third* I will try to define the concept of the collective worker, and in the *fourth* the concept of the collective capitalist: it is only in the *fifth* part, armed with the consistency of these definitions, that one will attain a more complete articulation of the theory of surplus value as a theory of exploitation and as a definition of the theory as the center, now and always, of Marxist theory. I will *conclude* this analysis by raising on the one hand a series of theoretical problems, which remain open (from the theory of surplus value to the theory of profit and of the crisis), and on the other hand a series of political problems which we must re-examine in the light of this reading (the problems of socialism and of communism). There is only one more thing to add: in the course of this phase of the project, we see the elements of Marx's methodology, such as we have defined them up to this point, developing more completely and extensively. The mechanism of the *neue Darstellung* becomes productive. We should thus pay heed to it and underline this productive materialization of the method.

One cannot consider, as does Rosdolsky, for example, that the way Marx introduces the question of "money as capital," which we have already considered above, is situated in the simple extension of the preceding pages on the "law of appropriation of the simple mercantile economy." From the point of view of the theme, it has to do rather with a resumption of the systematic exposé on "money as money" (see Lesson 2): in reality, one witnesses here an operation of the buoying of the terrain of the analysis which should concentrate all theoretical attention. What are its themes? *Money as universal material* and the ideology which hides its reality. That is, money, dominated and controlled antithesis, or money as political reality and command over exploitation. The *terrain of the analysis is thus political.* One can only found the theory of surplus value by beginning with the fact that exploitation structures political society, that it constitutes the basis of that society. By confronting the theme of money as capital—by beginning, in consequence, the analysis of the process of production—Marx *makes of command the very material of money.* This is a mode of exposition which attacks and reverses our habitual way of seeing the development of Marx's thought—politics and command are situated according to our tradition at the end of the analysis of the process of production, or, according to a more recent mode, politics is even considered as alien to the interest of the "economist" Marx. Just the contrary! Here the assumption of the command in all the intensity of its general political functioning is, on the contrary, primary. How can one be surprised by this? All that we have seen up to this point concerning the motivations and incitements which are at the origin of the *Grundrisse* and of their methodological foundation are conducive to making the political element the center of the analysis. And not only that: little by little the exposé is concentrated more and more on the specificity of the political. It is less the polemical raillery against "the socialists" that demonstrates this than the analysis of the crisis and of the financial restructuring in process, the articulation "exploitation-State-world market" which constantly underlies the analysis. *From* exploitation in general, *from* command *to* surplus value, this is the direction: *it is a class logic that governs this angle of attack of the exposition.* We witness in relation to the pages on money, of which the results are nonetheless entirely utilized, a logical and tendential displacement which thus broaches the theme of surplus value, the critique of production on the simplified terrain of the relation between the two classes, mediated by the tendency "command-State-world market." If, as we will see more than once, the world market is presented as a realization of bourgeois hegemony, it is precisely on this basis that the analysis of the class relations (an objective pursued by the theory of surplus value) should be approached and characterized: on the political pregnancy of that fact. *Thus from money to surplus value—this is the political path that furnishes class weapons.*

It is necessary to notice that the thought which discovers money as the fundamental moment and considers it as the center of the analysis of exploitation can be taken up in different ways in the workers' struggle. Here in Marx, as has already been said, money is taken as the form of bourgeois hegemony—as the monetary horizon of command within the acceptation which the Marxism of the 19th century, from Hilferding to Lenin, makes famous. But this position of money at the center of the project of domination of the capitalist class; we find it each time that *capital should restructure its command over the crisis—over the insurrection of workers' use value.* This perpetual tension of money in command is the exact parallel of workers' insurrection at the level of the world market and constitutes an attempt to restructure the form of domination. Because money is not only one of the forms in which capital is metamorphosed, but also is the general form of its command and of the development of that command, the eminent form in which the continuity of value exercises its reign and, with it, the continuity of command. The way in which Marx broaches the theory of surplus value could not be more pregnant and fitting: from the general form of domination to its productive specificity—there where the general, social, and global form of domination is that which characterizes the command—there where the productive specificity is that which demonstrates the place of antagonism. It is clear that if the trip out is so generalized, the trip back will be even more generalized and profound: *from the unveiled antagonism of surplus value to the destruction of the horizon of command, of mediation, of politics.*

A few pages further on (*Grundrisse*, p. 264; 175) at the beginning of the part on surplus value, Marx proposes again *a plan of work for analyzing capital,* a new plan after that proposed in the *Introduction* (*Grundrisse*, pp. 108–9; 28–29) and after the notes on the *chapter on money* (*Grundrisse*, pp. 227–8; 138–39). Here they are:

I. (1) General concept of capital.—(2) Particularity of capital: circulating capital, fixed capital. (Capital as the necessaries of life, as raw material, as instrument of labor.)—(3) Capital as money.
II. (1) *Quantity of capital. Accumulation.*—(2) *Capital measured by itself. Profit. Interest. Value of capital: i.e. capital as distinct* from itself as interest and profit.—(3) *The circulation of capitals.* (a) Exchange of capital and capital. Exchange of capital with revenue. Capital and *prices.* (b) *Competition of capitals.* (c) *Concentration of capitals.*
III. Capital as credit.
IV. Capital as share capital.
V. *Capital as money market.*
VI. Capital as source of wealth.
    The capitalist. After capital, landed property would be dealt with. After that, wage labor. All three presupposed the *movement of prices,* as circulation now defined in its inner totality. On the other side, the three classes, as production posited in its three basic forms and presuppositions of circulation. Then the *state.* (State and bourgeois society.—Taxes, or the existence of the unproductive classes.—The state debt.—Population.—The state externally: colonies. External trade. Rate of exchange. Money as international coin.—Finally the world market. Encroachment of bourgeois society over the state. Crises. Dissolution of the mode of production and form of society based on exchange value. Real positing of individual labor as social and vice versa.) [*Grundrisse*, p. 265].

Why is this plan important? Because, once again, as in the *Introduction,* the tendency from production toward the State, toward the world market as condition of analysis returns not only, or in a preferential way (here as distinct from the *Introduction*), in formal but in material terms (as already on p. 279: "The world market is the presupposition of all and the support of the whole"). *The new project thus situates us in the center of the terrain* of the analysis, the only one on which the theory of surplus value can be founded: the terrain which, through money, we have defined as the *terrain of command.* The State is the first level of synthesis for the contradictions of production; the world market is the second form of this synthesis of contradictions, but it is also, once again, the terrain of the crisis and of dissolution. The entire analysis *must* take this tendency into account, and be displaced *continually according to the rhythmn of the tendency.* The three classes as "premises of production and form of circulation" are situated within the mechanism of development as elements which are themselves transitory, if it is true that the fundamental antagonism will present itself at the level of the world market, in its pure form (antagonism between the two classes) as well as in its social form (socialization and diffusion of the antagonism from production to circulation). And again: "the movement of prices" is conceived on the basis of the value produced globally by society, that is, on the basis of the mass of surplus value and what it contains of command: money once again, with articulations which render the antagonism more and more precise; the antagonism that we want to define at this level of the development of the tendency; there can be no theory of surplus value which does not attain the level of generality which the theories of money and command possess. There can be no definition of the antagonism, if it is not at that level of radicality. The consequences which flow from the projects of the beginning and from the course of the work come to reassure Marx not only in terms of the coherence of analyses in each particular passage but above all in terms of its initial and final coherence, there *where the result should serve also as presupposition.* The result (crisis and dissolution at the level of the world market) should serve as a presupposition (antagonism and struggle at the level of the relations of production). Money is the black thread that joins together on that entire arc the command of capital; the theory of surplus value is the red thread that should remake the same operation from the workers' point of view, from the point of view of reversal.

"The only *use value,* therefore, which can form the opposite pole to capital is *labor (to be exact, value-creating, productive labor)"* (*Grundrisse,* p. 272; 183). A series of pages on the concept of productive and unproductive labor follows which contain the first formulation of a series of theoretical and polemical points which we will re-encounter as well in the *Theories of Surplus Value* and *Capital.* Why do we put forward this page for discussion while our analysis wants to stick with shedding light upon the dimension, the terrain, the horizon within which the theory of surplus value develops? Because *this Marxist approach of productive labor seems to contradict* out exposition and its divisions: here there is a contradiction which it's better to discuss right away. Now Marx maintains here (and even more in the note in the *Grundrisse,* pp. 305–6; 212) that only that work is productive which produces capital. "Productive labor is only that which produces capital"; "the productive laborer is the one who directly augments capital." In consequence, it is altogether stupid to consider as productive labor all exchange which *simply* concerns circulation or consumption.

> A. Smith was *essentially* correct with his *productive* and *unproductive* labor, correct from the standpoint of bourgeois economy. What the other econ-omists advance against it is either horse-piss (for instance, Storch, Senior even lousier, etc.), namely that every action after all acts upon something, thus confusion of the product in its natural and in its economic sense; so that the pickpocket becomes a productive worker too, since he indirectly produces books on criminal law (this reasoning at least as correct as calling a judge a productive worker because he protects *from* theft). Or the modern economists have turned themselves into such sycophants of the bourgeois that they want to demonstrate to the latter that it is productive labor when somebody picks the lice out of his hair, or strokes his tail, because for example the latter activity will make his fat head—blockhead—clearer the next day in the office. (*Grundrisse,* p. 273; 184).

But this sacrosanct insistence of Marx on productive labor as work imme-diately linked to capital, if it has a *direct political function,* which one can deny (it is probably the most workerist of Marx's positions) has as well *ambiguous effects:* the conception of surplus value seems thus to close itself up entirely on the inside of the level of production, and the entire theory seems to hold to this atomization of value, of the relation of value which always, since the end of the 19th century, the critics of Marx and of his thought have taken as an object of a scientific polemic and have tried to destroy politically. We have already insisted on the fact that the function of value can only exist at a general level, as general as is that of money: this within the development of the Marxist tendency (tendency in other respects largely realized today). One can only conclude that the definition of pro-ductive labor which we begin to find in these pages of the *Grundrisse* and which we will find in other works is a *heavily reductive definition* in the literal form it assumes. We reject it in the literal form which it takes because it is invalidated by an objectivist, atomized, and fetishist consideration of the theory of value: it is the consideration which is exactly the one one would want to attribute to Marx in order to make him an old materialist of the 18th century. The only merit of this Marxist definition, in its literal formulation, is to insist on the workers' opposition as a political opposition, on the political irreducibility of the force of workers and of the proletarian revolution.

Well, but then let us depart from here and see if it is not possible within the general frame of our exposition to apprehend certain terms which would permit us to advance and as well to take *the definition of productive labor to that level at once of abstraction and antagonism which seems essential for constructing the theory of surplus value.* I should say right away that it doesn't seem to me impossible to free Marx, in this case, from the weight of historical conditions, which lead him, in order to exalt workers' labor, to restrict in such a miserable way the conception of productive labor. In effect, always looking at these pages and keeping in mind the passage with which we opened this parenthesis, productive labor is presented there as well under another aspect: as workers' "use value," as work of a contracting party of the exchange which "is opposed to the other as capitalist." "Work is only productive in as much as it produces its contrary": but that is a way like any other of saying the concept of surplus value! It is, then, beyond the preeminence of certain literal forms in relation to others, it is to this substance of the reasoning and of the theory that one must refer and on it base the definition. It is on the level of the abstraction of labor that it is necessary to take up once again this definition: "In fact, of course, this 'productive' worker cares as much about the crappy shit he has to make as does the capitalist himself who employs him, and who also couldn't give a damn for the junk" (*Grundrisse*, p. 273; 166). And this is at *the level of the tendency of the development of capital in production,* in productive circulation or not, in capitalist socialization, it is at the level of capitalist society and of its constitution. Considered in this way, as an element constituted by the theory of surplus value and the dynamic of that theory, the concept of productive labor does not therefore constitute a limit of the field of analysis, of the general nature of that field— as we had envisaged it up to this point.

It is now time to enter into the merits of Marx's discourse: *"First section. Process of production of capital." "Money as capital* is an aspect of money which goes beyond its simple character as money" (*Grundrisse*, p. 250; 162). But in simple circulation the determination of money is never exceeded: "the simple movement of exchange values, such as is present in pure circulation, can never realize capital (*Grundrisse,* p. 254; 165).

> The repetition of the process from either of the points, money or com-
> modity, is not posited within the condition of exchange itself. The act
> can be repeated only until it is completed, i.e., until the amount of the
> exchange value is exchanged away. It cannot ignite itself anew through
> its own resources. *Circulation therefore does not carry within itself the principle
> of self-renewal. The moments of the latter are presupposed to it,* not posited by

it. Commodities constantly have to be thrown into it anew from the outside, like fuel into a fire. Otherwise it flickers out in indifference [*Grundrisse*, pp. 254–55; 166].

"Its immediate being is therefore pure semblance. *It is the phenomenon of a process taking place behind it*" (*Grundrisse*, p. 255; 166). The process which unfolds behind circulation is production.

It is commodities (whether in their particular form, or in the general form of money) which form the presupposition of circulation; they are the realization of a definite labor time and, as such, values; their presupposition, therefore, is both the production of commodities by labor and their production as exchange values. This is their point of departure, and through its own motion it goes back into exchange-value-creating production as its result. We have therefore reached the point of departure again, *production which posits, creates exchange values*; but this time, *production which presupposes circulation as a developed moment* and which appears as a constant process, which posits circulation and constantly returns from it into itself in order to posit it anew [*Grundrisse*, p. 255; 166].

From the exchange of equivalents, by way of the labor process, to the process of valorization: this thus means to go from labor to capital, which means M–C–M'. But what valorization consists of we do not yet know. We see it emerge, in quantitative terms, in the sphere of circulation. But money does not explain it to us. Certainly money has become the agent of a multiplying process whose basis is beyond itself. But that doesn't explain very much. We cannot presume *generically* that labor is the foundation of this multiplication: "It is just as impossible to make the transition directly from labor to capital as it is to go from the different human races directly to the banker, or from nature to the steam engine." "To develop the concept of capital it is necessary to begin not with labor, but with value, and, precisely, with exchange value in an already developed movement of circulation" (*Grundrisse*, p. 259; 170). In sum, the logical approach shows us the necessity of making a further step forward in the definition of the concept.

We can, we should, consider capital as objectified labor. But does that also permit us to understand valorization? *Can the theory of value identify the mechanism of valorization? No. In no case whatsoever.* When one advances on the terrain, it is there that "*capital is conceived as a thing not as a relation.*" "Capital is not a simple relation, but a process, in whose various moments it is always capital" (*Grundrisse*, p. 258; 170). Thus, it's neither a linear logic nor a simple conceptual extension of the presupposition. But what is the relation if it is not simply that of circulation? What is the relation of capital which multiplies itself not only quantitatively, in terms of the result, but equally genetically, in terms of production? Such that the reality of the process of valorization is itself a terrain vaguely connoted by acts of exchange which constitute in a productive way the circulation of value? We can perhaps now take up once again the question of labor and begin to regard it as the basis of the value which production prepares for circulation. But only on *condition of having submitted labor itself to the conditions of exchange.*

> Differently expressed: Exchange value, as regards its content, was originally an objectified amount of labor or labor time; as such it passed through circulation, in its objectification, until it became money, tangible money. It must now again posit the point of departure of circulation, which lay outside circulation, was presupposed to it, and for which circulation appeared as an external, penetrating and internally transforming movement; this point was labor; but [it must do so] now no longer as a simple equivalent or as a simple objectification of labor, but rather as objectified exchange value, now become independent, which yields itself to labor, becomes its material, only so as to renew itself and to begin circulating again by itself. And with that it is no longer a simple positing of equivalents, a preservation of its identity, as in circulation; but rather *multiplication* of itself. Exchange value posits itself as exchange value only by realizing itself; i.e., increasing its value. *Money* (as returned to itself from circulation), *as capital has lost its rigidity, and from a tangible thing has become a process.* But at the same time, labor has changed its relation to its objectivity; it, too, has returned to itself. But the nature of the return is this, that the labor objectified in the exchange value posits living labor as a means of reproducing it, whereas, originally, exchange value appeared merely as a product of labor [*Grundrisse*, p. 263; 174–75].

Labor can therefore be transformed into capital only if it assumes the form of exchange, the form of money. But that means that the relation is one of antagonism, that *labor and capital are present* only at the moment of exchange which constitutes their productive synthesis, as *autonomous, independent* entities. It is this antagonism which destroys the appearance of simple circulation: it is this antagonism which is the specific difference of the exchange between capital and labor. It is thus necessary to deepen the nature of this antagonism, given that only this analysis will be able to lead to a comprehension of the specificity with which the theory of value is presented within capital, that is, lead to a definition of the theory of surplus value.

Thus, "the first presupposition is that capital stands on one side and labor on the other, both as independent forms relative to each other; both hence also alien to one another. The labor which stands opposite capital is *alien {fremde}* labor, and the capital which stands opposite labor is *alien* capital. The extremes which stand opposite one another are *specifically* different" (*Grundrisse*, p. 266; 177). What does this antagonism consist of? It consists in the fact that capital must reduce to an exchange value that which for the worker is a use value. But:

> the use value which the worker has to offer to the capitalist, which he has to offer to others in general, is not materialized in a product, does not exist apart from him at all, thus exists not really, but only in potentiality, as his capacity. It becomes a reality only when it has been solicited by capital, is set in motion, since activity without object is nothing, or, at the most, mental activity, which is not the question at issue here. As soon as it has obtained motion from capital, this use value exists as the worker's specific, productive activity; it is his vitality itself, directed toward a specific purpose and hence expressing itself in a specific form. In the relation of capital and labor, exchange value and use value are brought into relation; the one side (capital) initially stands opposite the other side as *exchange value,* and the other (labor), stands opposite capital, as use value [*Grundrisse,* p. 267–68; 178].

The opposition takes two *forms:* first, that of *exchange value against use value,* but—given that the only use value of workers is the abstract and undifferentiated capacity to work—the opposition is also *objectified labor against subjective labor.* We will see it soon. But to conclude this first deepening of the opposition, let's insist once again on the *autonomous quality* of the factors which present themselves in the synthesis. The separation of labor as capacity, as immediate use value, is radical: its relation with exchange value, that is, with command, property, capital is immediately forced. It is necessary to be very insistent on this point, above all if one thinks of the habitual interpretation which considers the result of capitalist civilization as irrational. No, the result is only irrational in the sense that the foundation of the capital relation, the forced closure of radically distinct elements, is irrational, and also inhuman. Capital only sees use value as an "abstract chaos" which is opposed to it, and the only form in which use value permits capital to conclude it within itself, is the form of irrationality, "madness . . . as a moment of economics and as a determinant of the practical life of peoples" (*Grundrisse,* p. 269; 180).

The next point to deepen in the analysis is the nature of wage labor, its autonomy. This time, then, let us examine a little that "cursed difficulty" which confronts economists when they try to define the self-preservation and multiplication of capital. Well, from the moment when the problem is posed with substantial determinations and not in merely accidental terms, *we can fill the void of the development of capital as objectified labor only by having recourse to its opposite:* only the opposition can determine the completion of the analysis, and that opposition cannot itself consist in a particular commodity, because, in that case, the problem would not have a solution. If thus "the communal substance of all commodities, i.e., their substance not as material stuff, as physical character, but their communal substance as *commodities* and hence *exchange values*, is this, that they are *objectified labor*"; "the only thing distinct from *objectified* labor is *non-objectified* labor, labor which is still objectifying itself, *labor* as subjectivity" (*Grundrisse*, p. 271–72; 182–83).

It is the first time that we encounter this characterization of labor. With that we have entered into a central phase of Marx's analysis. The separation capital-labor was the first moment; here now is the second—*labor as subjectivity*, as source, as potential of all wealth. It is only on the basis of these passages that the theory of surplus value can be elaborated: these passages are already part of the theory of surplus value. Let us thus read a page that appears to us more important than any commentary:

> *Separation of property from labor* appears as the necessary law of this exchange between capital and labor. Labor posited as *not-capital* as such is: (1) *not-objectified labor {nicht-vergegenständlichte Arbeit}, conceived negatively* (itself still objective; the not-objective itself in objective form). As such it is not-raw-material, not-instrument-of-labor, not-raw-product: labor separated from all means and objects of labor, from its entire objectivity. This living labor, existing as an *abstraction* from these moments of its actual reality (also, not-value); this complete denudation, purely subjective existence of labor, stripped of all objectivity. Labor as *absolute poverty:* poverty not as shortage, but as total exclusion of objective wealth. Or also as the existing *not-value*, and hence purely objective use value, existing without mediation, this objectivity can only be an objectivity not separated from the person: only an objectivity coinciding with his immediate bodily existence. Since the objectivity is purely immediate, it is just as much direct not-objectivity. In other words, not an objectivity which falls outside the immediate presence *{Dasein}* of the individual himself. (2) *Not-objectified labor, not-value,* conceived *positively,* or as a negativity in relation to itself, is the not-*objectified,* hence not-objective, i.e. subjective existence of labor itself. Labor not as an object, but as activity; not as itself *value,* but as the *living source* of value. [Namely, it is] general wealth (in contrast to capital in which it exists objectively, as reality) as the *general possibility* of the same, which proves itself as such in action. Thus, it is not all contradictory, or, rather, the in-every-way mutually contradictory statements that labor is *absolute poverty as object,* on one side, and is, on the other side, the *general possibility* of wealth as subject and as activity [*Grundrisse*, pp. 295–96; 203].

But that doesn't suffice. This subjectivity of labor is that of "*labor pure and simple*, abstract labor; absolutely indifferent to its particular *specificity {Bestimmtheit}*, but capable of all specificities"; it is also "a *purely abstract activity,* a purely mechanical activity, hence indifferent to its particular form; a merely *formal* activity, or, what is the same, a merely *material {stofflich?}* activity, activity pure and simple" (*Grundrisse,* pp. 296–97; 204). The paradox is completed; and it is no longer a paradox, it is a dialectical development of an exceptional intensity: *the opposition determines subjectivity and this subjectivity of labor is defined as a general abstraction. The abstraction, the abstract collectivity of labor is subjective power (potenza).* Only this abstract subjective power (potenza), this prolonged refinement of the labor power in its entirety which destroys the partiality of labor itself, can permit labor to be presented as a general power (potenza) and as radical opposition. In this passage, the separation of labor from capital becomes the quality which defines labor. The two significations of "abstract," thus of "general," and of "separated," are found reunited and reinforced in this creative worker subjectivity, in the potentiality it possesses of being a source of all possible wealth. On the other hand, use value, in that it fundamentally qualifies the opposition capital/ labor, is with it found absorbed in this first attempt at a definition. Something quite different from the naturalist and humanist definitions of use value! In truth a great deal of ignorance or of complete bad faith is required in order to reduce "use value" (in Marx's sense) to being only a residue or an appendage of capitalist development! Here use value is nothing other than the radicality of the labor opposition, than the subjective and abstract potentiality of all wealth, the source of all human possibility. All multiplication of wealth and of life is linked to this type of value: there is no other source of wealth and of power. Capital sucks this force through surplus value.

Continuing the analysis of this opposition, one finds another determination of labor in as much as it is separated and antagonistic. *Use value is necessary labor* and vice versa. In what sense? In the sense that when worker use value is found changed by capitalism into exchange value, when the two autonomous entities must confront each other, and are forcefully tied together, a relation is established which contains a *specific measure:* the measure of labor necessary to the reproduction of the force of labor acquired by the capitalist and submitted to the general relation of capital.

> The exchange value of his commodity cannot be determined by the manner in which its buyer uses it, but only by the amount of objectified labor contained in it; hence, here, by the amount of labor required to reproduce the worker himself. For the use value which he offers exists only as an ability, a capacity *{Vermogen}* of his bodily existence; has no existence apart from that. The labor objectified in that use value is the objectified labor necessary bodily to maintain not only the general substance in which his labor power exists, i.e., the worker himself, but also that required to modify this general substance so as to develop its particular capacity. This, in general terms, is the measure of the amount of value, the sum of money,

which he obtains in exchange. The further development, where wages are measured, like all other commodities, by the labor time necessary to produce the worker as such, is not yet the point here [*Grundrisse,* pp. 282–83; 193–94].

The fact that the use value of labor is reduced by capital to this delimitation of exchange modifies neither its quality nor its relation: the worker in fact "is neither bound to particular objects, nor to a particular manner of satisfaction. The sphere of his consumption is not qualitatively restricted, only quantitatively. This distinguishes him from the slave, serf, etc." (*Grundrisse,* p. 283; 194). "But what is essential is that the purpose of the exchange for him is the satisfaction of his need. The object of his exchange is a direct object of need, not exchange value as such" (*Grundrisse,* p. 284; 195).

Immediate and satisfied need—necessary labor—use value: the relation expands. It expands to the extent that one could at this point think of reformulating the antagonism between workers and capital in mature terms, as a class antagonism. Marx grazes this idea when in these pages he sarcastically rejects the offers of abstinence, of saving, and of participation which the ideology of capital proposes to workers taken one by one but not to "workers *generally,* that is, as workers [*operaio collettivo,* 'collective worker,' in the Italian] (what the individual worker does or can do, as distinct from his genus, can only exist just as *exception*)" (*Grundrisse,* p. 285; 196). Here we are *at the heart of the problematic of relative wage,* and even if Marx adds, in relation to these themes, that this "is to be dealt with in the section *wage labor*" (*Grundrisse,* p. 288; 199)—and we will examine further on the ensemble of these elements which should constitute the chapter *"on wage and the working class"*—he also posits some elements of it. What are they? In the first place, necessary labor, as it is expressed in a mystified way in the monetary form of wage, is an immediate use value for the working class. In addition, this necessary level is continually restored by capital. Here is the second point: at the very heart of this restoration, there is a dynamic relation, an attempt by the working class to reaffirm the indispensable consistency and the necessity of its own composition, constant counterpart of that capitalist force which tries to under-value the workers and their necessary labor. This reconstruction of the equilibrium between capital and necessary labor (and wage) occurs *in a real way,* not ideologically. The advice given to workers to save is certainly ridiculous, but not the fact that the workers' opposition, the proletarian struggle, tries continually to broaden *the sphere of non-work,* that is, the sphere of their own needs, the value of necessary labor: "the worker's participation in the higher, even cultural satisfactions, the agitation for his own interests, newspaper subscriptions, attending lectures, educating his children, developing his taste, etc., his only share of civilization which distinguishes him from the slave, is economically only possible by widening the sphere of his pleasures" (*Grundrisse,*

p. 287; 197–98). Which means by the *ontological broadening of his use value, through the intensification and elevation of the value of necessary labor*. All of this in collective, abstract, general terms.

The chapter on wages should broach these themes. We will see further on once again which and how. For the moment we can only lament once again the absence of this chapter in Marx's work. (As we have already indicated, the pages of Book One of *Capital* cannot be considered to be that chapter unless it is in terms of the problematic of the struggle over the work-day and the effects which flow from its restructuring.) We can only regret the loss because it is evident that *the chapter on wages* finds its determination in this foundation of the theory of surplus value: it would have been a chapter on the working class, on the level of needs, pleasure, struggle, and necessary labor. In sum, *the chapter on wages* would have been *the chapter on not-capital, thus on not-work*.

"The real *not-capital* is *labor*" (*Grundrisse*, p. 274; 185). In the *Grundrisse*, the capital relation is antagonistic to the highest degree. Capitalist appropriation has a definitive antagonistic character. This antagonism finds its origin in the relation of scission between use value and exchange value—a relation of scission in which two tendencies are liberated from the forced unity to which they had been constrained: on the one hand, *exchange value is autonomised in money and in capital*, and on the other, *use value is autonomised as the working class*. We must, in what follows, confront the problem of surplus value in all its specificity, that is, carry the scission into the analysis of the working day of the collective worker. Let us pick up again therefore certain particularly important points and see the elements which derive from them and which permit the posing of certain conclusions at this stage of the enquiry.

In the first place, the moment of antagonism must be accentuated. When we speak of crisis, we will see how, in the last instance, completing and surpassing his analyses of realization and of circulation, Marx places the *fundamental cause of the crisis in the relation between necessary labor and surplus labor*, that is in the relation between the constitutive parts of the working day and in the class relation which constitutes it. The prerequisites of this conclusion are already filled: we read them in the critique Marx makes of abstinence. (*Grundrisse*, pp. 282–89; 195–200). In addition, Marx directly insists on the "chronological separation" of the two elements which form the labor/capital exchange, and for those who are familiar with the attention he pays to the disharmonies of the cycle, it is an extremely interesting point. (*Grundrisse*, pp. 274–75; 185). But another deduction must be argued apropos of this—a deduction which belongs to *the theory of catastrophe*, understood in Marx's sense as the actuality of communism, rather than to the theory of crisis. This is our deduction, that at a certain degree of fundamental antagonism, it is necessary *to break with any conception which has the pretension to link the development of the forces of production* (or of the productive force of human labor) *with the development of capital.* The capacity that capital possesses to absorb productive forces is purely historical—Marx would say "fortuitous"—that is, not endowed with a rational force, but "irrational," there where the antagonism which characterizes the formation of the relation is inclined to breakage, scission, explosion. Since 1857, much water has passed under the bridges of history: one must say that if this water does not carry the corpse of capitalism, if it is stupid to remain on the bridge to see it pass, waiting with the confidence of positivism for the relation between the forces of production and capital to deepen under the form of socialism, certainly then this waiting is rotted by the pestilent waters of our industrial rivers. In Marx, in that Marx who is beyond Marx, and who gives such a clear definition of the antagonism, we read the fall of that relation. The antagonism of the capital relation is not simply destructive. Deepening the meaning of Marx's discourse, we come to pose the antagonistic class tendency as winning. The side of the working class is the side of labor as not-capital. Alien to us, we have often repeated it, are all conceptions of development of the class which are posed in terms of "projection": it is not that for which we are looking; it is not the continuity but the leap which distinguishes the working class as such, as a revolutionary class. But it will be added that a certain mediacy (*medietà*) in the process by leaps must be underlined. In the pages we have read, Marx characterizes the working class as a solid subjectivity, which is at once collective use value and necessary labor, as an historical and social essence to which is owed on the one hand "the replacement for wear and tear so that it can maintain itself as a class" (*Grundrisse*, p. 323; 229); on the other hand, the working class is a social essence characterized by its particular status: its use value is creative; it is the unique and exclusive source of wealth. We are in consequence *exactly at the heart of a first definition of the dynamic of the working class,* where its essence as creator of value is engaged in a continual struggle which has as a result on the one hand the development of capital and on the other the *intensification of the class composition,* the enlargement of its needs and of its pleasures, the elevation of the value of labor necessary for its reproduction. And since capital finds itself constrained to repress and to devalue this productive force of the working class, and to delimit its impulsion into the intensification of its own composition (n.b.: the path of the intensification of the organic composition of capital passes by way of this repression), here then the struggle, the fundamental antagonism which is transformed into expanded proletarian struggle, constitutes at last a key to historical progress. Already in this preliminary definition of the antagonism alone, the theory of surplus value thus remains the most important law of the movements of capitalist development: *the antagonism alone determines the movement;* capital "is the process of this differentiation and of its suspension, in which capital itself becomes a process" (*Grundrisse*, p. 298; 205–6).

The law of value begins to take the form of the law of surplus value through the extreme accentuation of the antagonism of subjects. But it is defined in proper terms only when the process of labor is subsumed into capital. *The theory of surplus value is in consequence immediately the theory of exploitation.* None of the illusions which still leave open the theory of value survive at the level of the theory of surplus value. The creative power of labor, if it was at liberty, would certainly not tend to define capital: only exploitation as a political process of domination and constriction, as a generalized command over society, determines *at once value and surplus value.* The level of the initial antagonism is so strong that only exploitation, constraint, force can succeed in resolving it. "Labor is not only the *use value* which confronts capital, but, rather, it is *the use value* of capital itself" (*Grundrisse,* p. 297; 205): this is the moment when the theory of surplus value is born. It is clear that one speaks here of labor as it was defined in the ensemble of preceding pages: as *social, abstract, average labor.* The more these characteristics are accentuated, the more labor is apt to produce surplus value. Marx's discourse pauses at length over this determination of surplus value, over its origin in the creative nature of labor. This insistence goes along with the force of the political argument which dominates the entire analysis. Everything is in fact predisposed in such a way that the quantitative definition of surplus value, the division of the working day in two parts (*necessary labor* and *surplus labor*) do not appear as elements purely of doctrine but *as weapons in workers' struggle.*

When surplus value begins to be produced, it means that the workers' existence is definitively resolved into capital. Use value is reduced to the limits of necessary labor, to the conservation and reproduction of the working class. The remainder of the use value of workers' labor is completely subsumed by capital and by virtue of that produces surplus value. As much as the function of labor for this process of production is exclusive, that much is the capacity of capital to subsume this process into itself exclusive. *Every alternative existence to the control of capital is consumed in the process of production*—including the production of raw materials and instruments. "It is not the capitalist who does this consuming but rather labor. Thus the process of the production of capital does not appear as the process of the production of capital, but as the process of production in general, and capital's *distinction from labor* appears only in the material character of *raw material* and *instrument of labor*" (*Grundrisse,* p. 303; 210). Instruments of labor and raw materials are in themselves in reality only objectified labor, and the general appearance of capital, as constant capital, is simply a function of its entire reality (*constant capital and variable capital* both commanded by the category of capital as such). Once the unity of command, its unicity (process of production in general), and the concepts of constant capital and variable capital are established, it is possible to *quantify surplus value* in a definitive way.

How therefore is surplus value born from production? Marx has already created all of the presuppositions for the resolution of this problem; the only thing still missing is the division of capital into constant and variable capital. He will only use these terms later, but in fact this difference is already contained in the conditions of existence of surplus value. Confronting the excess of value of the product which exists as a result of the output of living labor, with the values of the raw materials, of auxiliary materials, and of the instruments of labor (constant capital!), Marx thus places the problem of the relation between the value which capital pays to the worker in the form of wages (variable capital!) and the value which living labor creates inside the process of production. Surplus value exists obviously only when the first is less than the second [*Vygodskij*, p. 69]. (In relation to this, see also Rosdolsky, p. 255.)

To quantify surplus value means, then, to consider the process of labor as productive of a global value of which one part serves to reproduce the working class, and the other comprises all the elements of the reproduction of capital and its immense growth. Nothing can escape the unity of the organizing command of capital: everything that labor, as use value, as necessary labor, as source of value, produces *is objectified and commanded by capital*. "As components of capital, raw material and instrument of labor are themselves already objectified labor, hence *product*" (*Grundrisse*, p. 299; 206). And labor? It "is not only consumed, but also at the same time fixed, converted from the form of activity into the form of the object; materialized; as a modification of the object, it modifies its own form and changes from activity to being" (*Grundrisse*, p. 300; 208). All of this "ferments" capital and in the course of this fermentation *all the elements of the initial antagonism are transmuted*: the use value of labor is use value of capital, necessary labor is commanded by capital through the wage. Quantifying surplus value is thus only possible at this point, because it is only capital that can quantify it when it has appropriated the entire process of production. If that had not occurred, there would be no quantification. Antagonism cannot be quantified. There is only exploitation which makes quantification possible, which gives it a meaning.

This is the occasion to draw attention to a moment which here, for the first time, not only arises from the standpoint of the observer, but is posited in the economic relation itself. In the first act, in the exchange between capital and labor, labor as such, existing *for itself*, necessarily appeared as *the worker*. Similarly, here in the second process: capital as such is posited as a value existing for itself, as egotistic value, so to speak (something to which money could only aspire). But capital in its being-for-itself is the *capitalist*. Of course, socialists sometimes say, we need capital, but not the capitalist. Then capital appears as a pure thing, not as a relation of production which, reflected in itself, is precisely the capitalist. I may well separate capital from a given individual capitalist, and it can be transferred to another. But, in losing capital, he loses the quality of being a capitalist. Thus capital is indeed separable from an individual capitalist, but not from *the* capitalist, who, as such, confronts *the* worker" [*Grundrisse,* p. 303; 210–11].

In effect, *the passage is here definitively accomplished.* Capital here has become the antithesis of the worker in an absolute and definitive way. Against the grain of the liberty of its nature, labor "itself is *productive only* if absorbed into capital;" "labor, such as it exists *for itself* in the worker in opposition to capital, that is, labor in its *immediate being,* separated from capital, is *not productive*" (*Grundrisse,* p. 308; 215), because capital has already become the force of "*transubstantiation,*" of the "*transposition*" of each vital element of the process of valorization. "Therefore, the demand that wage labor be continued but capital abolished is self-contradictory, self-dissolving" (*Grundrisse,* p. 308-9; 215).

But it is not enough to consider the unity of the process of production. Class struggle does not know synthesis, it only knows victories and defeats. It is a history of protagonists. All of that evidently applies to the history of capital if its concept rests upon antagonism. When the antagonism is overcome, *capital* does not appear simply as a unified process, but as itself a *subject.* "Value appears as subject" (*Grundrisse,* p. 311; 218). Capital is already self-valorized; it assumes the social costs of its conservation as elements of subjectivization which are owed it. Capital appears as a force of expansion, as production and reproduction, and always as command. *Valorization is a continuous and totalitarian process,* it knows neither limit nor repose. Labor is so dominated in the process of valorization that its autonomy seems reduced in all cases to an extreme limit, to the reduction of non-existence. Certainly, the theory of surplus value, at the same time that it defines the terms and the dynamism of the process of valorization, also defines the space (which can be something completely other than relative) of necessary labor, at least under the mystified form of wages. *But here the accent is placed on the unity of the process and on the subjectivisation of capital.* In the process of valorization, capital conquers a totalitarian subjectivity of command.

And yet *the initial antagonism cannot be negated.* Capital, after having tried in all possible ways to appear as the general representative of production and valorization, is nonetheless constrained to define itself by opposition. "The existence of capital *vis-à-vis* labor requires that capital in its being-for-itself, the capitalist, should exist and be able to live as *not-worker*" (*Grundrisse,* p. 317; 223). The antagonism reappears. And it reappears under the forms of the process of valorization we have learned to consider as more and more general: the antagonism returns within the entire field of valorization. *Worker and capitalist, collective worker and collective capitalist.* We are once again inside that political situation from which the *Grundrisse* is born: but a notable progress has already occurred, since this political situation begins to be articulated from the scientific point of view of revolutionary thought.

If we consider *the method* which informs these pages, we have—I think— a good example of Marx's way of proceeding. Above all, the materialist approach is fully respected: the antagonism of the elements that compose capital, the difference that founds the relation, are the *basis* of the entire analysis. But they are not only the basis, they are also the terms of the *dynamic* of the process. The difference is the motor of it. Here we have a series of operations of the *displacement* of the subject and the dislocation of the theoretical field. The first operation occurs when the synthesis is completed and the process of valorization begins. All the terms which constitute the theory of surplus value are detached here from the antagonism which constitutes them and drowned within the totality of valorization. In this operation they are transposed, translated, transubstantiated. *The categories of class struggle become the categories of capital.* The subject becomes object, activity becomes being. This passage is articulated on an analysis which operates the passage from quality (creative of value) to quantity (measure of value). Hence, in grounding itself on this result, the field tends once again toward a displacement and the reappearance of antagonism. The field of society characterized by valorization carries nevertheless, still and always, the mark of antagonism. First, with the rhythm of the passage from quality to quantity, use value and exchange value appeared as capitalist productions: necessary labor and surplus labor were dominated and mystified in the forms of the control of capital. Now, with the rhythm of this new passage from quantity to quality, the field tends to reacquire the tonality of antagonism. *The figures take the form of the opposition and of subjectivity:* worker and capitalist, collective worker and collective capitalist. Once capital attains the totality of the process of valorization and of reproduction, its process is in reality once again a process of the *reproduction of antagonisms.* Reproduction does not negate difference, does not annul antagonism; on the contrary, it exacerbates both. The result of this process is the expanded reproduction of antagonism and the reappearance of the subjective masks which the forces of history assume within the struggle. Inside this methodological frame, the theory of surplus value shows itself to be as well a fundamental acquisition for the method.

Evidently, there are at the present stage of the analysis *precise limits* to all of this. It is not simply a matter of the specific place of these passages in the articulation of the theory of surplus value: we will see this in a moment, as soon as we have concluded these remarks. Rather, I am thinking of the analysis of the antagonism in reproduction, of its total appearance. Now, in the lesson on the crisis (Lesson 5), we will see this point again. But one cannot think that a solution can be found on this level in exhaustive scientific terms, in a critical way, within a field where the antagonism re-explodes (in a way which is still essentially tendential). The passage must be deepened, and it occupies in fact the center of the entire second part of the *Grundrisse*. We will see it thus in the second part of the lessons (Lessons 6 and those following), where the object of the analysis will be precisely the antagonism in reproduction. It seems to us nonetheless that here we still have attained the ridge from which the new flow of reasoning descends: and the theory of surplus value is the ridge of the *Grundrisse*.

We are already in a condition to be able to define, with Marx, the *concept of surplus value* and to begin to articulate its consequences.

> *The surplus value which capital has at the end of the production process*—a surplus value which, as a higher price of the product, is realized only in circulation, but, like all prices, is realized in it by already being ideally *presupposed* to it, determined before they enter into it—signifies, expressed in accord with the general concept of exchange value, that the labour time objectified in the product—or amount of labour (expressed passively, the magnitude of labour appears as an amount of space; but expressed in motion, it is measurable only in time)—is greater than that which was present in the original components of capital. This in turn is possible only if the labour objectified in the price of labour is smaller than the living labour time purchased with it. The labour time objectified in capital appears, as we have seen, as a sum consisting of three parts: (a) the labour time objectified in the raw material; (b) the labour time objectified in the instrument of labour; (c) the labour time objectified in the price of labour. Now, parts (a) and (b) remain unchanged as components of capital; while they may change their form, their modes of material existence, in the process, they remain unchanged as values. Only in (c) does capital exchange one thing for something qualitatively different; a given amount of objectified labour for an amount of living labour. If living labour reproduced only the labour time objectified in the labour price, this also would be merely formal, and, as regards value, the only change which would have taken place would have been that from one mode to another of the existence of the same value, just as, in regard to the value of the material of labour and the instrument, only a change of its mode of material existence has taken place. If the capitalist has paid the worker a price = one working day, and the worker's working day adds only one working day to the raw material and the instrument, then the capitalist would merely have exchanged exchange value in one form for exchange value in another. He would not have acted as capital. At the same time, the worker would not have remained within the simple exchange process; he would in fact have obtained the product of his labour in payment, except that the capitalist

would have done him the favor of paying him the price of the product in advance of its realization *{Realisation}*. The capitalist would have advanced him credit, and free of charge at that, *pour le roi de Prusse. Voila tout.* No matter that for the worker the exchange between capital and labour, whose result is the price of labour, is a simple exchange as far as the capitalist is concerned, it has to be a not-exchange. He has to obtain more value than he gives. Looked at from the capitalists' side, the exchange must be only *apparent;* i.e. must belong to an economic category other than exchange, or capital as capital and labour as labour in opposition to it would be impossible. They would be exchanged for one another only as identical exchange values existing in different modes [*Grundrisse*, pp. 321–22; 227–28].

The worker alienates his capacity for labor, his creative force which is subsumed by capital under the appearance of an equal exchange relation: in the process of production capital puts to use this creative force for itself and pays for it a price independent of the result of the activity of labor. At best, thanks to the conceded price (wage), the worker succeeds in restoring his own use value: he responds to the necessity of his own reproduction—but even this price must be ceaselessly grabbed away. All the rest of the worker's activity is now in the hands of the boss.

Since we are dealing here not with any *particularly* qualified labour but with labour in general, simple labour, we are here not yet concerned with the fact that there is more labour objectified in his immediate existence than is contained in his mere vitality—i.e., the labour time necessary to pay for the products necessary to maintain his vitality—namely, the values he has consumed in order to produce a specific *laboring capacity*, a special *skill*—and the value of these shows itself in the costs necessary to produce a similar laboring skill [*Grundrisse*, pp. 323–24; 229–30].

Simple labor, raw material of wealth, labor objectified by the subjective necessity of the reproduction of labor power: we are again at the heart of Marx's way of conceiving use value as creative material. The link which this power of creation has with exploitation here, suggests, within the theory of surplus value, a *requalification of that material as a revolutionary subject. In fact, behind the appearance of exchange a theft takes place.*

Surplus value in general is value in excess of the equivalent. The equivalent by definition, is only the identity of value with itself. Hence surplus value can never sprout out of the equivalent; nor can it do so originally out of circulation; it has to arise from the production process of capital itself. The matter can also be expressed in this way: if the worker needs only half a working day in order to live a whole day, then, in order to keep alive as a worker, he needs to work only half a day. The second half of the labour day is forced labour; surplus-labour. What appears as surplus value on capital's side appears identically on the worker's side as surplus labour in excess of his requirements as worker, hence in excess of his immediate requirements for keeping himself alive [*Grundrisse*, pp. 324–25; 230–31].

Surplus labor is stolen from the worker and transformed into surplus value, into capital. "The discovery of surplus value marked the greatest revolutionary overturn in economic science. It permitted Marx, for the first time in the history of political economy, to discover and explain scientifically the mechanism of capitalist exploitation. To use the image of Vladimir Majakovskij, Marx grabs the hand of the robbers of surplus value and catches them red-handed" (Vygodskij, p. 71).

Nevertheless, here as well there is a *positive facet*, a revolutionary facet:

The great historic quality of capital is to *create* this *surplus labour*, super-fluous labour from the standpoint of mere use value, mere subsistence; and its historic destiny *{Bestimmung}* is fulfilled as soon as, on one side, there has been such a development of needs that surplus labour above and beyond necessity has itself become a general need arising out of individual needs themselves—and, on the other side, when the severe discipline of capital, acting on succeeding generations *{Geschlecter}*, has developed general industriousness as the general property of the new species *{Geschlect}*—and, finally, when the development of the productive powers of labour, which capital incessantly whips onward with its unlimited mania for wealth, and of the sole conditions in which this mania can be realized, have flourished to the stage where the possession and preservation of general wealth require a lesser labour time of society as a whole, and where the labouring society relates scientifically to the process of its progressive reproduction, its reproduction in a constantly greater abundance; hence where labour in which a human being does what a thing could do has ceased. Accordingly, capital and labour relate to each other here like money and commodity; the former is the general form of wealth, the other only the substance destined for immediate consumption. Capital's ceaseless striving towards the general form of wealth drives labour beyond the limits of its natural paltriness *{Naturbeduftigkeit}*, and thus creates the material elements for the development of the rich individuality which is as all-sided in its production as in its consumption, and whose labour also therefore appears no longer as labour, but as the full development of activity itself, in which natural necessity in its direct form has disappeared; because a historically created need has taken the place of the natural one. This is why *capital is productive; i.e. an essential relation for the development of the social productive forces*. It ceases to exist as such only where the development of these productive forces themselves encounters its barrier in capital itself" [*Grundrisse,* p. 325; 231].

Let us leave unprejudiced for the moment the question of the limits of the development of capital: we have insisted so much on the antagonistic nature of the process that it should no longer be surprising. What seems more interesting in this regard, and more in the spirit of Marx's argument, is to underscore the fact that *the limits can only appear to capital as insurmountable obstacles.*

> However, as representative of the general form of wealth—money—capital is the endless and limitless drive to go beyond its limiting barrier. Every boundary *{Grenze}* is and has to be a barrier *{Schranke}* for it. Else it would cease to be capital—money as self-reproductive. If ever it perceived a certain boundary not as a barrier, but became comfortable within it as a boundary, it would itself have declined from exchange value to use value, from the general form of wealth to a specific, substantial mode of the same. Capital as such creates a specific surplus value because it cannot create an infinite one all at once; but it is the constant movement to create more of the same. The quantitative boundary of the surplus value appears to it as a mere natural barrier, as a necessity which it constantly tries to violate and beyond which it constantly seeks to go [*Grundrisse,* pp. 334–35; 240].

It is in terms of this urgency that capital tries without let-up *to augment the productivity of labor,* and it is within this frame that the relation between living labor and objectified labor (for the worker or for the other elements of production) is ceaselessly intensifed. Within this diffusion of the productive force of capital the concept of *relative surplus value is born*: at that point, therefore, where surplus value does not correspond to an increase of surplus value in terms of an extension of working time, but in terms of a reduction of necessary labor.

> The increase in the productive force of living labour increases the *value* of capital (or diminishes the value of the worker) not because it increases the quantity of products or use values created by the same labour—the productive force of labour is its natural force—but rather because it diminishes *necessary* labour, hence, in the same relation as it diminishes the former, it creates *surplus labour* or, what amounts to the same thing, surplus value; because the surplus value which capital obtains through the production process consists only of the excess of surplus labour over *necessary labour.* The increase in productive force can increase surplus labour—i.e., the excess of labour objectified in capital as product over the labour objectified in the exchange value of the working day—only to the extent that it diminishes the relation of *necessary labour* to *surplus labour,* and only in the

proportion in which it diminishes this relation. Surplus value is exactly equal to surplus labour; the increase of the one [is] exactly measured by the diminution of *necessary labour* [*Grundrisse,* p. 339; 244–45].

I think little more need be said. We have seen the theory of surplus value develop as an exclusive, all-comprehending, and adequate theory of capital. The movement of exploitation alone explains the nature and the dynamic of capital. Antagonism alone makes capital and the rule of coercion of which it is the interpreter live. The theory of value, in order to exist, can exist only as a partial and abstract subordinate of the theory of surplus value. As for this last, its signification is entirely political: it is situated at the level of greatest generality, that of the critique of money, and contains an extraordinarily forceful antagonism. *An antagonistic force which is, in a materialist fashion, the correlative of the interpreted, real antagonism of the antagonism of existence.* Everything has been reduced to a relation between necessary labor and surplus value: this antagonism is at once the key to the dynamism of the process and the insoluble limit of capitalist production and of the social order that corresponds to it. Here the theory of surplus value can, must, open itself to other problems, which can be nothing other than the deepening of the antagonism. In particular, it is the theory of profit which is necessary here. "All these statements," Marx says, "correct only in this abstraction for the relation from the present standpoint," nevertheless, the entire argument *"actually already belongs in the doctrine of profit"* (*Grundrisse,* p. 341; 246–47). Here once again we are at the end of the definition of surplus value, on the ridge that will allow us to redescend to the terrain of circulation, to attain the second big problematic knot of the *Grundrisse,* the theory of profit seen as a theory of exploitation in circulation, of the exploitation of society. It is the principal direction, the essential woof of the problematic of the *Grundrisse,* but we must not forget nonetheless that this moment of passage is in force and is developed by proposing a revolutionary interpretation of the general development of capitalism.

Still, even if we forget it, Marx is there to remind us. It is not by chance that the part of the *Grundrisse* which is devoted to the definition of the theory of surplus value ends beyond the relaunching of the analysis toward the theory of profit (it is at this moment that Marx writes to Engels: "As for the rest, I am advancing with great strides. For example, I have thrown into the air the entire theory of profit as it has existed up until now") [January 14, 1858, *Selected Correspondence,* p. 121]—thus beyond the relaunching of the analysis towards the theory of profit, this part ends with a first, elementary but fundamental definition, which is a *theoretical allusion to the law of the tendency of profit to fall.*

The larger the surplus value of capital *before the increase of productive force,* the larger the amount of presupposed surplus labour or surplus value of capital; or, the smaller the fractional part of the working day which forms the equivalent of the worker, which expresses necessary labour, the smaller is the increase in surplus value which capital obtains from the increase of productive force. Its surplus value rises, but in an ever smaller relation to the development of the productive force. Thus the more developed capital already is, the more surplus labour it has created, the more terribly must it develop the productive force in order to realize itself in only smaller proportion, i.e., to add surplus value—because its barrier always remains the relation between the fractional part of the day which expresses *necessary labour,* the greater the *surplus labour,* the less can any increase in productive force perceptibly diminish necessary labour; since the denominator has grown enormously. The self-realization of capital becomes more difficult to the extent that is has already been realized [*Grundrisse,* p. 340; 246].

The more surplus value is developed, the less one can compress necessary labor, and less is the quantity and the quality of the creative activity which capital can subsume in the labor process. Why can the key to the interpretation of the theory of profit only be found in Marx's prefiguration, preliminary to the law of the tendency of profit to decline? We must obviously return at length to all of this. For the moment, it is sufficient to recognize the radicality of the antagonism which the theory of surplus value puts in play. We will soon see (Lesson 5) how the theory of crisis operates the first step forward toward the theory of profit.

Here we are then at the end of the first part of the seminar. Here, I would like to broach, at the end of this first development, and armed with this first conclusion concerning Marx's work, with this first complete definition of surplus value and of the movement of its antagonism—I would almost like to broach some other theoretical themes which are very important. But perhaps all these themes reduce themselves to one fundamental one, which one can state thus: *the subordination of the law of value to that of surplus value* is the revelation of the indestructible theoretical knot that lies behind the polemic with the Proudhonians. This means that the theory of surplus value demonstrates one thing: that socialism can only be a mystification of the competition and the social hegemony of capital, that—outside ideology, in reality—*socialism is as impossible as the functioning of the law of value.* The Marxism of the *Grundrisse* is in effect the contrary of socialism: as much as socialism is a hymn to the equivalence and the justice of social relations (constructed on the law of value), so much Marxism shows the law of value and socialism to be lies. The only reality we know is that ruled by theft, capitalist alienation and the objectification of living labor, of its use value, of its creativity. To make all of that function according to the law of value, supposing it were possible, would modify nothing. Because there is no value without exploitation. Communism is thus the destruction at the same time of the law of value, of value itself, of its capitalist or socialist variants. Communism is the destruction of exploitation and the emancipation of living labor. *Of non-labor.* That and it is enough. Simply.

Lesson Five
Profit, Crisis,
Catastrophe

Socialization of surplus value, that is towards a theory of profit. □ Ambiguity and/or correctness of the Marxist project. □ 1. New conditions (between Notebooks III–IV and VII) for the definition of "profit" as a category: circulation, rate and mass of profit. Law of the rate of profit and its double tension. □ 2. Profit as subordinate to the law of surplus value. Profit as objectified and socialized surplus value. Profit and "the capitalist class." For a theory of proletarian subjectivity. □ 3. Passage to the second section: circulation as form of the crisis. Phenomenology and types of crisis. The fundamental law of the crisis: the crisis as a product of class struggle. □ 4. From crisis to catastrophe: the red thread of revolutionary urgency in theory. Against objectivism and against reformism. □ 5. A verification of the law of the tendency of the rate of profit to decline. Different formulations of the law and class interpretations. □ 6. From the theory of profit in the crisis to the theory of communism: provisional conclusions and a leap of the analysis.

"All these statements correct only in this abstraction for the relation from the present standpoint. Additional relations will enter which modify them significantly. The whole, to the extent that it proceeds entirely in generalities, *actually already belongs in the doctrine of profit*" (*Grundrisse*, p. 341; 246–47). This is how the relation between surplus value and productive force leaves off—with the urgent demand for a modification of the field of investigation, for a global displacement of the fields of analysis. *From surplus value to profit, that is, to generalized and socialized surplus value:* originally a category of production, surplus value has now become a *social category*. A leap forward of the analysis becomes necessary, then. It is called for by the productive force of capital and by the force of expansion of surplus value from its place of origin to the general conditions of this formation. And it

85

goes without saying that this socialization, this displacement of the discursive terms, must reproduce the general rules of the approach, the criteria of the critique of exploitation. "We are the last to deny that *Capital* contains contradictions. Our purpose, rather, is to develop them fully. But Ricardo *does not develop them,* but rather shifts them off by considering the value in exchange as indifferent for the formation of wealth. . . . i.e., he regards exchange value as merely formal" (*Grundrisse,* p. 351; 257). No, the socialization of surplus value into profit is not formal, it is rather a process that extends socially the contradiction of surplus value: a contradiction similar in nature, but more extended, more in-depth, more antagonistic. It is not by chance, then, that between the first and the second sections of the *Book on Capital* in the *Grundrisse, the doctrine of profit* takes shape *along with the theory of the crisis.*

But let's proceed in order. Profit appears to Marx as surplus value detached from the conditions of its production and capable of self-valorization. Such an independence of capital from its constitutive relations represents the first paradox. A powerful paradox indeed: capital, in fact, manages to retain the value produced in the labor process and because of this appropriation presents itself, in so far as it is constant capital and constitutes domination, as social form, as form of the social relations. But this is just the paradox. "In a static state, this liberated exchange value by which society has become richer can only be money, in which case only the abstract form of wealth has increased." But,

> in motion it can realize itself only in *new* living labour (whether labour that had been dormant is set into motion, or *new workers* are created— population growth is accelerated—or again a new circle of exchange values, of exchange values in circulation, is expanded, which can occur on the production side if the liberated exchange value opens up a *new branch of production,* i.e. a new object of exchange, objectified labour in the form of a new use value; or the same is achieved when objectified labour is put in the sphere of circulation in a new country, by an expansion of trade). The latter must then be created [*Grundrisse,* p. 348; 253–54].

We must not be enslaved by this paradox. On the contrary, we must recognize that the more the independence of surplus value is consolidated and the more its impact is socially extended, the more exploitation is intensified: *capital* is not just specific exploitation within production, but it *also acquires for itself, gratuitously, social dimensions which are only produced by the force of living labor.* Living labor is subsumed and posed as a condition for the perpetuation of the social value of capital. "This preservation takes place simply by the addition of new labor, which adds a higher value" (*Grundrisse,* p. 357; 262): "Labor is the living, form-giving fire; it is the transitoriness of things, their temporality, as their formation by living time" (*Grundrisse*, p. 361; 266). But if it is *"on separation"* that *"the existence of capital and wage labour rests, capital does not pay for the suspension of this separation which proceeds in the real production process*—for otherwise work could not go on at all" (*Grundrisse*, p. 364; 269). The socialization of surplus value, then, is its extension and intensification, that is the extension and intensification of exploitation, a leap forward in its qualitative and quantitative definition. *Social surplus value* is surplus value from social capital and capitalist domination over social labor, present and future:

> *Money,* then, in so far as it now already *in itself* exists as capital, is therefore simply *a claim on future* (new) labour. It exists, objectively, merely as *money.* *Surplus value,* the new growth of *objectified labour,* to the extent that it exists for itself, is *money;* but now, it is money which *in itself* is already capital; and, as such, it is a *claim on new labour.* Here capital no longer enters into relation with ongoing labour, but with future labour. And it no longer appears dissolved into its simple elements in the production process, but as money; no longer, however, as money which is merely the abstract form of general wealth, but as a claim on the real possibility of general wealth— *labour capacity in the process of becoming.* As a claim, its material existence as money is irrelevant, and can be replaced by any other title. Like the creditor of the State, every capitalist with his newly gained value possesses a claim on future labour, and, by means of the appropriation of ongoing labour has already at the same time appropriated future labour. (This side of capital to be developed to this point. But already here its property of existing as value separately from its substance can be seen. This already lays the basis for credit.) To stockpile it in the form of money is therefore by no means the same as materially to stockpile the material conditions of labour. This is rather a stockpiling of property titles to labour. Posits future labour as *wage labour,* as use value for capital. No *equivalent* on hand for the newly created value; its possibility only in new labour [*Grundrisse,* p. 367; 272–73].

Hence we come to a crucial point in the construction of Marx's profit theory. Such a theory constitutes, first and foremost, a recognition of the *new quality* of exploitation which is contained in the social expansion of surplus value. This new quality cannot be simply defined nor can it be related to the values produced in the labor process: it is also constituted, *gratuitously,* by the *totality of social labor*—that is, the labor which preserves the value of capital as well as that which comes to be enriched in the cooporation of large masses, the labor which follows the scientific potential of society as well as that which results from the simple increase of the population. "In short, all the social powers developing with the growth of population and with the historic development of society cost it nothing" (*Grundrisse,* p. 765; 651). Thus, profit is, in the first place, the social expression of global surplus value, integrated by the gratuitous exploitation of the forces of social production.

The question has been raised, at this point, whether in the *Grundrisse* the profit theory emerges too much in submission to that of surplus value. Rosdolsky (p. 426) has noted how in the section on the process of production the expressions "rate of profit" and "rate of surplus value" are not rigorously distinguished from each other and seem even identical at times. It is true (see, in particular, *Grundrisse,* pp. 274–75; 341–54; 373–86): but we would not blame this excessively on Marx. Indeed, if the concept of surplus value—in its determined origin—must be kept distinct from the concept of profit and its social force, it is no less true that such distinction is actually operated out of the same conceptual nucleus, out of the same real substance: that of the social exploitation of social capital. Certainly, at this point of the analysis, the extension—from surplus value to profit—within which profit comes to be explained as social surplus value, represents an exasperation of the tendency. Profit is subsumed in surplus value before the analysis of the development of the capital relation has shown the implications of the socialization of capital. Once this is recognized, though, we must immediately add that with this passage (however rigid and precipitate it might seem) Marx shows how *the category of profit cannot be resolved* in the function *nor exposed in the categorial form of mediation.* The consequences of this approach are clear: profit is *also* mediation (and never just only mediation) as long as capital has invested the entire society with its mode of production. When capital has historically become social capital, profit can no longer be mediation: then profit becomes resolved mediation, social surplus value; it is the capitalist seal to an antagonistic relation which in reality involves the entire society.

The limit of this first definition of profit was superseded in the months of writing the *Grundrisse.* Other, more advanced theoretical conditions were needed—above all, the analysis of the costs of production and that of rotation; in short, a definition of the organic composition of capital had to be reached (see Rosdolsky pp. 425–433) for this elaboration to take place. Permit me here, then, to anticipate the timing of the commentary on the text and jump ahead to the section *"Capital as fructiferous: Transformation of surplus value into profit,"* which is almost at the end of the *Grundrisse* (pp. 745–778) in Notebook VII. This section represents the climax of the analysis of the circulation process (Notebooks IV–VII) and the *synthesis* between the results of this analysis and those reached in the analysis (Notebooks II–IV) of the process of capital production. Now, the analysis of the transformation of surplus value into profit, integrated with the analysis of socialization (through circulation), incorporates precisely the results of the production process: meanwhile, the analysis of the processes of socialization having been accomplished, the deduction of profit from surplus value does not submit the concept of the former to that of the latter, but on the contrary highlights their differences while showing their fundamental continuity. Thus the ambiguity ceases.

Here, then, capital

> relates to itself as positing new value, as producer of value. It relates as the foundation to surplus value as that which it founded. Its movement consists of relating to itself, while it produces itself, at the same time as the foundation of what it has founded, as value presupposed to itself as surplus value, or to the surplus value as posited by it. In a definite period of time which is posited as the unit measure of its turnovers because it is the natural measure of its reproduction in agriculture, capital produces a definite surplus value, which is determined not only by the surplus value it posits in one production process, but rather by the number of the repetitions of the production process, or of its production in a specified period of time. Because of the inclusion of circulation, of its movement outside the immediate production process, within the reproduction process, surplus value *appears* no longer to be posited by its simple, direct relation to living labour; this relation appears, rather, as merely a moment of its total movement. Proceeding from itself as the active subject, the subject of the process—and, in the turnover, the direct production process indeed appears determined by its movement as capital, independent of its relation to labour—capital relates to itself as self-increasing value; i.e. it relates to surplus value as something posited and founded by it; it relates as well-spring of production, to itself as product; it relates as producing value to itself as produced value. It therefore no longer measures the newly produced value by its real measure, the relation of surplus labour to necessary labour, but rather by itself as its presupposition. A capital of a certain value produces in a certain period of time a certain surplus value. Surplus value thus measured by the value of the presupposed capital, capital thus posited as self-realizing value—is *profit;* regarded not *sub specie aeternitatis,* but *sub specie capitalis,* the surplus value is profit; and capital as capital, the producing and reproducing value, distinguishes itself within itself from itself as profit, the newly produced value. The product of capital is *profit* [*Grundrisse,* pp. 745–46; 631–32].

Let's proceed in the definition of concepts. In the form of profit, surplus value must be measured against the total value of the capital presupposed in the process of production. "Presupposing the same surplus value, *the same surplus labour in proportion to necessary labor,* then, the *rate of profit* depends on the relation between the part of capital exchanged for living labor and the part existing in the form of raw material and means of production. Hence, the smaller the portion exchanged for living labor becomes, the smaller becomes the rate of profit. Thus, in the same proportion as capital takes up a larger place as capital in the production process relative to immediate labor, i.e. the more the relative surplus value grows—the value-creating power of capital—the more *does the rate of profit fall*" (*Grundrisse*, p. 747; 633). Consequently, "The rate of profit can rise although real surplus value falls" (*ibid.*). In conclusion, "while the rate of profit will be inversely related to the value of capital, the *sum of profit* will be directly related to it" (*Grundrisse*, p. 748; 634).

As one might note, between the concept of surplus value and the concept of profit there is a *distinction* that concerns the *quality* of exploitation: surplus value is the exploitation of living labor, the increase of its productivity, the exasperation of the intensity of labor, a total and totalizing drainage of working capacity; profit is the consolidation and fixation of surplus value, it is non-multiplying labor consolidated in a stable form, the theft of the productivity of labor, the indifference to living labor. But the distinction does not touch the *nature* of exploitation: both surplus value and profit are based on the subjugation of living labor—but in the case of surplus value living labor is considered within the production relation, while in the case of profit it is set against the conditions of production, to the totality of accumulation. "Profit is nothing but another form of surplus value, a form developed further in the sense of capital" (*Grundrisse*, p. 762; 648). The distinction does not touch the nature of exploitation, and evidence of this lies in the fact that the contradiction appears again at this point, not only opposing the exploited to the exploiters, as the category of surplus value has it, but also extending the antagonism to the relation between living labor and dead labor in socially comprehensive terms. *The more labor is objectified into capital* and capital is increased; in other words, the more labor and productivity have become capital, *all the more living labor opposes this growth in an antagonistic fashion.* The more capital posits itself as profit-creating power, as a source of wealth which is independent from labor (and in so doing represents each of its constitutive parts as being uniformly productive), then the more living labor estranges itself from capitalist growth in a social and compact form. We will see later on how Marx provides for a formation of the working class that is equal and contrary to the historical and real formation of the concept of social capital (the *Vergleichung* [equalization] of capital) which is implicit in capitalist development; it is a *Vergleichung* of the working class and its real and historical development into a revolutionary force. Here—and we will come back to this soon—the so-called law of the tendency of the profit rate to fall (in these pages Marx completes its elaboration together with the completion of the profit theory) shows this extension of antagonism from the relation producing surplus value to that producing profit.

The law of the rate of profit is a *double one: on the one hand* it exposes the tendency capital has to subsume more and more the conditions determined in the production process and made social in the circulation process; which is to say the tendency of capital to an ever more definitive appropriation of these conditions, as well as to the transformation of surplus value into a factor of profit. *On the other hand* it reveals the new antagonism which is determined by the development of profit from surplus value to social surplus value (profit), from capital to social capital. *The simultaneously progressive and destructive sign, of which the law of profit is the bearer, is determined by its relation with living labor.* On one side, profit is the tendency toward the most aggressive and productive expansion, toward an increasing utilization of living labor and an increase of its mass; on the other side, at this level, profit clashes against the conditions of its own production as well as against its own ferocious and extreme tendency toward subjugation, toward the expansion and the increase of the subjugation of living labor. Both these tendencies are dominated by living labor: the tendency of profit to expand goes hand in hand with a living labor directly exploited but creative nevertheless; the tendency to the fall in the profit rate bespeaks the *revolt of living labor* against the power of profit and its very separate constitution; a revolt against the theft and its fixation into a productive force for the capitalist against the productive force of the worker, into the power of social capital against the vitality of social labor: because of this *living labor reveals itself as destructive.* Too many "Marxists," for too long a time, have forgotten this and have thus suffocated the proletarian uprisings that were verifying this truth. Yet, Marx adds, "beyond a certain point the development of the powers of production becomes a barrier for capital; hence the capital relation a barrier for the development of the productive powers of labour" (*Grundrisse,* p. 749; 635). "This is in every respect the most important law of modern political economy, and the most essential for understanding the most difficult relations" (*Grundrisse,* p. 748; 634).

We must now make explicit some characteristics of the passage from surplus value to profit. We have seen how the category of profit, with its specific difference, is not an element that can be in any way separated from the category of surplus value; it is rather an expansion, an extension to a social level of the antagonism implicit in the law of surplus value. Yet, within the identical nature of the two categories, within the logically subordinated character that the category of profit has with respect to that of surplus value, there exist theoretical reasons which induce Marx to develop the analysis from the standpoint of *transformation.* The first of these reasons for Marx is the need to socially recompose, against the mystification of the anarchy of the market, the very concept of capital and the categories of its functioning. The second reason, closely tied to the first, highlights the need to bring the categories of capital and thus the real antagonism (and consequently the reasons for political opposition) beyond the transient passages and secondary crises (tied to the anarchy of the market) of the historical process of capitalist production. From this standpoint the category of profit is a category that takes shape methodically in dynamic, historical terms, that is, tendential terms. As in the *unpublished* Chapter VI of Book One of *Capital,* what is meant here by the word "tendency" is the necessary passage *from the formal to the real subsumption of labor by capital.* The tendency is that which views profit as being, at first, the mediation, the abstract equalization of the surplus values realized in the different branches of production; then, as capital invests the totality of social production, profit inexorably realizes the tendency, it becomes socially constituted surplus value, the exploitation of society under the control of capital. "At the present level of the relation," the movement of profit drives towards the unification of society under the rule of surplus value. Then, at a higher level of the relation, the movement of profit is determined by its essential capacity to be measured against the social working day—in the chapter on profit the analysis must not be a discussion of the single working day but of the *social working day*—and the categories of surplus value can be applied to the critique of the economic theory of the population:

> the newly created surplus capital can be realized as such only by being again exchanged for living labour. Hence the tendency of capital simul-taneously to increase the *labouring population* as well as to reduce constantly its *necessary* part (constantly to posit a part of it as a reserve). And the increase of the population itself the chief means for reducing the necessary part. *At bottom this is only an application of the relation of the single working day.* Here already lie, then, all the contradictions which modern population theory expresses as such but does not grasp. Capital, as the positing of surplus labour, is equally and in the same moment the positing and the not-positing of necessary labour; it exists only in so far as necessary labour both exists and does not exist [*Grundrisse* pp. 400–01; 304].

With the development of the capitalist mode of production, the category of profit loses its present configuration: or, to put it in a better way, it must be referred back to that of surplus value under the conditions of socialized production. Here, at this level, labor's *productive forces* present themselves, must present themselves, as *"social forces"* (*Grundrisse,* p. 400; 304): "in all stages of production there is a certain common quality of labour, *social* character of the same, etc. The force of social production develops later etc. (Return to this)" (*Grundrisse,* p. 398; 302). So *the category of profit has its origin in the equalization of individual surplus values,* in the simple units of surplus labor, but it tends, *it develops and ends in an ever closer approximation to surplus value, to social surplus labor.* The critiques to the first Marxist definition of profit (its category would overlap too much with that of surplus value) can be accepted as long as they do not claim a qualitative difference between surplus value and profit. *Rather, the relation must be inverted:* profit is a category that tends towards surplus value in so far as it is a social relation. Beyond that profit is a mystification and a category of the capitalist as such, it is "a further development of the inversion of subject and object which takes place in the production process already." Marx insists constantly on this formulation of the profit theory. On one hand he critically stresses the fact that we must not see in "the equalization of the rate of profit—which is to say in the constitution of profit by capital—more than it actually represents: a distributive phenomenon and not a creative one" (*Grundrisse*, pp. 668–69; 561). He says ironically: "if a single operation of exchange cannot increase the value of the thing exchanged, neither can a sum of exchanges do it" (*Grundrisse*, p. 632; 526). And he adds: "It is altogether necessary to make this clear; because the distribution of the surplus value among the capitals, the *calculation* of the total surplus value among the individual capitals—this *secondary* economic operation—gives rise to phenomena which are confused, in the ordinary economic books, with the primary ones" (*Ibid.*). A *secondary economic operation*, then. And so, on the other hand, we can no longer be satisfied with following the theoretical and categorical order of the argument; it is a matter, rather, of beginning *to define the dynamic, tendential, active figure of profit*, the element of the socialization of exploitation in which the essence of profit constitutes iself and unfolds. Profit, therefore, is always that of *"the capitalist class"* (*Grundrisse*, pp. 758–59, 766–67; 644, 653). In this *political figure of profit* the tendency of the development is anticipated: profit begins to concretize not only as the sum of surplus values and as the equalization of individual profits, but also as a political force, as a pole of social antagonism—political at this stage, but slowly ever more charged with reality. This passage is very important in that it represents the definitive demonstration that the theory of profit is subordinated to the theory of surplus value. The process leading to the political figure of capital is homologous with—and contrary to—the process that, in the theory of surplus value, led to the identification of living labor as the *"proletarian class."* Certainly Marx developed a theory of profit, which is to say a theory of the subjectivity of capital, while—in spite of his intentions—he did not develop a theory of the subjectivity of the working class—in the figure of wage, for instance. But this *asymmetry* of the *literary* development of Marx's work should not keep us from recognizing the *structural balance;* and from developing his proposed presuppositions, seeing in the social working day, in its division between social surplus labor and socially necessary labor, the basis for the deadly struggle that is put up by the two classes. We must see in these two spaces the formation of *opposed subjectivities,* opposed wills and intellects, opposed processes of valorization: in short, an antagonistic dynamism which is required by the very development of those conditions we have just considered here. A theory of the subjectivity of the working class and the proletariat constitutes then a presupposition and a duty *vis-à-vis* the theory of profit, opposing the reality of all this surplus labor extorted, objectified, socialized, through which capital simultaneously has achieved its own unification as a class and the control of exploitation. The *Grundrisse* aims at a theory of the subjectivity of the working class against the profitable theory of capitalist subjectivity.

Let's return, after this long digression, to the order of development of the *Grundrisse,* that is to the *second section ("The Circulation Process")* of the *Chapter on Capital.* This section formally begins with a long *Excursus on Crises.* Again the crisis, the present crisis, that critical reality which motivates the whole work and whose appreciation is its foundation! The *Grundrisse* had begun, in the emotion of the crisis, by fully exploring the theory of money as the privileged level of manifestation of the crisis. It developed then into the theory of surplus value and, through the first formulation of the profit theory and of the tensions implicit in the law of the profit rate, it returns again to the crisis and to its scientific explanation. Now, according to the preliminary plan, the process of capitalist production should make room for the analysis of the circulation process, and we should focus on this second thematic aspect of the *Grundrisse.* Marx's attention, however, is again arrested by the crisis: *before analysis unfolds extensively on it, circulation is seen exclusively as the form of the crisis.* Does this new and lengthy dwelling upon the crisis represent a shortcut in the development of the *Grundrisse?* Is it an abuse of the order of theoretical procedure by revolutionary subjectivity? Partially, this is undoubtedly so. But it's also something more and something different. A large step forward had been made in the first part of the *Grundrisse* and that is the subjectivization of the process. In other words, by virtue of the surplus value theory and its subsequent founding of the profit theory, we are now in possession of a conceptual network which allows us to bring into focus *the crisis in its relationship with economic growth and class struggle.* Unlike capital, which "has no awareness whatever of the nature of its process of realization, and has an interest in having an awareness of it only in times of *crisis" (Grundrisse,* p. 374; 277), the point of view of the working class is by now capable of considering the growth in the form of the crisis and the crisis as the privileged territory of class struggle. The thought of the crisis, Marx's fixation, breaks in at this point, that is, when the process of capital's valorization should extend into circulation: but, as the process of valorization is dominated by the antagonistic law of surplus value, so the circulation process must be referred back to it and be grasped above all in the crisis: in this crisis, which attests to the continuity of antagonism as well as to its ever-present subjective impetuosity. So the *second section* of the *Chapter on Capital,* the real elaboration of *"The Circulation Process,"* does not begin in coincidence with the appearance of the title, but it begins only after the *Excursus* on the crisis, about a hundred pages later, or better still (as we will see later in Lesson 6) even later than that, after the *Excursus* *"Formen,"* another hundred pages which, perhaps, represent a further expansion of Marx's interest in the definition of the crisis. The analysis of the *crisis as the form of circulation* is, then, a part of the fundamental analysis outlined by the surplus value theory. It is a research into the functioning of the antagonism which is proper to the production process in the crisis of circulation. The theory of surplus value therefore continues and undergoes a further definition in the crisis theory. The first part of the *Grundrisse* may be considered terminated only at the end of this *Excursus*.

"Looked at precisely, that is, the *realization process* of capital—and money becomes capital only through the realization process—appears at the same time as its *devaluation process,* its demonetization" (*Grundrisse,* p. 402; 306). "In any case, devaluation forms one moment of the realization process; which is already simply implied in the fact that the product of the process in its immediate form is not *value,* but first has to enter anew into circulation in order to be realized as such" (*Grundrisse,* p. 403; 308).

> Inside the production process, realization appeared totally identical with the production of surplus labour (the objectification of surplus time), and hence appeared to have no *bounds* other than those partly presupposed and partly posited within this process itself, but which are always posited within it as *barriers* to be forcibly overcome. There now appear barriers to it which lie *outside* it [*Grundrisse,* p. 404; 308].

Right away, then, we find ourselves in the middle of the problem. *Through the circulation process the contradictions of production are magnified:* contradictions are endlessly reproduced, relived in a new form, and even suspended, but they "are suspended only by force" (*Grundrisse,* p. 406; 309). "The main point here—where we are concerned with the general concept of capital— is that it is this *unity of production and realization,* not *immediately* but only as a *process,* which is linked to certain conditions, and, as it appeared, *external* conditions" (*Grundrisse,* p. 407; 310–11). Certainly "every limit appears as a barrier to be overcome" (*Grundrisse,* p. 408; 311). The fact that the crisis is immanent within the concept of capital represents not only its negative determination but also its positive one. The thrust towards relative surplus value, the tendency towards the world market, the "production of *new* needs and discovery and creation of new use values" (*Grundrisse,* p. 408; 312): all this represents *the positive tension* engendered by the very limits of the concept (of capital), limits which capital knows and must go through. Every period of crisis is therefore followed by an extensive period of *restructuration*.

> The value of the old industry is preserved by the creation of the fund for a new one in which the relation of capital and labour posits itself in a *new* form. Hence, exploration of all nature in order to discover new, useful qualities in things; universal exchange of the products of all alien climates and lands; new (artificial) preparation of natural objects, by which they are given new use values. The exploration of the earth in all directions,

to discover new things of use as well as new useful qualities of the old; such as new qualities of them as raw materials, etc.; the development, hence, of the natural sciences to their highest point; likewise the discovery, creation and satisfaction of new needs arising from society itself; the cultivation of all the qualities of the social human being, production of the same in a form as rich as possible in needs, because rich in qualities and relations—production of this being as the most total and universal possible social product, for, in order to take gratification in a many-sided way, he must be capable of many pleasures, hence cultured to a high degree—is likewise a condition of production founded on capital [*Grundrisse*, p. 409; 312–13].

But from the fact that capital posits every such limit as a barrier and hence gets *ideally* beyond it, it does not by any means follow that it has *really* overcome it, and, since every such barrier contradicts its character, its production moves in contradictions which are constantly overcome but just as constantly posited. Furthermore. The universality towards which it irresistibly strives encounters barriers in its own nature, which will, at a certain stage of its development, allow it to be recognized as being itself the greatest barrier to this tendency, and hence will drive towards its own suspension [*Grundrisse*, p. 410; 313–14].

To really overcome, to avoid the crisis: this is what capital *cannot do.* There are in fact two phenomenal forms in which the crisis presents itself: on one side *crises of disproportion* (which is to say, crises of the actual circulation, crises of unbalance among the various elements making up the circulation of capital), and on the other, *crises of realization* (which is to say, those crises ascribable to the capacity of consumption, where overproduction and inadequate consumption—and/or underconsumption—are combined). But beyond these phenomenal forms, it is in the very necessity of their endless self-reproduction that the fundamental law of the crisis is to be found. It rests in the contradiction between production and valorization, not as it is registered in "the individual moments of the process, or rather of the totality of processes" (*Grundrisse*, p.415; 318). There exists a limit which cannot be found within circulation or general production: we must go much further, for it is at the law of production based on capital that we must arrive. Now, from this immanent standpoint, the crisis derives from:

1) necessary labour as limit of the exchange value of living labour capacity; 2) surplus value as limit of surplus labour and development of the forces of production; 3) money as the limit of production; 4) the restriction of the production of use values by exchange values.

Hence overproduction: i.e., the sudden *recall* of all these necessary moments of production based on capital; hence general devaluation in consequence of forgetting them. Capital, at the same time, [is] thereby faced with the task of launching its attempt anew from a higher level of the development of productive forces, with each time greater collapse *as capital* [*Grundrisse*, p. 416; 319].

The fundamental law of the crisis lies therefore in the contradictory relation between necessary labor and surplus labor, that is, in the functioning of the law of surplus value.

It is with impressive violence that Marx evinces, in the subsequent pages, the effects of the fundamental law in determining the crisis. If capital is the dynamic and *"living contradiction,"* the working class represents the rigidity, the opposing force, *the limit.* The relationship is becoming more and more subjective. Development always has the form of crisis because, like crisis, it has, in the last instance, at its base "always *the relation of necessary to surplus labour,* or, if you like, of the different moments of objectified to living labour" (*Grundrisse,* p. 444; 348). "The original proportion"—how to divide these quantities—constitutes the problem which dominates both the development and the crisis of capital. "To restore the correct relation between necessary and surplus labour, on which, in the last analysis, everything rests" (*Grundrisse,* p. 446; 351) is the constant objective of capital. The destruction of capital, the devaluation of living labor, the reconstruction into more just (for capital) conditions of exploitation: this is the crisis for capital, this is the price that it is always willing to pay in order to retain its control, its subjective power.

Because this is precisely the case, if we analyze at a deeper level the mechanisms of the crisis, if we read the fundamental law in the way that the profit theory taught us to read it, we arrive at the *political relationship* that animates and sustains the entire analytic procedure. The objectivity of the laws shows, once again, the subjectivity of their course, because *the relation between surplus labor and necessary labor* is, as we have often seen, *the relation between the two classes.* On one side things are simple and clear cut: "capital thus appears as the product of labour, so does the product of labour likewise appear as *capital;* objectified labour as mastery, command over living labour. The product of labour appears as *alien property,* as a mode of existence confronting living labour as independent, as *value* in its being for itself; the product of labour, objectified labour, has been endowed by living labour with a soul of its own, and establishes itself opposite living labour as an *alien power:* both these situations are themselves the product of labour" (*Grundrisse,* pp. 453–54; 357). "This realization process is at the same time the de-realization process of labour" (*ibid.*). Therefore the problem on the capitalist's side is totally political. Power extends exploitation from production to the reproduction of the relations of power: "the result of the process of production and realization is, above all, the reproduction and new production of the *relation of capital and labour itself,* of *capitalist and worker"* (*Grundrisse,* p. 458; 362). But on the other side, also, things are simple and clear cut: "what is reproduced and produced anew is not only the *presence* of these objective conditions of living labour, *but also their presence as independent values, i.e., values belonging to an alien subject, confronting this living labour capacity*" (*Grundrisse*, p. 462; 366). The subjectivity of living labor opposes in such an antagonistic fashion the consolidation of dead labor into an exploiting power that it negates itself as a value, as an exploited essence, thus proposing itself as *the negation of value* and exploitation. "Living labour appears itself as *alien vis-à-vis* living labour capacity, whose labour it is, whose own life's expression it is, for it has been surrendered to capital in exchange for objectified labour, for the product of labour itself. Labour capacity relates to its labour as to an alien, and if capital were willing to pay it *without* making it labour it would enter the bargain with pleasure" (*ibid.*). But it's not enough: negation becomes *revolutionary insurgence*, consciousness of the inversion:

> The recognition of the products as its own, and the judgment that its separation from the conditions of its realization is improper—forcibly imposed—is an enormous (advance in) awareness, itself the product of the mode of production based on capital, and as much the knell to its doom as, with the slave, awareness that he *cannot be the property of another*, with his consciousness of himself as a person, the existence of slavery becomes a merely artificial, vegetative existence, and ceases to be able to prevail as the basis for production. [*Grundrisse*, p. 463; 366–67].

At this point the fundamental law of the crisis has been completely developed into the law of class struggle. "This to be developed later under wage labour" (*Grundrisse*, p. 465; 369). The internalization of the crisis of the development is such that both crisis and development are seen as a product of class struggle.

One cannot deny that an extraordinary, subjective and revolutionary tension runs through these pages and that, as a consequence, the above-mentioned shortcut between surplus value theory and crisis theory is taken and followed quite impetuously. We have seen how Marx achieves some important results, how he asserts at any rate—in this precise way—the subjective and strongly disruptive nature of the theory, particularly in the interpretation of the crisis. We must, however, stress right away the fact that this shortcut does not have (of course) the same clarity of the "long way." We can indeed understand Marx's subjective urgency, we can evaluate positively its effects, but we must also acknowledge how *paradoxes* and *ambiguities* do abound here. One paradox is particularly striking: and it is precisely that according to which the highest revolutionary subjectivity seems to parallel the highest contradiction in the growth of capitalist production, which is to say revolution combined with *catastrophe*. The crisis is potentially capable of making the two tendencies homologous and simultaneous. From a practical point of view this paradox is easily explained: it is an operation that aims at a convergence into focus of all the elements of the theory and subjectivity into a definitive act of persuasion. Marx and revolutionary Marxism are full, and for good reason, of these intentional political exclamations. It is a global verification which displaces all the terms of the critique and causes their convergence into moments of practical truth, which is called for by the subversive method of a revolutionary working class. This said, the fact remains that the concentration of focus—the more complex the more useful—should be a result and not a premise. And here the analogy of the tendencies appears often as a premise. It seems as though some sort of revolution from above on the workers' part—after it has been given rational motivations by the catastrophe—has to correspond to the revolution from above promoted by capital, that is, by its impetuous movement which, in the middle of the crisis, tends towards the social recognition of its own power. Yet the brevity of the shortcut and its implications are charged with other meanings that we must emphasize. It is easy for us to insist on the critique: but it is important to succeed in transforming its sense—especially since facing us we have one stage, one side, *and one only,* of Marx's approach. Marx himself senses the limits of his theoretical development. Why not try to understand the value and the positive determination of these limits as well? To move in the direction of such an understanding means the return *to the center of the revolutionary methodology of Marxist science.*

And so? Are we faced with an exasperated objectivism on Marx's part? Are we faced with a conception of subjectivity which is merely a residue of the determination of the critical elements of capitalist development—so that the former would emerge out of the latter as Minerva did from Zeus's head? Worse still, are we faced with an organic conception of capitalist growth, which combines the determinism of the crisis with a parasitic and subsequent genesis of the revolutionary project? We have already considered these objections from the standpoint of methodology. None of them appeared fearsome to us; because the tendency might well conceal the violence of its origin, but it cannot erase it; because the lack of historical forces adequate to the revolutionary project can indeed flatten it on the horizon of historical necessity, but it cannot keep the multilateral violence of its development from appearing. The immanence of antagonism, examined in the infinitely small detail of its conceptual framework, can indeed appear as a mere point: the trajectories, though, the antagonistic lines of its development are not erased by this. On the other hand, knowing how to read these pages, one can see such an acute and pressing attention paid to the genesis of the antagonism that negative conclusions can only be reached out of an excessive indifference. In sum, here, the urgency—the red thread of revolutionary urgency in the theory—has caused the analysis to precipitate, in a chemical sense, and to consolidate around some—perhaps too essential—reagents; but this precipitation is precisely posited against any sort of objectivism and reformism. One can denounce the paradoxes and the ambiguities that cluster in these pages: but if we want to solve them from a political point of view, we will recognize them as overflowing with revolutionary passion; if we want to solve them from a theoretical point of view, we must be careful not to understand them prevailingly in terms of objectivism or organicism. Rosdolsky has often told us that Marx's "catastrophism" is a keynote of revolutionary music. Having felt at times the rage of defeat and the theoretical exaltation of renewal, we can understand all of this.

From understanding to interpretation. Merely to understand, in fact, is not enough. We must have a clearer idea of it. Let's take a crucial problem, that of the *law of the tendency of the profit rate to decline,* perhaps one of the most ambiguous and paradoxical points of this Marx, and let's try to see whether the previously mentioned problems can be not only understood but also explicitly resolved, that is, whether among the different formulations a resolving one can be found—a resolving formulation adequate to the class point of view and in line with Marx's methodological presuppositions. The reason why we choose this particular point is clear. The law of the tendency of the profit rate to decline is, in fact, that which seems to best lend itself to the "atrocious vivisections" of the critics. We'll have made great progress if we succeed in showing, with respect to this, the correctness of the course of Marx's research, the continuity of the law of surplus value and of the class point of view.

Now, with the law of the tendency of the profit rate to decline Marx intends to demonstrate, as is well known, how *the rates of valorization of capital decrease proportionally to the variation of the ratio between constant capital and variable capital,* whereby the increase of the former impoverishes the latter in a proportional fashion and determines, accordingly, a proportional decrease in the realization of new value. Growing ever larger, constant capital sucks in, *proportionally,* less and less living labor, that is, valorizing labor, even if from the point of view of its sum it subjugates more and more. The sum total of profit can then increase in the presence of a decline of the rate. According to this law, capitalist growth *tends necessarily towards the crisis,* because the very reasons why capital assumes all the loads of production are precisely those same reasons which imply a devoiding of the values of capital. Upon its formation this law takes shape in the ratio between necessary labor and surplus labor, which is established by the *law of surplus value.* On this basis, the law of the fall of the profit rate derives from the fact that *necessary labor is a rigid quantity.* Capitalist growth may indeed urge the compression of its quantity, it can indeed multiply the productive force of labor, but after all the surplus value that can be extorted is limited: there is still the rigidity of necessary labor (necessary part of the labor day) to constitute the limit to valorization. A limit increasing to the extent that any increase in productivity and in the sum of profit is faced with a force less and less willing to be subjected, less and less available to compression. Such rigidity imparts its primary sense to the law of the tendency of the profit rate to decline. In this law we must read what Marx had acknowledged in the *Grundrisse* immediately preceding the first formulation of the law, that is, the radical estrangement, *the autonomy of the working class from the development of capital.* We must keep in mind how, in this perspective and in the light of the further development of capitalism, a new hypothesis can be made, which is, in our opinion, totally realistic and widely proved by the most recent experiences of class struggle. This is the hypothesis that the quantity of value of the necessary part of the working day is *not only* more and more rigid but also tends towards higher values and therefore tends to diminish—subjectively, actively—the surplus value that can be extorted. The sum of necessary labor is rigid and it is precisely on this rigidity that are based the possibilities for a higher valorization on the part of the class, *for a self-valorization of the working class and the proletariat.* In sum, for this Marx, the devaluation of labor power, in that it is a compression of the necessary part of the labor day, not only is not indefinite, but is, on the contrary, limited and reversible. Necessary labor can valorize itself autonomously, the world of needs can and must expand. There emerges an aspect of the law of the tendency of the profit rate to decline which combines the proportionality of the decrease of value of capital with the independent valorization of the proletariat. The law of the tendency to decline represents, therefore, one of the most lucid Marxist intuitions of the intensification *of the class struggle* in the course of capitalist development. The confusions on the subject will emerge later on when Marx, *reformulating the law,* instead of proposing the formula of the ratio between necessary labor and surplus labor, proposes the formula of *the organic composition of capital* (exclusive ratio between constant capital and variable capital) or that of the ratio between profit and wage. These two formulae are obviously present in the *Grundrisse* as well, but here they are subordinated to the quantities defined by the law of surplus value. Whenever, on the contrary, they become prominent or exclusive, the entire relation will be dislocated on an economistic level and objectified improperly. So that, as a consequence, a conception that *eliminates* the class struggle as a fundamental and rigid variable of the theory will be the result of an interpretation of the law of the tendency of the profit rate to decline, based on the formula of the organic composition; conversely, the unrealistic law of the increasing impoverishment will derive from an interpretation in the guideline of the ratio wage/profit. The confusion of the antagonistic causes will complete the picture, offering us such an unrealistic description of the crisis induced by the fall in the profit rate that more importance will always be attributed to the antagonistic causes than to the course of the law itself.

We started out from the need to interpret a series of Marx's oscillations in the discourse on the crisis. We understood *the sense of his catastrophism.* Now we can add that this catastrophism, together with the objectivism and the determinism that it implies, can be interpreted, on a theoretical level, only as a reflection of a later reformulation of his thought, that is, a formulation that upsets its foundations and denies the centrality of the law of surplus value as a foundation for all other Marxist categories. But if we take this law as a starting point, we can justly attribute Marx's catastrophism to the mere revolutionary urgency of his project, we can recognize the very seeking of the shortcut as a simple allusion to the extension of the theoretical argumentation, we can dissolve the objectivist and determinist residuals within the context of his militant materialism. Obversely, the image of the crisis is revealed to be based on the maximum intensity of the development of the class struggle, on the widest extension of the validity of the law of exploitation. We can at this point turn the picture around and recognize how *the immanence of the class struggle to both growth and crisis, to the very structure of capital*, has never been so evident at this stage of the discourse. It is an anticipation of what we will see studying the second part of the *Grundrisse,* which is to say the process of circulation and the reformulation of the categories of class struggle at the level of social capital. But for the time being let's insist on the importance of this approach.

Still on the subject of the law of the tendency of the profit rate to decline, another notation is to be made. Let's imagine that at a certain stage of the development of the class struggle, the rigidity of the proletarian front induces a stagnation and/or a fall of profit. Let's imagine that this situation lasts for a while and that the extension of class resistance is socially homogeneous. Now, on this terrain, we will have not only a decrease of the profit rate, but also a *decrease* of its *sum.* The last twenty years of class struggle in the advanced capitalist countries prove to us that the situation just described is not unrealistic.

It is important to stress all this in so far as it allows us to proceed to a deeper level of the rupture of any economistic scheme imposed upon Marxist theory. The law of the tendency of the profit rate to decline is ultimately correct only if it is interpreted in the light of the surplus value theory; its tendential character is that on which are organized the complexities of the tensions of the working class struggling against work under capitalism and for its own self-valorization. Moreover: only within these conditions is it possible to be "catastrophic" from the point of view of the working class. Only by not believing that communism is unavoidable will it be unavoidable. It is a paradox only in words. In practice only the freedom of necessary labor, the creativity of labor applied to itself, its force both creative and destructive, constitutes the real limit of capital and the manifold, recurrent cause of its crisis; up to the point of its irreversibility, that is, when, in the fundamental relation, the mass of exploited labor expropriates the expropriators of the mass of exploited labor. There's no theory of the crisis outside of this perspective.

But it's not enough. The Marxist outline of the crisis is germinative not only in that it reduces every economic phenomenology of the crisis to its class foundations. It is also incredibly fruitful, as we began to see, in that it defines the rich *phenomenology of the crisis* on the terrain of class struggle. Which is to say: once the study of the causes of the crisis has been reduced to the functioning of the law of surplus value, the analysis can open itself onto the forms of the crisis, keeping Marx's methodological elements in mind. At this point the pattern of the crisis (of the crises) will reveal itself to us as being interwoven by an enormous plurality of dialectical points, critical trajectories, significant segmentations. Of course, we will be able to follow this path only after we have reconsidered the crisis within a more articulated relationship between circulation and production. It is nevertheless worth stressing the importance of the consequences of the analysis developed above.

Through the theory of the rate of profit, with the dual tension it illus-trates—that is, the constructive and civilizing tension versus the destructive and coercive one—the surplus value theory has terminated its actual course in the theory of the crisis as a product of the class struggle. This much we have seen in this chapter. With this, the first part of the *Grundrisse* comes to an end, together with the elaboration of the surplus value theory from the point of view of the working class.

What is to be said? One has, at this point, the impression of sitting on a bomb. Some sparks have already flown, maybe prematurely, maybe rashly. Already some further directions have been glimpsed. But the potential of the surplus value theory must now explode, and—exploding—displace the whole field of analysis. Until now we have followed the thread of an analysis that has been stretched to the extreme of its elasticity. We have arrived at a point where the allusions to the continuation of the analysis, to the new horizon and new wealth that it promises, emerge almost only from nega-tivity. Communism in the glare of catastrophe: the dual scheme that splits and smashes every category of political economy by exposing it to the risk of the class struggle. The class struggle itself determines its project in the destruction of wage labor and here opens onto an extreme pluralism of extreme negations. At this turning point of the analysis we have a precise notion of the *destructive and critical effectiveness of Marx's analysis*. It is a *pars destruens* of Cartesian intensity. Everything has been destroyed and reduced in the name of the principles of class struggle, of the surplus value theory. And now? Now it is matter of coming back to the clash between *social capital and a recomposed class*. To go back means to make the theoretical approach rigorously concrete and historical. To go back must be *a passage into politics*. The negative allusion has the right and the duty of becoming an active and positive proposition. The allusion to communism, contained in the crisis theory, must be given content. We are faced with an image of capital which begins to move from production to circulation: but circulation is here blocked in the form of the crisis. A crisis that might be catastrophic: this is necessary to the urgency of the revolutionary project. But let's imagine that circulation stabilizes its course, even if in the irreversible form of the crisis; let's imagine that this immanence of the class struggle is stabilized and can only tendentially present itself as explosive; let's imagine, finally, that the relation between the normalization of circulation and crisis on one hand and the tendential development of the working class towards communism on the other is a given situation that can be theoretically estimated. The sudden insertion of the *Excursus* on the crisis is evidence of the trouble Marx goes through in ascertaining these presuppositions (we will see it in the initial pages on circulation): it is an indisputable moment of revolutionary impatience. It is clear, however, that the new terrain is that of normalization as well as that of another leap forward in terms of the socialization of capital— and of the class struggle. *To displace the analysis* is then necessary. Theoretical and historical motivations assemble as usual around crucial passages; do they become political motivation and intention? If I were to reply to this question, I would be inclined towards an affirmative. As a matter of fact—and the theory of the tendency of the profit rate to decline is for us a demonstration of it—Marx has reached the conclusion of the radical autonomy of the working class. The theory of exploitation, even though its socialization is demonstrated more emblematically than logically, leads to the antithetic emergence of the two forces in the field. The political fabric becomes at this point the fundament on which we can design our theoretical patterns, and concomitantly it begins to determine the binding conditions for this validity. The more a theory becomes abstract and comprehensive, the more it needs a real support. *It is inconceivable to think of a displacement of the analysis, what we have called the leap forward, which is not tied to a force, to a subject that makes this very leap.* Its difference, its singularity, is to be assumed as a condition of a comprehensive investigation. This series of presuppositions exists for Marx: the autonomy of the working class has been identified, allusively, perhaps, but with no less reality. Not so much as a part of a recompositional dialectic: in the crisis theory it appears as a rupture of any dialectic, as a foundation of the proletariat's independence, as a proposition of communism. I do not know how convincing this argumentation of mine is; I do know, however, that with every other argumentation it becomes impossible to bridge the gap dividing the surplus value theory from the theory of the revolution against social capital. Unless we are too fond of "Theory."

Social Capital &
World Market

From surplus value theory to circulation theory: passage to the second fundamental theme in the *Grundrisse*. ☐ Substantial and methodological aspects of the investigation. ☐ *"Forms which precede capitalist production":* a parenthesis necessary to proceed. ☐ Back to the subject: socialization as appropriation. ☐ From the formal to real subsumption. ☐ "Qualitative leap" towards social capital. ☐ From affirmation to negation: socialization as a barrier. ☐ "The permanent revolution" of capital and its law. ☐ Limit and barrier. ☐ Towards the world market. ☐ The expansion of capital as result and as condition. ☐ The collective form of capital and its antithetic form: social capital and class struggles. ☐ The synthetic moment of the argument as adequate and extreme development of the antagonism.

The crisis, then, has to be *normalized* in the theory of circulation. Circulation is nothing but the expansion of the fabric formed by the dynamics of exploitation. *The theory of circulation is the continuation and the expansion of the theory of surplus value.* The *Excursus* on the crisis had already exposed circulation to us, but it had done so only in negative terms, in a field still unmediated, highlighting the negative aspect of the separation and foregrounding its destructive effects. Now, instead, we must consider the mediation. Circulation is a capitalist victory over the crisis. But it does not eliminate the relation that constitutes crisis and capital itself, the schism between the two classes and their struggle. Capital must extend outward and multiply in the process of circulation in order to normalize the crisis, in order to contain the logic of separation which constitutes it and which is constantly about to explode—more and more impetuously. But every new territory invested by capital and its circulation constitutes one more class relation.

Circulation therefore entails the reproduction of capital, of the working class and of their struggle on a larger scale. Evidently difficult problems arise at this point, such as—in general—the definition of the relation between circulation and reproduction, or—if you will—the problem of the productive potential of circulation: we shall come to these problems later on. For the time being, we shall follow Marx's relative imprecision in attacking these themes. He is mostly concerned with the analysis of the expansive force of capital. It is not a process with only quantitative connotations, but also qualitative ones. Capital, in fact, becomes more and more a collective force through this expansion, and it subjugates ever more widely the productive forces— while, conversely, this testifies to its precariousness, to the precariousness of its growth—whenever a higher level is reached: the level of social capital, of the subjugation of the whole society. The second part of the *Grundrisse* is precisely this formidable passage forward of the analysis.

We must digress here, in order to insist on the *importance* of the *second part* of the *Grundrisse*. If, as Vygodskij puts it, the discovery of surplus value introduces the class struggle in economic theory, the analysis of circulation develops the theory of class struggle into a theory of the revolutionary subject. The surplus value theory, which is the object of the first part of the *Grundrisse,* is the definition of the possibility of the revolutionary subject, its negative definition. The *reality* of the *collective class-subject comes to be posited with the theory of circulation,* and, that is, within the context of normalized separation which the analysis (and the reality) of circulation is. In *this* and in the *next lesson* we will study this passage. In the two following we will discuss a further aspect instead: the theory of communism as a theory of the progressive realization of the subject, as a synthesis of both the theory of the crisis and of the subject.

The development of the argument in this direction entails a series of considerations which are only hastily touched upon by Marx's text: these elements, although belonging to Marx's methodology, have rarely been theorized in an explicit way by him. But here, within these passages, they accomplish a very relevant function. We shall have to insist particularly *on the constitutive character* of the various *theoretical displacements* we have been pointing out all along. We shall have to stress constantly the real character of these passages, and this amounts to saying that Marx's analysis tends more and more to the concrete. From the surplus value theory to that of circulation, from the analysis of the market to that of capital, from formal to real subsumption—it is the concrete, the political, to which we are drawing ever nearer. Too often Marx has been read as a direct history of capitalist development. This is not true. Now, in the midst of these formidable passages and displacements, we sense the true key of the knowing process: an ever closer approach to the complexity of the revolutionary subject, at the real level of the class struggle. An approach which realizes a fundamental criterion of Marx's methodology, a grasping of the essential relation in such a subjectively fruitful way that we can consider its possession as a key to real *transformation*. What we are after, then, is such a passage between the surplus value theory and the circulation theory: the subject becomes ever more real, ever more concrete; the cellular structure described by the surplus value theory becomes body, finished animal reality. Our expository problem is, of course, that of being able to proceed at the pace of this process. It won't be difficult if we follow Marx's argumentation.

But it is difficult for Marx. In fact, after having already formally begun the discourse on circulation (*Grundrisse*, p. 401; 305) by entitling it: *"Section Two—The Circulation Process of Capital"*, not only has he entertained us for a hundred pages with that *Excursus* on crises—which, as we have seen, is nothing but an appendix to the theory of surplus value/profit—but after this he still does not enter the heart of the analysis. In Notebooks IV and V, without interruption, in the continuity of Marx's exposition, we find ourselves faced with fifty more pages: *"Forms which Precede Capitalist Production"* (*Grundrisse*, pp. 471–514; 375–413), another long digression, another delay in the fulfillment of the obligation that was tacit in the opening title of the *Second Section* (this text, contained in the notebooks just mentioned, had presumably been written in February 1858).

Die Formen is a short essay on the productive process "which precedes the formation of the capital relation or of original accumulation." A short essay which has often been published and utilized in an independent form because, at first sight, it certainly has an individuality of its own. A short essay which is in any case quite impressive on account of the mass of readings it presupposes, and which ultimately opens up a series of peculiar yet extremely important (in their own way) problems. (see Sofri, G., *Il modo di produzione asiatico*, Torino 1969).

A discussion of the questions touched upon by *Die Formen* is not our concern here. Only we must not forget that *this essay is an organic part of the Grundrisse*, and as such it challenges us to understand its place in the unfolding of Marx's reasoning; that is, to understand why it appears at this point and not somewhere else, in short to ascertain its systematic function. Now we must immediately point out how this study is *yet another study on the crisis*. After the punctual and synchronic analysis developed by the *Excursus on Crises*, what unfolds here is a historical, diachronic analysis. After seeing the crisis in the form of circulation, Marx analyzes it in *Die Formen* in the figure of a long-term tendency, in the figure of genealogy. The method is perfect: at times, in the reading of these pages, one has the impression of being confronted with a direct, immediate exemplification of the methodological criteria exposed in the *Introduction*. A historiographic application. Here we find all the moments we stressed in *Lesson 3:* determinate abstraction—tendency—new exposition—displacement. The relevance of this essay, however, is not found (even if we leave aside the specificity of the subject matter) in its method, but in its substance. *Die Formen* is all too important, primarily for its enhancement of the reading and interpretation of the internal rhythm of the *Grundrisse:* it is a parenthesis that cannot be put in parentheses. We must therefore state again the role of this essay in the economy of the *Grundrisse,* in the project of the passage to the analysis of circulation and of the theoretical problems that such a displacement of the investigation involves. Its direction is towards the completion of *the analysis of the crisis,* by bringing it to the point where *the identification of the forces in the field,* of the classes making up the fabric of both development and crisis, can no longer be avoided or mystified. It is another step towards the concrete determination of the dialectic of separation that we cannot underestimate.

But let's look at some seminal points in *Die Formen.* It seems to me that we can proceed by identifying an abstract *general axis* and *two consequential and subsequent,* much more concrete, *positions.* The axis consists of the definition of *the general law of the historical development of the modes of production:* a community exists, a mode of production is stabilized as long as its reproduction is adequate to the objective conditions. But "production itself, the advance of population (this too belongs with production), necessarily suspends these conditions little by little; destroys them instead of reproducing them, etc., and, with that, the communal system declines and falls, together with the property relations on which it was based" (*Grundrisse,* p. 486; 386). The limits of production, reproduction, and crisis are determined by the degree of objective conditioning, that is, by *the predetermination of the conditions.* "Great developments can take place here within a specific sphere. The individuals may appear great. But there can be no conception here of a free and full development either of the individual or of the society, since such development stands in contradiction to the original relation" (*Grundrisse,* p. 487; 386–87). Each *"determined social formation"* is then *this complex of conditions and limits whose interrelationship is constitutive of both the existence and crisis of the given formation.* The general sign of civilization is the movement from nature to history, each formation is, by definition, "limited" while the direction of the development is towards the unlimitedness of human potential."

> In fact, however, when the limited bourgeois form is stripped away, what is wealth other than the universality of individual needs, capacities, pleasures, productive forces, etc., created through universal exchange? The full development of human mastery over the forces of nature, those of so-called nature as well as of humanity's own nature? The absolute working out of his creative potentialities, with no presupposition other than the previous historic development, which makes this totality of development, i.e., the

development of all human powers as such the end in itself, not as measured on a *predetermined* yardstick? Where he does not reproduce himself in one specificity, but produces his totality? Strives not to remain something he has become, but is in the absolute movement of becoming? [*Grundrisse*, p. 488; 387].

This is the general axis, abstract and tendential, which is presented here. The *law of movement* (like the law of tendency which promotes the passage from the limited to the unlimited) promotes the passage from *unity to difference*:

All forms (more or less naturally arisen, spontaneous, all at the same time, however, results of a historic process) in which the community presupposes its subjects in a specific objective unity with their conditions of production, or in which a specific subjective mode of being presupposes the communities themselves as conditions of production, necessarily correspond to a development of the forces of production which is only limited, and indeed limited only in principle. The development of the forces of production dissolves these forms, and their dissolution is itself a development of the human productive forces. Labour begins with a certain foundation—naturally arisen, spontaneous, at first—then historic presupposition. Then, however, this foundation or presupposition is itself suspended, or posited as a vanishing presupposition which has become too confining for the unfolding of the progressing human pack [*Grundrisse*, pp. 496–97; 396].

Difference and unlimitedness, difference and wealth are the homologous terms of *the general law of development*: "It is not the *unity* of living and active humanity with the natural, inorganic conditions of their metabolic exchange with nature, and hence their appropriation of nature, which requires explanation or is the result of a historic process, but rather the *separation* between these inorganic conditions of human existence and this active existence, a separation which is completely posited only in the relation of wage labour and capital" (*Grundrisse*, p. 489; 389). As we have said, the definition of the general law of development *is followed by two more concrete*, subordinate positions, and that is the analysis of at least *two fundamental groups of formations*, of their internal constitutive relation and the crises that cause their explosion. It is not our concern here to develop the analysis of ancient and Oriental communities that represents one of Marx's approaches to a type of determinate social formation—a precapitalistic one—nor is it worthwhile to note and stress how Marx resuscitates here the proto-romantic tradition of the "decay of empires."

It is more interesting to follow Marx's thread leading to the analysis of the *"original accumulation of capital,"* that is to the second subordinate theme, because it is around this that several generic (to say the least) presuppositions are made clear, ones which are at the base of the preceding general law and its subsequent exemplifications. Let us read these two passages:

> What concerns us here for the moment is this: the process of dissolution, which transforms a mass of individuals of a nation etc. into free wage labourers δυνάμει—individuals forced solely by their lack of property to labour and to sell their labour—presupposes on the other side *not* that these individuals' previous sources of income and in part conditions of property have *disappeared,* but the reverse, that *only* their utilization has become different, that their mode of existence has changed, has gone over into other hands as a *free fund* or has even in part remained *in the same* hands. But this much is clear: the same process which divorced a mass of individuals from their previous relations to the *objective conditions of labour,* relations which were, in one way or another, affirmative, negated these relations, and thereby transformed these individuals into *free workers,* this same process freed—δυνάμει—these *objective conditions of labour*—land and soil, raw material, necessaries of life, instruments of labour, money or all of these—from their *previous state of attachment* to the individuals now separated from them. They are still *there on hand,* but in another form; as a *free fund,* in which all political etc. relations are obliterated. The objective conditions of labour now confront these unbound, propertyless individuals only in the form of *values,* self-sufficient values. The same process which placed the mass face to face with the *objective conditions of labour* as free workers also placed these conditions, as *capital,* face to face with the free workers. The historic process was the divorce of elements which up until then were bound together; its result is therefore not that one of the elements disappears, but that each of them appears in a negative relation to the other—the (potentially) free worker on the one side, capital (potentially) on the other. The separation of the objective conditions from the classes which have become transformed into free workers necessarily also appears at the same time as the achievement of independence by these same conditions at the opposite pole [*Grundrisse,* pp. 502–3; 402–3].
>
> The *production of capitalists and wage labourers is thus a chief product of capital's realization process.* Ordinary economics, which looks only at the things produced, forgets this completely. When objectified labour is, in this process, at the same time posited as the worker's *non-objectivity,* as the objectivity of a subjectivity antithetical to the worker, as *property* of a will alien to him, then capital is necessarily at the same time the *capitalist,* and the idea held by some socialists that we need capital but not the capitalists is altogether wrong. It is posited within the concept of capital that the objective conditions of labour—and these are its own product—take on a *personality* towards it, or, what is the same, that they are posited as the property of a personality alien to the worker. The concept of capital contains the capitalist [*Grundrisse,* p. 512; 412].

In these pages *the entire discourse on diachronic transformation (crisis) becomes a discourse which constitutes class struggle in the modern sense*. The articulations of production and reproduction, far from simply being the rigid terms of "the determined social formation," represent the dynamism of class composition. The antagonistic dualism of development, which has been established so far around a sociological definition of compatibility and limits internal to "the determined social formation," is now personified, that is, subjectivized. As the synchronic analysis of the crisis, in the *Excursus* discussed above, had led us to consider the crisis as the product of class struggle, similarly this further development leads us to "personify" the actors of the relation of production as well as to consider both transformation and crisis as the products of the struggle between these "subjects." With the analysis of the original accumulation the concept of "determined social formation" becomes the concept of *"class composition":* it restores, in other words, the dynamism of the subject's action, of the will that structures or destroys the relations of necessity.

The *Die Formen* has often been attacked as some kind of remainder, in the *Grundrisse,* of a theoretical attitude which would be both naturalistic and humanistic, which is to say some kind of transplant of the first precritical Marx, the young Marx, into his mature thought. We cannot but recognize a certain amount of pertinence to these critiques. The general law smells of philosophy of history and sociology. The analysis of the ancient world and Oriental civilizations is an actual piece of historical sociology. We must say, however, that both its ambiguity and generality progressively decrease the closer we get to the analysis of the capitalist world and original accumulation. Here the sociological terminology of the social formation and the internal criteria of compatibility and limit (criteria which are totally adequate to a functional sociology) fade at first and dissolve thereafter into the *dialectic of separation*. Such a dialectic rarefies and annuls the initial humanism. The plenitude of needs and development is nothing but the plenitude of the rupture, the separation. But there is something more to it: for the first time the class dialectic not only shows its separate nature, but undergoes an implementation, a further specification and a superior meaning. It becomes *a dialectics of subjects,* and we cannot underestimate the political importance of this passage. We also come to understand the reason for this apparent interruption of the analysis on circulation represented by *Die Formen:* here, in *Die Formen,* the concept of subject was to be *intuitively* constructed before its *theoretical* exposition in the analysis on circulation. It was, in other words, necessary to hint at and somehow prefigure *the operation of displacement* that the section on circulation had in store. Thus the chapter *Die Formen* is not an outgrowth in the *Grundrisse,* it's not an interruption of its development; on the contrary, it is both an excellent instance of method (moreover, as it goes on, the argumentation corrects some of the philosophical and humanistic distortions at the beginning) and of substantial process as well: the theme of the subject, in fact, is here introduced which must form, and be formed in, that relationship of struggle constituting circulation. And, mind well, the subject here has nothing to do with the aforementioned substantialist and humanistic presuppositions: rather it is the product of class struggle, it is the result of the relation between the worker's extreme alienation and revolutionary insurgence: a short-circuiting caused by the separation, the subject is here the explosion of that inversion (of any naturalistic homology) which only the relation between difference and totality can interpret.

> It will be shown later that the *most extreme form of alienation*, wherein labour appears in the relation of capital and wage labour, and labour, productive activity appears in relation to its conditions and its own product, is a necessary point of transition—and therefore already contains in *itself*, in a still only inverted form, turned on its head, the dissolution of all *limited presuppositions of production*, and moreover creates and produces the unconditional presuppositions of production, and therewith the full material conditions for the total, universal development of the productive forces of the individual [*Grundrisse*, p. 515; 414–15].

At this point the analysis resumes its explicit thread: the circulation of capital and its process. It's a matter of studying the socialization of capital as a consequence of the contradictory dynamism of the law of the rate of profit. *A first stage of the analysis* concentrates on the process of increasing and continuous assumption of the social conditions of production by capital. It is the dialectical moment of the thesis, of the positioning, of the affirmation—in all the potency of its abstraction.

The circulation of money was a *"perpetuum mobile."* Such a characteristic belongs also to the circulation of capital; but capital structures its mobility in a substantial way, that is, it is a creative mobility. "The circulation of capital is at the same time its becoming, its growth, its vital process. If anything needed to be compared with the circulation of the blood, it was not the formal circulation of money, but the content-filled circulation of capital" (*Grundrisse*, p. 517; 416). Capital circulates in time and space determining flows which are ever more coalesced, ever quicker temporally and ever more integrated spacially. The social conditions of production are formed, organized and dominated by the organization of circulation, by the impulse capital gives to it. Therefore *circulation* is, above all, *the expansion of the potency of capital;* and for the same reason it entails the *appropriation* of all the social conditions and their placement in *valorization.* Even though circulation does not produce surplus value, it nonetheless enables capital to produce surplus value at every point of the circulation. The capitalistic appropriation of circulation, ever more totalitarian, determines circulation as the basis for production and reproduction until the *limit is reached* of a historical, effective (even though not logical) *identification of production with circulation*. "This pulling away of the natural ground from the foundations of every industry, and this transfer of its conditions of production outside itself, into a general context—hence the transformation of what was previously superfluous into what is necessary, as historically created necessity—is the tendency of capital. The general foundation of all industries comes to be general exchange itself, the world market, and hence the totality of the activities, intercourse, needs, etc., of which it is made up" (*Grundrisse,* p. 528; 426). Within a circulation so thoroughly invested by capital, labor itself comes to be unified, not only in that part which is directly expropriated and equalized by the rate of profit, but also in the part that constitutes necessary labor. The *Vergleichung* takes place in labor too. "If the whole society is regarded as one individual, then necessary labor would consist of the sum of all the particular labour functions which the division of labour separates off" (*Grundrisse*, p. 526; 425). *The circulation of capital unceasingly transforms necessary labor into "socially" necessary labor.* Circulation, then, invests capital and its components, with the result that capital achieves an internal homogeneity which constitutes an actual *displacement* of its category. The socialization of capital is a process which determines, through circulation, an irresistible compulsion towards expansion, appropriation and homogeneization—under the sign of a social totality. "The greater the extent to which historic needs—needs created by production itself, social needs—needs which are themselves the offspring of social production and intercourse, are posited as *necessary,* the higher the level to which real wealth has become developed" (*Grundrisse,* p. 527; 426).

It is necessary, however, to go a step further, at least in terms of clarification; which is to say that this process of socialization of capital cannot in any case be considered in a formal way. It represents *a real process.* Through circulation and socialization capital comes to be really unified. We must therefore begin to see "the degree to which the real community has constituted itself in the form of capital" (*Grundrisse,* p. 531; 430). *From the formal to the real subsumption*—this passage entails the effective, functional and organic subjugation of all the social conditions of production and, concomitantly, of labor as an associated force.

> The highest development of capital exists when the general conditions of the process of social production are not paid out of *deductions of the social revenue,* the state's taxes—where revenue and not capital appears as the labour fund, and where the worker, although he is a free wage worker like any other, nevertheless stands economically in a different relation—but rather out of *capital as capital.* This shows the degree to which capital has subjugated all the conditions of social production to itself on one side; and, on the other side, hence, the extent to which social reproductive wealth has been *capitalized,* and all the needs are satisfied through the

exchange form; as well the extent to which the *socially posited* needs of the individual, i.e. those which he consumes and feels not as a single individual in society, but communally with the others—whose mode of consumption is social by the nature of the thing—are likewise not only consumed but also produced through exchange, individual exchange [*Grundrisse*, p. 532; 431]. And quite obviously *adequate institutional forms* for capital and its state correspond to this progress in the subsumption [*Grundrisse*, p. 531; 430].

We must insist more on this development. Circulation, in fact, engenders here a first productive effect. If "the *constant continuity* of the process, the unobstructed and fluid transition of value from one form into the other, or from one phase of the process into the next, appears as a fundamental condition for production based on capital to a much greater degree than for all earlier forms of production" (*Grundrisse*, p. 535; 433)—this is also a *condition for a leap*, a mutation in capital's nature. In his pages on profit Marx had strongly insisted on the social conditions posed as a warranty of the continuity of production, of the preservation of value, etc. But in that analysis, capital was still a subject facing society, whose conditions of re-production gratuitously exploited. But such duality and separation no longer exist. *Capital constitutes society, capital is entirely social capital.* Circulation produces the socialization of capital. Marx fully appreciates this passage to social capital and stresses it: "there opened up for us the prospect, which cannot be sharply defined yet at this point, *of a specific relation of capital to the communal, general conditions of social production,* as distinct from the conditions of a *particular capital* and its *particular production* process" (*Grundrisse*, p. 533; 432). Therefore the leap to "social capital," like the leap to "social labor," is not a generic one. It is a *qualitative leap which permeates the category of capital.* Society appears to us as capital's society. It is through this passage that all social conditions are subsumed by capital, that is, they become part of its "organic composition." And besides the social conditions—which present themselves in their immediacy—capital progressively subsumes all the elements and materials of the process of circulation (money and exchange in the first place, as functions of mediation) and, thereafter, all those pertaining to the process of production, so that herein lies the foundation *for the passage from manufacture to big industry to social factory.* Subsumed in their turn are those elements pertaining to the process of the ideal and institutional structure: here, in fact, lies the origin of the passage to the *state of the ideal, collective capitalist,* of its realization. The real subsumption of labor and society by capital: it is a passage which transforms Marx's categories by giving them from the start an incredibly strong dynamism; a passage that constitutes somehow the keystone of his investigation; such a passage is here in the *Grundrisse* posited with extreme force and clarity. It is a passage that dominates Marx's enterprise; it is a passage of extraordinary foresight; for us, one of extraordinary relevance.

To stop at the characterization of the expansive force of capital is not enough. Capital is a relation, it's a synthesis of an opposition; it's an overdetermination of a separation. *The thesis is opposed by the antithesis,* negation opposes affirmation. After having stressed the expansive function of circulation, Marx submits its concept to dialectical analysis.

> *Circulation time* therefore determines value only in so far as it appears as a *natural barrier* to the realization of labour time. It is in fact a deduction from *surplus labour time,* i.e., an increase of *necessary labour time* [*Grundrisse,* p. 539; 437].
>
> *Circulation time thus appears as a barrier to the productivity of labour* = an increase in necessary labour time = a decrease in surplus labour time = a decrease in surplus value = an obstruction, a barrier to the self-realization process *(Selbstverwertungsprozess)* of capital. Thus, while capital must on one side strive to tear down every spatial barrier to intercourse, i.e., to exchange, and conquer the whole earth for its market, it strives on the other side to annihilate this space with time, i.e., to reduce to a minimum the time spent in motion from one place to another [*Grundrisse,* p. 539; 438].

Time and space, after constituting the fabric of capital's expansion in circulation, appear now as barriers, as obstacles. As obstacles to be eliminated, destroyed—*by reducing space to time,* by imparting to time the quickness of transfers and transformations. But that's not all. We have already seen how circulation is tendentially the entire society. In society, in the composition of the productive forces, and not only in their highly abstract spatio-temporal determinations, there exists *another series of obstacles* to the full development of capital. And capital is forced within these determinations. It must get rid of them in order to release its own potency—and again, always, the possibility of subversion.

> Capital posits the *production of wealth* itself and hence the universal development of the productive forces, the constant overthrow of its prevailing presuppositions, as the presupposition of its reproduction. Value excludes no use value; i.e., it includes no particular kind of consumption, etc., of intercourse, etc., as absolute condition; and likewise every degree of the development of the social forces of production, of intercourse, of knowledge, etc., appear to it only as a barrier which it strives to overpower. Its own presupposition—value—is posited as a product, not as a loftier presupposition hovering over production. The barrier to *capital* is that this entire development proceeds in a contradictory way, and that the working-

out of the productive forces, of general wealth, etc., knowledge, etc., appears in such a way that the working individual *alienates* himself *{sich entaussert};* relates to the conditions brought out of him by his labour as those not of his *own* but of an *alien wealth* and of his own poverty. But this antithetical form is itself fleeting, and produces the real conditions of its own suspension. The result is: the tendentially and potentially general development of the forces of production—of wealth as such—as a basis; likewise, the universality of intercourse, hence the world market as a basis. The basis as the possibility of the universal development of the individual, and the real development of the individuals from this basis as a constant suspension of its *barrier,* which is recognized as a barrier, not taken as a *sacred limit.* Not an ideal or imagined universality of the individual, but the universality of his real and ideal relations. Hence also the grasping of his own history as a *process,* and the recognition of nature (equally present as practical power over nature) as his real body. The process of development itself posited and known as the presupposition of the same. For this, however, necessary above all that the development of the forces of production has become the *condition of production;* and not that specific *conditions of production* are posited as a limit to the development of the productive forces [*Grundrisse,* pp. 541–42; 440].

Capital's *permanent revolution* discloses the motor of the movement. Every time we come to a global definition of it the picture undergoes a reversal. *Separation, not contradiction, moves the process.* Capital's expansion seems to be a power expressing itself, but it is, instead, a hostile relation which has to be resolved each time. The law of this movement does not consist of a solution of some sort, but, on the contrary, it consists of the reopening of the separation, in the endless re-positing of the obstacle. At this point the analysis of obstacles must develop as a study of the cause of the movement. Here, too, the argumentation develops rhetorically according to the triadic scheme which, first, situated the transcendental conditions of movement (space and time), and then indicated its concreteness and negation in the theme of the obstacle as specificity of the insurgence of determinate antitheses; determinate but, again, abstract. The synthesis of the argument must now be brought back to the foundation from which everything originates, to the law of class struggle. It is only class struggle that moves capital. The picture has been inverted. Thus we must go back to *the relations of living labor,* and see the implantation of the obstacle within them. Must we go through the relation of capital in order to arrive at this determination? Certainly yes, but only to separate it, to consider the contradictory and plural movement of its constitutive elements. So

circulation time in itself is a *barrier* to realization (*necessary labour time* is of course also a barrier; but at the same time an element, since value and capital would vanish without it); it is a deduction from surplus labour time or an increase in *necessary labour time* in relation to *surplus labour time.* The circulation of capital *realizes value,* while living labour *creates value.* Circulation time is only a barrier to this realization of value, and, to that extent, to value creation; a barrier arising not from production generally but specific to production of capital, the suspension of which—or the struggle against which—hence also belongs to the specific economic development of capital and gives the impulse for the development of its forms in credit etc. Capital itself is the contradiction, in that, while it constantly tries to suspend *necessary labour time* (and this is at the same time the reduction of the worker to a minimum, i.e., his existence as mere living labour capacity), *surplus labour time* exists only in antithesis with necessary labour time, so that capital posits necessary labour time as a *necessary* condition for its reproduction and realization. At a certain point, a development of the forces of material production—which is at the same time a development of the forces of the working class—*suspends capital itself* [*Grundrisse,* p. 543; 441–43].

The radicalness of Marx's development of the logic of separation is at this point totally evident. Again—but with an ever increasing power in proportion to the degree of complexity of the categories—again then it is the necessary labor/surplus labor relation that dictates the articulation of the process, of the moment of expansion of capital and its contradictions—the very contradictions that cause its movement. The articulation of capital is a dialectic of "limits" functional to the increase of profit, it is a dialectic of exploitation which can, must be blocked at the "limit" of the highest exploitation, of the highest expansion of capital. The reason why capital needs self-limitation for its self-valorization is clear: its process of valorization is *a strategy* that must take into account the separation constituting the concept of capital itself. The limit to the development has a strategic function in that it opposes the "obstacles" inherent in the production of surplus value—obstacles defined, at first, at the level of circulation, but in the last and decisive instance redefined and actively reconfigured on the terrain of production, in the most immanent moment of the relation of production, which is to say at the level of the separation between surplus labor and necessary labor.

Capital forces the workers beyond necessary labour to surplus labour. Only in this way does it realize itself, and create surplus value. But on the other hand, it posits necessary labour only *to the extent* and *in so far as* it is surplus labour and the latter is *realizable* as *surplus value.* It posits surplus labour, then, as the condition of the necessary, and surplus value as the limit of objectified labour, of value as such. As soon as it cannot posit value, it does not posit necessary labour; and, given its foundation, it cannot be otherwise. It therefore restricts labour and the creation of value—by an artificial check, as the English express it—and it does so on the same grounds as and to the same extent that it posits surplus labour and surplus value. By its nature, therefore, it posits a *barrier* to labour and value creation, in contradiction to its tendency to expand them boundlessly. And inasmuch as it both posits a barrier *specific* to itself, and on the other side equally drives over and beyond *every* barrier, it is the living contradiction [*Grundrisse,* p. 421; 324].

We understand now what it means to say that "the real obstacle to capitalist production is capital itself": *the real obstacle to capitalist production is the relation of force that constitutes the concept of capital,* it is the separation that constitutes its development. On this terrain the very concept of capital becomes the concept for a strategy, for a project that is constantly recalibrated for an adequate, proportionate and expansive production of profit in accordance with its *controlling power.* Limit, measure, proportion: these are the elements defining capitalist strategy, they are the figures in which it crystalizes. But, in crystalizing, the capitalist strategy confines the potential development of the productive forces within a capital-dominated relation. Will this limitation ever be capable of exceeding the terms of the initial relation? No. In this pattern capital can extend its power of determination up to the limit of war and destruction. Rosa Luxemburg wrote marvelous pages on this limit-obstacle relation. Here we want to bear in mind that the limit takes shape as the result of a strategy confronting the obstacle that the proletariat necessarily poses to the production of surplus value and reproduction of capitalist control.

The expansive process of capital and the "permanent revolution" that it must impose in order to overcome the obstacles to exploitation and to define its own winning strategy, tend towards the *building of the "world market."* More than once we have met this extension of the conditions of capitalist production towards the highest degree of its expansion, towards the constitution of a new realm of operation and control. We want to stop for a moment on this subject, taking it, as Marx does, as an exemplification of method on the theme of the expansive circulation of capital. It should be stressed right away that if profit is the organization of capital as determined by time, *the world market is the organization of capital as determined by space.* Therefore in Marx the constitutive process of the world market follows the rhythms of profit formation, both formally and substantially. There is a tension in Marx towards an *identification of these two concepts:* and the formidable relevance of this hypothesis is not impaired by the fact that in the *Grundrisse* (and even in the subsequent works) this identification is not fully elaborated. Consequently we are interested in introducing here the conception of the dialectic of the *Weltmarkt* because in and through it we grasp a new exposition of the problem of circulation, an exposition which emphasises some of the results so far produced by the investigation.

Now, the world market has been present in the *Grundrisse* since the first pages—already in the Chapter on Money—and has been untiringly reproposed at each fundamental passage, despite the fact that *a special book on it was contemplated*. On this subject, too, the expository rhythm follows that of the triadic logic: affirmation, negation, synthesis. By *affirmation* we mean the linear description of the constitutive process of the *Weltmarkt*, of "the autonomization of the world market" (*Grundrisse*, pp. 160–62; 78–81). In this first approach other elements are assembled rather confusedly together with the affirmation: here, for instance, the description of the substantially linear mechanism is mingled with the determination of the obstacles that it has to overcome somehow. Then the discourse becomes more impatient: "the formation of the world market already at the same time contains the conditions for going beyond it" (*Grundrisse*, p. 161; 79–80). And a page on communism, on the realized individual, comes immediately after this (*Grundrisse*, pp. 162–63; 81). The density of the argument should not be a reason for confusion; there's a thread organizing it, clarifying it: in fact both the moment of negation and of synthesis-supersession-subversion are present. The argumentation stretches out. But we are not concerned with the rhetorical and discursive movement: we are concerned with the substance, which is, again, *the emergence of the obstacle as the main theme*. This emerges at the level of both circulation and production: at the level of circulation as a global process of differences and subsequent *Ausgleichung*, and at the level of production as the impossibility of bringing the terms of production back to a material operation of equalization and mediation. In a passage on *"coin and the world market"* (*Grundrisse*, pp. 226–28; 137–39), Marx emphasizes how "coin" is blocked in its confrontation with the world market and, considering the stage of imperialist development that Marx refers to, this is the least we can say. Difficulties, obstacles and differences are so strong that, at the level of international exchange, "money has to be demonetized"; furthermore "it acquires a political title and talks, as it were, a different language in different countries," so that it loses its "symbolic" nature and becomes again "the universal commodity." But the moment of recession of its value engenders a crisis, because capitalist development tends always towards the world market, even in the absence of adequate instruments of control. Capital does not content itself with just overcoming its own obstacles: it wants also to overcome its own limits. All contradictions are then set in motion, "the world market" represents in many respects "the conclusion." "The world market then, again, forms the presupposition of the whole as well as its substratum." It is the *"Aufhebung,"* the generalized crisis of circulation which turns against production. Keeping in mind that we are still on a monetary level, the description cannot but be provisional, but later on in the *Grundrisse* (*Grundrisse*, pp. 408, 421–22, 449–50, 541–42;

324, 353–54, 440) the argument on the relation *Weltmarkt-Ausgleichung-Aufhebung* is translated to a superior level. The linearity of development unfolds now directly on the terrain of production: towards an international capital. Certainly we can't speak of a "universal capital", it would be a "non-thing"; we can speak, though, of "a capital in general" as the ideal term of the "permanent revolution" of the capitalist relations of production. The obstacles on this terrain have already become moments, key moments, real passages to more advanced stages of capitalist organization. *The linear development is simply a theoretical hypothesis,* while the reality of the *Ausgleichung,* of the comparison and equalization of values, is, despite countless obstacles, an ongoing process. But again, *the result of the process represents the highest potential of the contradiction.*

The argument should be developed and summarized once more. There is in the *Grundrisse* a constant tension towards the *Weltmarkt,* a tension which configures the expansive power of capital in the terrain of both circulation and production; an irresistible tension indeed. At times one might even reasonably denounce Marx for cynicism, considering how much the linearity of the process and the civilising function of capital are emphasized. This tension is present also in subsequent works, namely in *Capital.* Too often this reading has become an exclusive one: *the theory of the stages of development,* whether in its Oriental or Western version, follows as direct consequence of it. But this tension is not an exclusive one: *on the contrary,* it is completely dependent on a mechanism made of (proletarian) obstacles and (capitalist) limits whose interrelation must be closely investigated. Capital's circulation and expansion call for an endless and real reassumption of the social conditions of production which are subjected, always and again, to the expansion of capital. *This reassumption is a process of obstacles:* it is a formation of always renewed profit equalizations, *Ausgleichungen* and *Vergleichungen,* of always renewed determinations of the average profit. *Negation follows affirmation* in the dialectical rhythm of the argumentation. We must now look at this process of always renewed equilibria achieved by capital, of always renewed, self-imposed limitations (capital is always a "disproportioned proportion" or a "proportioned disproportion")—we must, then, look at this process from both sides. On one side we find the unbalanced rushing forward of capital, up to the conquest of the largest space that can be invested and occupied: it is the stage of accomplished *imperialism*—and it is the terrain on which the supersession-subversion of this basis must take place. On the other side we find that this spatial expansion of capital is nothing but *an ever broader process of constitution of the average profit:* and it is here that the contradiction inherent in profit, the antagonism of its constitutive forces, imposes itself. These two processes are collateral: in both their spatial, extensive and intensive dimensions they lead to the third moment of the dialectic, to the *Aufhebung.* We know that this expository form is abstract; yet it tells us about capital's motion with respect to its extreme tendency toward world occupation. On this terrain all the contradictions deepen. We must *insist*, then, in pursuit of analysis, *on these complications* and see how the dialectic of *Weltmarkt-Ausgleichung-Aufhebung* comes to be specifically determined each time. Each level of specificity determines an incredible richness of the field of analysis; therefore, each determining specificity entails a global displacement of the analysis. In the *limited terms* of the Marxist analysis, the imperialistic process was still confronted with an indefinite "frontier," which is to say that it still had to mediate the national realities constituting an effective barrier to the *Vergleichung* and the objective horizon of contradictions which always determine the perspective and the moment of the crisis. We are faced (and Marx himself comes close to our reading hypothesis in the third volume of *Capital*) with a multinational reality of exploitation which is enormously more advanced. We must, therefore, conclude that the more the capitalist unification of the world and the real subsumption of world society under capital advance, the more extensive and spatial theme of imperialism comes to match with the intensive theme of exploitation, of surplus value and class antagonism. Marx's terms are maintained, if not verified, beyond the punctual definition around which they have been determined. The expansive, imperialistic process of capital and its tension toward the constitution of average terms of world exploitation are then simultaneously the result and the premise for the conditions of revolutionary subjectivity. The imperialistic expansion of capital also represents its attempt to escape the resented opposition inherent in its determination as capital. Contradictions and antagonisms are motors which move capital toward ever higher levels of contradiction and antagonism. Every result is a premise, a new basis. Every regulative "limit" that capital poses to itself in this historical pursuit is the basis for the insurgence of new obstacles. This indefinite process encounters its blockage only in the class struggle. But the process of circulation has achieved such a broad and powerful expansion that it exposes the circulation of capital not only as an expression of its own collective potency but also as the privileged terrain for the emergence of the power antithetic to it. *The theme of the world market is the most mature exemplification of the revolutionary tendency of the capitalist development.*

"Social capital" is the form in which the expansive power of capital is consolidated through and upon circulation. An expansive power, which, as we have seen, is also and above all a collective power. In this relationship *social capital is the subject of development.* In operating circulation, capital posits itself as sociality, as the capacity to engulf within its own development, in an ever more determined manner, every socially productive force. The subjectivity that this synthesis confers on capital represents what capital itself has achieved through the process of subsumption, through the ever more coherent and exhaustive acts of subjugation of society. *The very mode of production is modified.* At first, capital assembles labor potentials which are given in society and reorganizes them in manufacture. Big industry, a further stage, represents a productive situation in which social capital has already posited itself as a subject, that is, it has prefigured the conditions of production. The working conditions and the labor process are preordained by the process of valorization: starting from a certain moment—the constitution of capital as "social capital"—it will no longer be possible to distinguish labor from capital, labor from social capital and the process of valorization. Labor is only that which produces capital. Capital is the totality of labor and life.

> *"This continual progression of knowledge and experience,"* says Babbage, "is our great power." This progression, this social progress belongs [to] and is exploited by capital. All earlier forms of property condemn the greater part of humanity, the slaves, to be the pure instruments of labour. Historical development, political development, art, science etc. take place in higher circles over their heads. But only capital has subjugated historical progress to the service of wealth [*Grundrisse*, pp. 589–90; 483–84].

But let's follow the articulations of Marx's thought. The pages immediately before the above quotation are a summary of the very broad analysis that in the First Book of *Capital* and in the unpublished sixth chapter describes in detail the passage from manufacture to big industry, from the formal to real subjugation of labor—in short these pages constitute a succinct yet complete scheme of a *continuous categorial displacement*, which is pertinent to the particular historical passage Marx had in mind (from manufacture to big industry), but which shows simultaneously *the method* of analysis and definition of each subsequent passage (those present to us).

> Like all productive powers of labour, i.e. those which determine the degree of its intensity and hence of its extensive realization, the association of the workers—the cooperation and division of labour as fundamental conditions of the productivity of labour—appears as the *productive power of capital*. The collective power of labour, its character as social labour therefore the *collective power* of capital. Likewise *science*. Likewise the division of labour, as it appears as division of the occupations and of exchange corresponding to them. All social powers of production are productive powers of capital, and it appears as itself their subject. The association of the workers, as it appears in the factory, is therefore not posited by them but by capital. Their combination is not *their* being, but the *being* [Dasein] of capital. Vis-à-vis the individual worker, the combination appears accidental. He relates to his own combination and cooperation with other workers as *alien*, as modes of capital's effectiveness. Unless it appears in an inadequate form—e.g., small, self-employed capital—capital already, at a certain greater or lesser stage, presupposes concentration both in objective form, i.e. as concentration in one hand, which here still coincides with accu-

mulation, of the necessaries of life, of raw material and instruments, or, in a word, of money as the general form of wealth; and on the other side, in subjective form, the accumulation of labour powers and their concentration at a single point under the command of the capitalist. There cannot be one capitalist for every worker, but rather there has to be a certain quantity of workers per capitalist, not like one or two journeymen per master. Productive capital, or the mode of production corresponding to capital, can be present only in two forms: manufacture and large scale industry. In the former, the division of labour is predominant; in the second, the combination of labour powers (with a regular mode of work) and the employment of scientific power, where the combination and, so to speak, the communal spirit of labour is transferred to the machine etc. In the first situation the mass of (accumulated) workers must be large in relation to the amount of capital; in the second the fixed capital must be large in relation to the number of the many cooperative workers [*Grundrisse*, p. 585; 479–80].

Hereafter Marx specifies in a thorough way (even from the point of view of terminology) the passage from the formal to real subsumption. Here then *capital* is a real subject, it is *a collective social force. Circulation gave us this first subject.* Marx's argumentation leaves off thus on this subjective element of antagonism. Never has such a recognition been attributed to capital. Justly.

But even if at this point it is no longer possible to distinguish labor from capital, the reasoning is nonetheless still open. The other subject, the working class subject, must emerge, since capitalist subsumption does not efface its identity but just dominates its activity; this subject must emerge precisely at the level to which the collective force of social capital has led the process. *If capital is a subject on one side, on the other labor must be a subject as well.*

Above all, it must be *a subject modified by its relation with capital.* In the successive process of the subsumptions, capital modifies the class composition, driving it to ever higher degrees of unity under and within its domination. At first.

the unification of their labours appears as a particular act, alongside which the independent fragmentation of their labours continues. This is the *first condition* necessary for *money* to be exchanged as capital for free labour. The second is the suspension of the fragmentation of these many workers, so that the *individual capital* no longer appears towards them merely as *social collective power in the act of exchange*, uniting many exchanges, but rather, gathers them in one spot under its command, into one manufactory, and no longer leaves them in the *mode of production found already in existence*, establishing its power on that basis, but rather creates a mode of production corresponding to itself, as its basis. It posits the *concentration* of the workers in production, a unification which will occur initially only in a common location, under overseers, *regimentation, greater discipline, regularity and the posited dependence in production itself on capital.* Certain *faux frais de production* are thereby saved from the outset. (On this whole process compare Gaskell, where special regard is had to the development of large industry in England.) Now capital appears as the collective force of the workers, their social force, as well as that which ties them together, and hence as the unity which creates this force [*Grundrisse,* pp. 586–87; 481]. Here no distinction between labor and capital can be made yet, even from a proletarian standpoint (it is the stage of the union).

Subsequently, however the situation changes. We have a unity of the working class which, although created by capital, has rid us of the isolation of single workers and has brought us to the level of the unity of interests, *to the material basis of political unity.* "Thus from the outset (capital) appears as the *collective force,* the social force, the suspension of individual isolation, first that of exchange with the workers, then that of the workers themselves. The workers' individual isolation still implies their relative independence. Hence their regroupment around the individual capital as the exclusive base of their subsistence implies full dependence on capital, complete dissolution of the ties between the workers and the conditions of production" (*Grundrisse,* p. 589; 483).

Now, a further step forward. This objective process, dominated by capital, begins to reveal *the new subjective level of the working class.* A qualitative leap occurs: the unity of working class behaviors begins to be self-sufficient. Capital's socialization is faced with the insurgence of working class antagonism. Working class subjectivity is revealed by the fact that: (1) the unity capital has created allows the workers to break the exchange relation with capital. *In the capitalist process the exchange relation is superseded by the relation of force between the classes.*

> When competition permits the worker to bargain and to argue with the capitalists, he measures his demands against the capitalists' profit and demands a certain share of the surplus value created by him; so that the *proportion* itself becomes a real moment of economic life itself. Further, in the struggle between the two classes—which necessarily arises with the development of the working class—the measurement of the distance between them, which, precisely, is expressed by wages itself as a proportion, becomes decisively important. The *semblance of exchange vanishes* in the course [Prozess] of the mode of production founded on capital [*Grundrisse,* p. 597; 491].

(2) In addition to this, the working class' subjectivity is revealed by the fact that the exchange relation is not valid *among* workers. We'll see this in detail

in the next chapter: for the time being we just need to put it forth as an essential complement to the fall of the exchange relation between workers and capital.

The chapter on circulation reaches here a first conclusion. The capitalist tendency is paralleled by the working class tendency, the extension of the exchange relation through circulation is paralleled by its destruction. The constitution of social capital is paralleled by the emergence of the social class of workers, who are at first unified by capital at the level of its social development, and secondly by themselves—in material composition and identity—by the destruction of the exchange relation as a basis of the associated existence of the workers. We have thus seen the explosion of the *form antithetic* to the collective force of capital, to its expansion: a new subject is now on the terrain. Marx has presented the genealogy of this new subject to us, he has offered us a model of analysis which proposes constant displacements of investigation and reality. The organic composition of capital does *not* enclose the political composition of the working class, *but* it indicates it as its external antagonist. *Again the dialectic of separation is posed at the very center of the methodical logic and real development.* The synthesis of the analysis of circulation presents an extreme and adequate development of the antagonism to us. It is here only a potentiality. But let's proceed with Marx and with the *Grundrisse;* we'll find ourselves in the presence of formidable developments.

Lesson Seven
The Theory
of the Wage
& Its Developments

A. The antithetical form of capitalist development once again: an essential articulation of the *Grundrisse*. □ B. The Book on the Wage and the polemic it stirs up: its central position in the genesis and the development of Marxian thought. □ The Book on the Wage as foundation and as development. □ From the wage to the subject. □ C. Circulation and small-scale circulation. □ Money and small-scale circulation. □ The logic of separation in the theory of circulation: the theory of the wage, the guiding thread of the theory of the subject; it permits us to give the theory a new foundation. □ D. The "Fragment on Machines": the logic of separation at work. □ The collective power of subjectivity and the constitution of the social individual of the communist revolution. □ E. Notes disguised as a conclusion: the metamorphoses of the theory of value, the path of subjectivity, the methodology confirmed.

We must deepen the analysis undertaken in Lesson 6 and the conclusions of that lesson. The antithetical form of capitalist development, the explosion of the logic of separation, could appear to be more a description than a proof. It is now a question of attaining the level of the *neue Darstellung,* the level at which all of the terms of the proof are displaced. It is a question of seeing that the antithetical character of capital is not only a result: it is a result, but *this antithetical form is also the key, the general characteristic of development.* In certain of its aspects, the constituting process which led us to the definition of social capital must be completely reversed. This is absolutely obvious if we cling to the simple coherence of Marx's approach. That approach, as we have often repeated all along the path of our argumentation, proposes the thematic of surplus value as the basic law to be

127

fully developed. This is what gives to the concept of social capital the distinct mark of duality and of antagonism. This is what allows a second moment of explaining the law: the more capitalist socialization expands, the more its antagonistic character deepens (qualitatively) and grows (quantitatively). The synthesis of the spacial-temporal categories integrates the fundamental contradiction of the law of profit. The actual structure of the *Grundrisse* is based on this integration through successive stages. We enter here into the conclusive stage of the argumentation. This stage comes after the expansive effects of the theory of surplus value or of the theory of exploitation have undergone—in the *Excursus on Crises* and in *Die Formen*—a first synchronic and categorial contraction and then a second diachronic and historical contraction—after these expansive effects have undergone those contractions necessary to their presentation and their examples. Now these effects develop in a new space, a space which is social, collective and general. *The rule of antagonism must now appear in all its originality and with all its force.* The process of valorization, when it reaches this totalitarian dimension, must allow proletarian *self-valorization* to appear. It must allow its own antagonism to develop in all its potential. We will analyse this articulation of Marx's thought at length in the following pages. Its resolving character will appear clearly. We could say that the *Grundrisse* comes to completion with this "Fragment on Machines" (which is precisely the terms of our analysis in this Lesson), and thus that the logical rhythm of Marx's argument here reaches its fullness. What follows the "Fragment on Machines" (there is almost all of Notebook VII) is mostly complementary to these conclusions. What follows is a deepening and development of various partial lines of argument begun in other earlier phases of the work. The material is certainly very important, but not essential. We are thus at a fundamental articulation in the center of this *second part,* of this second side of the analysis of the *Grundrisse* represented by the *theory of circulation.* Let us take up the text where we left it at the end of Lesson 6. The progression of Marx's argument appears here to surge forward. The argument proceeds by waves which advance and subside. The wave that now subsides brought us social capital, and in subsiding it uncovers its antithesis: *working class subjectivity.* Let us go discover this category of the logic of separation in its most developed form, there where the condensation of capital is strongest: this is the same procedure as Marx's.

That necessary labor and its creativity are hidden under the form of the wage—this is what we learn by dwelling on the theory of surplus value. This reality which is hidden—but still unique and powerful as a productive force—is found everywhere the law of surplus value operates. It joins in all the law's movements. This means that in order to attain working class subjectivity, in order to illuminate its role, we must above all explore the wage-form in order to break the envelope that hides the vitality of value, that pumps out its substance and gives it the appearance of the productivity of capital. That means, essentially, to discover the laws of movement of the wage, which, by developing itself independently (or relatively independently) from the general movement of commodities, can lead us to that particular reality which is now covered up. This project was present, as we have seen, in the "outline" of the *Grundrisse,* in the plans Marx had for the development of his research. Then, in the drafting of *Capital,* it disappeared. This specific Book which would have been consecrated to the wage disappeared from *Capital* as a separate Book. Why? Roman Rosdolsky (pp. 57–62) has asked the question explicitly, or rather he has asked two questions: (1) What were the themes that should have been developed in this book? (2) Why did Marx renounce his plan for a special "Book on Wage Labor"? The response that Rosdolsky gives to the first question is satisfying. That which he gives to the second is less so. We will see this a little further on. But first let us see which themes would have been included in this book on waged labor. A long and careful analysis allows us to make up a list. Here are the essentials:

Grundrisse, p. 264; 175: the wage as a form of existence of the proletariat face to face—in circulation—with the two other classes.

Grundrisse, pp. 281–82; 193–94: the forms of the wage. Piece wages: the demystification of the illusion of participation that it contains.

Grundrisse, pp. 398–401; 302–04: the relationship wage/global population and the relation necessary labor/surplus labor. Towards the payment of necessary labor as a payment of the reproduction of a social totality.

Grundrisse, p. 416; 319: necessary labor as the limit of the exchange value of living labor power (downward rigidity of wages?).

Grundrisse, p. 426 and footnote; 329: on the other side, on the laws of the reduction of the wage beyond the limits of necessary labor. The historical evolution of the forms of the wage.

Grundrisse, pp. 464–65; 368–69: again on the historical evolution of the wage-form: the demystification of the wage as the appearance of exchange between equals. Labor power as "property" of the worker.

Grundrisse, pp. 520–21; 420: "small-scale circulation," or the wage as revenue in the sphere of circulation.

Grundrisse, pp. 607–08; 501: the wage and the excess of workers.

Grundrisse, pp. 817–18; 702: the hypothesis of the minimum wage. The fluidity of this hypothesis in the development of the analysis.

Taking account of these points and of other fundamental problems (such as the reduction of concrete labor to abstract labor and the reduction of particular human workers to simple, undifferentiated average labor. On the question of skilled labor also see Rosdolsky, pp. 506–20), Rosdolsky moves to the resolution of the second problem and concludes that Marx dropped the special book on wage labor because "the strict separation of the categories of capital and wage labor, which the old outline envisaged, could only be taken up to a certain point and then had to be abandoned." Which means that all these listed themes must be considered as elements subaltern to the analysis of capital.

But this is not true. It is not true, as we have already underlined here and there, for some of these themes; nor is it true for the others, as we will see. But it is also not true in general; because all these elements must be considered to be subordinated, not to the laws of capital but, to the laws of the class struggle. As we have already seen: "the *proportion* itself becomes a real moment of economic life itself. Further, in the struggle between the two classes—which necessarily arises with the development of the working class—the measurement of the distance between them, which, precisely, is expressed by wages itself as a proportion, becomes decisively important. The *semblance of exchange* vanishes in the course *{Prozess}* of the mode of production founded on capital" (*Grundrisse,* p. 597; 491).

At this stage we need to restate the problem. Rosdolsky can help us through a remark that he makes, which for him is secondary. He notes that the reduction of concrete labor to abstract labor and the reduction of particular workers to average social labor do not demand, strictly speaking, a chapter on the wage. These reductions involve the elaboration of the theory of surplus value. They were thus *at the base of the theory of capital.* Fundamental reductions, yes, veritable foundations: why repeat it? We can respond to the rhetorical question of Rosdolsky. We must repeat it because the fundamental character of Marx's discovery of surplus value (and of the reductions which found it) *cannot* be exhausted in the book on capital. Because each time this fundamental element appears, it imposes a different logical rhythm on the analysis: the *logic of separation* against an all-resolving dialectic. Perhaps we should say, from this point of view, that if *"the Book on the Wage"* was not written, it was not because it represented—at the level of the theory of capital—a problem that had already been resolved, but because on the contrary, *the whole theory of capital can only base itself and develop by way of the theory of the wage.* The former refers constantly to the latter and contains it. My point of view is an extreme one, I know this: beginning with Lesson 1, I already deplored the absence of this "Book on the Wage" which introduced an essential element of ambiguity. But now, here, we are perhaps able to show that this ambiguity has tripped up almost all interpreters of Marx, but not Marx himself.

Let us return to the heart of the problem. *The chapter on the wage founds the chapter on capital* in so far as concrete labor is transformed into abstract labor, in so far as distinct and skilled labor is transformed into simple average labor. This transmutation is not a completed synthesis, a given on which to build: it is a *tendency*—an antagonistic tendency. Productive labor, labor power, do not constitute an immobile motor out of which capital is created:

they exist throughout the articulations of capital, they animate in a contradictory fashion all the objectifications of capital. The formation of the relation of force between the classes—at a certain level of capitalist development—expresses in a real and collective way what was already present in the capitalist relation from the beginning. The circulation of capital intervenes—spatially and temporally (as an averaging factor)—to allow the dualism of the concept to explode and to take the form of a duality of subjects. But always on the same basis, that of a continuous process that never stops. There is not a single category of capital that can be taken out of this antagonism, out of this perpetually fissioning flux. Nor can we subordinate a supposed theory of the wage to the theory of capital. When the wage actually does appear in the first volume of *Capital,* taking over a number of themes explicitly launched in the *Grundrisse,* it appears as an "independent variable." Its laws flow from the condensation into a subject of the revolt against work contained in capitalist development. They present themselves immediately as rules of independence. The whole system of categories such as it exists when the wage is introduced must therefore change. We must pass from the extraction of absolute surplus value to the organization of the extraction of relative surplus value, from the formal subsumption to the real subsumption of society by capital. The increase in the value of necessary labor that results from the struggle over the working day and over its reduction demands a *general displacement* of the categorical forms of accumulation and of capitalist reproduction. The foundation of the theory of capital is continually forced to submit to this dynamic.

This is true so far as the categories are concerned. But this is not sufficient. The fact that the wage must appear, always and despite everything, as a variable that is independent of the process of capital engenders a *sequence of effects* that we can follow on all levels of development. The chapter on the wage is not only the implicit foundation, but also *the guiding thread to the development* of Marx's theory of capital. At the very moment that we succeed in defining the first categorical themes, we must deal with their historical variations and their particular determinations: the point of view of the wage dominates here. The opposition is given from the beginning: "The exchange of a part of the capital for living labour capacity can be regarded as a particular moment, and must be so regarded, since the labour market is ruled by other laws than the product market, etc." (*Grundrisse,* p. 521; 420). Here, in fact, the main problem is that of necessary labor, which consolidates itself more and more fully, at ever more irreversible levels. And all this "belongs to the section on wages." What does it mean, "other laws"? It means that the logic of separation dominates. In other words, the wage is, as far as its social quantities are concerned, an *independent magnitude* that varies independently. Its rigidity is irreversible and given in the analysis.

It is true that this rigidity can change. Let us suppose, for example, that in order to obtain some constancy in the law of profit necessary labor is fixed at the necessary minimum of wages. This is only a totally abstract hypothesis. In reality, we must study historically the rigidities that are based on a real relation of force. "All of these fixed suppositions themselves become fluid in the further course of development" (*Grundrisse*, p. 817; 702). In practice then, "the standard of necessary labour may differ in various epochs and in various countries." For capital, on the contrary, "at any given epoch, the standard is to be considered and acted upon as a fixed one. To consider these changes themselves belongs altogether to the chapter on wage labor." (*Grundrisse*, p. 817; 702).

But the contrast between these contradictory assertions leaves a potentiality hanging undeveloped—yes, *the reality of the class struggle. The wage is an independent variable in so far as the quantity, the quality, the value of necessary labor "must" be a fixed dimension for capital.* The contradiction constituted by the capitalist relationship evolves within this contradictory relation. There is no alternative: capital can only mature through the logic of separation. The pole of separation is formed by the wage, by this mass of necessary labor whose value capital must absolutely fix, no matter what—and which is in fact mobile, variable. Its value is not determined once and for all in exchange, but is *the result of the class struggle,* when it fails to become the dictatorship of the proletariat. Independence determines the struggles, fixes the possibilities and the development. It is the struggle which consolidates the values of necessary labor and poses them as historical entities: the sign of a totality of needs, of behaviors, of acquired values that only the struggle succeeds in modifying and developing—and this according to the possibilities that living labor contains, as a function of the historical transformations it has undergone, possibilities that are always linked with the productive transformations of capital. Let us examine this *power of living labor:* in the form of the wage it shows only the mystified aspect of its existence, this fixity that capital demands in order to measure it. But once we go beyond this necessity that capital imposes, we can see in the wage, beyond the wage, the palpitation of living labor in all its social reality, with all the power of its antagonism. And we can see this at every stage of Marx's reasoning. We can perceive these never-ending pulsations at each moment of capitalist development. The complexity of the problem is dizzying. In so far as we refuse the objectivist interpretations of the *"school of capital-logic"*—which infinitely assert the power of capital to possess and command all development—in so far as we reject this, it seems to us that we must also avoid the *path of subjectivity* which imputes capital to an objectification *tout court.* But those are not the theoretical tensions—terrible simplifications—that interest us. What does interest us, on the contrary, is the ambiguity of the process, the absence of a solution, the exhaustion of any law of command at this level. In the *Grundrisse* we can read each theoretical passage within this *extreme variability of the relationship of force*. We can, with reason, regret the uncertainty of *Capital* on this question: that book gives only a fragmented clarification. It only shows moments of this singular whole that is the development of the categories. What it fails to give us—and what the *Grundrisse* does give us—is the global framework, the background within which this antagonism is situated. The wage, the quantity of necessary labor are not only the basis of capitalist development, they also determine, in a general way, the fundamental laws. There lies the *creative function of necessary labor,* its irresistible *upward* bias. From being a condition, the theory of the wage becomes the rule of development. We cannot read the *Grundrisse* (as an anticipation of the course of history) without inducing that separation dominates the whole process. The separation, from the workers' point of view, is the consolidation of a historically given reality; it is the productive power of the free subject which dominates on this terrain.

The analysis progresses. The veil of mystery which enveloped work when it had the form of the wage has been torn, now we need to rip it away completely. All the elements that we have underlined as we have gone along converge here to form a combination rich in creativity. In the first place, the *power of living labor,* the real key to the whole dynamic of production, is the motor that transforms nature into history. Remember how, from the first pages of the analysis, when money began to represent the rarified but powerful space of social command, living labor began to rise up untiringly before it? Remember how, in its development, living labor takes the form of *"real" abstraction,* of workers' society, of mediator of production? *The red thread of abstract labor traces a constituting process.* The more work becomes abstract and socialized—this is the second element that displaces the analysis—the more the sphere of needs grows. Work creates its own needs and forces capital to satisfy them. The progressive evolution of needs gives a concretization to the unity, to the different composite unities created by the progression of abstract and social labor. The *wage* is formed on the basis of these needs—to *mystify* the individuality, henceforth clear, of the masses of necessary labor that this process has consolidated. A third element: this individuality tends to become subjectivity. This means that the connection between needs and the individual materiality of their composition must come to life. The relation with capital breaks the subjection to economic necessity, comes to life in the only way that matter can come to life: as behavior, *as power (potenza)*. This power is subjectivity. It is irreducible. Capital is forced to see itself as relation, as proportion, as a rule imposed on a separation. *The form of the relation is both sides of the struggle.* The class struggle and politics are henceforth at the center of economic theory. *If the theory of surplus value introduces into economic theory the fact of expoitation, the Marxist theory of circulation introduces the class struggle.* It is at this stage that we can fully understand what the *book on waged labor* is for Marx. It is the theoretical reasoning that leads from economics to politics, it is the immersion of the political in the economic and vice versa. The theory of surplus value brought out and described the cell-form of bourgeois society; here it is a question of analysing and unveiling the organic, developed, mature relation of capital. All the threads come together. As we will see further on, the fruits of this discovery are inestimable. It may have been difficult to cross over the line separating this second side of Marx's work: we can now progress more easily in the vast landscape that opens up before us. The theme of the *book on waged labor* is this and this alone: *from the wage to the subject, from capital relation to the class struggle.* Marx didn't write a separate book on the wage because his whole work constantly returns to this theme. Without ever relaxing it seeks to approach the class struggle, subversion, revolution. Now we must examine how the worker-subject develops an independent logic.

Let us take up the analysis of the text at the point where we left it at the end of *Lesson Six. The chapter on "small scale circulation."* We find here an immediate example of the *possibility of inverting* the reading of capital *from the point of view of subjectivity.* Whether this possibility actually develops obviously depends on the state of the historical class relations. What we want to underline here is that these terms outline the theoretical (tendential) possibility of proletarian independence within capital.

"Within circulation as the total process, we can distinguish between large-scale and small-scale circulation. The former spans the entire period from the moment when capital exits from the production process until it enters again. The second is continuous and constantly proceeds simultaneously with the production process. It is the part of capital which is paid out as wages, exchanged for labouring capacity" (*Grundrisse,* p. 673; 565). *What are the characteristics* of this second and "small-scale" circulation? What are its effects? Above all small-scale circulation is the sphere where the *value of necessary labor is reproduced* and determined. "The labour time contained in labour capacity, i.e. the time required to produce living labour capacity, is the same as is required—presupposing the same stage of the productive forces— to reproduce it, i.e. to maintain it" (*Grundrisse,* p. 673; 565–66). This production and reproduction-conservation of labor power are present in circulation but in a particular manner. This implies that "the circulation of the part of capital which is posited as wages accompanies the production process, appears as an economic form-relation alongside it, and is simultaneous and interwoven with it" (*Grundrisse,* p. 674; 566). This means that *the capitalist relation, exchange and exploitation do not annul the independence of the proletarian subject.* Better: the tangling up which is born out of the dualism of the forms of circulation is characteristic of the emergence of an irreducible subject, one that nothing can pacify. The values that are linked with the subject influence the capitalist process. "Here is the only moment in the circulation of capital where consumption enters directly." (*Grundrisse,* p. 675; 567). Productive consumption? It is not a question of entering onto this uncertain terrain. We must simply and always underline the immediate and insoluble aspect of the relationship. It is present in all of Marx's reflections: "Thus the circulating capital here appears directly as that which is specified for the workers' individual consumption; specified for direct consumption generally, and hence existing in the form of finished product. Thus, while in one respect capital appears as the presupposition of the product, the finished product also at the same time appears as the presupposition of capital—which means, historically, that capital did not begin the world from the beginning, but rather encountered production and products already present, before it subjugated them beneath its process. Once in motion, proceeding from itself as basis, it constantly posits itself ahead of itself in its various forms as consumable product, raw material and instrument of labour, in order constantly to reproduce itself in these forms. They appear initially as the conditions presupposed by it, and then as its result. In its reproduction it produces its own conditions. Here, then—through the relation of capital to living labour capacity and to the natural conditions of the latter's maintenance—we find circulating capital specified in respect of its use value" (*Grundrisse,* p. 675; 567).

In respect of its use value: this is what founds the insoluble character of the relation. Necessary labor touches products and transforms them, through its own consumption, into use values. Only necessary labor has this capacity to oppose its own resistance to capitalist valorization, a resistance that is its own conservation and reproduction. A resistance that does not consist of simply a point of immobility, but rather is itself *a cycle*, a movement, a growth. "The payment of wages is an act of circulation which proceeds simultaneously with and alongside the act of production" (*Grundrisse,* p. 676; 568). *Simultaneity and parallelism distinguish the independence of the worker-subject, its own self-valorization face to face with capitalist valorization.* Modern economists outline this relationship between the two opposed forms of valorization as a *double spiral* or a double windmill of parallel convergences; they well know how many crises are by this process determined, a process which at any rate always contains the formal possibility of crisis. And it has this possibility increasingly as the power of the proletariat grows. The relation is no longer dialectical, it is an antagonistic relation, always dominated, but full of risks and insurrections. Capital cannot separate itself from this relation. It must recompose it, and in order to do this it must bend to the relation, not only in its abstract form but also in its contents. "Small-scale circulation between capital and labour capacity. This accompanies the production process and appears as contract, exchange, form of intercourse; these things are presupposed before the production process can be set going. The part of capital entering into this circulation—the ap-provisionnement—is circulating capital. It is specified not only in respect to its form; in addition to this, its use value, i.e. its material character as a consumable product entering directly into individual consumption, itself constitutes a part of its form." (*Grundrisse,* p. 678; 570). The *two faces* of the wage (*Grundrisse,* pp. 593-94; 639–40; 759) dissolve. It appears rather as a *second* face completely redone as worker *revenue*; it denies all comple-mentarity with respect to capital and rises up in opposition to it. The insistence of Marx on this dynamic of small-scale circulation is very important for us. The theoretical hypothesis is as usual rigid *and* flexible: rigid in the indicative tendency; flexible in the historical relations it experiences. From this last point of view, we should not be astonished that Marx returns frequently to the real conditions of the process and insists, showing punc-tually his sharp sense of history, on the fact that capital, at the stage that was present to him, dominates petty circulation and recuperates it within the overall process of circulation. But this in no way undermines the an-tagonistic power with which small-scale circulation appears: not only as a fact but as a dynamic process, as a tendency. It is this passage from fact to dynamic process which characterizes small-scale circulation. We have seen in the abstract how the creative power of labor becomes subject; we can now see how this movement is accomplished concretely. Small-scale circulation is the space within which the sphere of needs related to necessary labor develops. Thus it takes form and constitutes itself dynamically, consolidates itself in the composition of labor power, in the composition of the working class. It reproduces itself and grows, finally defining itself as the potential of struggle.

Several problems appear here. The *first* is that of deepening the constituting articulation described here. The *second* will be to analyse the general antag-onistic consequences which flow from this first apparition in the completed form of the proletarian subject. It is not the place to deepen these points: as far as I am concerned, I have tried to formalize some of them in the last part of my book *La forma Stato* (Milan: Feltrinelli, 1977). We will sometimes return to this but always with haste. Yet we should nevertheless remember that we are touching here one of the *central points* in the political debate of Marxism. It is on the issue of how these questions should be developed that revolutionary Marxists *are divided.* I am not so much concerned for the moment with which side one prefers (supposing that such similar theoretical situations exist); I only want to underline that on these questions we must go our different ways. For Marx the historical judgment passed on the phase of self-valorization is an *objective* one. For us, at the level of composition (and of power) reached by the working and proletariat class, it has become totally *subjective.* This means that each relation is maintained by the will, that each determination founds a development, that each episode is significative of a tendency. Moreover, the basis of self-valorization has expanded to the point where we can define the revolutionary project as *the construction of an opposition power based on the class dynamic. A dynamic of power.* Of power: because use value is for the proletariat an immediate revindication and immediate practice of power. Necessary labor can only be defined—even if it is a purely abstract definition—in terms of power: rigidity, irreversibility, pretension, subversive will to insurrection. Use-value. Use-value is indispensable for defining small-scale circulation. The dualism is complete from the point of view of the tendency: a new proclamation of power. The dualism is the actuality of the crisis for capital or, at any rate, the precariousness of its development.

Let us examine this carefully. We are already beyond Marxism. It is around these propositions that a large number of vulgar Marxists fail to understand Marx. These are theoretical problems which lead us—at a minimum—to regret the split in Marxist thought between an objectivist (economic) position and a subjectivist (political) position and to denounce—thereafter—the lack of an adequate and sufficient political perspective. Marx is seen as objectivistic and economistic and interpreted as an alibi for the paralysis of revolutionary thought and action. It thus becomes necessary to demand the *unity of Marxist thought* beyond Marxism, beyond the orthodoxy of a suffocating tradition. We do not want to deny that partial examination can find aspects of Marx's thought that are apparently separated from the unity of the project. Nor do we want to deny that one can read numerous pages of Marx (especially those collected and published in the German circles of the Second International) purely and simply through the spectacles of objectivism. We have, ourselves, often brought out the gap that exists between the *Grundrisse* (and the unity that marks its project) and *Capital* (whose development is not without lapses in the dialectic). On the other hand what we want to say is that there is no possibility of giving a general interpretation of Marx's thought by employing objectivist considerations and by always returning his analysis to that of the economy. It is from this point of view that we radically critique the recent rising tide of vulgar Marxism with its catastrophic and consoling aspects, its objectivist and opportunist aspects, and its always economistic bent. Should we take the field against some of the common elements of these recent interpretations? Why not. We have everything to win. Let us consider, for example, while remaining within the theme of small-scale circulation and proletarian self-valorization, the Marxist treatment of the *"reproduction schemes"* of Volume II of *Capital*. It is clear that the logic of separation that we see at work in the *Grundrisse* denies that these schemes can really work. It considers them only as an approximation, as adequate as it can be for a reality that is in fact profoundly broken up and rent by antagonism. This does not mean that we should throw garbage on these schemes: it means simply that they can serve to *approach* productive circulation and its concept from the point of view of economic unity, or, of the *accounting* unity of the process. To make of these abstractions, which are situated at a very high level of abstraction, schemes that can be used to interpret the class struggle; to try—in negative or positive ways—to find the logical coherence in order to obtain a necessary force to recognize the spaces and objectives of the class struggle; this is an error and a pettiness. This single piece of fabric within which reproduction grows, in an antagonistic manner, is something else, we have seen this. It is something else and far more complicated.

The *concept of self-valorization,* with all its density, refers us back to the concept of money as it was elaborated in the first pages of the *Grundrisse.* Money is general, social, abstract and antagonistic. From both sides we have forms that are opposed to each other in a contradictory way. *We must underline the antagonistic aspect of the relationship.* Money is the great mediator of capitalist development (the quantity theory is linked with this function) and it even represents the command of capital in this mediation constituted by the class relation (the Keynesian theory of money represents this aspect). Confronted with self-valorization, these functions fade. *Small-scale circulation seems to reject the functions of money,* even though money can function within it in terms of simple commodity circulation. Within this small-scale circulation, the sequence M-C-M' does not hold: money exchanged between proletarians is use-value. *Money is subordinated to self-valorization.* Naturally this analysis will seem abstract and full of utopianism if it does not take account of the way in which a contradictory relation is established between the collective forces. It is less abstract as soon as we situate it at this level. It is, for example, impossible today to appreciate the antagonistic class relations that run through the social functions of capitalist exploitation (State-as-entrepreneur, public expenses, etc.) if we do not take account of these dimensions of the problem. *The reduction of money to the pure and simple function of command,* on one side of the relation, *equals its subordination to self-valorization* on the other side of the relation. And this occurs in antagonistic terms. Well, it is all this that Marx begins to examine theoretically in these chapters. The conditions are all given: the emergence of the subjectivity of the two classes, the general and social character of their formation, the antagonistic nature of their confrontation in circulation and in reproduction. The possibility of defining the categories of capital in a new way, by beginning with Marx's teaching, the possibility of giving new foundations and a new and adequate formulation to the character of *social capital* in our time, depends on this thematic: *money (command)—self-valorization,* more than on any other Marxist moment. It is only by taking this thematic as point of departure that we can perhaps grasp the actual class antagonism in its real dimensions. Here, too, we will discover the possibility of raising the level of analysis such that we can understand the political mechanisms of capital and the *problem of power.* At the heart of this relationship, the capitalist relation is immediately a relation of power. The same is true from the working class point of view. This means that after having seen the potential of the *Marxist theory of the wage* develop with the elaboration of the theory of the subject, we are now going to be able to take it as a point of reference in order to revise and found the *most important categories of the theory of the class struggle*. It is a question of implementing the logic of separation at every level. It is a question of understanding the crisis as a constituting moment of every apparition, of every concretization of capital. It is a question of reviewing the whole outline of *Capital* and of confronting it point by point with the modifications implied by the development of the class struggle today. As far as I am concerned, I am always stupified to see the power of Marx's intuitions, the extraordinary anticipations of the *Grundrisse*. But that does not allow us to avoid the work of creation that we must give here.

To Summarize. It seems to me that the Marxist theory of the wage and the theoretical openings it creates allow us to define the fundamental moment where the theory of the class struggle enters into the theory of circulation. Once the social determinations of capital and its progressive power are solidly set out and reviewed, then we come face to face with the rule of antagonism. Important results follow. Above all from the point of view of the analysis of the working class: little by little a *subjective direction* emerges which takes on more and more materiality, to wind up determining the real composition of the class. The path that runs in this direction is open, and we will see in the following pages how Marx proceeds. In the second place, the logic of separation defines the general space where the analysis can develop; the space where we find a few anticipations that tend to found anew the main categories. At this point all we can do is follow the development of Marx's thought in the *Grundrisse*, in the pages that follow the analysis of "small-scale circulation."

Basing ourselves on what we have obtained so far, we can now take up the *"Fragment on Machines."* This is, without doubt, the highest example of the use of an antagonistic and constituting dialectic that we can find, certainly in the *Grundrisse*, but perhaps also in the whole of Marx's work. The chapter on machines covers the last pages of Notebook VI and the beginning of Notebook VII (*Grundrisse*, pp. 690–712; 582–600). This chapter was written at the end of February 1858 and is located, we have already pointed this out, at the peak of Marx's theoretical tension in the *Grundrisse*. It is also a moment of logical conclusion. Henceforth the process of capital develops through a series of critical elements, as much from the point of view of synchronic construction of the categories as from the point of view of their diachronic, historical determination: to the point where the antagonism takes on the form of working class subjectivity. At this point the antagonism opens into subversion. It is now a matter of bringing the different threads together, to harvest the totality of the process in all its richness. Let us begin again at the beginning and move forward.

The analysis begins with the dialectic of *living labor*. This living labor finds itself inserted into "the dynamic, constituting unity of the labor process". This unity deepens, and changes form as capital, through the machine, or the *"automatic system of machinery,"* subsumes labor. The automatic system of machinery is

> set in motion by an automaton, a moving power that moves itself; this automaton consisting of numerous mechanical and intellectual organs, so that the workers themselves are cast merely as its conscious linkages. In the machine, and even more in machinery as an automatic system, the use value, i.e., the material quality of the means of labour, is transformed into an existence adequate to fixed capital and to capital as such; and the form in which it was adopted into the production process of capital, the direct means of labour, is superseded by a form posited by capital itself and corresponding to it. In no way does the machine appear as the individual worker's means of labour. Its distinguishing characteristic is not in the least, as with the means of labour, to transmit the worker's activity to the object; this activity, rather is posited in such a way that it merely transmits the machine's work, the machine's action on to the raw material—supervises it and guards against interruptions. Not as with the instrument, which the worker animates and makes into his organ with his skill and strength, and whose handling therefore depends on his virtuosity. Rather, it is the machine which possesses skill and strength in place of the worker, is itself the virtuoso, with a soul of its own in the mechanical laws acting through it; and it consumes coal, oil etc *(matières instrumentales),* just as the worker consumes food, to keep up its perpetual motion. The worker's activity, reduced to a mere abstraction of activity, is determined and regulated on all sides by the movement of the machinery, and not the opposite. The science which compels the inanimate limbs of the machinery, by their construction, to act purposefully, as an automaton, does not exist in the worker's consciousness, but rather acts upon him through the machine as an alien power, as the power of the machine itself. The appropriation of living labour by objectified labour—of the power or activity which creates value by value existing for-itself—which lies in the concept of capital, is posited, in production resting on machinery, as the character of the production process itself, including its material elements and its material motion. The production process has ceased to be a labour process in the sense of a process dominated by labour as its governing unity. Labour appears, rather, merely as a conscious organ, scattered among the individual living workers at numerous points of the mechanical system; subsumed under the total process of the machinery itself, as itself only a link of the system, whose unity exists not in the living workers, but rather in the living (active) machinery, which confronts his individual, insignificant doings as a mighty organism. In machinery, objectified labour confronts living labour within the labour process itself as the power which

rules it; a power which as the appropriation of living labour, is the form of capital. The transformation of the means of labour into machinery, and of living labour into mere living accessory of this machinery, as the means of its action, also posits the absorption of the labour process in its material character as a mere moment of the realization process of capital. The increase of the productive force of labour and the greatest possible negation of necessary labour is the necessary tendency of capital, as we have seen. The transformation of the means of labour into machinery is the realization of this tendency. In machinery, objectified labour materially confronts living labour as a ruling power and as an active subsumption of the latter under itself, not only by appropriating it, but in the real production process itself; the relation of capital as value which appropriates value-creating activity is, in fixed capital existing as machinery, posited at the same time as the relation of the use value of capital to the use value of labour capacity; further, the value objectified in machinery appears as a presupposition against which the value-creating power of the individual labour capacity is an infinitesimal, vanishing magnitude; the production in enormous mass quantities which is posited with machinery destroys every connection of the product with the direct need of the producer, and hence with direct use value; it is already posited in the form of the product's production and in the relations in which it is produced, that it is produced only as a conveyor of value, and its use value only as condition to that end. In machinery, objectified labour itself appears not only in the form of product or of the product employed as means of labour, but in the form of the force of production itself. The development of the means of labour into machinery is not an accidental moment of capital, but is rather the historical reshaping of the traditional, inherited means of labour into a form adequate to capital. The accumulation of knowledge and of skill, of the general productive forces of the social brain, is thus absorbed into capital, as opposed to labour, and hence appears as an attribute of capital, and more specifically of *fixed capital,* in so far as it enters into the production process as a means of production proper. *Machinery* appears, then, as the most adequate form of *fixed capital,* and fixed capital, in so far as capital's relations with itself are concerned, appears as *the most adequate form of capital* as such. In another respect, however, in so far as fixed capital is condemned to an existence within the confines of a specific use value, it does not correspond to the concept of capital, which, as value, is indifferent to every specific form of use value, and can adopt or shed any of them as equivalent incarnations. In this respect, as regards capital's external relations, it is *circulating capital* which appears as the adequate form of capital, and not fixed capital [*Grundrisse,* pp. 692–694; 584–86].

To simply comment on these quoted pages would necessitate going back over everything we have said already; it's not worth the trouble. It is more useful to underline a few particular points which appear here and to understand how Marx used them to move forward. The first point is an intensive one: *the labor process is taken as a simple element of the process of valorization*. The second point is extensive: *productive capital extends into circulation*. Real subsumption of labor can't but be (in the same moment) real subsumption of society. Of society, in other words of the productive social forces, especially of science. "The entire production process appears as not subsumed under the direct skilfulness of the worker, but rather as the technological application of science" (*Grundrisse*, p. 699; 587). And Marx continues, insisting on the subsumption of the social productive forces—in their totality—on their being totally functional to the development of capital. The moment arrives when the whole system *is displaced* and advances. First from the point of view of an intensive analysis, that is with respect to *the labor process* and its subsumption to the process of valorization. Here, the displacement of categories signifies the capitalist dissolution of working class use value.

> To the degree that labour time—the mere quantity of labour—is posited by capital as the sole determinant element, to that degree does direct labour and its quantity disappear as the determinant principle of production—of the creation of use values—and is reduced both quantitatively, to a smaller proportion, and qualitatively, as an, of course, indispensable but subordinate moment, compared to general scientific labour, technological application of natural sciences, on one side, and to the general productive force arising from social combination *{Gliederung}* in total production on the other side—a combination which appears as a natural fruit of social labour (although it is a historic product). Capital thus works towards its own dissolution as the form dominating production [*Grundrisse*, p. 700; 587–88].

Furthermore, in the second place, from the point of view of an extensive analysis. Here circulating capital appears as productive capital by taking *the form of planning* and of control of the reproduction of society. The subsumption of society has become the production of that same society. The displacement is total. "So does it now appear, in another respect, as a quality of *circulating capital,* to maintain labour in one branch of production by means of *co-existing* labour in another" (*Grundrisse*, p. 700; 588).

> This exchange of one's own labour with alien labour appears here not as mediated and determined by the simultaneous existence of the labour of others, but rather by the advance which capital makes. The worker's ability to engage in the exchange of substances necessary for his consumption during production appears as due to an attribute of the part of circulating capital which is paid to the worker, and of circulating capital generally. It appears not as an exchange of substances between the simultaneous labour powers, but as the metabolism *{Stoffwechsel}* of capital; as the ex-

istence of circulating capital; the productive power of labour into fixed capital (posited as external to labour and as existing independently of it (as object {*sachlich*})); and, in circulating capital, the fact that the worker himself has created the conditions for the repetition of his labour, and that the exchange of this, his labour, is mediated by the co-existing labour of others, appears in such a way that capital gives him an advance and posits the simultaneity of the branches of labour. (These last two aspects actually belong to accumulation.) Capital in the form of circulating capital posits itself as mediator between the different workers [*Grundrisse,* pp. 700–701; 588].

At this stage, *the capitalist appropriation of society is total.* The subjectivity of capital has been violently activated. Machines and science have constituted and produced it. *But the separation within the category has not been suppressed.* The antagonism must reproduce itself at the highest level of power. The displacement of antagonistic dialectic must be totally revealed and operate fully at this stage. You can criticize all you like this way Marx has of proceeding via large *tranches* of argument which appear as relatively exterior one to another, this somewhat mechanical way of linking up the developments. We would sometimes wish to find a more interior, more subtle, more refined dialectic. We could skip these improvised displacements which emerge suddenly and leave us breathless, reminding us of the taste of a certain "catastrophism." Yet, it seems to us difficult to imagine that we could develop a logical argument as powerful, or such an incredible capacity of prediction of capitalist development, in terms that would not be necessarily rigid but would still be strong, powerful, marked by an exceptional scientific tension. Here thought possesses such strength that it cannot be reduced to a simple caricature. The cleavage reappears and the process advances. *The separation occurs within the process.* "But to the degree that large industry develops, the creation of real wealth comes to depend less on labour time and on the amount of labour employed than on the power of the agencies set in motion during labour time, whose 'powerful effectiveness' is itself in turn out of all proportion to the direct labour time spent on their production, but depends rather on the general state of science and on the progress of technology, or the application of this science to production (*Grundrisse,* pp. 704–705; 592). But from within the process where it was hidden the separation *is suddenly displaced to the outside* and there takes the form of an independent subjectivity. In the conditions of the process described already

real wealth manifests itself, rather—and large industry reveals this—in the monstrous disproportion between the labour time applied, and its product, as well as in the qualitative imbalance between labour, reduced to a pure abstraction, and the power of the production process it superintends. Labour no longer appears so much to be included within the production process; rather, the human being comes to relate more as watchman and regulator to the production process itself. (What holds for machinery holds likewise for the combination of human activities and the development of human intercourse.) No longer does the worker insert a modified natural thing *{Naturgeganstand}* as middle link between the object *{Objekt}* and himself; rather, he inserts the process of nature, transformed into an industrial process, as a means between himself and inorganic nature, mastering it. He steps to the side of the production process instead of being its chief actor. In this transformation, it is neither the direct human labour he himself performs, nor the time during which he works, but rather the appropriation of his own general productive power, his understanding of nature and it is, in a word, the development of the social individual which appears as the great foundation-stone of production and of wealth. *The theft of alien labour time, on which the present wealth is based,* appears a miserable foundation in face of this new one, created by large-scale industry itself. As soon as labour in the direct form has ceased to be the great well-spring of wealth, labour time ceases and must cease to be its measure, and hence exchange value [must cease to be the measure] of use value. The *surplus labour of the mass* has ceased to be the condition for the development of general wealth, just as the *non-labour of the few,* for the development of the general powers of the human head. With that, production based on exchange value breaks down, and the direct, material production process is stripped of the form of penury and antithesis. The free development of individualities, and hence not the reduction of necessary labour time so as to posit surplus labour, but rather the general reduction of the necessary labour of society to a minimum, which then corresponds to the artistic, scientific etc. development of the individuals in the time set free, and with the means created, for all of them. Capital itself is the moving contradiction, [in] that it presses to reduce labour time to a minimum, while it posits labour time, on the other side, as sole measure and source of wealth. Hence it diminishes labour time in the necessary form so as to increase it in the superfluous form; hence posits the superfluous in growing measure as a condition—question of life or death—for the necessary. On the one side, then, it calls to life all the powers of science and of nature, as of social combination and of social intercourse, in order to make the creation of wealth independent (relatively) of the labour time employed on it. On the other side, it wants to use labour time as the measuring rod for the giant social forces thereby created, and to confine them within the limits required to maintain the already created value as value. Forces of production and social relations—two different sides of the development of the social individual—appear to capital as mere means, and are merely means for it to produce on its limited foundation. In fact, however, they are the material conditions to blow this foundation sky-high [*Grundrisse*, pp. 705–706; 592–94].

The first result produced by the logic of separation is to displace the relationship necessary labor/surplus labor to situate it at the level of the capacity of capital to subsume society, and to *transform the relation between two complete, opposed subjectivities* that are hostile to the point of destroying each other reciprocally. This is *impossible* for capital, which lives on exploitation. It is *possible* for the proletariat, whose power (potenza) becomes more and more immense as capital tries to destroy its identity. Capital seeks a continual reduction in necessary labor in order to expand the proportion of surplus value extorted, but the more it succeeds individually with workers taken one by one, the more necessary labor benefits the collectivity and is reappropriated by absorbing the great collective forces that capital would like to determine purely for its own account. *The compression of necessary individual labor is the expansion of necessary collective labor* and it constructs a "*social individual,*" capable not only of producing but also of *enjoying* the wealth produced. After a first analysis, Marx returns to the argument, retraces the path that he had at first jumped, takes up again each category of the threads that allowed the displacement of the analysis and redefines the law of value at this new level of complexity. Various indices—sometimes allusive, sometimes precise—allow us to advance in our research. Each time the categories work in a reversed way: to surplus labor, the motor of development, is opposed non-work; to capitalism is opposed communism.

The creation of a large quantity of disposable time apart from necessary labour time for society generally and each of its members (i.e. room for the development of the individuals' full productive forces, hence those of society also), this creation of not-labour time appears in the stage of capital, as of all earlier ones, as not-labour time, free time, for a few. What capital adds is that it increases the surplus labour time of the mass by all the means of art and science, because its wealth consists directly in the appropriation of surplus labour time; since *value directly its purpose*, not use value. It is thus, despite itself, instrumental in creating the means of social disposable time, in order to reduce labour time for the whole society to a diminishing minimum, and thus to free everyone's time for their own development. But its tendency always, on the one side, *to create disposable time, on the other, to convert it into surplus labour.* If it succeeds too well at the first, then it suffers from surplus production, and then necessary labour is interrupted, because *no surplus labour can be realized by capital.* The more this contradiction develops, the more does it become evident that the growth of the forces of production can no longer be bound up with the appropriation of alien labour, but that the mass of workers must themselves appropriate their own surplus labour. Once they have done so—and *disposable time* thereby ceases to have an *antithetical* existence—then, on one side, necessary labour time will be measured by the needs of the social individual, and, on the other, the development of the power of social production will grow so rapidly that, even though production is now calculated for the wealth of all, *disposable time* will grow for all. For real wealth is the developed productive power of all individuals. The measure of wealth is then not any longer, in any way, labour time, but rather disposable time. *Labour time as the measure of value* posits wealth itself as founded on poverty, and disposable time as existing *in and because of the antithesis to surplus labour time;* or, the positing of an individual's entire time as labour time, and his degradation therefore to mere worker, subsumption under labour. *The most developed machinery thus forces the worker to work longer than the savage does, or than he himself did with the simplest, crudest tools* [*Grundrisse,* pp. 708–709; 595–96].

Some want to see, in this fierce *demand* by Marx for a *communism that is liberation from exploitation,* the mark of individualism and of humanist compassion. Even if that were so, there is certainly no evil there. However, it is not the case. It is not the case because, if we stay at the level of categories, we must remember that the communist destruction of the law of value (or better, its overthrow and reversal) suppresses and denies the individual elements of individual productivity on which—from the capitalist point of view and the corresponding Marxist analysis—it is based. The *displacement* is here totally completed. To social capital corresponds the collective worker. Once more the temporal dimension demands and implies an extensive spatial dimension. "As the basis on which large industry rests, the appropriation of alien labour time, ceases, with its development, to make up or to create wealth, so does *direct labour* as such cease to be the basis of production since, in one respect, it is transformed more into a supervisory and regulatory activity; but then also because the product ceases to be the product of isolated direct labour, and the *combination* of social activity appears, rather, as the producer" (*Grundrisse,* p. 709; 596–97). *In the communist revolution, the individual is social.* Social but concrete, he is exaltation and overdetermination, expansion of enjoyment, founder of that expansion.

Real economy—saving—consists of the saving of labour time (minimum (and minimization) of production costs); but this saving identical with development of the productive force. Hence in no way *abstinence from consumption,* but rather the development of power, of capabilities of production, and hence both of the capabilities as well as the means of consumption. The capability to consume is a condition of consumption, hence its primary means, and this capability is the development of an individual potential, a force of production. The saving of labour time [is] equal to an increase of free time, i.e. time for the full development of the individual, which in turn reacts back upon the productive power of labour as itself the greatest productive power. From the standpoint of the direct production process it can be regarded as the production of *fixed capital*, this fixed capital being man himself. It goes without saying, by the way, that direct labour time itself cannot remain in the abstract antithesis to free time in which it appears from the perspective of bourgeois economy. Labour cannot become play, as Fourier would like, although it remains his great contribution to have expressed the suspension not of distribution, but of the mode of production itself, in a higher form, as the ultimate object. Free time—which is both idle time and time for higher activity—has naturally transformed its possessor into a different subject, and he then enters into the direct production process as this different subject. This process is then both discipline, as regards the human being in the process of becoming; and at the same time, practice *{Ausübung}*, experimental science, materially creative and objectifying science, as regards the human being who has become, in whose head exists the accumulated knowledge of society. For both, in so far as labour requires practical use of the hands and free bodily movement, as in agriculture, at the same time exercise [*Grundrisse*, pp. 711–12; 599–600].

It is time to draw some conclusions about this important book on the wage—that is to say the unfolding of the logic of separation. We can now outline in its totality the path followed by the antithetical form of capitalist development. In the first place, beginning with the theory of surplus value, in other words in the terms and categories of the theoretical framework of the first part of the *Grundrisse*, a framework which is completely reversed in the second part. *The theory of surplus value is reversed.* Where, in capital's project, labor is commanded by surplus labor, *in the proletariat's revolutionary project reappropriated surplus labor is commanded by necessary labor.* In the first part of the *Grundrisse*, the theory of value appeared to us as an abstract subordinate of the theory of surplus value, from the point of view of the exploited class. Here, the theory of value is no longer simply subordinated. It undergoes, in this subordination, an important displacement and is subjected to a fundamental metamorphosis. In other words, when the theory of value can not measure itself by a quantity of labor time or by an individual dimension of labor, when a first displacement leads it to confront social time and the collective dimension of labor, at this moment the *impossibility of measuring exploitation modifies the form of exploitation.* The emptiness that appears in the theory of value, the evacuation of any element of measure which is not a generic reference to social industriousness, the liberation of social industriousness and its constitution in collective individuality, does not suppress the law of value but reduces it to a mere formality. Of course, formality does not mean a lack of efficacy. Formality does not mean a lack of meaning. The *form of the law of value* is, on the contrary, efficient and full of meaning, but efficacy and meaning are given to it only by its *irrationality*, by the end of the progressive and rationalizing function of exploitation. The form is the empty, miserable base of exploitation. The *form of value is pure and simple command, the pure and simple form of politics*—of the "essential inessentiality," as the young Marx would say in Hegelian terms. We are here at the culminating point of a process in which the power relations— rationally established—regulated and included within the development of capital—are reversed. Where the relation of rationality inverts itself. *The inversion is total.* The law of surplus value continues to rule, but in reversed terms. Non-work, the refusal of work becomes the worker's point of view, the basis from which the law of value can be inverted and the law of surplus value reinterpreted. The second part of the *Grundrisse* is this process in action. We could have entitled our Lesson: "*The Metamorphoses of the Law of Value*" and the following Lesson, which we consecrate to "the *concept of communism*," could be called "the refusal of work"; finally, the Ninth Lesson, in which we will treat the mechanisms of "*enlarged reproduction*," could also have as title: "*Worker Self-valorization.*" All in all we have here rapidly traced the whole path of liberation and communism. But when we speak of this path, we speak of a subject which is linked to it. A subject which materially possesses as a power the keys to the reversal of the law of surplus value. Nevertheless, above all let us remember the result at which we have arrived, that is to say this law of value which is emptied, which is reduced to being only an empty form of capitalist command. Empty and efficient. Efficient and irrational. Irrational and cruel.

What does it mean, from the class point of view, to possess the key to the reversal of surplus value? Some have thought that this proposition allows us to say this: *capital, when there is a reversal, becomes working class use-value.* This is *false.* Whoever tries to prove it must work within the logic of separation and will find himself stuck in the dualism of the capital relation. On another side it would be to stop before the inversion occurs: that is, it would be to invert the concept of capital instead of its reality, instead of its relation. This would not definitively split the capital relation but would globally attribute an opposed valence to its concept by hypostatizing a superior will to the relation. By imagining it. By self-illusion. By mystification. Mystification, because along this path worker behavior appears as an "equivalent" to capitalist behavior? Worker behavior becomes command over the capital relation and not destruction—by necessary labor—of the capitalist appropriation of surplus labor. It is a *typically sophistic treatment:* in so far as it is a question of critique, capital is a relation that must be broken; when we pass from critique to theory, capital becomes something to be dominated. But that is only possible for capital, which can objectify its own negation. It is not possible for the working class, which denies that which is its negation. It is possible for capital, which mystifies the relation and encloses it in objectivity. It cannot be possible for the worker-subject who unveils the mystification and moves the relation to the foreground.

We insist on this critique for several different reasons. In the first place, because of the falsity of the results that are obtained from the point of view we have criticized: this view hypostatizes capital when it makes it a working-class use value, whereas there can only be working-class use value in the accummulated part of surplus labor that it is possible to reappropriate, that part which can be reduced to non-work, to working class liberty, to self-valorization. This part is negation, the wealth of negation. In the second place, because the point of view that I have criticized winds up giving autonomy to the political in a very mystified way: the political in this case is not the new form of the law of value but rather is a relation superior to capital and independent of it. In the *Grundrisse* there are no relations superior to capital that are not functions of capitalism, that are not forms taken by capital's command as it develops. To break it from inside, to not seek outside points of references, to smash it beginning with worker subjectivity as negation and as potential wealth (which is already used in its global aspect by capital); in sum, *to deepen the rupture of the capital relation from within this relation;* basing oneself on the contradictory essense of the law of surplus value: this is the only path that we find in Marx, in the *Grundrisse,* and in all his work. A work in which we can find contradictions, divisions and in which we can—and we freely admit to this—prefer some parts to others. But not because in the other parts we can not find the same unity of the *critique of political economy* and the *critique of the political* that we see in the *Grundrisse.* At the point we have reached, and this can be seen in the present polemic, we begin to *master subjectivity, Marx's acceptance of subjectivity, its working class and proletarian development.* Here we have accentuation of separation which is implicitly contained, as an element of definition in the theory of surplus value, which shows us the theory of the wage, the development and dynamism that gives to the working-class pole—liberated from the capital relation in the theory of the wage—the theory of "small-scale circulation." The general displacement undergone by this antagonistic terrain through the theories of machinery, of social capital, and of real and global social subsumption—well, all that leads to the theory of the *social individual* and of *communism* as the negation of the capital relation. *Not* as an inversion of capitalist command, *but* as an inversion of the relation between necessary labor and surplus labor, as the negation and reappropriation of surplus labor. The path of subjectivity lies within the capital relation, it does not try to imagine alternatives, but knows how, as it deepens its separation, to destroy the relation. The path of subjectivity is an intensive path. It is a continual and coherent recomposition of successive negations. It raises necessary labor to the point where it can destroy surplus labor.

In this intensity which characterizes separation we find maximum liberty. The social individual is *multilaterality.* The highest intensity of difference is the highest approach to communism. When the capital relation has reached the point where it explodes, the liberated negation is not a synthesis. It knows no formal equivalences whatsoever. *Working-class power is not the reversal of capitalist power, not even formally.* Working-class power is the negation of the power of capital. It is the negation of the centralized and homogeneous power of the bourgeoisie, of the political classes of capital. It is the dissolution of all homogeneity. This methodological "plural", this multilaterality triumphs. We cannot impose on liberated subjectivity any uniform and flat scheme for organizing social reality. Surplus labor had a uniform aspect in the capitalist project. The wage refigured the shape of capital. When the *wage* as it developed became *self-valorization* and *reappropriation* of surplus labor, it was the end of all rules useful for development. There is no more profit because labor productivity is no longer translated into capital. There is no more capitalist rationality. Subjectivity not only liberates itself, it liberates a totality of possibilities. It draws a new horizon. Labor productivity is founded and spread socially. It is both a magma which gathers and recomposes everything, and a network of streams of enjoyment, of propositions and inventions which spread out across a land made fertile by the magma. The communist revolution, the emergence in all its power of the social individual, creates this wealth of alternatives, of propositions, of functions. Of liberty. Never has communism appeared as synonymous with liberty as in these pages of the *Grundrisse* that we have just studied.

Lesson Eight

Communism &
Transition

The problem of communism and the problem of transition in the
Grundrisse. ☐ Synthesis of the material covered? A critique of this
synthesis and of the way of posing the problem. ☐ (a.) On the
humanism of Marx. A new thematic proposition: transition rather
than utopia, or demystification and inversion. The great dynamic
themes; from prehistory to history, communism building itself. ☐ (b.)
The demystification and development of the categories of the critique
of political economy. The great substantial themes. The content of
communism. From demystification to inversion, from substantial
themes to the form of the transition. ☐ (c.) Transition and subjectivity. Transition and constituting praxis. The power *(potenza)* of
the inversion: the suppression of work. ☐ (d.) The refusal of work
as the communist mode of production. ☐ Giving the dialectic back
to capital and the destruction of utopia.

From the world market to communism. Where we have arrived in our
reasoning, after all our insistence on bringing out the subjective dimension
of the process, is a kind of path that always appears as a veritable paradox.
It is nevertheless a path that Marx indicates more than once: in the outline
of the *Grundrisse* (pp. 227–28; 139) and in the outline of page 264 (175):
"At last, the world market. Bourgeois society dominates the state. Crises.
The dissolution of the mode of production and of the form of society founded
on exchange-value. Individual work seen clearly in its social form and vice
versa." Communism springs forth from the intensity of the contradictions
that are contained in the concept of world market: at once a moment of
maximum capitalist integration and a moment of maximum antagonism,
a synthesis of the temporal and spatial determinations of capital's process.
*Posed in these terms, the problem of communism does not even recognize the problem
of the transition,* it does not know the problem of subjectivity: it can pose

them as moments internal to capital, as symptoms, as detours of objectivity, it can not pose them as specific problems. The question of "what is communism?" which runs through Marx's discourse from the *Manuscripts* up until the *German Ideology* in a very central way (and we must not forget that it is a question which is at the center of Hegel's thought after the *Umrisse der Nationalokonomie* of 1844), this question, in the form in which it is being posed here, seems more an objective than a methodical function, more a transcendental object of research than its motor. What is communism? How does the passage to this "superior form of the mode of production" that we call communism work? The traditional response to these two problems takes the form of *a unique process, internal to capital's dialectic.* Communism is seen as beyond a leap, beyond a catastrophe produced by the antagonistic development of capital. The problem of the transition disappeared behind that of defining communism, and this last is presented as a transcendence in relation to capitalist development. Paradoxically, what unifies the path to communism and to transition is their common negation of capital, the objective side of this negation. Both constitute, in some sense, an "afterwards."

Obviously this way of posing the problem does not please me at all. It seems unrealistic and utopian. Above all, this position is situated very much outside the overall development of the *Grundrisse,* as we have read it up to this point. The points of this theme that defines communism are all derived from the growing antagonism of capitalist development. Their development follows the different determinations of subjectivity, of its constitution in global and antagonistic terms, within the radical inversion of the law of surplus value. It is thus that I can understand the subjective insistence of Marx's discourse on catastrophe as a prospective determination marked by revolutionary passion. It is around this concept of crisis and catastrophe that are combined, as we have seen, the elements that meet in the genesis of the *Grundrisse.* Once that is said, the problem still remains completely open. *To confuse these paths means to deny another fundamental characteristic of Marx's thought.* To think through the transition in the form of communism leads in reality to *the suppression of the problem of the transition.* It means (for better or worse) to cut it into two fragments, one which serves as an introduction and is situated within capital, in the interstices of its contradictions, the other which finally comes after and reveals itself in a space beyond the catastrophe in the full liberty of communism. Now, what interests us is *the process of liberation,* that which lies between the introduction and the conclusion. Putting the two paths together has an enormous theoretical implication: it homogenizes the two concepts, suppressing all possibility of separating the logical substance and the historical quality or hypostatizing them in some dialectic of stages and hierarchy. By combining the two paths we recognize implicitly the communist character of the process of liberation.

But what is the point if this combining offers me no space for determining this process of liberation?

Let us examine the *Grundrisse* on this question of communism: we must now present our hypothesis. And it is the one that emerges from all the research that we have done until now, and that we must still verify here: *it is not the transition that reveals itself (and eliminates itself) in the form of communism, but rather it is communism that takes the form of the transition.*

Rosdolsky (pp. 413–35), when he treats the problem of communism in Marx, underlines—putting aside the two characteristics usually brought out, the centrality of communism in the work of Marx and Engels, and the struggle against *both* opportunism and utopianism—the importance and the pertinence in Marx, in the dialectic, *both* his *descent* from and his *divergence* from *the utopians*. In other words, for Rosdolsky the Marxist dialectic is entirely permeated by a *positive utopia*, by the power of utopia, simply tempered by the conscience of having to give it a materialist force. It is surprising that Rosdolsky—a Marxist grown up in the school of leftist communism of the 1920s—knows how to see in Marx the important function of positive utopia! And we can not deny a certain power to this suggestion: positive utopia always sets very precise limits between the camp of revolutionaries and that of opportunists. And yet his insight is not entirely convincing. Because it does not see, it does not sufficiently underline the indeterminacy of the proposed synthesis and of the dialectical process. This dialectic which becomes one with communism, with obstinancy, but which does not embrace the process, is a key too general and too generic. It risks giving new force to that "bewitchment of method" in the name of which all distinction—and the process that only differences can animate—fades, flattens out to the point of disappearing. On the one side we have the *flattening* of communism, of its concept that we reduce to the dimension of objective logic, of determinism; on the other side and in opposition, we find the "leap," the new quality, politics and voluntarism posed in all their fullness and violence. Let us remember—as Rosdolsky does (p. 424)—the positions of Marcuse. On the one side, the increasingly consistent power *(potenza)* of capital over work, the terrible Moloch taking form; on the other side, again a "bewitching," but no longer the one produced by the determinist method. Rather, a "qualitative leap" into the beyond. To the capitalist exaltation of the organization of work is opposed the abolition of work. The dice are cast, Marcuse's romanticism is satisfied. Yet the problem is not to be found there. It is not a matter of detailing this leap: we must overthrow everything, the process, its antagonism the constituting logic, the appearance of subjectivity, and everything that exists between the organization of work and its abolition. The Marxist method is not based on paradox, but on the total and original unity of economics and politics, on the capacity to follow the path according to *the point of view of the transformation*. In the second place, Marx's method is affirmed by a continual displacement of the terms of analysis, a displacement that results from the multiplicity of forms that the relations of force take on. The categories are modified as the subjects are modified. That is, along with—and this is the third important point— the historical determinations of the process. It is not a question of defining the transition in terms of communism but rather, after having homogenized the two terms (and this does not mean that they are the same), *to define communism by the transition.* When we have thus reposed the problem, *it is a question* of *subject,* of its struggle, of its displacement. It is the process that globally constitutes communism which steps to the front.

If, on the contrary, we accept the Marxist *fiction* of the transition in the form of communism, we are inevitably thrown back to positions that have nothing to do with the dialectic. There we find happily gathered all the models of *humanism.* A generic humanism which reigns there where the method of the tendency seems to be incapable of transforming itself into a method of displacement: the tendency becomes the organic unfolding of human nature (even if it is defined historically). The orgy of totality, rebirth, and plenitude to which we give ourselves over has quite justly aroused indignation. Althusser is not wrong to consider as a decisive sign of good Marxism the tracing of clear limits and the exclusion of this insipid blub-bering from theory. But let us not exaggerate either the importance of these elements, let us not introduce ulterior, fictional classifications into the de-velopment of Marxist thought! We will have occasion to return to the so-called humanism of Marx: but it is interesting to see it already for what it is—the fruit of impatience with theory, a usage of positive utopia destined to homogenize transition and communism, the *contradictory residue* of the materialist method of separation, of the constitutive method of subjectivity. *To say that communism takes the form of the transition means for us following the red thread that serves as woof to antagonistic subjectivity.* In avoiding humanism, some would also seek to avoid the theoretical areas of subjectivity. They are wrong. The path of materialism passes precisely through subjectivity. The path of subjectivity is the one that gives materiality to communism. The working class is subjectivity, separated subjectivity, which animates devel-opment, crisis, transition and communism.

We must thus take this theme of communism in the *Grundrisse* and separate from it all considerations, all methodologies (however patiently justified by Marxist fictions) that do not bring to the fore the materialist process of subjectivity. The *synthesis of the paths* that Marx proposed—the path that passes through the determinism of the world market and the one that leaps toward communism—must be separated and reversed. We can only confront these paths if we analyse the determinations which subjectively represent the process of transition. We must resolutely demystify and over-throw all kinds of necessity and determinism attributed to the process of transition.

What does it mean to *demystify?* It means to follow the formation of communism through all of the particular moments of the critique of political economy. From this point of view, the *Grundrisse* is fundamentally a work of demystification.

> Our method indicates the points where historical investigation must enter in, or where bourgeois economy as a merely historical form of the production process points beyond itself to earlier historical modes of production. In order to develop the laws of bourgeois economy, therefore, it is not necessary to write the *real history of the relations of production.* But the correct observation and deduction of these laws, as having themselves become in history, always leads to primary equations—like the empirical numbers e.g. in natural science—which point towards a past lying behind this system. These indications *{Andeutung},* together with a correct grasp of the present, then also offer the key to the understanding of the past— a work in its own right which, it is to be hoped, we shall be able to undertake as well. This correct view likewise leads at the same time to the points at which the suspension of the present form of production relations gives signs of its becoming—foreshadowings of the future. Just as, on one side the pre-bourgeois phases appear as *merely historical,* i.e. suspended presuppositions, so do the contemporary conditions of production likewise appear as engaged in *suspending themselves* and hence in positing the *historic presuppositions* for a new state of society (*Grundrisse,* pp. 460–61; 364–65).

The path along which the categories advance seems clear: while progressing in history, they continually take the historical phases as conditions, the present as history, the future foreseen as movement of becoming. We must thus examine, even if it is by fits and starts, *the great dynamic themes* of the formation of communism. This is the moment when the categories of the critique of political economy are demystified—we will see shortly the moment when these categories invert themselves as a result of the practical recognition of the subject.

Making use now of this approach, and of the methodology such as we have presented and delimited it, we can easily work through numerous passages which allow the specification of the Marxist definition of communism and of its historical evolution. Almost all the chapters that we have read include a *logic of communism,* beginning with the Chapter on Money. At that point where money is considered a social relationship (*Grundrisse,* pp. 156–63; 74–82)—let us remember well these passages: it is from the very power of *extraneation* that the "law of three stages" is engendered, and from this emerges the power of a radical alternative—where money appears as a social collective relation, beyond the mystification that it presents, we can see outlined the third stage of the development of individuality. "Free individuality, based on the universal development of individuals and on their subordination of their communal, social productivity as their social wealth, is the third stage" (*Grundrisse,* p. 158; 75). Some of the characteristic aspects of money—its sociality, the representation of collective productivity, the measure and symbol of social patrimony—are immediately inverted. We might say that the category "money" only lives for the possibility of inverting itself. To demystify means to understand the category as an inversion. This is what happens with the category of "money": it refers to the possibility, to the necessity of inversion, it deploys itself to control this inversion, given the violence of this tension, of this rupture. (And, in parenthesis, let us underline the fundamentally anti-humanist sense of terms such as "universal individual". This term depends more on the overthrow of the brutality of money relations, of their socializing force, than on some naturalist or historicist consideration, or on some continuist consideration. *The separation* is radical, and it serves not only as a key to achieving the *inversion,* but also as a *matrix of constitution.* If we really want to find something of humanism or of ambiguity in Marx's thought, we must look for it in those moments where the dialectical process pretends to function in terms of recomposition and sublimation.) The idea of communism, to return to our reasoning, functions as a pole of rupture for each category of capital, as its critical antithesis. Here, when it comes to money, the idea of communism takes the form of inversion of a fully developed sociality, as is that of money. *The passage from prehistory to history,* which is also the passage to the domination of man over nature and over history, the passage to communism, depends on the total *facticity* of the operation: it is the efficacy of the liberated subject which opposes and inverts the mystified efficacy of capitalist socialization.

Grundrisse (pp. 487–89; 387–88): here again is an example of what the theme of communism takes from the inversion, from the critique of the categories. It is nothing less than the category of "universal exchange," the category itself of the "bourgeois world," which is to be inverted here.

> In fact, however, when the limited bourgeois form is stripped away, what is wealth other than the universality of individual needs, capacities, pleasures, productive forces etc., created through universal exchange? The full development of human mastery over the forces of nature, those of so-called nature as well as of humanity's own nature? The absolute working-out of his creative potentialities, with no presupposition other than the previous historic development, which makes this totality of development, i.e. the development of all human powers as such the end in itself, not as measured on a *predetermined* yardstick? Where he does not reproduce himself in one specificity, but produces his totality? Strives not to remain something he has become, but is in the absolute movement of becoming? In bourgeois economics—and in the epoch of production to which it corresponds—this complete working-out of the human content appears as a complete emp-

tying-out, this universal objectification as total alienation, and the tearing down of all limited, one-sided aims as sacrifice of the human end-in-itself to an entirely external end. This is why the childish world of antiquity appears on one side as loftier. On the other side, it really is loftier in all matters where closed shapes, forms and given limits are sought for. It is satisfaction from a limited standpoint; while the modern gives no satisfaction; or, where it appears satisfied with itself, it is *vulgar* [*Grundrisse*, p. 488; 387–88].

The bourgeois world is emptiness, alienation and vulgarity; communism is richness of needs, expansion, abstract (though seeking to concretize itself) universality of needs. The abstract category refers to concrete inversion. Prehistory to history. The "true community" that we find a few pages further on (*Grundrisse*, p. 496; 396) forms the woof of the category of progress in bourgeois society: it is in so far as it is the inversion. And: "It will be shown later that the *most extreme form* of alienation . . . already contains in *itself*, in a still only inverted form, turned on its head, the dissolution of all *limited presuppositions of production,* and moreover creates and produces the unconditional presuppositions of production, and therewith the full material conditions for the total, universal development of the productive forces of the individual" (*Grundrisse*, p. 515; 414–15). It is here that we find rising up those terms both magical and marked by the brand of infamy, "in an inverted form," "upside down," terms that some have sought to give an exhaustive or metaphysical explanation: for our part, the course of our analysis leads us to a more lucid explanation—it is evident that these terms are those of a language that speaks of the reversal of categories, of revolutionary tension pointed beyond them, totally inside of development. The woof of inversion is everywhere, everywhere the point of view of the worker-subject imposes its power.

It is when we arrive at those moments where Marx's description of capitalist development, as development of the productive force of capital and conclusion of human prehistory, is strongest and most complete—for example in the *Grundrisse* (pp. 584–90)—that the great dynamic themes of communism, which find their source in the exasperation of the separation contained in the capital relation, appear with the most formidable clarity. Let us reread the cited pages: capital with all its power of expansion extends abstract labor to the whole of society, pushing cooperation and the division of labor to its extreme limits. Each category of this passage is *double:* thus the cooperation as well as the division of labor is at once richness of needs and incessant displacement of the concept of individuality. But this duplicity is not false, it is not a case of competition. *It is double on all sides,* such that capitalist development is the reverse image of the communist process, an image which is as disfigured and insane as the progression of capital is advanced. When this opposition reaches its extreme point, when subversion remains the only path to follow, associated human labor achieves its palingenesis. We must not with false modesty deny the value of terms such as palingenesis or catastrophe at this level of development. Capital is just too ugly for that.

Further on, Marx analyses the fundamental law (and the mystification) of capitalist development, *the law of competition,* and in so doing he insists on the power of capitalist liberty: but this liberty has *a narrow base.* "It is nothing more than free development on a limited basis—the basis of the rule of capital. This kind of individual freedom is therefore at the same time the most complete suspension of all individual freedom, and the most complete subjugation of individuality under social conditions which assume the form of objective powers, even of overpowering objects—of things independent of the relations among individuals themselves" (*Grundrisse,* p. 652; 545). The law of competition is also an outline of what the development of capital contains as force of opposition and of separation: communism, a potent reversal of everything.

To demystify the categories of capital means to expose to the light of day the *laws of movement* of history. The fundamental law is that which constructs the possibility of communism. From this point of view, to remain at demystification, communism is *building itself.* It is in the process of building itself as radical and extreme antithesis. The theme of liberty and the wealth of needs, of the contradictory development of the forms of production, and finally the theme of crisis, all meet here. They are present within each category as its reversal. Here, when we speak of communism, *the reversal is powerful and synthetic.* The contradictory form has the appearance of an insurmountable obstacle, of an obstacle that grows larger along with the development of the "permanent revolution" of capital. There is no solution to this process. No capitalist equilibrium can hold. Even less can a proposition that seeks socialism remain solid: the theory of state property, of planning, of equality in exploitation are all derived from the permanent revolution of capital. There is no possible equilibrium, not even a categorical one, when each element of the ideal synthesis is invalidated by antagonism. This emerges because the development of opposition is at least as tendentious as is the development of capital. Each one has its objectives. We know that of capitalism, and that of the working class and the proletariat we begin to see as a reversal of poles. It is not enough. In the *Grundrisse,* beyond this reaffirmation of the categories (reversal of the categories of capital, a new workers' foundation to these categories) we can still read passages where this term of demystification begins to *constitute itself as subject* and to convert the process which consists of defining "communism" as a residue—incompressible perhaps, but still a residue—in order to make it the motor of an alternative.

At this point we must begin to *speak of the subject.* But we are not yet up to it. So let us advance with Marx, be measured steps. Let us take, before everything else, the great dynamic and antithetical theme of communism: its reversed model. But we still lack the *research and the definition of the contents of communism*. Before tackling again the theme of the communist subject, we need to illuminate the antithetical *character* and also the antithetical *root* of communism. This antithetical rooting consists of the synthesis of the liberation of the productive forces and the appearance of the antithetical subject. *Liberation of the productive forces?* What does that mean? It means that at a certain level of capitalist development, capitalist command ceases to be necessary. "Capital appears as the condition of the development of the forces of production as long as they require an external spur, which appears at the same time as their bridle. It is a discipline over them, which becomes superfluous and burdensome at a certain level of their development, just like the guilds etc." (*Grundrisse*, p. 415; 318). *The appearance of the antithetical subject.* What does that mean? It means that communism can only found itself on the birth, between the steps of development, of a *new collective individuality*, which invents *new rules* of production and of development. *The liberated subject opens a new world* of new collectively unfolded needs.

Surplus value in general is value in excess of the equivalent. The equivalent, by definition, is only the identity of value with itself. Hence surplus value can never sprout out of the equivalent; nor can it do so originally out of circulation; it has to arise from the production process of capital itself. The matter can also be expressed in this way: if the worker needs only half a working day in order to live a whole day, then, in order to keep alive as a worker, he needs to work only half a day. The second half of the labour day is forced labour; surplus labour. What appears as surplus value on capital's side appears identically on the worker's side as surplus labour in excess of his requirements as worker, hence in excess of his immediate requirements for keeping himself alive. The great historic quality of capital is to *create* this *surplus labour*, superfluous labour from the standpoint of mere use value, mere subsistence; and its historic destiny *{Bestimmung}* is fulfilled as soon as, on one side, there has been such a development of needs that surplus labour above and beyond necessity has itself become a general need arising out of individual needs themselves— and, on the other side, when the severe discipline of capital, acting on succeeding generations *{Geschlechter}*, has developed general industriousness as the general property of the new species *{Geschlecht}* and, finally, when the development of the productive powers of labour, which capital incessantly whips onward with its unlimited mania for wealth, and of the sole conditions in which this mania can be realized, have flourished to the stage where the possession and preservation of general wealth require a lesser labour time of society as a whole, and where the labouring society relates scientifically to the process of its progressive reproduction, its reproduction in a constantly greater abundance; hence where labour in which a human being does what a thing could do has ceased. Accordingly, capital and labour relate to each other here like money and commodity; the former is the general form of wealth, the other only the substance destined for immediate consumption. Capital's ceaseless striving towards the general form of wealth drives labour beyond the limits of its natural paltriness {*Naturbedurftigkeit*}, and thus creates the material elements for the development of the rich individuality which is as all-sided in its production as in its consumption, and whose labour also therefore appears no longer as labour, but as the full development of activity itself, in which natural necessity in its direct form has disappeared; because a historically created need has taken the place of the natural one. This is why *capital is productive; i.e. an essential relation for the development of the social productive forces*. It ceases to exist as such only where the development of these productive forces themselves encounters its barrier in capital itself. [*Grundrisse*, p. 324–25; 230–31].

Work is no longer work, it is work which is liberated from work. The content of communism thus consists in a reversal which suppresses at the same time the object reversed. Communism is only reversal of work in so far as *this reversal is suppression: of work.* Liberation of the productive forces: certainly, but as a dynamic of a process which leads to abolition, to negation in the most total form. *Turning from the liberation-from-work toward the going-beyond-of-work forms the center, the heart of the definition of communism.* We must not be afraid to insist on this theoretical moment: the liberation of living labor exalts its creative power, *the abolition of work is what gives it life in every moment.* The content, the program of communism are a development of universal needs which have emerged on the collective but miserable basis of the organization of waged work, but which in a revolutionary way signify the abolition of work, its definitive death.

We have advanced in this way in our definition of the communist project. We have been able to grasp not only the power of reversal, on the level of history or of theory, but also the *content* of this reversal. Now we must go further. Conditions have sufficiently matured that we can see this reversal become dynamic, by itself, independent and autonomous. The communist subject emerges as the conclusion of this reversal.

From the *demystification* of the process to *its inversion.* It is no longer a question of the road which leads from prehistory to history, but of revolution in its synchronic and punctual aspect. The inversion receives subjectivity as a result of demystification and makes of it the condition of communism. *The transition appears here as the exclusive form of the formation of communism.*

There are two orders of considerations to be developed here. The first concerns method. Here, above all we must see that Marx's method arrives at its most developed definition. It is when Marx takes on the thematic of communism that the method exposed in the *Introduction* finds its full application. It functions fully when communism takes the form of the transition. *There is no other exposition of communism possible except that of the transition.* Otherwise it is an *ineffable* concept. All Marxist categories are categories of communism. It is thus that they escape from the possibility of "scientific use"—in the bourgeois sense of the term—but also from a reformist usage. Marxist categories are not only permeated by a permanent and irreducible duality, but this duality appears in the form of antagonism, and that antagonism in the form of reversal. To make use of Marxist categories means to push them to this necessary reversal, to allow oneself to be pushed to this incredible experience. Marxist categories are *subversive categories;* categories that emerge from the process of subversion. The categories are taken in the logic of the antagonistic tendency whose development is made up of successive displacements of the system of categories. The theory interrupts the historical process to the point of making its continuity impossible, to remodel it completely in the process of rupture and of transformation. It is not only the substantial categories (money, work, capital, etc.) that are revolutionary, there are also those belonging to the mode or to the method (limit, obstacle, process, transformation, etc.). In the interaction which occurs, the concept becomes the element of a movement which in developing takes the form of an antagonism, of an antithetical power *(potenza).* The transformation, within this logic of rupture, constitutes an opposition taken at its strongest level. Materialist logic—in so far as it is adequate to grasp the real—is rich with the power *(potenza)* of creation of the real, of the class struggle. Communism is only *concept* from the point of view of method, in so far as it remains a dynamic term of transformation.

The second order of consideration concerns the *historical* concretization of the thematic of transformation which is inherent in the concept. We must once again trace the whole theoretical path, already examined in its other aspects, and see how this path is, at each moment, for each category, marked by this element of revolutionary becoming. Nevertheless we will see here only a few essential elements. (*Grundrisse*, p. 157; 77): we are still in the analysis of "money as social relation." All oppositions seem to disappear into its universality. So much so that there are those—such as socialists, such as Proudhonians—who consider money as a "reverse face" of communism. There is nothing more false: the category is only the face of a quite opposite essence.

> But within bourgeois society, the society that rests on *exchange value,* there arise relations of circulation as well as of production which are so many mines to explode it. (A mass of antithetical forms of the social unity, whose antithetical character can never be abolished through quiet metamorphosis. On the other hand, if we did not find concealed in society as it is the material conditions of production and the corresponding relations

of exchange prerequisite for a classless society, then all attempts to explode
it would be quixotic.) [*Grundrisse,* p. 159; 79–80].

This, as concerns money, exchange value by *autonomasia.* But all this is
also true for work. With *Grundrisse,* pp. 167–68; 88–89, we are at the heart
of the analysis that elaborates the concept of abstract labor, and thus the
mediation between the time of work and social production. The forms are
ever more antithetical as the mediation progresses. Communism appears as
the concept of the overthrow of work, of its subtraction from command.
That which seems the conclusion of a process—the constitution of social
production—has as its only effect to produce another, the social liberation
of the subject. The subject thus begins to constitute itself. In order to rid
itself once and for all of its antithetical character and to become hegemonic,
it only lacks one element: *recognition.*

> The recognition *{Erkennung}* of the products as its own, and the judgement
> that its separation from the conditions of its realization is improper—
> forcibly imposed—is an enormous [advance in] awareness *{Bewusstsein},*
> itself the product of the mode of production resting on capital, and as
> much the knell to its doom as, with the slave's awareness that he *cannot
> be the property of another,* with his consciousness of himself as a person, the
> existence of slavery becomes a merely artificial, vegetative existence, and
> ceases to be able to prevail as the basis of production. [*Grundrisse,* p. 463;
> 366–67].

Recognition, consciousness, revolution. It is the moment in the method
where the "obstacle" materializes. This passage is extremely important because it is where *subjectivity appears as a specific and organic element of the material
class composition:* the subjectivity which expresses itself here is an element
certainly revolutionary, but which is situated completely within the contradictory structure of the relations of production. The subject is able to
develop itself, to liberate itself from the relations of production in so far as
it liberates them and dominates them. The self-valorization of the proletarian
subject, contrarily to capitalist valorization, takes the form of *auto-determination* in its development. Marx follows this process. He attempts to en-
compass it by approximation. He grasps auto-determination in the capacity
of the social body to present itself as the activity that regulates universality.
(For example: *Grundrisse,* pp. 612–13; 505). But this way of seeing the
process of the transition as a process rooted in science, understood as an
activity regulating all natural and material forces, is, in effect, an approximation. We must go to the heart of the matter: *science,* incorporated in
work, *its productive force,* subsumed by capital, *must only be more radically
liberated* in so far as the contradictory process which founds its development
is at its end. It is only at a very high level of integration that there is the

possibility of a rupture sufficiently profound and efficacious to construct a perspective of auto-determination. Approximation, allusion is not adequate. Often (for instance, *Grundrisse,* p. 540; 439) the way in which Marx deals with science is humanistic and scientistic; the deepening of the contradictory nature of the concept of science is weakened by this. But this does not happen, the analysis is even very expressive and very powerful, at the moment when the antithetical force—the process of proletarian auto-determination— begins with the definition of the highest level of the subsumption of society (and thus also of science) within capital. Here again is the "Fragment on Machines" (see *Lesson Seven*). *Communism has the form of subjectivity, communism is a constituting praxis.* There is no part of capital that is not destroyed by the impetuous development of the new subject. This subject shows such a power of subjective upheaval that all the vestiges of the old order are carried away. The transition is a constituting process in the fullest sense, which is based entirely on that space defined by the most radical alternatives. *Marx beyond Marx.* Beyond vulgar determinism. Beyond all hypotheses implying homogeneity. The most ingenuous revolutionary consciousness can find here plenty for the most sublime exaltation. The *inversion of the inversion* that capital has operated against work is, in the "Fragment on Machines," not an operation of overthrowing, but an operation of constitution. The capitalist inversion, with alienation, plays not only on distribution but finds itself at the foundation of the mode of production: the inversion of the inversion reaches this foundation.

Returning, still in Notebook VII, to the examination of this relation, Marx reasons as follows:

> The fact that in the development of the productive powers of labour the objective conditions of labour, objectified labour, must grow relative to living labour—this is actually a tautological statement, for what else does growing productive power of labour mean than that less immediate labour is required to create a greater product, and that therefore social wealth expresses itself more and more in the conditions of labour created by labour itself?—this fact appears from the standpoint of capital not in such a way that one of the moments of social activity—objective labour—becomes the ever more powerful body of the other moment, of subjective, living labour, but rather—and this is important for wage labour—that the objective conditions of labour assume an ever more colossal independence, repre- sented by its very extent, opposite living labour, and that social wealth confronts labour in more powerful portions as an alien and dominant power. The emphasis comes to be placed not on the state of being *objectified,* but on the state of being *alienated,* dispossessed, sold {*Der Ton wird gelegt nicht auf das* **Vergegenständlichtsein,** *sondern das* **Entfremdet-,** *Entäussert-, Veräussertsein};* on the condition that the monstrous objective power which social labour itself erected opposite itself as one of its moments belongs

not to the worker, but to the personified conditions of production, i.e. to capital. To the extent that, from the standpoint of capital and wage labour, the creation of the objective body of activity happens in antithesis to the immediate labour capacity—that this process of objectification in fact appears as a process of dispossession from the standpoint of labour or as appropriation of alien labour from the standpoint of capital—to that extent, this twisting and inversion {Verdrehung und Verkehrung} is a real {phenomenon}, not a merely supposed one existing merely in the imagination of the workers and the capitalists. But obviously this process of inversion is a merely historical necessity, a necessity for the development of the forces of production solely from a specific historic point of departure, or basis, but in no way an absolute necessity of production; rather, a vanishing one, and the result and the inherent purpose of this process is to suspend this basis itself, together with this form of the process. The bourgeois economists are so much cooped up within the notions belonging to a specific historic stage of social development that the necessity of the objectification of the powers of social labour appears to them as inseparable from the necessity of their alienation vis-à-vis living labour. But with the suspension of the immediate character of living labour, as merely individual, or as general merely internally or merely externally, with the positing of the activity of individuals as immediately general or social activity, the objective moments of production are stripped of this form of alienation; they are thereby posited as property, as the organic social body within which the individuals reproduce themselves as individuals, but as social individuals. The conditions which allow them to exist in this way in the reproduction of their life, in their productive life's process, have been posited only by the historic economic process itself; both the objective and the subjective conditions, which are only the two distinct forms of the same conditions.

The worker's propertylessness, and the ownership of living labour by objectified labour, or the appropriation of alien labour by capital—both merely expressions of the same relation from opposite poles—are fundamental conditions of the bourgeois mode of production, in no way accidents irrelevant to it. These modes of distribution are the relations of production themselves, but sub specie distributionis. It is therefore highly absurd when e.g. J. St. Mill says (Principles of Political Economy, 2nd ed., London, 1849, Vol. I, p. 240): 'The laws and conditions of the production of wealth partake of the character of physical truths . . . It is not so with the distribution of wealth. That is a matter of human institutions solely.' (p. 239, 240.) The 'laws and conditions' of the production of wealth and the laws of the 'distribution of wealth' are the same laws under different forms, and both change, undergo the same historic process; are as such only moments of a historic process.

It requires no great penetration to grasp that, where e.g. free labour or wage labour arising out of the dissolution of bondage is the point of departure, there machines can only *arise* in antithesis to living labour, as property alien to it, and as power hostile to it; i.e. that they must confront it as capital. But it is just as easy to perceive that machines will not cease to be agencies of social production when they become e.g. property of the associated workers. In the first case, however, their distribution, i.e. that they *do not belong* to the worker, is just as much a condition of the mode of production founded on wage labour. In the second case the changed distribution would start from a *changed* foundation of production, a new foundation first created by the process of history.

One can develop no more clearly the Marxist thesis. The revolutionary subject *emerges* from the relation with capital at this stage. The inversion that this—the subject—operates against capital is an operation which is not even any longer a reappropriation. Reappropriation is a term which becomes insufficient and ambiguous when there are new foundations. *Auto-determination of the subject thus qualitatively modifies the process.* The subject deploys its power to the point of reappropriating the objectified labor itself—which until now was the enemy of living labor—and is henceforth dominated by living labor. There is no more room, at this stage of the analysis, for themes of demystification: the thematic inversion is so radical that it creates an incommensurable distance from the misery of exploitation.

We arrive then at the end of Marx's discourse on communism in the *Grundrisse*. As we have seen, *communism is in no case a product of capitalist development, it is its radical inversion.* It is the demystification which becomes the reversal of capitalist development. Communism is neither a teleology of the capitalist system nor its catastrophe. It is a new subject which takes form, which transforms reality and destroys capital. Communism is thus a concept that we can only formulate within the form of the transition. The movement of inversion is powerful, so much so that the form of the transition is not simply antithetical, but rather constitutive of a new subject, and of its potential for total transformation. To mark this transformation in the most rigorous way possible, Marx insists on the abolition of work. Work which is liberated is liberation from work. The creativity of communist work has no relation with the capitalist organization of labor. Living labor—by liberating itself, by reconquering *its own use value,* against exchange value— opens a universe of needs of which work can become a part only eventually. And in this case, it is a question of work as essential, collective, nonmystified, communist work: instead of work as capitalist construction. The reversal is total, it *allows no kind of homology whatsoever.* It's a new subject. Rich and joyous. *Marx said it:* there is no need to exaggerate it. Marx said it ten times, a hundred times. The only funny thing about the whole affair is the shame that too many—almost all—Marxists need to repeat—to read these passages. As for the rest there is nothing funny, there is only the enormous pain of the struggle to abolish work.

Beginning there, we can make a few remarks on the consequences that result from this way of approaching communism. Which is to say the central space occupied by the abolition of work in the thematic of transition implies the need to examine the theoretical conditions peculiar to this articulation. We must now, faced with all the current stereotypes, pose the problem of the relation between communism and planning. What is this problem doing in the articulation of the "abolition of work and of the transition"? There is no doubt that Marx considered planning as a quality of communism. Nevertheless, too often based on Engels, this relation has been understood either in the simple terms of socialization "statilization" of the relations of production, or in terms of "superior economic rationality." It is evident if we examine the *Grundrisse* that this is not the point. Communism is planning only in so far as it is the planned abolition of work. *Planning is an expression (and a condition) of the associated character of work which must suppress the alien characters of command and its reification.* It is thus an economic rationality which is *not superior, but different.* So different that there can be no homology between them. When the conditions and the objective of the abolition of work do not exist, planning is only a new form of capitalist command—its socialist form. It is here that the *Marxist critique of socialism* exerts all its force. Socialism is not—and can in no case be—a stage or a passage toward communism. Socialism is the highest form, the superior form of the economic rationality of capital, of the rationality of profit. It still thrives on the law of value, but carried to a degree of centralization and of general synthesis which connects the forms of socialist planned economic management to the functioning of the political and juridical machinery of the State. *Socialism keeps alive, and generalizes, the law of value. The abolition of work is the inverse mark of the law of value.* This question of the abolition of work renders impossible all homogeneity between capitalist planning and communist planning. We must again strongly criticize the dialectical logic which authorizes levels of homogeneity in the development of oppositions; it is on the contrary the logic of radical dualism that we must see at work. The extinction of the law of value—which the "Fragment on Machines" allowed us to see in the *Grundrisse*—is at the base of the transformation of its functioning (in the capitalist involution) into the law of pure command. But the expression of the functioning of the logic of antagonism is already there. Each relationship, each movement of homogeneity, each element of relative rationality is suppressed by the disappearance of the law of value. The continuity of the capitalist relation is definitively broken. There is only the logic of antagonism—based on opposed and irreducible subjects—that can function here. Each polarity possesses its own criteria for planning. An independent planning. *Worker and proletarian auto-valorization is the planning of the abolition of work.* The saturation of social spaces produced by the socialist planning of capitalism is a result of monstrous fragility: each segment is contradictory, not only with regard to the immediacy of the antagonism that it reveals but also with respect to the framework of opposition, of the planning to abolish work, to which it is linked. The refusal of work, its planned organization by the working and proletarian class, measures the quantity and quality of the transition, measures not this stupid approach of utopia, but the concrete constituting process determined by the subject. The process thus undergoes a displacement; really a dislocation. Planning becomes something irreducible to capital, socialism a term (when it represents an economic category) irreducible to communism. The communist subject takes form in this process, on the same base as these radical displacements. Its *multilaterality* is not only rich in needs, it is also (as the theory of class composition teaches us) rich with successive syntheses.

The analysis returns to the subject and to its constitutive force. Beginning with the refusal of work—which has transformed itself into a planned and rational abolition of work—we have seen the subject pose the conditions of its own self-constitution. But the outline is of a strategic order. The *refusal of work* constitutes the subject—in that it projects into the world, in that it *constitutes a mode of production.* It is not up to Marx, nor to us, to offer previews of this subject. What we can say is simply that the communist mode of production includes the totality of the social and economic determinations which belong to the definition of each of these modes of production. We can only embrace the specter of future relations in all its breadth at the level of totality. It is important to underline that—in this precise situation of the extinction of the rationalizing function of the law of value— the measure, the proportions, and the finality of the development of the communist mode of production emerge entirely from the refusal of work, from the subjective practice of the suppression of work which is more and more planned collectively.

To reintroduce the idea of totality does not mean that we place all discourse on communism at the level of totality, it does not mean that we reduce the whole of development to the unfolding of strategy. In fact, it means the contrary. The refusal of work shows—with the totality of the project which characterizes it, and in a way that is happily contradictory with this project— a great *multiplicity* of aspects, a great wealth and liberty of movements of a complex autonomy. Each step toward communism is a moment of extension and of expansion of the whole wealth of differences. *Differences and ruptures.* I would like, at this point, to suggest the consideration of the explosive metaphors of Marx (the capitalist world must "explode" etc.). It is a theme which comes back continually, not as a mark of a certain catastrophism, but rather as the growth of the movement of liberation of the subject toward communism. The rebellion, the subversion which is rooted in the necessity of the antagonism, forms a process of liberation by acts which are just as important as the totality of the process. How else can we understand a revolutionary mechanism whose method is the suppression of work, unless it is as a process of liberation? How can we imagine the totality of communism if it is not as a risk which is continually assumed and repeated in all its plenitude? Communism in the form of the transition is a process of which we know the origin, with which we share the path. No one can tell us, outside of the way that we proceed and fight, what will be the conclusion. No homology in objective terms can hold: *the communist future can only be constructed.* All of its quality resides in the solidity of its foundations, in the power of the project which animates it.

This result, to which Marx's considerations on communism come, appears convincing to me. There is no doubt that the framework has changed from what we had at the beginning of this analysis. We have left this joining of paths which from time to time held communism back between the links of objective necessity and of its catastrophic development, or even in the rose fingers of utopia.

While digging into these themes, while pausing on the subjective articulation of the process, while displacing the emphasis from the theoretical to the practical level, *the theme of communism has melted into that of the transition,* it has rooted itself in the antagonistic nature of Marxist logic. All the determinations, little by little, have converged toward this new space, around this new process. All the remnants of a dialectical, continuist logic have disappeared. Let us admit nevertheless that often Marx's examination of communism is marked by dialectical residues and allusions: but these are not decisive "in the last instance." On the contrary, the path is sketched— on the basis of many methodological and substantial determinations—in terms of antagonism. The center of Marx's path is to be found there, where we have noted the passage from *demystification to inversion.* When the inversion exerts all its power on all the levels and categories essential to Marxist analysis and invests categories like "money, abstract labor, machines, science," etc., there is no longer the shadow of any ambiguity. *The dialectic is returned to capital. Materialism becomes the only horizon, entirely animated by the logic of antagonism and by subjectivity.* The communist transition follows at this stage the path which leads from auto-valorization to auto-determination, to an ever greater and more total independence of the proletarian subject, to the multilaterality of its way. The transition is the terrain of the final demystification of all utopias, be they idealist or scientist; it founds communism as it traverses subjectivity in all its complexity, in all its multilaterality. It is the refusal and the inversion of all dialectic. It is Marx who demystifies himself as well. Marx beyond Marx. *The content of this process is perfectly adequate to its form: the antagonistic and subjective process of the suppression of work.* Communism is the destruction of capital in every sense of the term. It is non-work, it is the subjective, collective and proletarian planning of the suppression of exploitation. It is the positivity of a free constitution of subjectivity. All utopias become impossible.

Lesson Nine
Capitalist Development &
Revolutionary Class

The problem of the dynamic of communism. ☐ Its positive and negative determinations: from the crisis of the law of value to the reappearance of use value. (Indetermination.) ☐ Theoretical conditions necessary to resolve the problem: social production as productive circulation; productive circulation and its contradictions as the foundation and constituting process of the proletarian social individual. ☐ Conditions of method and limits to the Marxist discourse. ☐ Displacement of the category of "productive labor": the revolutionary class. ☐ New historical conditions so that the transition can be translated into the dynamic of communism. ☐ Self-valorization, the theoretico-practical kernal of the project. ☐ Communism as motor and agent of destruction of capitalist development. ☐ (For the critique of communism: the categories of the overthrow of capital.)

The power to invert capitalist development that communism, with its own dynamic and process, sets to work, is immense. But that must not make us forget the dampening effect of the dialectical residue of Marxist discourse. We must liberate ourselves from it and give a definition, and explication of the dynamic of communism, that is not generic. *We need to achieve a new exposition of communism through the form of the transition.* We have clarified the logic of antagonism, the plural logic at work in Marx's discourse. We have seen it literally explode. We have seen it clear away numerous obstacles that are the stubborn fruit of dialectical habits. Let us now see how that logic is simultaneously reinforced by certain general determinations, upheld by some original theoretical conditions, and verified by new historical conditions. Let us now seek to see how the analysis advances, by displacing itself theoretically and liberating itself from its limits. To root the analysis of the transition in materiality will signify that we will truly speak of the dynamic

171

of communism. Whatever has been the power of the inversion—and we have seen that it is immense—it is however only an allusion, a risk, an horizon. To materialize communism by transforming it into a process: there is the new problem. We need to go to the heart of that problem.

And, in fact, there are diverse determinations which can help us do this. Above all those determinations which have a negative function—which emphasize the crisis in capitalist development, but which at the same time concretely define the framework. The Law of Value dies. The force and the efficiency with which it appears, at the level of the socialization of capital, such as we have seen in the *Grundrisse,* are demystified. The Law of Value passes over from appearance to misery: both are efficient, but the first form is rational, the second only constraining. There is no longer any relationship with the (average) time of (abstract) labor, there is no longer any determinant proportionality between necessary labor and surplus labor. The progressive appearance of the Law of Exploitation depended on that. Once capital and global labor power have completely become social classes—each independent and capable of self-valorizing activity—then the Law of Value can only represent the power *(potenza)* and the violence of the relationship. It is the synthesis of the relationships of force. All positive determinations have become negative. Command, the planning of command, the forced over-determination of crisis: there is the Law of Value at the stage of the "Fragment on Machines." The Law recognizes its own emptiness and defines the negativity of those who are opposed to it as antagonism. The appearance, the illusion of synthesis, must recognize itself as being pure appearance and illusion. It is not a synthesis that is produced, but an act of strength that forces a conclusion. Thus the pole which is that of the working class liberates itself, makes itself independent. We can see there an enormous power that corresponds to the inversion. But does this supposition take into account the real power that it expresses? We can found a positive dialectic of development on this moment of independence and of liberation; but the movement of liberation tells us nothing of the content or of the positivity of this liberation. Nothing of its dynamic, of its process. *The truth that we can deduce from the extinction of the Law of Value, and of its metamorphosis into a Law of Command, is a partial truth.* The shortening of the horizon of exchange value risks having as a consequence the rendering opaque of any framework of reference. (It is not by accident that many, faced with the depth of the crisis of capitalism, cry out warnings of the rebirth of fascism at every corner of the street. We will not resolve the problem by denying it. If the allusion to communism is founded only on the extension of the Law of Value, it will remain a fruitless, unpassable allusion.)

On the other hand it is certain that the extinction of the Law of Value effectively liberates *a real space for proletarian independence.* A space constellated and nebulous but nevertheless real, one which accumulates use values, needs, and more or less immediate acts. But *the simple demand for use value does not*

by itself result in a solution, in something determinate. It has been by remaining
at this level that many in the history of Marxism have come to a dead stop
in the theme of transition, have gotten stuck in an unsolvable scientific
puzzle. It has seemed desirable that the movement of inversion has, in itself,
the necessary force to describe the path to communism. As a result we have
seen the exaltation of one characteristic of bourgeois thought by recuperating—in the description of communism—the framework, reversed but still
homologous, of the market. Capitalism, crisis, subversion: the unspecified
effect was the creation of a free but empty space. Empty: it is filled only
by a new spontaneity, overthrown and reversed. Just like the market. In
this framework, "the universal individual" is an empty positivity. A dialectic
of inversion that continues to live in the immediacy of use value has no
significance. Certainly, here the determination wants to be positive—but
it fails. The process of inversion is qualitatively different from the process
which produces the crisis of value and of its Law: the second process has
only a critical and allusive potency. It is not simply because of this that the
first process fulfills its task; it is not satisfied with the inversion. The attempts
of those theoreticians who have tried to find a solution to this puzzle have
not been very satisfying. The most famous of these attempts has been that
based on the idea of the *overdetermination of process,* which consists of opposing
to the capitalist violence of the synthesis the proletarian violence of the
inversion. But what can this extreme tension of proletarian violence mean—
when it is not organized on the material power *(potenza)* of real inversion—
other than the tragically efficient and terrible reappearance of the domination
of value? By staying purely and simply at the level of the inversion, we can
not succeed in liberating ourselves from the emptiness of a use value totality
which is immediately indifferent, and we fall, inevitably, into voluntarist
and terrorist solutions to the problem. *Use value, taken by itself, can resolve
nothing.* The immediacy of the child who denounces is just as naked as is
the king. By saying this I am not confusing one with the other. I hold
myself resolutely on one side. But I am not, because of that, satisfied with
this immediacy. It is a beginning, a rediscovered origin, a felicitous moment.
But if it is not transformed into the dynamic of communism, it is only
empty and dangerous. The only element it has in common with the dynamic
of communism and with the process of inversion is to affirm the violence
of the passage, to demystify all possibilities of pacifist hypotheses, to pose
force as the decisive element. It is in this that we find its primordial link
to communism. Proletarian violence, insofar as it is a positive allusion to
communism, is an essential element of the dynamic of communism. To
suppress the violence of this process can only deliver it—tied hand and
foot—to capital. Violence is a first, immediate, and vigorous affirmation of
the necessity of communism. It does not provide the solution, but it is
fundamental. It is perhaps the only means, insufficient but appropriate, for
use value to emerge on this level of analysis (and on the interpreted reality)

from the indistinct horizon of behaviors. Proletarian violence is a symptom of communism.

   We cannot pose and resolve the problem of the dynamic of communism by placing it on very strong theoretical and categorical oppositions. The only result, as we have seen, would be indeterminacy. Approaching the terrain of a solution, the adequate conditions of a solution, implies deciphering concretely the terrain of the dynamic of communism. And with appropriate terms. It is not a question of following indefinitely the transformations in the class composition and the modes of production, a path which privileges static analysis, within which each change in worker behavior hypostatizes abstractly the definite categories. "Bewitch the method, freeze research." Nor is it a question of being satisfied with an objective definition of the crisis of the Law of Value and of the totalitarian extension of the sequences of power to the whole society. "After me, the flood!" Marx is conscious of all that. In the *Grundrisse* he poses the problem and defines the conditions of solution. The elements of a solution can only still be terribly far off, something which limits his approach. Nevertheless the solution is, after all, indicated with a very great precision and a very strong approximation. Even if he cannot give it in a very determined form, Marx comes close to the solution to the problem of the dynamic of communism. Let's look at this at various points. In the *Grundrisse* Marx follows from the beginning the theme of surplus value, up to the crisis and to catastrophe, up until the moment when the antagonism traverses each of the categories of exploitation and finds an historical anchor. Next, after a second great movement of his analysis, Marx takes the theme of circulation to show the great antagonistic social forces at work up to the final explosion of communism. From the two sides it is still an abstract discourse. From the two sides, in order to arrive at communism, there must be a jump. Even when the vision of the path is, as in the second phase of the reasoning, subjectivized, there too it is the triumph of indeterminacy. *Marx is conscious of this limit and wants to go beyond it.* If he can not go beyond it, his whole theoretical approach risks falling into objectivism, a deformation of method from which not even *Capital* is exempt. The indeterminacy at which the analysis arrives must not engender a lack of resolution. Now, says Marx, let's try to put together under the same yoke the process of surplus value and its enormous and odious quantity of exploitation (and the extreme logic of antagonism it produces)—let us try to put that together with the other process, that of socialization within the circulation of capital and of global labor power. The antagonism must become social, *global labor power must become a revolutionary class* against capitalist development. Throughout the final part of the *Grundrisse* Marx tries hard to reach this new level of exposition. Let us say immediately that the results are not completely satisfying. We will see why.

But they are not less consistent. It is here, in reality, at this stage of the analysis, that on the side of capital the category of profit takes form, and on the side of the working class the categories of social antagonism and self-valorization begin to emerge. Within this process, we can correctly tackle the problem of the dynamic of communism: for Marx and for ourselves. The fact that Marx himself could only achieve partial results must not block us, but rather, on the contrary, it should stimulate us to follow his hypothesis.

Putting together, within the perspective of proletarian subjectivity, the thematics of exploitation and circulation constitutes the fundamental theoretical condition for solving the problem of the dynamic of communism. Already within the perspective of capital, Marx had advanced in this direction. As we saw in Lesson 5, the definition of the category of profit—whose most developed definition is to be found in the pages we are now considering—was derived from the close conjugation of the theory of surplus value with that of circulation. The *Ausgleichung* of exploitation, its internal equalization at the mean, the construction in this mode of the law of capitalist development, is born from the distension of the relation of exploitation within the social circuit, or better, in the circuit of the socialization of capitalist production. The *Ausgleichung* of subversion and of proletarian valorization must take the same path, but in the other direction. And taking account of this reversal is only a beginning. There is no possible homology between the two paths, that of capital and that of the proletariat. This decides the logic of the antagonism. The moment of inversion ruptures all possibility of homology, and liberates absolute diversity. We must, however, examine this moment of reversal. It is not insignificant that it appears, and can only appear—as we saw—there where the law of exploitation dissolves itself into circulation, and there where productive circulation transforms itself into the antagonism of social subjects. Marx—within the historical limits inherent in his project, but with the force of exploration and anticipation which characterizes him—is able to advance on the two terrains. He fully resolves the first problem (which is to say that of the constitution of productive circulation) and approaches a solution to the second (that of antagonism at the social level). If he resolves the first problem, it is because the theoretical base which he uses is the same that serves to pose the problem of profit. If he can only *approach* the solution to the second problem, it is because at this point the theoretical base is not sufficient. As long as one could accumulate, by drawing on the arsenal of givens, the means of defining the independence of the proletarian subject, Marx accumulated. But here, in order to advance, there is only a *mature revolutionary practice that can allow us to displace the problem completely,* to fully develop the subject. The tendency wants to verify itself in a concrete determination, exactly as abstraction seeks to determine itself. The historical limits to the experience of class struggle block this process where the tendency verifies itself. The power of the analysis can nevertheless push forward the tendency, can expose it in such a provocative way within reality that it will only require very little for workers' struggles to realize the fully determined category that Marx indicated: that of the "other" workers' movement. But let us leave this until later.

Money—negative relationship with circulation. When Marx begins to introduce this theme he sees immediately its great importance. According to a first interpretation, this affirmation signifies that circulation is not sufficient to money, that money maintains a relation with circulation that does not exhaust the meaning of circulation. Circulation, in fact, is an intermediary of production. In this sense, money is presented positively as an *"instrument of production,* since circulation no longer appears in its primitive simplicity, as quantitative exchange, but as a process of production, as a real metabolism. Thus money is itself stamped as a particular moment of this process of production" (*Grundrisse,* p. 217; 130). But here is a second point to explore. Negative money becomes positive. Even more, this mutation must change the general concept of circulation. "The *constant continuity* of the process, the unobstructed and fluid transition of value from one form into the other, or from one phase of the process into the next, appears as a fundamental condition for production based on capital to a much greater degree than for all earlier forms of production" (*Grundrisse,* p. 535; 433). In this situation, the power of capital shows an unbelievable fluidity, interchangeability, inventiveness.

Before everything, from an objective point of view, within the perspective of capital itself:

> But while capital thus, as the whole of circulation, is *circulating capital,* is the process of going from one phase into the other, it is at the same time, within each phase, posited in a specific aspect, restricted to a particular form, which is the negation of itself as the subject of the whole movement. Therefore, capital in each of its particular phases is the negation of itself as the subject of all the various metamorphoses. Not-circulating capital. *Fixed capital,* actually *fixated* capital, fixated in one of the different particular aspects, phases, through which it must move. As long as it persists in one of these phases—[as long as] the phase itself does not appear as fluid transition—and each of them has its duration, [then] it is not circulating, [but] fixated. As long as it remains in the production process it is not capable of circulating; and it is virtually devalued. As long as it remains in circulation, it is not capable of producing, not capable of positing surplus value, not capable of engaging in the process as capital. As long as it cannot be brought to market, it is fixated as product. As long as it has to remain on the market, it is fixated as commodity. As long as it cannot be exchanged for conditions of production, it is fixated as money. Finally, if the conditions of production remain in their form

as conditions and do not enter into the production process, it is again fixated and devalued. As the subject moving through all phases, as the moving unity, the unity-in-process of circulation and production, capital is *circulating* capital; capital as restricted into any of its phases, as posited in its *divisions,* is *fixated* capital, *tied-down* capital. As circulating capital it fixates itself, and as fixated capital it circulates [*Grundrisse,* pp. 620–21; 514–15].

Let us now see what follows from the subjective point of view. In fact, capital appears here as subject, as a dynamic and creative unity. *But capital is a relation. Inside this relation, proletarian antagonism must develop itself to attain full and complete subjectivity.* The subsumption of circulation by the production of capital must liberate the antagonism at this same level. To these conditions of socialization (which we examined in Lesson 6) we must add that the *emergence of the other subject,* of the *proletarian subject, can't but extend itself to the whole sphere of circulation.* At the same time the movement of the proletarian subject is such that it engenders a complex dynamic of natural and historical powers that confront it. Naturally, this is a general definition. But a stable one. At this degree of socialization, production is so profoundly mixed with circulation that they constitute a capitalist relation whose social efficiency continues to grow. It is precisely at this stage that the proletarian subject also takes a social dimension.

If social production subsumes circulation and poses it as productive circulation—and therefore also proposes at this level an equally profound and extensive conception of the movement of the working class—in sum, if all of that is given, we must proceed to see how Marx works on this canvas and what results he draws concerning the fundamental problems that we have posed. *Does there thus exist an area of expansion for the socialized class that the level of antagonism has rendered independent?* To say that Marx resolved this problem would be (as we have recalled) false. But that takes nothing from the fact that Marx constantly comes close to the solution, that he is expressly looking for it. Furthermore, it is true that the results of this research are partial. But we must add that, if we have only approximations that are essentially negative, if they take form primarily in the analysis of the new contradictions that socialized capital has engendered, it is always easy to see that these are not residual results, not simply negations of the positive definition of capital and of its development. These are scattered elements, but nevertheless true, of a compact class reality that we have begun, through the contradictions, to grasp. Their episodic character does not prevent them from being significant. It is thus time to examine how, in the face of and in the interior of productive circulation, the subject—as proletarian subject—conquers autonomous space and dynamics.

The *first point* which requires our attention is Marx's examination of the contradiction between exchange value and use-value in productive circulation. He notes:

> The *particular nature of use value*, in which the value exists, or which now appears as capital's body, here appears as itself a *determinant* of the *form* and of the action of capital; as giving one capital a particular property as against another; as particularizing it. As we have already seen in several instances, nothing is therefore more erroneous than to overlook that the distinction between use value and exchange value, which falls outside the characteristic economic form in simple circulation, to the extent that it is *realized* there, falls outside it in general [*Grundrisse*, p. 646; 539–40].

We must concretize this analysis:

> One and the same relation appears sometimes in the form of use value and sometimes in that of exchange value, but at different stages and with a different meaning. To use is to consume, whether for production or consumption. Exchange is the mediation of this act through a social process. Use can be posited as, and can be, a mere consequence of exchange; then again, exchange can appear as merely a moment of use, etc. [*Grundrisse*, p. 647; 540].

In summary: "Use value itself plays a role as an economic category" (*Grundrisse*, p. 646; 540). What sense must we give to this enlarged field of action of use value? Certainly not that of recognizing—as "Monsieur Proudhon and his social-sentimentalists" would like—that exchange value and use value are identical at this degree of socialization. On the contrary, the social extension of capitalist circulation makes exchange value and use value appear above all as *contradictory*, always contradictory. The most important case of this dynamic contradiction is described in the *chapter on small-scale circulation* (*Grundrisse*, pp. 673–78; 565–71) that we examined at length in Lesson 7. But this relationship can also become antagonistic, as we have already seen. In fact, capitalist reproduction must submit here to a double movement: on one side, reproduction through valorization, on the other, the reproduction that the working class operates on and of itself. The difference, which is contradictory by principle, can become antagonistic as it develops.

When does the *possibility* of antagonism become *actualized?* It seems to me that this development begins to appear when Marx returns the analysis of the contradiction to the question of the nature of the class composition, of the nature of the quality of exploitation. "As to production founded on capital, the greatest absolute mass of necessary labour together with the greatest relative mass of surplus labour appears as a condition, regarded absolutely" (*Grundrisse*, p. 608; 502). It is the relationship between mass and rate of surplus value which is in question. A relationship which (as we saw in Lesson 5) is completely internal to the theme of the crisis; capital is pushed by the law of profit (as law of appropriation) to extend its power to the maximum, but at the same time it finds itself completely exposed to suffer the countercoup of exploitation. When the law disappears from the abstract horizon of the "tendency" to descend to the level of historical relations between classes in struggle, necessary labor, its massification, the articulation between its definition and use value—all that completely subjectivizes our relation. It gives it a maximum subjective intensity. It is here that many of the threads that we have followed begin to come together: necessary labor, use value, up to and including the negative determination derived from the extinction of the law of value. *On this level, capitalist relations are reduced to a relation of force.* Not only because capital fails to impose the law of value, and thus to reaffirm its own legitimacy, but above all because the working-class side of the relation has subjectivized itself and rises up as an antagonistic force.

We must now consider a *third element:* it is an important element because it allows us to make progress on the question of working class composition at this stage of socialization. Now, Marx asks himself, at this stage of the analysis, in the presence of such a strong interpenetration of circulation and production, before such dramatically accentuated antagonisms—what happens? The most important phenomenon to underline is that in these conditions the function of intermediary played by the equivalent is reduced. Capital, which has always seen the time of circulation as an obstacle for production, which has always tended to reduce to the minimum the contradiction between the time of production and the time of circulation, finds itself stuck in a relationship of force which, while needing to continue the game, also sees the *mortal character* of this solution. "It is the necessary tendency of capital to strive to equate circulation time to 0; i.e. to suspend itself, since it is capital itself which posits circulation time as a determinant moment of production time. It is the same as to suspend the necessity of exchange, of money, and of the division of labour resting on them, hence capital itself" (*Grundrisse,* p. 629; 522). Horizontal equivalence must dominate circulation, just as vertical equivalence must dominate exploitation: *one can not follow both paths at once.* The simultaneity of circulation and production, the antagonism in production, renders impossible the attribution of a sign to equivalence. They destroy all the functions of control which can influence these contradictions before they become antagonistic: and especially those of money. (See on this subject *Grundrisse,* pp. 659 and following; 551.) Inversely, the power of opposition that we have seen root itself in use value and in the massification of necessary labor, finds here an enormous space of collective liberation. The more constraining and efficient aspect of capitalist control withers: that of the determination of inequality by the use of equivalents.

But this is not enough. A new contradiction appears here. We know that fixed capital contains the potential for reproducing the totality of society. We also know that it does not enter into circulation as use value (*Grundrisse*, p. 717; 604). We also know that fixed capital commands, organizes hierarchically, and renders functional all the mechanisms of reproduction of capitalist society. But we also know that this reproduction is only possible under the pressure of human needs (*Grundrisse*, pp. 741–43; 629–30). Now, at the point where we have arrived, these relations become impossible, because on the one side capital no longer possesses the key to interpret development (equivalence), and on the other, workers' use value becomes very strongly antagonistic as it develops the sense of its own subjectivity. *Fixed capital opposes itself as an enemy to worker subjectivity. Tension is at its maximum, it becomes the theoretical base of a struggle where each of the adversaries suppresses the other.* The contradiction, which in the beginning only appeared as a possibility, has shown its reality, to the point of transforming itself into antagonism. The terms of antagonism, rigidified in the expectation of violence, have henceforth as their basis the exclusion of the adversary.

We have made a good forward step. We begin to see how the dynamic of communism is an independent process within the contradictions of mature capitalist development. The dynamic of communism rests on the emergence of subjectivity allowed by the crisis of mature capitalist development— passively, simply allowing it space—but which also finds in this crisis the possibility to expand and enrich itself. *Capitalist production, when it takes over society, renders inextricable the linkage of production and circulation.* Circulation and production become, little by little, concepts which imply each other in the manner of production and reproduction. The social antagonism of the capital relation eventually ruptures this *compact universe* by exploding. *The concept and the reality of the working class are displaced and reach the level where this explosion occurs.* It is not simply the new antagonism between "worker" and "proletarian" which is displaced, but the *composition* of the proletarian class. Within this space, it is a process of collective constitution of the class which develops. It is evident that it is only its recomposition into a unity which gives it a sense. It is evident that only the complex and subjective way in which all these aspects find themselves unified, only the punctual pertinence of the antagonism and its violence, allow this emergence to develop in its totality . . . But that does not imply that we must not also follow the different passages that the pages of the *Grundrisse* have already indicated. The universal individual of the class begins to appear here as an activity which valorizes him/herself through use value, then massifies and raises the value of necessary labor to very rigid levels. His/her power carries in itself the end of all capitalist laws of equivalence, of all possibility of rationally mystifying exploitation. Finally, still in these pages of the *Grundrisse, the process that constitutes the universal individual* presents itself in a totally conflictual relation with the functioning of fixed capital: it is a question of determining who controls it, who commands the necessary intermediary which fixed capital needs to reproduce society. In the same process where the social, universal individual constitutes him/herself, he/she shows the capacity and the strength for this command.

Communism thus begins to descend from the clouds, insofar as the inversion of the capitalist process—which the Marxist method requires for defining communism—is achieved, and it invades the horizon of the constituting process. The universal individual *can no longer appear* as the fruit of a humanist nostalgia: *he/she is the product of a materialist process* and we must connect to the materialist character of this analysis, every leap of quality, every qualitative deepening of the subject. A last remark: there is nothing "socialist" in this process. In socialism there is only the development of mature capitalism. Communism does not come in a "subsequent period," it springs up contemporaneously as a process constituting an enormous power of antagonism and of real supersession.

Nevertheless, we remain with an approximation. I mean that Marx shows us a path more than he proceeds down it himself. The theoretical elements he gives us are more ideas tossed out than systematic developments. *Even if this path which goes from the inversion to constitution is of fundamental importance.* From this point of view, the most consistent limit of Marxist thought is perhaps of a methodological order. This means that this formidable unification of the theory of surplus value with that of productive circulation is not able to completely displace its own terms. Each time that we meet these great theoretical moments we have the impression that an enormous force of gravity holds us back, preventing us from penetrating the quality of the synthesis, from arriving at a new understanding of the composing elements. So that, each time that we seem to have finally traversed a segment of the constituting process, we find Marx at the same moment giving us a new illustration—with theoretical improvements at an extraordinary level— either of the theory of surplus value, or of the theory of productive circulation. The displacement is not conscious of itself, the results are not able to stand by themselves. And yet, Marx possesses the instruments of the *neue Darstellung,* he was drawn to this operation of the displacement of terms which might have allowed him to transform the basis of his research and to attain the end he sought. Just as his dialectical logic has been replaced by the logic of separation, which permitted him—around the wage, small-scale circulation, the theme of needs—to construct the antagonistic figure of the subject, similarly, the relation between subjectivity and cycle, the passage from the law of value to the law of self-valorization, the exhaustion of all the possibilities carried in the operation of going beyond the law of value— all this must have been able to appear, must be theoretically possible. And it was in part, as we have seen. But not completely. In fact, the Marxist method remains at the limits traced by the historically possible experience, and the most advanced theoretical figure that it draws remains at this limit. As we have already remarked with respect to the "Book on the Wage," and even more so here with relation to the *Book on the Constitution of the Social Individual of Communism, it is the lag of workers' organization that blocks the further development of theory.* We can almost suspect Marx of being afraid of falling into utopianism. Of being afraid of the non-commensurability of theory and of organization, of possible organization.

Two remarks on this subject. *First,* a new verification of what we already said in Lesson 1, that is: there is never with Marx, and above all in the *Grundrisse,* a theoretical attitude detached not so much from practice (from the possibility of verification in practice) as from organization (from the possibility of conversion into organization). That appears to be foolish if we remember the political conditions under which Marx worked. And yet, that's the way it was. And it is a good lesson. The *second* observation that we need to make, with reference to the limits implicit in the method, here too is of extraordinary theoretical consequence: the process of self-valorization and of constitution of the communist individual succeeds in displacing not only the general terms of discourse but also the central motor of its development. Which means that the theme of constitution forces us to penetrate into a theoretical phase where the concrete determination of proletarian behavior, the collective praxis of the proletariat becomes a theoretical motor, the woof of a theoretical proposition, a subject with an extraordinary power of freedom and self-presentation. At this stage of theoretical displacement, it is the presupposition that changes. It is a mutation of the subject that is produced. Without a concrete experience of this mutation, it is difficult to go beyond simple allusion. We would not want to attribute to Marx a clear and sharp consciousness of this evolution of the theory, and thus justify in some way its limits. I repeat, these limits derive from the lag of workers' organization. Besides, the theoretical imagination of Marx went well beyond this, as we have seen. This said, it remains true that the *neue Darstellung* in this process— henceforth ripe with the constitution of the collective individual of communism—must transform itself, more and more, into a *Selbst-Darstellung.*

Let us return again to this limit of Marxist thought. Even when Marx conjugates most narrowly production and reproduction, *he is not able to illuminate,* in sufficiently explicit terms, *the social labor process in all its materiality.* The relationship between production and reproduction still remains fairly generic. That is, Marx shows us how the system reproduces itself and how the antagonism reproduces itself, on the whole, but he never redescends to examine *the nature of the labor process* at this stage of productive circulation, nor does he examine the nature of productive labor. Now, let us pause to examine this concept of *productive labor*. What Marx tells us we have often had occasion to examine. Productive labor is that which produces *surplus labor*. With this we are in agreement. The problem appears when we seek out where we can find *surplus value* and what are its circuits of production. Now, when production and reproduction are so closely mixed one with the other, we can no longer distinguish productive labor from reproductive labor. Productive circulation gathers, in the *assembly line of social capital,* all social work defined as directly or indirectly, immediately or mediately productive. Here average, social abstract labor, which forms the very first categories of Marxist analysis, displaces itself to take a very dense historical dimension, a concrete dimension: which is itself an element of the constitution of the universal individual of communism. The extension of the concept and of the reality of productive labor, to circulation, to reproduction, forces the appearance not only of the historical character but also of the multiple variety of the constituting process of the historical individuality of the communist subject. Well, this process in the definition, in the theoretical level that he reached, allowed Marx to accomplish this extension. But he did not do it. In fact, the Marxist definition of productive labor is a reductive definition, which is linked to the socialist axiology of manual labor. It remains conditioned by this axiology even when the theoretical conditions have changed. And how profoundly! There was only one *complete displacement* of the concept of *productive labor* which would permit the definition of the *revolutionary class.* To conserve this socialist axiology in order to define this concept, while all the other equipment and definitions of the system have been displaced forward, was frankly useless and sterile. Marx suffered the noxious effect of the limits of the workers' movement.

But let us continue to examine, on the other side, the theoretical possibilities implicitly contained in the concept of productive labor. Its evolution from production to reproduction through productive circulation is a *precious* index of the development of the *constituting praxis* of the social individual of communism. Within this development, the revolutionary class will be the category whose independent development will include the multiplicity of forms and of productive labor relations and will accumulate them as potential and as alternative powers to capitalist valorization. The *refusal of work,* as the content of communism and as measure of the process of liberation which leads to its realization, appears here, when it is placed in relation with the universality of productive labor, as also having a productive essence. This is due to its exercising of its massified power to destroy the universality of exploitation and to liberate its creative energies, creative energies that the universality of cooperation in production, that the successive displacements of production have produced, have enormously enlarged. *The revolutionary class, by self-valorization, takes on a significance whose intensity and expansion make it appear as the result of development and of its total inversion.* The abstract and generic aspects of the Marxist definition of the universal individual, taken in the literal sense, are here completely eclipsed. We can recuperate here completely, if not to the letter, Marx's method: it is that which leads us to analyse the deepening of productive cooperation, to always consider collective force as a constituting praxis. It seemed at one moment that the formidable expansion of the theoretical framework, an expansion capable of taking into account the antagonism of the whole society, was not able to link up in its own analysis the intensity of the thrust toward the deepening of cooperation and the expression of its power both creative and destructive. But all the necessary conditions to correct this deviation are now present and can be recuperated. In this sense, I think that the definition that Marx gives of the dynamic of communism leads in new directions. The global displacement of all the terms of capitalist development must be simultaneously the displacement of all the terms of the constitution of the subject. This no longer appears as a simple antagonistic pole: rather it appears very much as revolutionary class, wealth, and self-valorization.

To materialize communism, to make it into an historical force more fully than was possible for Marx, is the project for today. Today, where the conditions of capitalist development and the conditions of worker organization have matured. *A project for today, but one that is still based on the theory of Marx.* We can imagine this as a trajectory that the real movement traverses. It is only the real movement that transforms the indication of communism contained in the discourse on the transition into the constituting process: the *dynamic of communism.* It is the further development of capitalism, the maturing of tendencies defined by Marx which gives a reality to the fully developed effort to materialize the definition of communism. In terms of dynamism, of path, in terms of class. It is evident that we are not taking into account here the theme of transition such as we find it in the history of orthodox political Marxism. Here the critique of the political, far from representing a terrain that Marx should have one day covered, is presupposed. The "orthodox" transition is a pure and simple invention, a horrible mystification. In Marxist analysis, the dynamic of communism appears as an antagonistic process which invests the totality of capitalist domination over society and takes over from it the subjective position of the proletariat in order to render it independent, free, rich. The path to traverse becomes a repeated but continuous accumulation of moments of rebellion and of the expression of needs, where subjective functions are distributed which sometimes determine and take over new spaces of valorization. Multilaterality, difference are a substantial attribute of the development of proletarian wealth. Today, we have before our eyes, both the very high level of capitalist integration of society and the wealth of needs and movements of reappropriation of the proletariat: it is at this level that we can varify the Marxist path. And it is there. It is sufficient to have the desire and the strength to see it. It is a path that is a source of permanent war among classes, probably a very long path, material at every point. There is no possibility whatsoever of taking away from the proletariat this process, this path of revolution.

A revolution which has finally recuperated the importance of its definition: a revolution which is based on the materiality of the collective subject. The irreversibility of the path traced by Marxist science is rooted in the materiality of the class composition and strengthens it in its necessary combat—"fatal" combat, Marx says—determined against the enemy. The eternal and boring discussions to discover if it is possible or not (and it is always the latter conclusion which is reached not by passion but by reasoning) are closed. Here there is no decision to take: in the revolution one is or is not, in communism one lives or does not. The decision is forward, in the conditions of the class war.

To materialize communism, to make it an historical force, is thus to have as resolved, in reality, the Marxist problem of its dynamic. We can pose this problem from another point of view and in an equivalent manner, in terms of the composition of class. It is a matter of showing how the composition of class determines in an irreversible manner the direction of the communist movement. All the theoretical conditions are now brought together. The problem is posed from the historical point of view and we can only resolve it through a constitutive phenomenology of collective praxis which is able to recuperate in itself the determinacy of the historical development of the class, given the present conditions of class composition. Not to celebrate them: but for exploring the concrete determinations, more and more concrete, of the process of self-valorization. We always return to the same point: the independence, the autonomy of working-class valorization. Capital sees it emerge; capital sees in it, without difficulty, the fundamental key for explaining the crisis, the loss of efficiency of all its categories relevant to control. It is more difficult to turn this consideration around to the workers point of view, because here the negative, the force of destruction is not enough to furnish an explanation. It is the proper character of the wealth of the development of self-valorization to achieve a positivity, strong and rational, to explain its own development. And it is a difficult demand to satisfy. It is simpler to consider the limiting movements of capital, to define the stategy which appears on the border between the warring classes. But when we must descend to this tangle of tactical initiatives which constitutes the woof of self-valorization we only succeed in giving ourselves vague and scattered definitions. Certain positive elements are purely and simply given. In the *first place,* the character—both multilateral and cumulative—of class composition. A strategy of self-valorization must be based on the variety of dynamics which flow from this level of workers' sociality, from the wealth and diversity of pressures, from needs, from behaviors. The capacity to attack each of the articulations of the incessant capitalist recomposition of the cycle.

The manner in which this wealth and this variety express themselves imposes on capital a total flexibility in the control it exerts. But beware, the flexibility is only on capital's side: the variety, the multilaterality, the dynamism, the wealth of the workers' side are not flexible, but rather rigid. And that is the *second point* to keep in mind. The syntheses which, displacing themselves, form within the permanent process of the constitution of the composition of the class the qualitative leaps that this development effects, all that is constituted materially in the composition of class. Capital can control, can block this process of constitution, but it can never invert it. The moment of blooming of the antagonistic class pole that Marx pointed out to us in the development of the hypotheses of the socialization of the dialectic, this moment is inscribed materially: in the reality of necessary labor. In the *third instance,* at last, we must keep in mind that the class composition adds to its multilaterality and rigidity a supplementary element: *the productive violence of the highest level of cooperation it presents.* We can finally name the class composition for what it has become: communist composition. Its dynamic is marked by the communist character of the premise, it is continuously animated, stretched by this characteristic. Nothing can explain better than this element the incessant alternation of violence and program, of war and of the massification of objectives, of the attack of the avant-garde and of the resistance, in the historical expression of the movement of proletarian self-valorization.

In order to better outline the character of this dynamism, *let us now look to see how the class enemy behaves.* It is sensitive to the autonomy assumed by the social cooperation of the proletariat in the movement of self-valorization. It is so sensitive that it continuously remakes the frame of reference and strategic perspective of capital, taking account of this insurgence. Capital will attempt to respond to the multilaterality of worker initiative by trying to continually recompose the social framework, in terms of a socialized, diffused and enlarged assembly line. It will thus try to bring together various indefinite stimuli, but by decomposing them, segmenting them in production and reproduction. It amounts to a purely artificial, political control because, as we have seen in the second point, the rigidity of autonomy is such that it blocks all operations that would make cuts or impose recessions. The political and violent character of the relation of capital will be shown at least by the impossibility of planning the tension of workers' cooperation in the phase of self-valorization. Here capital will simply be constrained to attempt to make an end by using force against force, in opposing violence to violence. All of this demonstrates in my view that communism—the communist reality of the class composition—already anticipates and conditions the forms that will be taken on by capitalist development. Communism appears, in its role as dynamic and constituting element, as the motor and the force which destroys capitalist development. All the dynamics that Marx has indicated—which we have seen in the last movement of the

Grundrisse and which represent the initial articulation of a process which was developing—all these dynamics find here their conclusion. The contradiction is no longer indicated but actual: its terms are antagonistic, but even more are they separation, difference and contary development. The conditioning which self-valorization imposes on capitalist development is no longer an effect of the dialectic resolved within capitalist relations; it is on the contrary a veritable conditioning, a logic imposed on the adversary through positions of force—separate positions which are self-determining. We can thus advance today "beyond Marx" on this path that Marx posed from the first few cobblestones. But once the leap is done, the image of the realization of communism, its dynamic, has such a strong connotation that we must really, despite our own incredulity, repeat to ourselves: yes, we have gone beyond Marx.

Many have said that *Capital* functions poorly to help us understand contemporary capitalist development. Especially revisionists—who did not wait for the modern transformations of capitalism to say it. Revisionism repeats it by loathing the revolutionary spirit that animated Marx's work. But beyond these malicious motivations revisionism—and after it numerous tendencies attached to the same orthodox analysis—have found sufficient space to support their complaints. Some say we must modernize, that we must reposition, at the present phenomenological level of capital and within the social development of capital, the fundamental concepts of the Marxist tradition: *the concept of capital, of working class, of imperialism*. How can we respond other than in the affirmative? All of my discourse is located on this terrain of modernization. But is this way of looking at things sufficient? Let's see. In the first place, there is no doubt that *we must give new foundations to Marxist categories* by taking account of the social character of capitalist development. From this point of view the *Grundrisse* is in advance of *Capital* because *in it the social character of the categories appears immediately as fundamental*. The heavy threads of the private-public dialectic that a legal critique allows to survive in the Marxist critique of political economy are almost absent in the *Grundrisse*. That said, it does not mean that we can find in the *Grundrisse* a total reformulation of the categories. Surely not. There are moments that show a very great originality in the definitions, but it is beyond doubt that even where Marx goes farthest, he only—as we have underlined—makes an allusion to the new social reality of capital. Where the *Grundrisse* goes far beyond the efforts made on the first point (new bases for categories in the necessity of socialization) is rather around the definition of *social antagonism*. There the categories break with any possible reformist conception and define a second fundamental element of the modernization of Marx's categories.

Let us pause a moment and examine this last element. This gives not only the originality but also the modernity, the *actuality* of the *Grundrisse*.

Marx's insistence emphasizes here the union of the theory of socialization and the theory of surplus value. The latter makes it possible to consider the former in antagonistic terms. The first allows us to carry the second to universal levels. "To universal levels" means that the work of modernization and the refounding of Marxist categories must be able to grasp in its object the *development of capital managed by the state* and that the *increasingly impetuous multinational mode of production is growing to the international level.* The critique of political economy can't but be, simultaneously a critique of the political, a critique of socialism, a critique of the multinationality. But these universal levels are nevertheless levels of real antagonism. The development of capital within the state-form, the insertion of political mechanisms within the dynamic of accumulation, the elaboration of the way of producing (that some call "post-Taylorism") where at center is the question of political control, all of that places the antagonism worker-State at the center of the critical dynamic. Marx indicated, and often too frequently, especially in the *Grundrisse,* that to say State is only another way of saying capital. The development of the mode of production leads us to recognize that to say State is the *only* way to say capital: a socialized capital, a capital whose accumulation is done in terms of power, a transformation of the theory of value into a theory of command; the launching into circuit and the development of the State of the multinationals. *The development of Marxist categories,* their *refounding,* must not make us forget, at the risk of destroying all theoretical effort, *this centrality.* We must reformulate the concept of capital starting from the statist centralization of the mechanisms of accumulation and planning, starting from the massive reorganization of the multinational capitalist centralization of all instruments and changes in production and reproduction. From the *Grundrisse* to *Capital?* Yes, but in this one precise sense. And in another sense which is complementary to this, organically complementary: the analysis of the dynamic of communism. It is only at this level that we can propose to analyse the dynamic of communism, at this degree of intensity of antagonism. We must grasp the progress of capitalist accumulation in a reversed form. But we can not do this if we do not reduce this concept of inversion to that of *separation.* The relation of capital is a relation of force which tends toward the separate and independent existence of its enemy: the process of workers' self-valorization, the dynamic of communism. *Antagonism is no longer a form of the dialectic, it is its negation.* There's much talk of "negative thought" these days. Well, negative thought, ripped from its bourgeois origins, is a fundamental element of the workers' point of view. Let us begin to use it, it will give some fruits! Some fruits to harvest, to nourish the development of the healthy solidity of worker cirtique, in all its independence.

   Even more so, once all that is admitted, we still must traverse the most interior and most important path: that which demands *the analysis of collective praxis,* of proletarian independence. Let us re-examine on this point a fundamental passage of Marxist methodology:

To begin with, capital forces the workers beyond necessary labour to surplus labour. Only in this way does it realize itself, and create surplus value. But on the other hand, it posits necessary labour only *to the extent and in so far as* it is surplus labour and the latter is *realizable* as *surplus value*. It posits surplus labour, then, as the condition of the necessary, and surplus value as the limit of objectified labour, of value as such. As soon as it cannot posit value, it does not posit necessary labour; and, given its foundation, it cannot be otherwise. It therefore restricts labour and the creation of value—by an artificial check, as the English express it—and it does so on the same grounds as and to the same extent that it posits surplus labour and surplus value. By its nature, therefore, it posits a *barrier* to labour and value-creation, in contradiction to its tendency to expand them boundlessly. And in as much as it both posits a barrier *specific* to itself, and on the other side equally drives over and beyond *every* barrier, it is the living contradiction [*Grundrisse*, p. 421; 324].

We have already read and commented on this passage for another point. We now want to reread it, to reverse it, convinced that this methodology can permit us to rediscover the direction of development of this *new "living contradiction" that is the working class and the proletariat on the communist path*. A path where each limit—rigidity of the composition of class, determined level of necessary labor, etc.—appears as an obstacle. But where for capital limits exist and are considered as obstacles only in order to found again limits and proportions, here, from the worker point of view, the limit appears as an obstacle in its proper sense, as coming from the other side. This manner of seeing is that of the antagonism, where the overcoming of the obstacle does not tend to create new limits but rather to develop most fully the use-value and the power of living labor. In this passage, with this method, worker subjectivity becomes the revolutionary class, the universal class. *In this passage, the constituting process of communism finds its full development.* We must immediately underline that in this light the antagonistic logic ceases to have a binary rhythm, ceases to accept the fantastical reality of the adversary on its horizon. *It refuses the dialectic* even as a simple horizon. *It refuses all binary formulae.* The antagonistic process tends here to hegemony, *it tends to destroy and to suppress its adversary. Deny the dialectic:* that eternal formula of Judeo-Christian thought, that circumlocution for saying—in the Western world—rationality. In Marx we have read the most advanced project of its destruction, we have seen enormous steps forward in this direction. We must now engage ourselves completely. It is only on this terrain that we will be able to begin to speak of new categories: not of capital but for the overthrow of capital.

Here, at the end of our work, it seems to me that we can consider as satisfied the intuition with which we began. We must liberate the revolutionary content of the Marxist method. The path of the *Grundrisse* offers for this a fundamental basis. Advancing within it, rediscovering the mechanisms

190 MARX BEYOND MARX

which push Marxist thought forward, we arrive at last at the central point: *the Marxist critique of all dialectical forms*. It is there, finally, that we find the practical character of Marx's thought. The end of the dialectic? Yes, because the act of thinking here does not have any autonomy from the collective force, from the collective praxis which constitutes the subject as dynamism tending toward communism. The adversary must be destroyed. Only communist practice can destroy it, and must, accomplishing that and developing itself, liberating the rich independent multilaterality of communism.

Epilogue

The Theory of Autonomy in Negri's Other Writings

Marx Beyond Marx is more easily understandable when it is situated in the context of Negri's other writings on the theory and practice of autonomy, only a small number of which have been translated into English.[1] Here, I will give an account of those writings and relate them to the themes of *Marx Beyond Marx*.

Workers and the State (1972) contains two essays by Negri, one of which—"Marx on the Cycle and the Crisis"—is crucial for an understanding of his later work. Here, in an embryonic form, one encounters several of the concepts which will be essential to the later, more elaborated theory of autonomy. The most important emphasis is the active role played by workers' struggle *(lotta operaia)* in determining economic development and its crisis. This once established, Negri can argue that workers already possess sufficient power to overthrow the capitalist State, since the State planning economy rests on a precarious antagonistic relation between capital and labor, in which labor plays the determining role.

Negri reads the economy politically. What seems, in purely economic terms, an equilibrium is in fact a relation of antagonistic forces; what seems an objective structure is in fact the product of subjective activity. The economy is not a system of "objective" laws operating independently of social agents. It is, rather, an antagonistic relation between subjects. Thus, he argues that economic development is a problem and a project of capitalist *power*. Development is determined by the antagonism between capital and labor, more specifically by the relation between surplus value and the wage. That irreducible dualism imposes crisis as a necessity on capital. After 1917 and the example of Russia, Negri sees emerging an increasing autonomy of the working classes of western Europe, and this calls forth responses on the part of the bourgeoisie to reorder this antinomy into an equilibrium. Keynes represents the promotion of development, based on the use of artificial instruments according to a formal model of equilibrium, as an alternative to crisis. Schumpeter, in his theory of business cycles, represents a political

191

definition of development as a means of attaining class domination. Capital uses the crisis to rearrange the fundamental relation of forces. The cycle contains crisis as a function of its process.

Negri finds both Keynes and Schumpeter foreshadowed in Marx's writings on the crisis. Marx sees capitalism's periodic cycles as containing necessary crises. Equilibrium is in fact a median or an accident; "normal" development is in fact the anormal possibility of crisis. More significantly, Negri emphasizes the active role Marx attributes to the working class in inducing crises. Marx argues that wage pressure produces a falling rate of profit and that this tendency is produced solely by competition between the classes. Negri adds that since development is dependent on the desire for profit, in the seemingly objective process of development one must read an antagonistic class relation—a political relation of force between subjects, in other words, not an objective law. The crisis of the falling rate of profit is the result of a relation of forces, of the tendencies and counter-tendencies of subjects in struggle. The working class raises the level of the necessary labor wage, and capital is constrained by this action to diminish the amount of living labor incorporated into production. The workers' struggle constitutes an irreducible limit to capitalist development. And even as capital uses the crisis to reassert the fundamental relation of forces, this merely displays the precariousness of capitalist development. The use of the crisis also realigns social segmentation—"the political composition of the classes"—and this radicalizes the class antagonism and extends it throughout society. Capital is irreducibly given over to this dialectic of development and crisis.

The solution Negri sees emerging is the "social planning State." Political violence and repression overcome the precariousness of capitalist economic development in a way which is not possible in mere economic practice. The organization of development has become the development of organization. Planning is central to this process. The more capitalism is planned and socially organized, the less it requires the crisis as a weapon. Because the planning State has become so necessary to capital, it must become an object of working class subversion. Negri bases this political call on his previous economic argument. First, he assumes that worker power is already possible because of the determining role workers' struggles play in current capitalist economic development. He assumes the subjective determination of objective movements. Negri privileges mass actions over intuitive vanguardism. He recalls Luxemburg's concept of the worker struggle as "continuity of independent power, the vitality of irrepressible action." Negri occasionally speaks of the necessity of mixing Lenin and Luxemburg, and it is fitting that at this point he should also call for a rediscovery, on the part of the working class, of Lenin's emphasis on breakage (*spezzare*), of violent rupture. This leads to the second economic basis for the political call to move against the planning State. If capital is dependent on development, which rests on a precarious fundamental relation, so that capital demonstrates the necessity of crisis for its own salvation, then breakage is both necessary and possible. Capital cannot have development except in the form of crisis, of an antagonism of classes which makes necessary the role of the planning State. Because it is founded on the forced closure of an irreducible antagonism, the State constitutes the weakest link in capitalism. It is the last resort of capital, and, hence, its breakage becomes the first recourse of workers power *(potere operaia)*.

The other essay in *Workers and the State* is "John M. Keynes and the Capitalist Theory of the State of '29." Negri sees 1929 as a fundamental moment in the development of the modern State. It was in many ways a response to 1917, a crisis which allowed capital to develop measures for controlling the working class. Taylorism (the rationalization of production) and Fordism (the massification of production—hence, the "mass worker") were designed to take Bolshevism away from the workers, but such measures only relaunched class composition on a higher level. A higher degree of control was needed, so that workers' autonomy could be channeled to serve the interests of capital. By assuming a Keynesian norm of equilibrium, capital merged the economic and the juridical, and made out any working class action which disturbed equilibrium to be illegal. The Keynesian instruments of state interventionism and the management of circulation turned all of society into a factory. And economic development was assured by an alliance between the bourgeoisie and the socialists.

Negri congratulates Keynes on recognizing the autonomy of the working class, but he points out a paradox in Keynes' attempt to use the working class for capitalist development. The attempt works not because the working class is always inside capitalism, but because it can always be outside. It always threatens to be outside, to assert its autonomy, and the political project of Keynesianism consists of recuperating this threat. Capital cannot do without labor, but the working class can do without capital.

In *Crisis of the Planning State* (1974) the central concern is the question of *organization*. It was written at a time when the "area of autonomy" was beginning to hold national meetings in Florence and Bologna, partly to discuss the relationship between the spontaneous mass movement and the traditional workers' organization.[2]

Negri begins with an analysis of the way money reflects the irrepressible contradiction of capitalism, the antagonistic social relation upon which it is based. Money indicates capital's power over that relation in the form of the law of value. Since wage labor is the essential basis of production, money also points out the crisis of that domination. Rising wage pressure encroaches upon the seemingly independent (mystified, because value is simply an expression of political force) operations of the law of exchange value. The myth of equivalence (and political equality) which conceals the extraction of surplus value cannot be maintained. The tendency of capital at this point, Negri argues, is to seek control beyond money, and this takes the form of planning.

The rule of planning is broken by the emergence of the autonomy of the working class. "Socialist" planning should give rise to a harmony which descends from the law of value to the determination of the social whole. This can only be given as the reduction of difference (between the classes) into unity. Nevertheless, irrationality cannot be expunged from the crisis of circulation. And, Negri argues, this is not simply a crisis of structural proportion, but a manifestation of the proportion between the classes, of their antagonism. Capitalist planning ultimately is impossible because of the heterogeneity of the organic composition of capital. The independence of the labor force is irrepressible, and this means that the relation between the extraction of labor value and profit must remain indeterminate. The recognition that capital cannot be determined apart from workers' struggles, from the actions of the total labor force, leads to the demand that capital overdetermine the system, as a mature rule of development. Keynesian "socialism" is a response to this exigency. Crisis is wielded to put limits on the productive force of labor; destruction serves the self-conservation of capital. Keynesianism becomes a permanent desire to block a potential development of the productive force of labor whose explosion could only mean the triumph of communism, conceived here in the terms Marx uses in the *Grundrisse* as the unfettered production of wealth and the consequent full development of each individual. Such a development would destroy capitalism by breaking the limits on production and on human development which the law of value requires. Over-production and disproportionate wages reduce profit within the regime of the law of value. Hence, the permanence of crisis and of stagnation becomes a condition of the permanence of capital.

This concept of productive labor, as the immanent possibility of communism (defined as the full realization and reappropriation of human wealth) and as, in consequence, a *political* threat to the law of value and to capital, is essential to the theory of autonomy. It is followed in the text by another essential concept: as capital attempts to recompose itself, to resolve in its autonomy the contradictions of practice, the contradictions reappear at a deeper level. The antagonism is irreducible; the totality of power of capital merely means that on the other side will stand the totality of power of a recomposed proletariat. The ultimate solution to this problem is its containment by the State.

The tendency Negri sees at work in Italy in the early 70s resides in labor as a revolutionary subject, representing the unique source of wealth and the actuality of communism in its productivity, contradicted by capital's need to reduce the amount of living labor incorporated into production in order to counter the falling rate of profit. Socialism is thus impossible because no relation between labor and exchange value can escape being antagonistic.

And communism is necessary as the untrammeled production which is subversive of the limits imposed by exchange value. Productive forces and social relations, which, for capital, are merely a means toward maintaining production on a limited basis, can become conditions for making this basis explode. What would emerge would be a communism where, as Marx put it, labor time would cease to be a measure of wealth, or exchange value a measure of use value. The theoretico-practical task which accompanies this assessment of the tendency implicit in the potency of the process of labor productivity is *direct appropriation,* as a practical recognition of the social conditions of production. Labor is already an immediate participation in the world of wealth, and to recognize this is to propose to the proletarian organization a necessary mass content for its program: the direct appropriation of produced social wealth by the producers.

In the next chapter of *Crisis,* Negri addresses the relation between the workers' organization and the political composition of capital. The political composition of capital is characterized by the metamorphosis of the planning State into a *crisis State* marked by the free managment of *command* for the survival of capital. The crisis State presents itself today as the crisis of the national State in relationship to the multinational corporation. With the demise of Keynesianism as a form of internal policy, the multinational corporation assumes the general command over development. This is in reaction to the actions of the mass workers. Capital reintroduces the division of labor against the mass worker. As massification was used in the 20s against the professional base of the workers' struggle, now selective participation is used against the mass base. The norm of the command over labor in the factory is spread throughout society. The political project of the proletarian organization must therefore break the political support of capital—the corporation and the factory. Just as earlier the assertion of autonomy was the proper character of class behavior against the planning State, of the proportion of necessary labor to surplus value, now direct social appropriation is the proper character of class behavior against the State of "disvalue" and of enterprise-command.

For Negri, the concept of the productive, creative, and inventive subject of labor is inseparable from the political task which derives necessarily from that concept. If labor is the living source of value and of wealth, and if exchange value-cum-enterprise command sets limits on the realization of that productive potential for wealth, then the concept of a revolutionary organization requires a consciousness of the growth of a new revolutionary subject, one rich in inventive potential, accompanied by a consciousness of the monstrosity of the rule of the law of value. This entirely political reading of the tendency implicit in capitalist economic development would see the class' potential for invention as in itself destructive of capital's power. Capital attempts to contain labor, but only because it is itself contained (and determined) by labor. For example, the arbitrariness of command reflects the destruction of the stability between the State and the unions, indicates the precariousness of the institutional functions of the State, and reveals the extreme condition into which the working class has put the State. The process which first saw the working class as entirely within capital, now sees capital as entirely within the working class.

Along with the essay on Marx's theory of crisis, Negri's "Workers' Party Against Work" (1974) is a key text of the theory of autonomy. In it he discusses the problem of moving from the mass autonomous workers' movement to a workers' party organization.

He beings with a definition of crisis, not as a mechanistic breakdown, but rather as something which can only be understood in terms of the relations of force between the classes and their internal political composition. The crisis is caused by the developed composition of the working class. If capital depends on value extracted from labor, then crisis occurs when the working class no longer valorizes for capital. It is on the basis of an analysis of the relationship between crisis and working class action that the tasks of a workers' party organization can be determined. At this point, Negri praises Lenin's concept of the "determinate social formation," but he also argues that the present-day working class composition requires a new concept of organization. Reformist organizations (i.e. the CPI) have blocked the continuity of organization within the class. The new organization must live the life of the class in an adequate way. Hence, although it is necessary to move from class composition to organization, the reverse must also be true.

Negri next describes the coming into being of a mass working class subject as a result of the actions of capital in reaction to the worker-induced crisis of the falling rate of profit. As always, Negri's point of reference here is Marx's description in the *Grundrisse* of a communism of the direct appropriation by workers of the value they produce, thus abolishing the regime of value and of work. The falling rate of profit can be countered by increasing the mass of products, but this makes evident the contradiction between production and valorization, since not all the value of the mass of products can be realized. Too great a mass leads to a crisis of realization and overproduction. The resolutive mechanism of the capitalist process is broken by the necessary presence in production of a unified worker subject, the result of the massification of social productive forces in response to the falling rate of profit. This subject presents itself as a power which puts in increasingly drastic terms the possible alternative of the appropriation of the mass of products. The contemporary crisis is thus a combination of the falling rate of profit and the mass attacks carried out by a subject capital itself was constrained to construct in order to secure valorization. The working class has become a radical obstacle to capitalist development. As Negri puts it, the catastrophe of capital is the working class.

The most important point here is the contradiction between the expansive mass productivity of labor and the limits capital must place on it in order to guarantee the realization of value. That massification of productive forces *is* already the communism Marx describes, only without the direct appropriation by workers of their product. What capitalists see as *over*-production is simply communist production, an excess which guarantees a fully developed social individual and an end to the necessity of wage work. But the massification of production also constructs the subject capable of breaking the constraints capital puts on this potential communism.

Capital's reaction to the obstacle to profit which the working class poses is planning and reformism, but these fall apart as a result of stagnation (due to the falling rate of profit) and inflation (due to wage demands), both symptoms of the appropriation of profit by the new proletarian mass reunited in a productive subject. Beyond planning and reformism lies command, the logic of the power of the State, as capital's only recourse. The fall of value is the result of the struggles of the massified class, and value can only be restored by making the factory/enterprise into the moment of the complete recuperation of the social product. The command form of the enterprise is applied to all society. The enterprise State thus accepts crisis and recomposes itself on the basis of that crisis.

Today, Negri goes on to argue, the fundamental character of class composition in Italy is the irreducibility of the autonomous actions of the class. He sees in the mass tendency to refuse work—the movement from factory work to the tertiary or service sector, the spontaneous refusal of the regime of training for abstract labor—a prefiguration of Marx's descripton of communism as enjoyment not discipline, as the absence of work in free, creative activity. In relation to this, the unions and the reform parties merely constitute a redistribution of the law of value. Negri perceives the tendency which is in the process of realizing itself and the political needs which derive from the political class composition as being the unification of the class, the destruction of wage labor, and the political struggle for appropriation.

On the basis of the two processes at work in the contemporary situation— the social massification of the productive forces and the imposition of the enterprise as the form of social organization (corporatism)—Negri concludes that the vanguard of the proletariat is the workers of the large factories, who are the principal object of exploitation and whose labor is most valorized. (At this time in the early 70s, the workers most active in the "area of autonomy" were the chemical, machine tool, and automobile workers. Negri will later change this position in light of the emergence of the "social" worker.)

Because command has replaced the law of value as the means of assuring capitalist domination, the working class, in constituting itself as an organization, must develop a force of command and a capacity of violence equal to that of the *padroni*. Negri considers the possibility of a Leninist party, organized "from above," and rejects it. The Leninist question of workers' alliances has been transformed into a problem of the unification along the internal lines of the proletariat, from below or inside, not from above. And because the refusal of work is taken as a given, the Leninist concept of the party as the director of a passage to socialism conceived as a higher organization of work must be rejected. Today, communism consists of the *immediate* use of accumulated wealth, outside and beyond any logic of the labor process. This is the express exigency of workers' power, as well as the direct cause of capital's crisis. Therefore, appropriation, the thematic of the contemporary workers' organization, comprehends the Leninist thematic of insurrection, as that which induces economic crisis and, potentially, breaks the political character of capital's control. It is a science, not an art.

This identification of an "economic" activity—appropriation—with political power is another major principle of the theory of autonomy. The workers organization now bases struggle not on the errors of the bosses (as in Lenin's conjunctural theory), but rather on its own potential *(potenza)*. Negri dislikes the word "party" for this new organization because it suggests the formal character of the Leninist party, its centralization, discipline, and division of labor. Nevertheless, the word should be used, he concludes, because it indicates the independence of the proletariat as an organization as well as the uninterrupted character of the revolution.

At this point, he argues, the political task is to articulate factory struggle with struggles in the social terrain, wage actions with subversion. (This book was written at a time when the Italian urban struggle was expanding to include issues of services, public expenditure, housework, housing, etc.) In addition, the vanguard and the mass process, Lenin and Luxemburg, must be combined. The concept of a vanguard party of the mass must unify the struggle for the wage and the revolutionary struggle for power. It must also include armed struggle, since the law of value, once it is stripped of its capitalist mystification, is revealed to be a law of terrorism, the violence of a mere relation of force. Because the "State of law" of the liberal tradition and the "State of labor" of the reformist tradition are impelled to transform the disaster of the falling rate of profit into the permanence of capitalist command, only armed struggle can revise the structure of power.

At this point in "Workers' Party Against Work," Negri proceeds to elaborate upon what he means by such an organization. A party based on the present political class composition cannot be a top-down Leninist organization, as we have seen. The composition of the class is that of an independent variable in planning and an obstacle in development. The party, therefore, must undertake the reversal of the capitalist management of the extinction of the law of value from below, through mass actions. Because the working class, in its autonomy, is an obstacle to profit, the task of the party is to break the mystifying image which capital's power has over the class, to break its command. The growth of working class power in society is thus acknowledged as being inseparable from the affirmation of its power against the State. Because the autonomous activity of the class is based in material needs, the communist content of its political program is already expressed in absenteeism, sabotage, and direct appropriation. The party ceases its function of representation; it is no longer the consciousness of the class. The mass vanguards, already in the immediacy of their actions, contain the totality of revolutionary consequences which derive from them; these actions become organisms of workers' power which already expresses the program of communism. The party, therefore, is merely the executive organ of workers' power *(potere operaia)*. It is the specular opposite of the capitalist process of valorization; its object of attack is the law of value as domination over labor; thus, it seeks to empower workers' autonomy as "the communist power of non-work."

This does not constitute, Negri insists, an old consecration of the party; rather, what is acknowledged is "the paramount necessity of its function." With the State, the party should also be extinguished. And prior to that moment, the party is subordinated to the movement of the working class. Negri describes Lenin's Bolshevik party as a party based on a class composition determined by the importance of the professional worker. It imposed the law of value and the discipline of the professional worker on the revolutionary movement. With the crisis of 1929, the period of the central party came to an end, and with it, the socialism of the professional worker. The impoverishment of the social composition of the working class in Europe, due to its massification after 1929, marks the beginning of a new practice of the party. The class vanguards at the level of the mass discover the use of the wage and the identification of democratic struggle with political struggle. For the center is substituted the circulation of the mobility of inexhaustible wage objectives and factory guerilla warfare. All this derived from the new consciousness the class had in the socially planned economy (in Italy after 1948). This gave rise to a new figure of unity, of an integral and autonomous subject, of the mass worker and of the vanguards of the masses. In reaction to this autonomy—that is, the slow erosion of profit—capital eventually developed the separation of command.

On the basis of this configuration of political class compositions, the vanguard workers are not officers of a red army, but instead functions of workers' power. The more the working class constitutes itself as a social individual, the less there is a problem of power, the less party vanguard delegation is conceded. Worker recomposition is at this point directly political; the class' management of its own power requires no mediation. The party is only an aspect of this necessity. The working class can use it, but only when its activity dominates the party.

The problem the movement faces (in the early 70s), according to Negri, is that of bringing autonomy to the level of political direction. He describes three phases of the autonomy movement. During the first, in the 60s, there was a diffuse molecularity of struggles. This diffusion tended toward re-unification in a party during the second phase in the late 60s. The third

period consists of the building of institutions of attack for the party and of
the attempt to build a cycle of armed struggle and appropriation. The
problem at this stage is how to construct an organization without the fe-
tishization of the party. Like other Italian theorists, Negri turns to the
example of the IWW. Such examples show that liberation is not something
which awaits communism; it can grow in the process of struggle as the form
and the result of workers' power.

The appendices published with "Workers' Party Against Work" are worth
noting. One is entitled "Theses on the Crisis: the Multinational Worker."
Negri analyzes the right-wing attack against Keynesianism and the workers'
response to it. That response aims at productivity and the division of labor
founded on it. The capitalist counterattack takes place on the international
level as monetary reorganization and the development of an international
division of labor. The power of multinational corporations extinguishes the
concept of national sovereignty and abolishes any notion of "the autonomy
of the political" (a reformist theme in Italy, where it is used to justify
participation in government with Christian Democrats). Negri describes
social democracy as the specific form of terror of the multinationals, the
militarization of command over labor. He goes on to criticize the theory of
"State monopoly capitalism" which describes the internationalization of capital only in the market. This permits a fascization and isolation of internal
national relations, as well as the development of revolutionary alliances with
the bourgeoisie. The theory lacks any sense of international capitalist production, hence of an international proletariat. Failing to note the socialization
of capitalist production, it sees centralization without socialization, and
hence, the State seems fascist and technocratic. This leads to the claim that
revolution is possible on a national basis through a strategy of democratic
recomposition uniting all progressive forces (essentially the CPI strategy).
Negri calls instead for a multinational organization of workers and for the
use of autonomy against social-democratic terrorism. He thinks it is essential
to use the weapon of the social wage, and to move from the factory to
society. The wage struggle then becomes a struggle for appropriation (for
public expenditure—services and a social wage—without a wage work equivalent exchange) and an attack on bourgeois property principles, as well as
an attack on the process of profit realization in commodity circulation.
Capital responds by segmenting labor and by curtailing the social wage. The
factory is separated from society and the workers from the proletariat. (The
CPI doctrine of "productive labor" participates in this exclusion of the
unemployed.) Consequently, Negri emphasizes the importance of the marginalized proletariat (students, unemployed, house workers) in the struggle.
Because the wage struggle encounters an increasing rigidity on the part of
capital, the struggle is shifted to the terrain of reappropriation (in the sphere
of reproduction). And, Negri concludes, armed struggle becomes a necessity
of the multinational worker.

"One Step Forward, Two Back: The End of the Groups" is a critique of the groups which formed in '68 and dissolved in the early '70s. These militants were too individualistic, according to Negri, and out of touch with the workers' movement. They lacked a theoretical analysis which could have linked them to the movement of the masses. Negri describes their history, from the Spring of 1969 to the Spring of 1973 and the occupation of the Fiat Mirafiori plant, in terms of three phases. The first phase was characterized by an autonomy of workers' actions; the project was unified as an indentification with the object. The object was egalitarianism, and the movement itself was egalitarian. The refusal of the contract and the refusal of work became one. The vanguard was interchangeable with the mass. During the second phase, demands were extended to include the guaranteed wage. But the organizing process which sought to co-ordinate the discontinuities of the movement was broken. The groups of militants went on the attack without mass support and failed. The Spring of 1972 marked the end of the groups, but the movement of proletarians and workers continued without them. It was at this time that the need for a continuous and organized conscious political relation was felt. The plant occupation at Mirafiori in 1973 marks out the third phase. Direction for the attack resided entirely within the movement. Negri reads the event as manifesting a unifying function which at this point began to form the nervature of an organization. Autonomy, as he puts it, began to write its own *What Is To Be Done?* It is predicated upon the constant expansion of wage demands and the consciousness that the wage is power. And he points out that the newer young workers bring to the organization a new consciousness of the relation between wage struggle and the struggle for power, as well as between factory struggle and struggle in the community.

It is in the final appendix—"Organizational Articulations and Whole Organization: the Party of Mirafiori"—that Negri offers an example of what he means by a "workers' party." The problem he poses is that of the relation between the necessary disarticulation of the instances of attack and the level of workers' power of the whole organization. There can be no workers' concept of a party which does not involve the immediate exercise of power. In this light, it is necessary to demystify the neo-Leninist Third Internationalist concept of delegational representation. The Mirafiori occupation indicated an alternative—a party where the workers trust in their own mass power. Negri argues that this does not reflect spontaneism because the movement was informed and interpreted by the conscious initiative of the vanguards who staked out the terrain and provided direction. The need now is to attend to the "continuous discontinuity" of the relation between the moments of attack and the mass movement. And this is especially true in terms of moving from the factory to society, of joining the different functions of attack (houseworkers, unemployed, students, marginals) against capital's attempts at disarticulation. Finally, what Negri privileges in the Mirafiori experience is the mass character of the movement, that it was an immediately working class organization, that it was vertically integrated from the level of attack to the mass level (overcoming spontaneism), and that it had a directly political character as the exercise of power.

Although not published until 1977, Negri's critical study of Lenin—*The Factory of Strategy*, which is in many ways a companion piece to "Workers' Party Against Work"—was originally a course of lectures given in 1973. Negri criticizes Lenin, but through a close consecutive reading of Lenin's writings, he also finds much that is of value to his own theory of revolution.

Negri praises Lenin for correctly determining the form of political organization suited to the particular class composition of the Russian proletariat. But he also points out that the composition of the Italian working class is quite different, and this historical transformation makes necessary a new organizational strategy. By political class composition here, Negri means the determinateness of needs, actions, and levels of political consciousness that the working class as a subject reveals at a determined moment of history. Whereas Negri's referent is the revolutionary mass worker, Lenin's was the vanguard of industrial workers. The isolated and minoritarian status of that vanguard (its political class composition) determined the necessity of an organization external to the proletariat. The diffusion of spontaneous struggle in Russia also made necessary a central party to unify the diverse struggles and to accumulate them into a more powerful and destructive force. For Lenin, the party is a factory because, Negri argues, of its capacity to act as a multiplier on the revolutionary spontaneity of the workers, turning this primary material of insubordination into a revolutionary accumulation, and transforming it into a general capacity of attack against the adversary. Workers learn the discipline and organization required for the party in the factory. Lenin's use of the analogy of the factory is thus representative of the technico-political composition of the class in Russia at the time. The composition of the class determined the need for external direction. And the underdeveloped condition of Russia determined that the struggle against exploitation should be a struggle for economic development. Negri defines Leninism as the capacity of a party, of a subjective will transformed into a collective brain, to assume workers' needs and to invert them, through adequate organizational means, from the impotence of demand into the force of attack, from the subversion of the State to the practice of power. Defined in this way, Leninism can be seen as a permanent feature of the Marxist political project.

The contemporary political class composition of the Italian proletariat is rather different, and this means that a different form of organization is required. The working class is no longer isolated; the mass worker turns the abstractness of labor into a general, intersectoral and territorial mobility. Also, planning has transformed the nature of capital. Control is no longer centralized, but instead extended beyond the factory to all society. The isolation of the Russian vanguard was determined by a large pre-capitalist sector, but today there is no outside to capitalism. For Lenin, all economic struggles are political, but political struggle is not only economic. Now, economic struggle and political struggle are identified completely. The move from particularity (the minority vanguard) to generality (the unifying party), the economic to the political, loses all significance in the present context. Capital has conquered society, operating a real subsumption of labor, but in so doing it has developed a social individual directly capable of communism. It is possible now to read communism in the class. Lenin's party, on the other hand, belongs to the period of the merely formal subsumption of labor, and this imposed the necessity of further development before a class composition could be attained which was capable of communism. Today, Lenin's vanguard has become a vanguard of the mass. The concept of organization has become internal to class composition. This, Negri suggests, is a much more dialectical concept of the relation than Lenin's (who always risks separating the subjective and the objective). But the modern party is defined by a higher level of class homogeneity. Whereas Lenin's party was delegational, there is no longer a need for representatives of the working class' interests. Acting autonomously, the working class itself becomes an obstacle which constructs contraditions to capitalist development.

On a more general level, Negri thinks that a revision of the concept of the party is necessary. The new party is a mass-determined organization, and he points for examples to the Paris Commune and the Mirafiori occupation. The Russian Soviet as an organization of immediate workers' power, although it could not last in Russia, applies today because it indicates in the masses a possible source of legitimate power based on the activity of the masses. Lenin believed the Soviets should be mediated by the generality of the insurrectional process organized in a party. Today, the traditional party is no longer a solution. Now, there is a sovietization of the masses against the decentralization of capital. In Lenin's time, the Soviets were characterized by two contradictions: that between the diffusion-socialization of power and insurrection, and that between the Sovietism of the masses (without delegation), that is, the socialization of workers' power, and the mediating organization of insurrection. Lenin could not solve these contradictions because of his definition of power as a natural, non-dialectical absolute—a definition very close to a bourgeois conception. The first contradiction can be solved by a concept of power as a dialectical absolute, a relation of forces; the second by recognizing that one needs not one instrument of mediation, but many continuous and punctual functions of the management of civil war. The Leninist notion of a single party insurrection is today replaced by a concept of permanent civil war. Where Lenin drew a straight line of mediation from spontaneism to the Soviets through the party for an insurrection against autocracy, today, autonomy moves from the Sovietism of the masses to the self-organizing proletariat of the extinction of work through a civil war against the contemporary form of bourgeois dictatorship. Autonomy consists of a plurality of points of organization, a plural mobilization of all legal and illegal kinds of struggle, the coordination of an entire "molecular web," and the progressive accumulation of moments of encounter. The highest class consciousness today consists in the realization that power resides not in a representative or a delegate but in the class itself.

Lenin's greatest limitation, according to Negri, is that it was impossible for him to show the struggle against the State as a struggle against work. Hegemony over development, as Lenin's socialist organization of work, is not yet liberation from development. But the highly developed level of the productive forces today means it is possible to move directly to communism, skipping an intermediate "socialist" stage and extinguishing the law of value once and for all. Whereas planning was a positive value for Lenin, today it is the first thing to be attacked, since it is simply a form of capitalist command. This need lays the ground for determining the significance of contemporary autonomy conceived as proletarian liberation born from the particularity of a subject, the autonomous particularity of its interests. Lenin's greatest contributions to revolutionary theory are the necessity of constructing organizations in terms of the political composition of the class, the location of revolutionary potential in a class subject capable of transforming reality, and the notion that the best method of revolution is that of the tendency as a theoretico-practical anticipation based on an anaysis of the existing social formation. Class composition determines organization, although an underdeveloped class composition can mean that the relation must be inverted, as was the case in Russia.

Proletarians and the State (1976) is Negri's critique of the CPI strategy of historical compromise with the Christian Democrats. He begins by describing the current crisis of the falling rate of profit and capital's restructuring in reaction to it. The major strategy of reaction is socialization, the extension of the command over labor into the domain of circulation. Command becomes the planning of crisis through money. But capitalist control fails in the face of stagflation. Energy and automation supply additional modes of control which help place capital beyond workers' struggles. But by far the most important means of control is the centralization of the world market. The multinational corporation disarticulates the unity of capital's control, and the State is replaced by the multinationals. Control is achieved through the world markets and money.

Negri sees the historical compromise as an integral part of this capitalist restructuring of the relations of production. In the face of the autonomous refusal of work, the "socialism" of the compromise could only be repressive, since it is committed to the norm of capitalist development. The compromise assumes an ideology of work—of employment and of productive labor. It would exercise control over the crisis by the weapon of unemployment, thus isolating the workers from the proletariat, the factory from society, preventing the coming to unity of the proletariat. The new planning State, Negri says, would simply amount to workers' participation in the exploitation of workers. It rests on a mystification of the neutrality of the State as a mechanism which can be taken over. But, Negri argues, the State is in fact organic with capitalist development and the world market; there is no "autonomy of the political" of the sort preached by CPI theorists. Today, there is no such thing as "civil society," a domain distinguishable from the political; civil society has become subsumed to the State. Because of the irreducible antagonism between the State as the center of command for production and the proletarian force of social production, all revolutions from above within the State (like the compromise) must necessarily be directed against the other pole, that is, the working class. Hence, now, class struggle must be directed against the State, and therefore, against reformism, in as much as reformism is part of the State.

In the next section of *Proletarians and the State,* Negri describes the effects of the restructuring of capital on the working class. In response to the workers' struggles of the 60s, capital has restructured itself in order to gain more flexibility against labor and to reduce the cost of labor. Restructuring has taken the form of increased technical control and segmentation, the integration of individual and collateral enterprises (credit), and the international reorganization of industry (decentralization of labor). All of this amounts to greater socialization, tertiarization, and flexibility. It has produced a separation of workers from unemployed, separation between enterprises, the proletarianization of the social strata of labor, the making unproductive of productive labor through tertiarization, the territorial decentralization of mass production, the introduction of capitalist production into all sectors of society, the destruction of all working class concentration, and reformism. But it has also meant the emergence of the social (as opposed to the mass) worker, as well as a new proletariat. Since the working class must always reverse the intention of capital, greater articulations, to counter division, must be sought. More and more, the movement must pass from a fight for wages to a fight for power over production. Now, the struggle becomes entirely political, and it moves against the State as the instance of command over production.

The historic compromise is part of this restructuring process. Negri calls the CPI the party of order and of work, a contention sustained by the party's support for the police State measures undertaken against the Autonomy Movement. Its public management would rationalize the relations of planned exploitation. The party acts against the needs of the working class, just as it did after the war and in 1968. Because the efforts of the class are inserted in an *interclass* scheme, the party's project can only be understood as benefiting capital's restructuring. The antagonism cannot be pacified; hence, today, the State is always repressive. Negri concludes that there can be no possible working class use of State institutions of the sort proposed by the CPI.

In the following section, Negri describes a central point of the theory of autonomy: the elaboration of a politics based on labor and class composition. The passage from the mass worker to the social worker brings with it a new horizon of needs. But increased needs under the reign of exchange value merely increases the power of capital (by increasing demand). Work-labor is a use value which is not a reflection of exchange value. It is the only source of wealth independent of capital. The use value of labor as activity, force of production, and inventiveness is the opposite of exchange value. In the subordination of the use value of labor to exchange value, Negri sees the only possibility of rebellion. It is only through the use value of labor that one can subtract from capital its control over itself, so that capital becomes a use value for labor. Against the system of needs, then, is defined the system of struggle. When exploitation is strongest, insubordination becomes greatest. Labor is the only productive force which is opposed to the reigning productive relations. Set opposite the dictatorship of exchange value is the hegemony of the useful particularity of living labor. This implies the possibility that labor can valorize itself against capital, moving from need to struggle. Class composition thus becomes the cagegory of communist transition. The proletariat becomes the subject of the successful reappropriation of the productive forces by the class. The realization of enjoyment contains the possibility of revolution. It is important therefore that the composition tends toward organization. But, Negri cautions, the emerging "party" must be conceived not as a vanguard, but as the motor of transformation of a system of mass struggles, an organ for the mass reappropriation of power— against wage labor and as the invention of communism.

It is in this context that the historic compromise's intention to retain wage labor must be understood. Struggle should instead move against necessary labor through the wage. And the wage struggle tends to transform itself into a struggle for appropriation. Negri says that the dictatorship of the proletariat cannot be understood outside such an appropriation. It does not mean a capitalism of the State. The CPI, he argues, opposes the dictatorship of the proletariat because it would imply the dissolution of the party into the legitimate materiality for generating workers' power. Autonomy, on the contrary, implies direct appropriation. The new class composition makes necessary a redefinition of the theme of mediation which underlies the exteriority of the Leninist party in relation to the class. Now, the antagonism is not mediated by delegation or by being delayed into the future. And the mediation of class consciousness is replaced by a directly collective and practical knowledge which is moving toward the construction of an alternative to capitalism. Consciousness is insinuated materially into reality, denying the mediation of abstract theory and reducing mediation to a tendential function. The historic compromise constitutes another form of mediation. Against this, proletarian action shifts the center away from the party. The only real pluralism is the plurality of the organizations of workers' power and not the plurality of electoral parties crowding together into a single catch-all government.

Working class recomposition focuses on the wage, but it leads to wider demands and objects (a widening of the social wage, for example) which point toward the demand for a new mode of production. The manipulation of capital by labor through the refusal of work leads to a fundamental law of the transition to communism. It becomes possible when the working class subordinates capital to its actions, producing crises rather than economic development. The proletariat tends in its own actions to break the chains of reformist mediation. But repression is organic to capital, and the reformists, through the compromise, participate in repression. In addition, Negri argues that up against the power of multinational capital, the historic compromise would lose.

Autonomy defines its tasks against the historic compromise. It emphasizes that the marginal disarticulation of labor produces new needs which are not reducible to those of wage labor (the social wage, public expenditure for services). Against the capitalist image of separation and division, autonomy insists that all are exploited. In political terms, it acts against the institutions of capitalist command, and seeks to transform contradictions into antagonisms. It tries to show how all attempts at State solutions to the crisis of legitimation merely amount to an increase of exploitation. Autonomy is moving tendentially toward the organization of a party, but this can only be a party in action, without neutrality or mediation, and conceived as an accumulation of struggles. The road moves from practice to the theory of practice. Negri outlines three points of attack: the attack against wage labor, the destruction of the legitimacy of restructuration (the compromise), and the preparation for the militant struggle against capital's use of force. He suggests a party form which would be the development of an effective directive function, but, he adds, only mass power can decide this directive capacity.

The subtitle of *The State Form* (1977), Negri's next work—"For a Critique of the Political Economy of the Constitution"—indicates the direction the book takes in further undermining the CPI theory of "civil society" and of the "autonomy of the political." The State form, particularly the Italian constitution of 1948, is embedded in the capitalist economy. Therefore, it is not a neutral political mechanism which can be occupied by means of compromise; the State is a direct function of political economy, and it must be uncompromisingly attacked if capitalism is to be overcome.

Negri begins with a consideration of the implications of the CPI's attempt to assume a place in the constitutional government. The phenomenon indicates the development of a new form of domination—the corporate State—which absorbs civil society into the State, following in the wake of a new form of worker insubordination. The workers' movement of the 60s was characterized by worker self-valorization against capital, the self-recognition of the mass worker and the formation of the social worker. Since Negri assumes class composition to be fundamental, he sees the constitution of the State changing according to changes in class composition. The constitutional reaction to '68, for example, was the development of the crisis State. The need for a new concept of legitimation led to corporate codetermination between classes, the social democratic solution which saw the constitution and administration become direct functions of capital command. This meant that anyone opposing economic development was criminalized. The new constitutional reforms amount to exploitation with political legitimation. The critique of political economy is therefore necessarily a critique of administration, the constitution, and the State. All law relates to changes in social relations. In this light, the purpose of the 1948 constitution was to disarm the working class. The CPI theory of civil society fails to grasp this relation; it does not realize that civil society cannot function outside the reproduction of capital. In consequence, Negri calls for a "revolutionary function of theory" to combat the "Italian ideology" with its concepts of hegemony, war of position, historic compromise, democratism, the autonomy of the political, the long march through the institutions, and the neutrality of the State.

Negri does an exegesis of the Italian constitution which underscores the way it disarms the working class through rhetorical and conceptual manipulation. It terms Italy a "democracy founded on labor," but this basis in productive labor is sublated into the terms of the bourgeoisie—liberal economic development. Labor becomes a bourgeois category. By making social production out to be for the good of all, the constitution suppresses class antagonism. The "socialist" obligation to work is thus related to democracy and equality by the bourgeoisie. Negri argues that this "social State" of the constitution permits a resolution of the contradiction between the rationality of law and the irrationality of capitalist accumulation by substituting an integration of classes for economic self-regulation in the market. All of society becomes a medium of accumulation, a social factory.

The material productivity of the law consists in the overcoming of struggle and conflict. This is the function of making labor the basis of social production. The subordination of labor is a condition of social organization and of capital accumulation. Capital wants to be the only wealth, but it is bound up with labor as the unique producer of wealth. This contradiction is overcome through the constitution which recognizes the valorization of labor, but simultaneously integrates it into capital through a social factory organization. However, to the concentration of capital necessarily corresponds a growth in workers' power. The constitution seeks integration, but the increasing valorization and development of capitalism reproduces struggle on increasingly higher levels. This leads to a crisis of legality. Command then becomes the general exigency of economic development. The more capital is socialized, the greater adequation exists between law and reality, the more imperative and consensus coalesce. The integration of labor into the constitution implies a concomitant subordination. The socialist concept of the disappearance of the State here becomes the capitalist utopia of total consensus for the management of accumulation.

The homogeneity of this corporate social factory would seem to be belied, however, by modern labor legislation, the necessity of which seems to betoken the inevitability of conflict. Capital is forced to recognize the necessity of its other and of conflict with it. The constitution, then, seeks to substitute a norm of collective administration for open-ended contract negotiation. The purpose of the production of law—to resolve conflicts—is made clearer. It is born from an accord, and it reproduces it—for the sake of organized production. Negri concludes by pointing out an aporia, or irresolvable contradiction, in the constitution's assumptions about itself. If, as the constitution implicitly acknowledges, labor is the general origin of value and of social production, and if the constitution presents itself as a general science, that is, as law, then the fact of labor legislation cannot be written off as a merely particular episode. It relates to the general level, and what it indicates—against the corporatist mystification of the constitution's claim to social integration—is the necessity of contradiction and of class conflict. Negri relates this aporia to changing class composition. When the constitution was written, the mass worker, the subject of autonomy, had not yet been created by capitalist production. Hence, it was still possible to imagine a social order based on collective contracts.

The solution to the aporia is the social planning State. Negri plots its emergence in this way. Capital moves toward a general model of abstraction, which includes the complete alienation of labor on the social level. The capitalist project always responds to contestation and seeks its overcoming. Hence, the massification of abstract labor is perennially threatened by its transformation into a totality of content, of living labor force, as opposed to the abstract labor capital requires in its mass production base. To the massification of the formal intensity of the unification of economic development in the capitalist model must correspond unavoidably a maximum of unification of the labor force. The constitution tries to ignore the insubordination of labor; labor appears in the constitution as abstract, as a formal moment in social production, without any analysis of the concrete conditions of production. The formalism of the constitution operates an a priori elimination of the accidentality labor contestation might introduce into the abstract generality of the constitutional model of social production in a social State.

The problem is that in passing from the formal unification of the constitution to the functional effectivity of unification in reality, conflicts have to be recognized which contradict the formality of the legal system. The abstract unifies; the concrete separates. And the more the concrete separates (the greater the level of worker contestation), the more there is a tendency in capital toward the unification of abstract labor. But equally, abstract labor necessarily indicates revolt and insubordination in relation to capital. The question then is how to restore the totality which the abstract formal generality of constitutional law afforded? Capital, Negri argues, makes use of the very mobility of labor which opposes it. It recognizes the right of labor and of unions, and in this way, it resolves conflicts. The formal constitutional model of corporate social production can be realized only as a negation of a negation (labor contestation). The positive result is the social planning State which assures accumulation, realizes the abstract model, orients the entire activity of social normativity, and affirms the unicity of the labor force in determining the process of valorization. The planning State completes the "constitutionalization of labor." It makes labor the basis of the social State through planning and ordering for a total process. Through a dialectical mediation, continuity is achieved; contestation and conflict are eliminated. And it shows that beyond consensus lies power.

There is, then, an antinomy between abstract and concrete labor, between formal integration and substantive conflict. The constitution must be understood as operating against the desire to attack the social totality based on labor. Only authority can guarantee the working of the formal model. This is the function of juridical science which, in the service of imperativism, lends normativity to the interests of capital. The role of the constitution in all this is to guarantee the continuity in society which capital requires. The possibility of civil war must be reduced. All conflict must be resolved in favor of economic development. The contradiction of abstract and concrete labor is mediated by the transcendence of the State. But the unity of the State can be turned inside out; then, there exists only the irreducible contradiction of the two forms of labor. Negri concludes that the bourgeois world is dialectical and integrative, while the world of workers' struggles is not, because it depends on keeping the contradiction open.

In another chapter of *The State Form,* Negri takes issue with Pasukansis' theory of law and the Bolshevik theory of transition; it is another crucial moment in the development of the theory of autonomy. He argues that law is not superstructural; in the form of law, the command of capital as exploitation is exercised. There is, then, a direct link between law *(diritto)* and surplus value. Law is the form of relation between the organization and command of exploitation. As violence and command, it is necessary for production. The relations of production are produced by law. This means, however, that at the moment when an identity of law and command seems to be attained, the antagonism implicit in capitalist social relations expresses itself. Law is therefore both the identity of authority and the first line of crisis. In relation to this antagonism within the unity of capitalist society, law becomes general domination. There is no proletarian law. Therefore, in the transition to communism, law founded on antagonism will become extinct. The State of law will no longer be possible. Negri criticizes the

Bolsheviks for conceiving of the transition in terms of a mere socialization of property, a replacement of the relations of the market with relations of the organization of social property, of social work. This is not enough; workers' struggles must move against the basis of property itself, the law of work-value, the regulator of exploitation. Property is nothing more than determinate concentration of capitalist command, of the enforcement of the law of value. At this point, Negri cites a highly significant passage in Marx: "The suppression of private property is thus realized only when it is conceived as the suppression of work. . . . An 'organization of work' is therefore a contradiction." In Pasukansis, law is saved by the myth of social work which exists outside the process of valorization. But, Negri counters, the work process and the valorization process cannot be separated. In the transition, law cannot be separated from exploitation. The communist struggle against work and the State must also be against law as the specific authoritative form of the relation between the State and organized labor.

At this point, Negri once again takes up the Communist Party theory of State monopoly capitalism in order to demonstrate its political paucity. The theory pitches civil society against the monopoly State in favor of democracy as a defense against fascism. The theory fails to see the complete process of the social reproduction of capitalism; instead, it concentrates on specific areas like science and technology. The only goal it can project is the restoration of the rationality of capitalist development—"socialism"—purged of the monopoly deviation. In this scenario, the workers' struggle against exploitation is marginalized.

The Marxist alternative, Negri argues, sees the State as being integral with capitalist exploitation and accumulation. The State is not separate from production, and the planning State in particular is necessary for capitalist valorization. "Stamokap" misses this point, fetishizes civil society, and substitutes a struggle in circulation for the struggle against wage labor. The relative autonomy of the State is nothing more than the continuity and permanence of capitalist command. In planning, objectified command becomes a part of the labor process, and the capitalist machine becomes "political" through and through.

Negri goes on to argue that one form of State control—public expenditure, the social wage—can be used by workers against the State. By increasing the quantity of needs and the level of demands, a point of qualitative explosion, a "fiscal crisis of the State," can be reached. Economic attacks of this sort (for work or social wages) are immediately political because they are against the State organization of the relation between consensus and production. Consensus is an internal function of the relations of production. Mutations in legitimation have led to an increased role of the State, as a response to the falling rate of profit. The State becomes directly productive through the oligopolistic investment of public expenditure. This helps the accumulation of social capital, and "productivity" is the legitimating term of the complete process. But a gap opens between the productivity of business (the rallying cry which legitimates capitalist development in the "general interest") and the real terrain of accumulation (the cooperating social whole controlled by the State), and this becomes a space for struggle through the reduction of productivity and the accentuation of the dysfunctions of the social accumulation of the capital State. Both the work wage and the social wage become potentially destructive. But this struggle requires a recognition of society as a factory and of the State as a boss, as well as a breaking of the fetish of productivity as a weapon of legitimation. Instead, legitimation must be referred to the complete needs of the proletariat.

In terms of the tendency of class struggle to move against the State, Negri criticizes Gramsci's notion of hegemony and the use the CPI makes of it in promoting calls for alliances and compromise. Hegemony is in fact subsumed under the capitalist command for profit, which makes civil society into a project of the productive process and of the structure of power. Civil society is dead; it is assumed into capitalist development and the social unity of productive labor. On the other hand, Negri sees the struggle for radical democracy, against the increasingly authoritarian nature of consensus, as a fundamental matter of class struggle, because such struggle affects the relation between necessary labor and surplus value (upon which the whole system hangs).

Negri views Italian socialism as the utopian subsumption of social labor into capital, as itself a moment in class struggle. It merely raises to a higher level the new antagonism between labor and capital. It is at this higher level today that subjectivity becomes the key to the process of communist prefiguration. As the increasing demand for wages (both relative and social), the reappropriation of work time, autoreductions (the highest form of struggle of the mass worker), resistance, and appropriation, the consciousness of class manifests itself as the immediate recuperation of the wealth of labor. Appropriation thus liquidates the socialist mediation of social domination.

The Marxist theory of the State, then, consists of the imputation of a tendency to a revolutionary subject. It centers on the necessary transformation of productive relations. Negri calls for a dictatorship of the proletariat which he defines in terms of a radical transformation of the law of value. Unlike bourgeois democracy, which is merely the shell of capitalist domination over the working class, this dictatorship can only be the capacity of the masses to manage their own power. This does not exist in the East, where there is instead a dictatorship of the party bureaucracy. The law of value still obtains in the USSR, and the working class there is used to increase social productivity.

Negri concludes *The State Form* with a chapter whose subtitle is "Toward a Critique of the Material Constitution: worker self-valorization and the party hypothesis." He argues that two forces act against capitalist development based on co-management between capital and the parties and unions of the working class: the social dimension and the emancipatory quality of the labor force. These two forces demonstrate that exchange is inadequate to put the collective power of socially cooperating labor in action; only communist production, beyond the law of value, can realize the full potential of productive labor. The constitution of 1948 was founded on the social organization of value, conflictuality, and exchange. But the constitution collapses around the failure of the law of value due to the growth and rigidity of necessary labor through capitalist socialization. The class' refusal of work defines modes of worker self-valorization (as opposed to contributing labor for the valorization of capital) in reproduction which disturb the proportion required for the law of value to function. The solution is command and co-management. The restored corporate form mystifies the break-up of the constitution and stabilizes capital.

As capital becomes socialized, reproduction becomes a sphere of antagonism and struggle. Capital's dependence on the reproduction of the worker opens the possibility of the relative independence of the needs, consumption, and use values of the working class in response to capitalist development. The process of reproduction, which subsumes circulation, presents conditions for antagonism, for a manifestation of the independence of the working class. Circulation is reduced to production, but this means that it also is contaminated by the antagonisms of production.

Negri believes it is possible to break reproduction. This is the role of the "other" workers' movement.[3] Because of the automomous quality of this movement (that, for example, it refuses to be repressively controlled by reformist institutions such as "workers" parties and unions), capital loses the possibility of neutrality, democratic containment, and the quantitative weapon of the wage; it must become repressive. The form repression takes is public administration. New constitutional forms, ones which function as factory-enterprise-command, are required today because only an open affirmation of inequality can overcome the crisis. Since the State subsumed civil society (eliminating law, liberty, and equality), the working class is no longer part of civil society. The "other" workers' movement constructs in itself its own society (self-valorization). There is no longer an exchange between labor and capital. Its place is taken by command.

Negri ends *The State Form* by calling for the organization of the diverse self-valorizing autonomous workers' struggles into a party. If the State is the party of capital, then the party is the State of the working class. The essence of the party is the subjectivity of the class, and it accumulates workers' actions until they culminate in a qualitative leap to power. Breakdown is never automatic; only workers' struggles (refusal of work, self-valorization, appropriation) channeled by a party can bring it about. The task of the party is to centralize the various proletarian sectors (workers as well as unemployed, house workers, students, etc.) in a project for wages which spreads the base of struggle for a complete re-appropriation of social productivity.

Negri was unjustly imprisoned as a terrorist, despite his written criticisms of terrorism. In light of this accusation, it is interesting to note the tactics he privileges in *The State Form:* throwing nuts into machinery as a part of general factory sabotage, delaying the production line, "urban guerillas without guns," the use of laws, takeovers, and squatting—in short, "legality as a weapon."

In *Domination and Sabotage* (1978), Negri defines autonomy as a dual project: destructuration of the economic system and destabilization of the political regime. This dual project provokes an effort at restructuration on the part of capital which aims at an elimination of the antagonistic element in the working class. But the working class tends to separate itself from the process of capitalist development, to refuse capitalist valorization and to engage instead in self-valorization, which Negri defines here as the form power assumes in an advanced workerist position, the global, mass, productive figuration of a project of insurrection for the abolition of the State. The personal is political, in that proletarian self-love merges with class hatred.

Negri formulates his argument in terms of the thematic of discontinuity which has been making its way into Italy from France in the 70s. Whereas the orthodox dialectic, which provides a basis for communist party thinking, operates in terms of homology, totality, and resolution, the philosophy of discontinuity emphasizes non-homologous otherness or heterogeneity, the fractured and incomplete nature of "totality," and the impossibility of full resolution. It is in many ways the philosophic equivalent of autonomy and is in France associated with the names of Deleuze, Derrida, Foucault, and Lyotard. Negri writes that it is only by insisting on his difference and otherness, and on the otherness of the class movement, that there can be ruptures of the sort that provide hope for renewal. The workers' movement is discontinuous; it is continuously remaking itself by destroying its old organizational forms. By defining itself as other than the totality of capitalist development, the movement operates a destructuration-sabotage of it. There can be no homology between the movement and capitalist development. The totality of capitalism is thus seen as a "forced relationship"; it is structured by a destructuration which is the product of the proletarian subject. The purpose of capitalist restructuration is to reimpose conclusiveness on this destructuration, but working class self-valorization is irreducibly discontinuous; it has nothing to do with the homologies of rationalist or historicist progressivism. As autonomy, it refuses the goal of economic development. "The rupture and recognition of the class' own productive force removes any possibility of a resolutive dialectic."

Capitalist power resides in the simultaneity of the processes of production and reproduction, whereas "for the proletariat it means developing the independence of its own processes of reproduction, its dis-symmetry, its discontinuity." Negri calls for a linkage between wage struggles and the struggle for public expenditures as part of a program designed to disrupt the simultaneity of production and reproduction. This would develop the unity of productive labor against the attempt by capital to divide workers from other proletarian sectors. Negri argues that the unemployed must oppose the arrogance of salaried income; the privileged position of the factory and the wage must be extended to include the majority of proletarians. If, as Negri believes, the proletarian movement represents the extreme dissolution of the concept of power, then within the movement, the wage struggle must become political, general, and egalitarian. It must act principally on the terrain of public spending, for the self-valorization of the overall reproduction of the entire proletariat.

Negri returns to the problem of autonomous organization. He defines the party as a function of proletarian power, a guarantor of the process of self-valorization, and an army that defends the frontiers of the independence of the proletariat. Only working class self-valorization (as wage and public spending pressure, the refusal of work, direct appropriation, etc), however, can exercise the logic of separation, and this is the sole source of proletarian power. Negri points out that whenever in history the party becomes uppermost, the revolution is finished. In autonomy, power dissolves into a network of powers; only a diffuse network of powers can organize revolutionary democracy. The independence of the class is to be constructed via the autonomy of single, individual revolutionary movements. Unity will be the product of moments of power which are pluralistic.

For Negri, the question of violence is fundamental, as the immediate refusal of work, the inducement of capitalist crisis through the class' reappropriation of the mechanisms of its own reproduction (via public expenditure), and the eventual exclusion of the enemy. To waylay hasty accusations of "totalitarianism," it should be pointed out that Negri also speaks here of democracy and freedom as necessary components of self-valorization, whose object is the total use of wealth in the service of collective freedom. The bourgeoisie excludes violence even as it practices it. For Negri, the only way to overcome the violence of history is to acknowledge its reality.

Negri concludes this book on a note of optimism. The balance of power, he contends, has been reversed; the working class is now the stronger power. The more the form of domination perfects itself, the more empty it becomes, the more working class refusal grows and becomes full of rationality and value. And the goal of refusal is to unleash the proletariat's productive potential which is now constrained by capitalist domination.

Marx Beyond Marx (1979) is the most comprehesive statement of the theory of autonomy. One point that Negri makes that is necessary to bear in mind in order to understand his next book on Spinoza is that communism is immediately given in inverted form in the categories of capital. For example, the specific characteristics of money (sociality, the representation of collective productivity, the measure and sign of social patrimony) can be immediately reversed into communism. Capitalist development is the inverse image of the process of communism, as a radical and extreme antithesis (liberation, the wealth of needs, the reverse of the crises of "over"-production). When the opposition becomes extreme, then associated labor will be transformed. The emergence of an antithetical subject and the liberation of the forces of production will legislate that capitalist command is no longer necessary. There will be new rules of production and development. The two most important features of Negri's communism are first, that it is the result of the activity of a constituting subject, and second, that it consists of the liberty of this subject's labor from the capitalist form of value and of work. The communist future can only be constructed; it is not the product or teleology of capitalism's logical development, but rather a new subject forming itself by destroying capital and transforming reality. (As Negri puts it, communism is not inevitable; hence, it is all the more inevitable.) The communist refusal of work unleashes the multiplicity of free movement of this subject, its complete autonomy. But what is necessary to see is that this multiplicity and potential "over"-productivity is already contained (in the dual sense of limited and housed) in capitalism. Communism, as a dynamic and constitutive subjective element—human productive potential—is the motor of capitalist development; this is why Negri is so optimistic. The materialization of communism will thus consist of the development of the use values of living labor beyond the limits capital value imposes. The transition to communism is the material self-construction of an autonomous subject.

At first glance, *The Savage Anomaly: Essay on Power and Potential in Baruch Spinoza* (1980), the study of Spinoza which Negri wrote while in prison, seems to mark a radical break from his preceding works. In it, he returns to the analysis of 17th-century politics and philosophy which was his concern in *Descartes politico* (1970), before he undertook a more engaged form of writing. Yet *Savage Anomaly* is not all that anomalous. In it, Negri constructs a reading of Spinoza which justifies his own political and philosophical position.

Negri reads Spinoza as privileging "potential" (*potenza*) against power. One can see immediately how this relates to Negri's notion of communism as the liberation of human collective productive capacity from the law of value and capitalist work, two forms of power. Potential is the materialist production and constitution of being in Spinoza. It also names collective human activity as a world-constituting practice. Potential has both an ontological and a political dimension, and the two necessarily articulate. Ontologically, it describes the constitutive collective practice that produces the world as an open-ended dynamic activity. The collectivity is the "multitudes," and the activity is progressive liberation. Politically, therefore, potential is the basis of a revolutionary democracy, constituted by consensus. By interweaving the concepts of material production and political constitution, Spinoza demystifies the philosophical basis of the 17th-century bourgeois absolute State, that is, the rational idealist dualism of mind and body, mind and world. Elevated, like the mind, above the world of material production, the State becomes transcendental command and power, beyond determination by the collective practice of the masses. It is for this reason that Negri will argue that Spinoza's political theory is actually to be found in his metaphysics. The metaphysical concept of potential in a non-dualist materialist philosophy necessarily leads to an ethics of need, passion, and generosity, as well as to a politics of republican constitution and liberation. Hence, Negri argues, Spinoza puts the problem of democracy on a material basis, within the problem of production and against all the current mystifications of the State. He is anomalous in relation to the new 17th-century capitalist order of production because his work represents the transgression of all ordering which is not freely constituted by the masses. His "new rationality" consists of a constitutional ontology founded on needs and the organization of the collective "imagination" (a principle of inventive production). Philosophy and politics, therefore, like constitution and production, are inseparable in Spinoza. The fact that the writing of the *Tractatus Theologico-politicus*. a political tract, interrupts the writing of the *Ethics,* a philosophical document, is not an accident as far as Negri is concerned. It simply shows that the activity of discovery mimes the discovery of activity.

I will discuss only those parts of the book which relate to the theory of autonomy; I won't enter into historical or textual detail. It is enough to say that Negri has performed a fine materialist and historical analysis. He describes the development of Spinoza's work in terms of the political economy of the Dutch Republic, the cultural milieu of the counter-Reformation, and Spinoza's own perambulations. And he outlines an antagonistic dual tradition of political theory—Hobbes/Rousseau/Hegel vs. Machiavelli/Spinoza/Marx—which clearly is pertinent to the current situation in Italy.

For Negri, Spinoza is a post-bourgeois philosopher who writes against the grain of the ideological requirements of the Dutch bourgeoisie. Rather than a utopia which merely idealizes the capitalist market in the face of a crisis, Spinoza writes a dystopia which acknowledges the practical material basis of human life in need and desire, the conflictuality which is the consequence of this basis, and the collectivity of human production which is the only possible ethical solution to that conflictuality. Spinoza is radically anti-transcendental. His method follows the diffuse expansion of material potential rather than taking the form of a finalist, teleological dialectic, which mediates difference, conflict, and the plurality of modes of being into an abstract resolution which would be the identity of power. Potential is always at odds with power in Spinoza. The power of dialectical mediation subsumes the individual into the universal. The emphasis on potential reverses this transcendental metaphysic by promoting an insertion into the world, an exaltation of the plurality of modes, in politics, history, and in the phenomenology of singular and collective life. Spinoza's logic follows the constitutive process of reality. It posits material being as *potenza*, activity, a construction, within which human productive activity is situated. The political implication of the emphasis on human production as potential is that it opposes the subsumption of that activity into a principle of transcendence, of power. Political society will not be based on obedience, but rather on consensus. For Spinoza, the State is not founded on law, but instead on liberation, which is equatable with constitution, the free expansion of human productive potential.

The notion of potential is subversive of power because it implies an open-endedness and a counter-finality of constitution and production which foregrounds the principles of displacement and transformation, both of which undermine the bases of power in stability and absolutism. Philosophical finalism always makes a historical world order out to be of the indissoluble order of nature; hence, it legitimates power and command. Spinoza's concept of the human being as an activity, as a subject of construction and the producer of the world, dislocates any finality assigned to a particular world order. The horizon of human constitutive potential is open; the world is what is not yet. This, according to Negri, is what makes Spinoza an anomaly in terms of the dominant culture of the 17th century. With its emphasis on the collectivity of the multitude, and its opposition to the rigid individualism of the capitalist market, Spinoza's metaphysic is a declaration of the irreducibility of the forces of production to the bourgeois order. It is an affirmation of the productive force of humankind and a demystification of all bourgeois ideology which hides domination exercised over that productive force. As in Negri's other writings on the problem of the antagonism between capitalist command and worker autonomy, the problem of the crossing between productive force and productive relation appears here as crucial. In Spinoza, there is no possibility of a separation of productive relations from productive forces (as in the absolutist State of the 17th century bourgeoisie). He negates the distinction between civil society and the State. Civil society and politics are completely interwoven.

This argument has two important consequences which set off echoes in the theory of autonomy. The first is that the 17th-century order of capitalist development, as a result of economic crises, required an ideology of ascesis and ordering which placed limits on productive accumulation. Spinoza's philosophy of potential as an infinite activity of constructive production which remained open counters this bourgeois necessity. The limitlessness of potential is posed against the limitations imposed by power. The second consequence is that power can only be determined as subordinate to the social potential of the "multitude." The collapsing of the distinctions between civil society and politics, productive forces and productive relations, in Spinoza implies that State power can only be constitutionally organized. This represents a negation of the absolutist State, of the separation of State of capitalist "original accumulation" (the exercise of State force to consolidate early capitalism) from society, and an espousal of a constitution founded on opposition to power and the affirmation of autonomy. The modernity of Spinoza's concept of the political constitution of the real resides in its destruction of the notion of the autonomy of the political and an affirmation of the hegemony and autonomy of the collective needs of the masses.

Spinoza's metaphysic, then, presents being as a productive force and ethics as the phenomenological articulation of productive needs. It affirms productive forces as a terrain of liberation, much like the theory of autonomy. In Spinoza, as in the theory of autonomy, production and constitution, collective human productive activity and the political arrangement of society, are presented as inseparable. Production is inside the structure of being, and human activity extends nature by transforming it into second nature, something produced by human kind. The political constitution in Spinoza is what mediates the passage from nature to second nature. Therefore, according to Negri, it is the productive machinery of the destruction of power, conceived as transcendence and control over the productive masses. In this frame, power is seen as contingent in relation to the truly constitutive principle of the world, which is potential. The legitimation of command is based on the separation of the relation between relations of production and forces of production, and in Spinoza such a separation cannot obtain. Productive force, once liberated from the constraints of bourgeois productive relations, shows itself to be immediately constitutive, and it shows the possibility that the world can be transformed according to desire. And this last, one might say, is the conclusion of the theory of autonomy. As Negri words it in his political writings: "Communism as a minimal program."

The first major political piece that Negri published in prison is entitled *Class Politics: Motor and Form, The Five Campaigns Today.* It is an appendix to a forthcoming book to be called *War and Communism.* He calls for a critical reassessment of the 70s. He repudiates the Red Brigades' strategy of armed terrorism, blaming it for the current straits in which the movement finds itself. He argues that a new level of class composition has been attained which calls for a new "class politics" that would be "the conscious mediation of the constitutive activity of the proletarian practice of needs." The period of pure-auto-valorization is over, and now is a time requiring auto-determination through a political mediation of the movement. Hence, the "fifth campaign" he outlines calls for the formation of a political stratum for the direction of the communist movement, the strategic definition of its functions, and the political mediation of the class struggle. Once again arguing for the refusal of work and for the constitutive communist potential of the proletariat within capitalism, Negri emphasizes that this political mediation must grow directly out of the class' activity. The taking of power can only be the form of this material. The seizure of State power alone, without an anchor in the composition of the class, merely reproduces the bourgeois autonomization of the political, places the vanguard before the mass, and leads to socialism as planned capitalism.

Negri's argument is characteristically optimistic. The crisis, he writes, must be made the key to reconstructing the movement. It should not be seen as a catastrophe, but rather, as a source of creativity. Once one sees the possiblity of communism in the crisis, then peace itself, not armed struggle, becomes a weapon against capitalist development. The revolutionary passage can only grow out of the long, material process of the class composition of the proletariat. That composition has now reached a higher level that requires a higher level of political mediation, not that of the micro-groups of the 70s, but one that is more unitary in character, not a party, but a political mediation of counter-power that would translate the constitutive mobility of the class subject into a political mobility.

Of the two traditional options which offer themselves now as possible strategies—tyrannicide or the right of resistance—Negri chooses resistance, "destruction through mass insubordination," rejecting the Brigades' brand of tyrannicide. Collective revolt, he argues, will constitute communism. The political struggle comes first, and it assumes the immediacy of needs as an essential moment in the revolutionary passage. And there is a political need in the proletariat for wealth and liberty that is not answered by either the Brigades' terrorism or the CPI's statist alternative.

Negri concludes by listing the five "campaigns" that are needed today: first, the struggle against work as the exercise of counter-power and as the immanence of communism; second, the fight over public expenditures for services that affect the proletariat's reproduction of itself; third, the nuclear struggle and the critique of science as power; fourth, the struggle against the authoritarian State through education and the construction of a mass front; and finally, the creation of a political stratum for directing the movement. At a time of great pessimism in the Italian movement, Negri still sees grounds for hope within oppression. "Every suture," he writes, "opens new wounds."

Michael Ryan

Notes

1. The conference of Socialist Economists has produced an excellent volume entitled *Working Class Autonomy and the Crisis* (Red Notes, 1979), which contains several short texts by Negri, as well as a full translation of *Il dominio e il sabotaggio*. A short resume of Negri's works is available in French—Benjamin Coriat, "l'opéraisme italien," in *Dialectiques*, no. 30.

2. See *Potere Operaio: Per una internazionale della avanguardie rivoluzionarie* (Florence, 1974) and *Autonomia Operaia* (Rome, 1976). For an account of the role young workers and the student movement played in transforming autonomy from a primary workers' orientation to a broader social worker strategy, see Paolo Bassi and Antonio Pilati, *I giovanni e la crisi degli anni settenta* (Rome, 1978).

3. See Karl-Heinz Roth, *Die 'andere' Arbeiterbewegung* (Munich, 1974), a book Negri frequently refers to. Roth argues through a history of the German working class movement from the time of the Second International down to the present that the methods now being used to control the "other," autonomous workers' movement in Germany are essentially those developed during the Fascist period.

Bibliography

Edited by Harry Cleaver, Jim Fleming & Conrad Herold

I. Writings by Antonio Negri
(in chronological order)

1958   *Stato e diritto nel giovane Hegel: Studio sulla genesi illuministica della filosofia giuridica e politica di Hegel.* Cedam, Padova.

1959   *Saggi sullo storicismo tedesco: Dilthey e Meinecke.* Istituto Giangacomo Feltrinelli, Milano.

1962   *Alle origini del formalismo giuridico.* Cedam, Padova.
_____   *Hegel: scritti di filosofia del diritto (traduzione e cura).* Laterza, Bari.
_____   *Alle origini del formalismo giuridico: Studio sul problema della forma in Kant e nei giuristi kantiani fra il 1789 e il 1802.* Cedam, Padova.

1964   "Alcune riflessioni sullo 'Stato dei partiti,'" *Rivista trimestrale di diritto pubblico*, A. Giuffrè, Milano, pp. 1–60. Reprinted as capìtolo terzo: "Lo stato dei partiti," in Antonio Negri, *La forma stato: per la critica dell'economia politica della Costituzione*, Feltrinelli, Milano, 1977, pp. 77–98.

1967   "Studi su Max Weber (1956-1965)," in *Annuario bibliografico di filosofia del diritto*, A. Giuffrè, Milano.

1968   "John M. Keynes e la teoria capitalistica dello stato nel '29," *Contropiano*. Reprinted in S. Bologna, et al., *Operai e stato: Lotte operaie e riforma dello stato capitalistico tra rivoluzione d'Ottobre e New Deal.* Feltrinelli, Milano, 1972. Available in English as "John M. Keynes and the Capitalist Theory of the State in 1929," in Toni Negri, *Revolution Retrieved: Selected Writings on Marx, Keynes, Capitalist Crisis and New Social Subjects, 1967–83,* Red Notes, London, 1988, pp. 9–42.
_____   "Marx sul ciclo e la crisi," *Contropiano*, La Nuova Italia, Firenze. Reprinted in *Operai e stato.* Available in English as "Marx on the Cycle and on the Crisis," in *Revolution Retrieved*, pp. 47–90. Also available in German as *Zyklus und Krise bei Marx*, Merve Verlag, Berlin, 1972.
_____   "Lotte e Stato nel nuovo gius-sindacalismo," *Contropiano*, #1, La Nuova Italia, Firenze, pp. 207–216. Reprinted as capìtolo quarto: "Lotte e Stato nel nuovo gius-sindacalismo," in *La forma stato*, pp. 99–110.

1970   *Descartes politico o della ragionevole ideologia.* Feltrinelli, Milano.
_____   Scienze politiche 1 (Stato e politica) «Enciclopedia Feltrinelli-Fischer» #27 (a cura di) Feltrinelli, Milano.

1971   "Crisi dello Stato-piano: comunismo e organizzazione rivoluzionaria," *Potere operaio* No. 45, September 25, 1971. Available in English as "Crisis of the Planner State: Communism and Revolutionary Organization," in *Revolution Retrieved*, pp. 94–148. Also available in German as *Krise des Plan-Staats*, Merve Verlag, Berlin, 1973.

1974   Crisi dello Stato-piano: communismo e organizzazione rivoluzionaria. *Opuscoli marxisti* #1, Feltrinelli, Milano.
_____   "Rileggendo Pasukanis: note di discussione," Critica del diritto, #1, Musolini, Torino, pp. 90-119. Reprinted as chapter 5 in *La forma stato*.
_____   "Su alcune tendenze della più recente teoria comunista dello Stato: rassegna critica," *Critica del diritto*, #3, Musolini, Torino, pp. 84–120. Reprinted as chapter 6 in *La forma stato*, pp. 196–232. Also available in French as "Sur quelques tendances de la théorie communiste de l'état la plus récent: revue critique," in Association pour la Critique des Sciences Economiques et Sociales, *Sur L'État*, Colloque de Nice, 8–10 septembre 1976, Contradictions, Bruxelles, 1977, pp. 375–427.
_____   "Partito operaio contro il lavoro," in Sergio Bologna, Paolo Carpignano and Antonio Negri, Crisi e organizzazione operaia, Feltrinelli, Milano. Appendix 1 on "Riformismo e ristrutturazione: il terrorismo dello Stato-impresa," Appendix 2 on "Tesi sulla crisi: la multinazionale operaia," Appendix 3 on "Un passo avanti, due indiertro: la fine dei gruppi," and Appendix 4 on "Articolazioni organizzative e organizzazione complessiva: il partito di Mirafiori," are available in English as "Reformism and Restructuration: Terrorism of the State-as-factory-Command," "Theses on the Crisis", "One Step Forward, Two Steps Back...", and "The Workers' Party of Mirafiori," in Red Notes, *Working Class Autonomy and the Crisis*, Red Notes and Conference of Socialist Economists, London, 1979, pp. 33–37, 39–54, 55–59, 61–65.

1975   "Ambiguità di Panzieri?" *Aut–Aut*, #149–150, settembre–dicembre, pp. 141–155.
_____   "Stato, spesa pubblica e fatiscenza del compromesso storico," *Critica del diritto*, #5–6, Musolini, Torino, pp. 32–68. Reprinted as chapter 7 in Antonio Negri, *La forma stato*, pp. 233–269.

1976   "Simplex sigillum veri. Per la discussione di «Krisis» e di «Bisogni e teoria marxista»," *aut aut*, n. 155-156, settembre–dicembre, pp. 180-195.
_____   *Proletari e Stato: per una discussione su autonomia operaia e compromesso storico*, Opuscoli marxisti n.13, Feltrinelli, Milano. Also in French as "Prolétaires et Etat," in A. Negri, *La Classe Ouvrière Contre L'Etat*, Éditions Galilée, Paris 1978, pp. 221–306.
_____   "Esiste una dottrina marxista dello Stato?," *Aut–Aut*, #152–153, marzo–giugno, La Nuova Italia, Firenze, pp. 35–50. Reprinted as chapter 8 in *La forma stato*, pp. 273–287. Available in English as "Is There a Marxist Doctrine of the State? A Reply by Antonio Negri," in Norberto Bobbio, *Which Socialism?* University of Minnesota Press, Minneapolis, 1987, pp. 121–138.
_____   "Il marxismo e la questione criminale. Intervento nel dibattito promosso da 'La questione criminale'," *Il Mulino*, Bologna, 1976. Reprinted as chapter 9 in *La forma stato*, pp. 288–296.

224 MARX BEYOND MARX

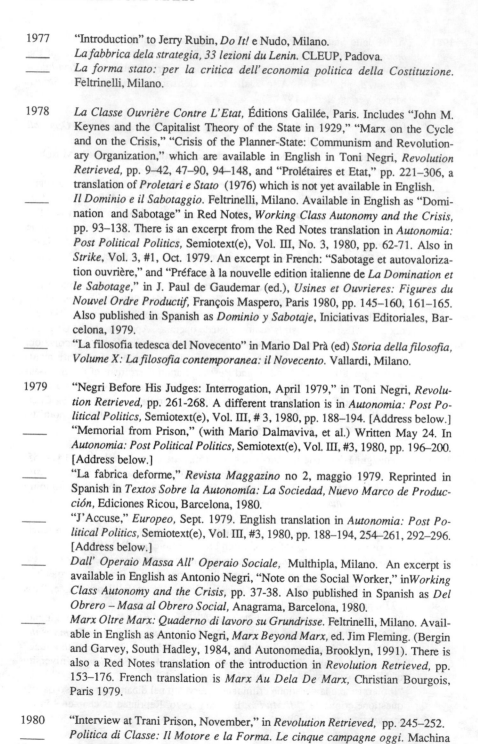

1977   "Introduction" to Jerry Rubin, *Do It!* e Nudo, Milano.
____   *La fabbrica dela strategia, 33 lezioni du Lenin.* CLEUP, Padova.
____   *La forma stato: per la critica dell'economia politica della Costituzione.* Feltrinelli, Milano.

1978   *La Classe Ouvrière Contre L'Etat,* Éditions Galilée, Paris. Includes "John M. Keynes and the Capitalist Theory of the State in 1929," "Marx on the Cycle and on the Crisis," "Crisis of the Planner-State: Communism and Revolutionary Organization," which are available in English in Toni Negri, *Revolution Retrieved,* pp. 9–42, 47–90, 94–148, and "Prolétaires et Etat," pp. 221–306, a translation of *Proletari e Stato* (1976) which is not yet available in English.
____   *Il Dominio e il Sabotaggio.* Feltrinelli, Milano. Available in English as "Domination and Sabotage" in Red Notes, *Working Class Autonomy and the Crisis,* pp. 93–138. There is an excerpt from the Red Notes translation in *Autonomia: Post Political Politics,* Semiotext(e), Vol. III, No. 3, 1980, pp. 62-71. Also in *Strike,* Vol. 3, #1, Oct. 1979. An excerpt in French: "Sabotage et autovalorization ouvrière," and "Préface à la nouvelle edition italienne de *La Domination et le Sabotage,*" in J. Paul de Gaudemar (ed.), *Usines et Ouvrieres: Figures du Nouvel Ordre Productif,* François Maspero, Paris 1980, pp. 145–160, 161–165. Also published in Spanish as *Dominio y Sabotaje,* Iniciativas Editoriales, Barcelona, 1979.
____   "La filosofia tedesca del Novecento" in Mario Dal Prà (ed) *Storia della filosofia, Volume X: La filosofia contemporanea: il Novecento.* Vallardi, Milano.

1979   "Negri Before His Judges: Interrogation, April 1979," in Toni Negri, *Revolution Retrieved,* pp. 261-268. A different translation is in *Autonomia: Post Political Politics,* Semiotext(e), Vol. III, # 3, 1980, pp. 188–194. [Address below.]
____   "Memorial from Prison," (with Mario Dalmaviva, et al.) Written May 24. In *Autonomia: Post Political Politics,* Semiotext(e), Vol. III, #3, 1980, pp. 196–200. [Address below.]
____   "La fabrica deforme," *Revista Maggazino* no 2, maggio 1979. Reprinted in Spanish in *Textos Sobre la Autonomía: La Sociedad, Nuevo Marco de Producción,* Ediciones Ricou, Barcelona, 1980.
____   "J'Accuse," *Europeo,* Sept. 1979. English translation in *Autonomia: Post Political Politics,* Semiotext(e), Vol. III, #3, 1980, pp. 188–194, 254–261, 292–296. [Address below.]
____   *Dall' Operaio Massa All' Operaio Sociale,* Multhipla, Milano. An excerpt is available in English as Antonio Negri, "Note on the Social Worker," in *Working Class Autonomy and the Crisis,* pp. 37-38. Also published in Spanish as *Del Obrero – Masa al Obrero Social,* Anagrama, Barcelona, 1980.
____   *Marx Oltre Marx: Quaderno di lavoro su Grundrisse.* Feltrinelli, Milano. Available in English as Antonio Negri, *Marx Beyond Marx,* ed. Jim Fleming. (Bergin and Garvey, South Hadley, 1984, and Autonomedia, Brooklyn, 1991). There is also a Red Notes translation of the introduction in *Revolution Retrieved,* pp. 153–176. French translation is *Marx Au Dela De Marx,* Christian Bourgois, Paris 1979.

1980   "Interview at Trani Prison, November," in *Revolution Retrieved,* pp. 245–252.
____   *Politica di Classe: Il Motore e la Forma. Le cinque campagne oggi.* Machina Libri, Milano.

_____ *Il comunismo e la guerra*. Feltrinelli, Milano.

1981   "Riflessioni su un Fantasma," (con Luciano Ferrari Bravo) in *Metropoli*, 3, Anno 3, Numero 3, Febbraio, pp. 21–25.

_____ "Terrorismo? Nein, Danke. Un Documento dal Carcere di Toni Negri," *Il Manifesto*, 22 March. Available in French in Toni Negri, *L'Italie; Rouge et Noire: Journal, Février 1983 – Novembre 1983*, Hachette, Paris, 1985, pp. 111–117.

_____ "Erkenntnistheorie: Elogio dell'asenza di memoria," *Metropoli*, 5, Anno 3, Numero 5, Giugno, pp. 50–53.

_____ "Noi e l'europa," *Metropoli*, 6, Anno 3, Numero 6, Settembre, pp. 4–5.

_____ *L'Anomalia Selvaggia, saggio du potere e potenza in Spinoza*. Feltrinelli, Milano. French edition is: *L'Anomalie Sauvage: Puissance et pouvoir chez Spinoza*, PUF, Paris.

_____ "Crisi di Stato-crisi: Ipotesi sugli anni '80," in AA.VV. *Crisi delle Politiche*, Pironti, Napoli. Reprinted as chapter 10 in Negri, *Macchina Tempo: Rompicapi, Liberazione, Costituzione*, Feltrinelli, Milano, 1982. Available in English as "Crisis of the Crisis-State," in *Revolution Retrieved*, pp. 177-197.

1982   *Macchina Tempo: Rompicapi, Liberazione, Costituzione*. Feltrinelli, Milano. Chapter 8 on "Archeologia e progetto. L'operaio massa e l'operaio sociale," and Chapter 10 on "Crisi di Stato-crisi," are available in English as "Archaeology and Project: The Mass Worker and the Social Worker," and "Crisis of the Crisis-State," in *Revolution Retrieved*, pp. 199–228.

1983   "Do You Remember Revolution?" (with Paolo Virno et al) *Il Manifesto*, 20-22 February. Available in English in *Revolution Retrieved*, pp. 229-243. Available in French in *L'Italie: Rouge et Noire*, pp. 55–68.

_____ "L'instituzione logica del collettivo e le fatiche dell'estetica (a proposito del libro su Frege di Roberta de Monticelli)," *Aut–Aut*, #197-98, settembre–dicembre, pp. 133-142.

_____ *Pipe-Line, lettere da Rebibbia*. Einaudi, Torino. Letter 19 has been published in French as "Ferocious Alphabets," in *Change international*, no 1, 1983.

1985   "Réaction à 'A propos de Logos et théorie des catastrophes' de Jean Petitot" *Babylone* n. 4, 10/18 Union Generale d'Editions, Printemps–Été, Paris.

_____ "Deliqua Desiderantur: Congettura per un definzione del concetto di democrazia nell'ultimo Spinoza," *Studia Spinozana*, n. 1, pp. 143-181.

_____ *Les Nouveau Espaces de Liberté*. (avec Félix Guattari). Bedou. English translation is *Communists Like Us*, [New York: Semiotext(e), 1990].

1986   "Vers de Nouvelles Valeurs?" *Terminal* 19/84, No. 26, Juin, pp. 3–7.

_____ "Lettre a Félix Guattari," in Marie-Blanche Tahon et Antre Corten, *l'Italie: le philosophe et le gendarme*, Actes du Coloque de Montreal, VLB editeur, Montreal, 1986, pp. 95–110.

_____ *Diario di Un'Evasione*. In French as *L'Italie: Rouge et Noire*.

_____ "Postmoderno," in José Tono Martínez (ed.) *La Polemica de la Posmodernidad*, Ediciones Libertarias, Madrid, pp. 125–135.

1987 *Fabbriche del soggetto: profili, protesi, transiti, macchine, paradossi, passaggi, sovversioni, sistemi, potenze: appunti per un dispositivo ontologico*, XXI SECOLO Bimestrale di politicae cultura n. 1, Settembre-Ottobre.

_____ *Lenta ginestra: saggio sull' ontologia di Giacomo Leopardi*. SugarCo, Milano.

1988 *Revolution Retrieved: Selected Writings on Marx, Keynes, Capitalist Crisis and New Social Subjects, 1967–83*. Red Notes, London, 1988.

1989 "Gauche et Coordinations Ouvrières (Nouveau mouvements sociaux)," *Lignes*, n. 5, Février, pp. 86–96.

_____ "Ocho Tesis Preliminares para una Teoría del Poder," *Contrarios*, n. 1, April, (Madrid).

_____ "Review of Norberto Bobbio's *Future of Democracy* and *Which Socialism? Marxism, Socialism and Democracy*," *Capital & Class*, #37, Spring, pp. 156–161.

_____ *The Politics of Subversion: A Manifesto for the Twenty-First Century*, Polity Press, Oxford.

_____ "Postscript, 1990," trans. Jared Becker, in Félix Guattari and Toni Negri, *Communists Like Us* , trans. Michael Ryan [New York: Semiotext(e)].

II. Selected Texts of the Italian New Left from Other Authors

1960 Unita Proletaria, "Italie: Juillet 1960," *Socialisme ou Barbarie*, No 31, Vol. VI (12e année] Décembre 1960 – Février 1961.

1961 Romano Alquati, "Relazione sulle 'forze nuove': Convegno del PSI sulla FIAT," *Quaderni Rossi*, n. 1, Settembre 1961, pp. 215–240. Reprinted in Romano Alquati, *Sulla FIAT e Altri Scritti*, Milano: Feltrinelli Editore, 1975, pp. 27-53.

_____ Raniero Panzieri, "Sull'uso capitalistico delle macchine nel neocapitalismo," *Quaderni Rossi*, No. 1, 1961, pp. 53–72. Reprinted in Panzieri, *La Ripresa del Marxismo Leninismo in Italia*, Milano: Sapere Ed. 1975, pp. 73–80. Available in English as "The Capitalist Use of Machinery: Marx Versus the 'Objectivists'," in Phil Slater (ed), *Outlines of a Critique of Technology*, Atlantic Highlands: Humanities Press 1980, pp. 39–68.

1962 Mario Tronti "Marx ieri e oggi," *Mondo Nuovo*, n. 1, 1962. Reprinted in Mario Tronti, *Operai e Capitale*, Turin: Einaudi, 1966, 1971, pp. 31–38.

_____ Mario Tronti, "La fabbrica e la società," Quaderni Rossi, No. 2, giugno 1962, pp. 1–31. Reprinted in *Operai e Capitale*, pp. 39–59.

_____ Romano Alquati, "Composizione organica del capitale e forza-lavoro alla Olivetti," *Quaderni Rossi* #2, giugno 1962 e #3, giugno 1963, pp. 63–98. Reprinted in *Sulla FIAT e Altri Scritti*, pp. 81–163.

1963 Mario Tronti, "Il Piano del Capitale," in *Quaderni Rossi*, No. 3, Giugno 1963, pp. 44–73. Reprinted in *Operai e Capitale*, pp. 267-311. Available in English as "Social Capital," *Telos*, #17, Fall 1973, pp. 98–121.

1964 Romano Alquati, "Lotta alla FIAT," *Classe Operaia*, #1, Gennaio 1964, pp. 6–8. Reprinted in *Sulla FIAT e Altri Scritti*, pp. 185–197.

—— Mario Tronti, "Lenin in Inghilterra," *Classe Operaio*, #1, Jan. 1964, pp. 1, 18–20. Reprinted in *Operai e Capitale*, pp. 89-95. Available in English in *Working Class Autonomy and the Crisis*, pp. 1–6.

—— Mario Tronti, "Vecchia tattica per una nuova strategia," *Classe Operaio*, 4–5, maggio 1964, pp. 1, 31–32. Reprinted in *Operai e Capitale*, pp. 96–102.

—— Mario Tronti, "1905 in Italia," *Classe Operaio*, 8–9, settembre 1964, pp. 1, 15–16. Reprinted in *Operai e Capitale*, pp. 103-109.

—— Mario Tronti, "Classe e partito," *Classe Operaio*, 10-12, diciembre 1964, pp. 2–6. Reprinted in *Operai e Capitale*, 110–120.

—— Raniero Panzieri, "Plusvalore e pianificazione: Appunti di lettura del Capitale," in *Quaderni Rossi*, #4, pp. 257-288. Reprinted as Chapter 25 in *Ripresa del Marxismo Leninismo in Italia*, pp. 329–365. Available in English as "Surplus Value and Planning: Notes on the Reading of *Capital*," in *The Labour Process and Class Strategies*. CSE Pamphlet, #1, London: Stage 1, 1976, pp. 4–25.

1965 Romano Alquati, "Ricerca sulla structtura interna della classe operaia," *Classe Operaia*, #1, Anno II, gennaio–febbraio 1965, pp. 8–14. Reprinted in *Sulla FIAT e Altri Scritti*, pp. 219–228.

1966 Mario Tronti, "La strategia del rifiuto," and "Poscritto di problemi," in *Operai e Capitale*, pp. 234–252, 267–311. Available in English as "The Strategy of Refusal," in *Working Class Autonomy and the Crisis*, pp. 7–21, and as "Workers and Capital," *Telos*, #14, Winter 1972, pp. 25–62..

—— Mario Tronti, *Operai e Capitale*, Turin: Einaudi, 1966, 1971. Also in French: Mario Tronti, *Ouvriers et capital*, Paris: Christian Bourgois editeur, 1977.

1967 Romano Alquati, "Capitale e classe operaia alla FIAT: un punto medio nel ciclo internazionale," in *Sulla FIAT e Altri Scritti*, pp. 315–341. Originally written in May 1967.

1968 Bologna, Sergio and Daghini, Giairo, "Maggio '68 in Francia," *Quaderni Piacentini*, #35, anno VII, Iuglio 1968, pp. 2-41.

—— Alberto Asor Rosa, "A Separate Branch of the Working Class," *International Socialist Journal*, Year 5, No. 26–27, July 1968, pp. 191-200.

—— Luigi Bobbio and Guido Viale, "Student Political Organization," *International Socialist Journal*, Year 5, #26–27, July, pp. 220–231.

—— Massimo Cacciari, "Sviluppo capitalistico e ciclo delle lotte. La Montecatini–Edison di Porto Marghera. I. La 'fase' 1950-1966," *Contropiano* #3, pp. 579–627.

1969 Rita di Leo, "I bolscevichi e 'il Capitale'," *Contropiano* #2, pp. 273–344.

—— Massimo Cacciari, "Sviluppo capitalistico e ciclo delle lotte. La Montecatini–Edison di Porto Marghera. I. La 'fase' 1966–estate 1969," *Contropiano* #2, pp. 397–447.

—— Adriano Sofri, "Quelle Avant-Garde? Quelle Organisation?" *Les Temps Modernes*, #279, Octobre, pp. 435–445 with "Réponse a Sofri" by R. Luperini, pp. 445-454.

1970   Potere Operaio, "Italy 1969–1970: A Wave of Struggles," A Supplement to *Potere Operaio*, #27, June 22–July 3.

____   Il Manifesto, "For Communism: Theses of the *Il Manifesto* Group," *Politics & Society*, August 1971, pp. 407–440. Originally in *Il Manifesto*, Sept. 1970.

____   Comitato Operaio di Porto Maghera, *Lotte Operaie e problema dell 'organizzazione: Iuglio '68–Febbraio '70*, Milano: Edizioni Della Libreria. (PCL: HD 6713, C45, L6)

____   Renzo Gianotti, *Lotte e organizzazione di classe alla FIAT (1948–1970)*, De Donato Editore, Bari.

1971   Mario Tronti, "Poscritto di problemi," in Mario Tronti, *Operai e Capitale*, Einaudi, Torino 1966, 1971, pp. 267–311. Available in English as "Workers and Capital," *Telos*, #14, Winter 1972, pp. 25–62.

1972   Guido Viale, "Class Struggle and European Unity," *Lotta Continua*, #7–8. In English in *Autonomous Struggles and the Capitalist Crisis*, Toronto 1974.

____   Sergio Bologna, "Composizione di classe e teoria del partito alle origini del movimento consiliare," in *Operai e Stato*, pp. 13–46. In English as "Class Composition and the Theory of the Party at the Origin of the Workers Councils Movement," *Telos* #13, Fall 1972, pp. 14–21.

____   Potere Operaio, "The Communism of the Working Class," (typescript).

____   L. Ferrari-Bravo e A. Serafini, *Stato e Sottosviluppo: Il Caso del Mezzogiorno Italiano*, Milano: Feltrinelli.

____   S. Bologna, G.P. Rawick, M. Gobbini, A. Negri, L. Ferrari Bravo e F. Gambino, *Operai e Stato: Lotte operaie e riforma dello stato capitalistico tra revoluzione d'ottobre e New Deal*, Milano: Feltrinelli.

____   Mariarosa Dalla Costa, *Potere femminile e sovversione sociale* (con "Il posto della donna" di Selma James). In English as Mariarosa Dalla Costa, "Women and the Subversion of the Community," *Radical America*, Vol. 6, #1, January–February 1972, pp. 67–102; with an introduction by Selma James, pp. 62–67.

1973   Sergio Bologna, "Questions of Method for Analysis of the Chemical Plan," *Quaderni Piacentini*, January. Available in English typescript.

____   Potero Operaio, "Italy 1973: Workers' Struggles and the Capitalist Crisis," *Radical America*, Vol. 7, #2, March–April, pp. 15–32. (Whole issue on Italy.)

____   Sergio Bologna, "Moneta e Crisi: Marx Corrispondente della New York *Daily Tribune*, 1856-57," *Primo Maggio*, No. 1, Settembre, pp. 1–15. An expanded version was published in S. Bologna, P. Carpignano and A. Negri, *Crisi e Organizzazione Operaia*, Milano: Feltrinelli, 1974, pp. 9–72.

____   Sergio Bologna, "Il rapporto societa-fabbrica come categoria storica," *Primo Maggio*, No. 2, Ottobre 1973, pp. 1–8.

____   Raniero Panzieri, *La Ripresa del Marxismo Leninismo in Italia*, Sapere Ed., Milano.

1974   Sergio Bologna, "Petrolio e mercato mondiale: cronistoria di una crisi," in *Quaderni Piacentini*, #52. First half available in English typescript as "Oil and the World Market: Chronology of a Crisis."

____   S. Bologna, P. Carpignano & A. Negri, *Crisi e Organizzazione Operaia*, Feltrinelli, Milano.

____ Paolo Carpignano, "Note su classe operaia e capitale in America negli anni sessanta," in S. Bologna, P. Carpignano and A. Negri, *Crisi e Organizzazione Operaia*, Feltrinelli, Milano. Available in English as "U.S. Class composition in the 1960s," *Zerowork* #1, December 1975, pp. 7–32.

____ A. Serafini, et. al., *L'Operaio multinationale in Europa*, Feltrinelli, Milano.

____ Mariarosa Dalla Costa, "Riproduzione e emigrazione," in A. Serafini, et al., *L'Operaio Multinazionale in Europa*, Feltrinelli, Milano, pp. 207–242. Reprinted in Mariarosa Dalla Costa e Leopoldina Fortunati, *Brutto ciao! Direzioni di marcia delle donne negli ultimi 30 anni*, Edizioni delle donne, Roma.

____ Romano Alquati, *Sindadato e partito*. Ed. Stampatori, Torino.

1975   Raniero Panzieri e M. Tronti, "Tesi Panzieri–Tronti," *Aut–Aut*, No. 149–150, Sett.–Dic., pp. 6-10.

____ Paolo Carpignano, "Note su classe operaia e capitale in America negli anni sessanta," in *Crisi e Organizzazione Operaia*,. Available in English as "U.S. Class composition in the 1960s," *Zerowork* #1, December 1975, pp. 7–32.

____ Luciano Ferrari Bravo, "Utopia e progetto loro possibilità e rapporti," *Quaderni del Progetto* #1, dicembre, pp. 59–79.

____ Collectivo Internazionale Femminista (a cura del), *Le Operai Della Casa*. (Salario al lavoro domestico: strategia internazionale, #1) Marsilio Editori, Venezia.

____ Collectivo Internazionale Femminista (a cura del), *8 Marzo 1974: giornata internazionale di lotta delle donne*. (Salario al lavoro domestico: strategia internazionale, #2) Marsilio Editori, Venezia.

____ Massimo Cacciari e Paolo Perulli, *Piano Economico e composizione di classe: il dibattito sull'industrializzazione e lo scontro politico durante la NEP*, Feltrinelli, Milano.

1976   Alquati, Romano "Universita, Formazione della Forza Lavoro Intellecttuale, Terziarizzazione," in Roberta Tomassini, *Studenti e Composizione di classe*, Milano: edizioni Aut-Aut, 1977, pp. 12–76. (Originally written maggio 1976)

____ Leopoldina Fortunati, "La famiglia: verso la ricostruzione," in *Brutto ciao!* pp. 71–144.

____ Quaderni del Territorio, "Ristrutturazione produttiva e Nuova Geografia della Forza-lavoro," *Anno I*, #1.

____ Collectivo Internazionale Femminista (a cura del), *Aborto di stato: strage delle innocenti*. (Salario al lavoro domestico: strategia internazionale, #3) Marsilio Editori, Venezia.

____ Danilo Montaldi, *Saggio sulla politica comunista in Italia (1919–1970)*. Edizioni Quaderni Piacentini, Piacenza.

____ Gruppi Femministi, *Coordinamento Emiliano Per il Salario al Lavoro Domestico*, Bologna.

____ Gisela Bock, Paolo Carpignano e Bruno Ramirez, *La formazione dell'operaio massa negli USA 1898/1922*. Feltrinelli, Milano.

1977   Sergio Bologna, "Proletari e stato di A. Negri: una recensione," *Primo Maggio*, #7.

____ Sergio Bologna, "La tribù delle talpe," *Primo Maggio*, #8, Spring, pp. 3–18. Available in English as "The Tribe of Moles: Class Composition and the Party System in Italy," in*Working Class Autonomy and the Crisis*, pp. 67–91 and in

Semiotext(e), Vol. III, #3, 1980, pp. 36–61. [Address below.]

_____ Rita di Leo, _Il modello di stalin: il rapporto tra politica e economia nel socialismo realizzato,_ Feltrinelli, Milano.

1978   Collectivo Internazionale Femminista (a cura del), _Lotta all'ospedale di ferrara: diertro la normalità del parto._ (Salario al lavoro domestico: strategia internazionale, #5) Marsilio Editori, Venezia.

_____ Paolo Carpignano, "La classe operaia americana e la degradzione della teoria," _Aut–Aut,_ #172, Luglio-Agosto, pp. 96-108.

_____ Silvia Federici e Nicole Cox, _Contropiano dalle cucine._ Collectivo Internazionale Femminista (a cura del) (Salario al lavoro domestico: strategia internazionale, #6) Marsilio Editori, Venezia.

_____ Lapo Berti (ed.), _Moneta, Crisi e stato capitalistico,_ Opuscoli marxisti 22, Feltrinelli, Milano.

_____ Sergio Bologna (ed.), _La Tribu delle Talpe,_ Opuscoli marxisti 23, Feltrinelli, Milano.

_____ Giovanna Franca Dalla Costa, _Un lavoro d'amore; La violenza fisica componente essenziale del 'trattamento' maschile nei confronti delle donne,_ edizioni delle donne, Roma.

_____ Bruno Ramirez, _When Workers Fight: The Politics of Industrial Relations in the Progressive Era, 1898–1916,_ Greenwood Press, Westport.

1979   Bruno Cartosio, "L'Altra faccia della 'degradazione'," _Aut–Aut,_ #172, Luglio–Agosto, pp. 109–117.

_____ Mariarosa Dalla Costa, "Forza-lavoro femminile e formazione de proletariato urbano a Trieste," _Primo Maggio,_ #13, Autunno, pp. 61–62.

1980   Oreste Scalzone, "From Guaranteeism to Armed Politics," _Autonomia: Post Political Politics,_ Semiotext(e), New York, pp. 80–83. [Address below.]

_____ Franco Berardi ("Bifo"), "Anatomy of Autonomy," _Autonomia: Post Political Politics,_ Semiotext(e), New York, pp. 148–170 [Address below.].

_____ Franco Piperno, "The Naked Truth About Moro's Detention," _Autonomia: Post Political Politics,_ Semiotext(e), New York, pp. 202–205 [Address below.]

_____ Roberto Battaggia, "Operaio massa e operaio sociale: alcune considerazione sulla 'nuova composizione'," _Primo Maggio,_ #14, Inverno 1980-81, pp. 71–77.

_____ Giovanna Franca Dalla Costa, _La riproduzione nel sottosviluppo: un caso il venezuela,_ CLEUP, Padova.

1981   Bologna, Sergio "Composizione di classe e sistema politico," in _Crisi delle Politiche e Politiche nella Crisi,_ Pironti, Napoli, pp. 119–128.

_____ Leopoldina Fortunati, _L'Archano Della Riproduzione: casalinghe, prostitute, operai e capitale,_ Marsilio Editori, Venezia. In English as _The Arcane of Reproduction: Housework, Prostitution, Labor and Capital,_ trans. Hillary Creek (Brooklyn: Autonomedia, 1990).

1983   Mariarosa Dalla Costa, _Famiglia, welfare e stato tra progressismo e New Deal,_ Franco Angeli Editore, Milano.

1984   Silvia Federici e Leopoldina Fortunati, _Il Grande Calibano: Storia del corpo sociale ribelle nella prima fase del capitale,_ Franco Angeli, Milano.

1986 Sergio Bologna, "Qu'est-ce que l'operaisme aujourd'hui?" in Marie-Blanche Tahon et Antre Corten, *L'Italie: le philosophe et le gendarme,* Actes du Coloque de Montreal, VLB editeur, Montreal, pp. 63–80.

_____ Franco Berardi ("Bifo"), "Communication et autonomie," in *L'Italie: le philosophe et le gendarme,* pp. 111–121.

_____ Franco Piperno, "Innovation technologique et transformation de l'être social," in *L'Italie: le philosophe et le gendarme,* pp. 123–132.

_____ Bifo, Piperno et Bologna, "L'Autonomie sociale au-delà de l'autonomie," in *L'Italie: le philosophe et le gendarme,* pp. 219–231.

_____ Marie-Blanche Tahon et Antre Corten, *L'Italie: le philosophe et le gendarme,* Actes du Coloque de Montreal, VLB editeur, Montreal.

_____ B. Cartosio, "Il peso dell'emergenza: il sistema dei partiti e il '77," *Primo Maggio,* #26, Inverno 1986/87.

_____ S. Bologna, "Memoria operaia e nuova composizione di classe, Atti del Convegno di Mantova, Ottobre 1981" *Primo Maggio,* #26, Inverno 1986/87.

1988 G. Lavanco, "Il soggetto, l'evento, il progetto, l'ambiente ed altri preamboli, Note sulle lotte ecologiste all'inizio del XXI secolo," *Notebook: Quaderni di Autonomia,* Supplemento Autonomia #43, Novembre, pp. 49–52.

_____ Bobbio, Luigi *Storia di Lotta Continua,* Feltrinelli, MIlano.

_____ Materiali per una nuova sinistra, *Il sessantotto: La stagione dei movimenti (1960-1979),* Edizioni Associate, Roma.

1989 Balestrini, Nanni e Primo Moroni *L'Orda d'Oro: 1968-1977, La grande ondata rivoluzionaria e creativa, politica ed esistenziale,* Milano: SugarCo.

III. Selected Works in English in or about the Autonomist Marxist tradition

1933 C.L.R. James, "The Case for West-Indian Self Government," in C.L.R. James, *The Future in the Present, Selected Writings,* Westport: Lawrence Hill, 1977 and London: Allison & Busby, 1977, pp. 25–40. Excerpt from C.L.R. James, *The Case for West Indian Self Government,* London: Hogarth Press, 1933, an abridgement of C.L.R. James, *The Life of Captain Cipriani,* Lancashire, 1932.

1938 C.L.R. James, *A History of Negro Revolt,* London: Race Today, 1985. (Originally published in 1938; this is a reprint of the 1969 Drum and Spear Press revised version.) [Available from Race Today, address below.]

_____ C.L.R. James, "Revolts in Africa," in C.L.R. James, *The Future in the Present,* pp. 70–85. Originally a chapter of *A History of Negro Revolt,* FACT Monograph #18, London, September 1938. Revised and reissued as *A History of Pan-African Revolt,* Drum & Spear Press, Wash., D.C., 1969.

1942 Raya Dunayevskaya, "Labor and Society," typescript. [Available from: News & Letters, address below.]

_____ F. Forest [Raya Dunayevskaya], "An Analysis of Russian Economy: A Contribution on the Discussion on Russia," Part II: 2 articles in the *New International* Dec. 1946 and Jan. 1947. These articles, along with three others [see above] were reprinted by News & Letters in 1973 as a pamphlet: *The Original Historical Analysis: Russia as State-Capitalist Society*. [Address below.]

1947   Paul Romano and Ria Stone, *The American Worker*, Detroit: Facing Reality Publishing Company. Translated and published in France by Socialisme ou Barbarie, and then in Italy (from the French) by Danilo Montaldi.

———   Johnson–Forest Tendency, *Balance Sheet: Trotskyism in the United States, 1940-47,* The Workers Party and the Johnson–Forest Tendency, August 1947.

———   C.L.R. James, "Dialectical Materialism and the Fate of Humanity," in C.L.R. James, *Spheres of Existence: Selected Writings,* Westport: Lawrence Hill & Co., 1980, pp. 70–105. Originally published as a pamphlet in September 1947.

1948   C.L.R. James, *Notes on Dialectics: Hegel–Marx–Lenin,* Westport: Lawrence Hill & Co., 1980. First published 1948.

———   C.L.R. James, "The Revolutionary Answer to the Negro Problem in the USA," New York. Reprinted in *The Future in the Present,* pp. 119–127.

1950   C.L.R. James, with Raya Dunayevskaya and Grace Lee, *State Capitalism and World Revolution,* Chicago: Charles H. Kerr, 1986. Originally published 1950.

1952   Martin Glaberman, *Punching Out,* Detroit: Correspondence Publishing Committee. Reprinted 1973 by Bewick Editions. [Address below.]

———   C.L.R. James, *Mariners, Renegades and Castaways: The Story of Herman Melville and the World We Live In,* Detroit: Bewick Editions, 1978. Originally written in 1952 and published in 1953.

1955   Martin Glaberman, *Union Committeemen and Wildcat Strikes,* Detroit: Correspondence Publishing Committee. [Available from Bewick Editions.]

1956   C.L.R. James, *Every Cook Can Govern: A Study of Democracy in Ancient Greece,* Correspondence Pamphlet #2, June. Originally published in *Correspondence,* Vol. 2, #12.

1958   C.L.R. James, Grace C. Lee, and Pierre Chaulieu [pseudonym of Cornelius Castoriadis], *Facing Reality: The New Society... Where to look for it, How to bring it closer. A Statement for Our Time,* Detroit: Bewick Editions, 1974. Originally published by the Correspondence Publishing Committee in 1958. [Available from: Bewick Editions, address below.]

———   Raya Dunayevskaya, *Marxism and Freedom,* London: Pluto (4th edition: 1975).

1961   J.R. Johnson [C.L.R. James], *Marxism and the Intellectuals,* Facing Reality Publishing Company, May 1962. Originally written in 1961.

1964   Martin Glaberman, *Negro Americans Take the Lead,* A Facing Reality Pamphlet, Detroit: Facing Reality Publishing Committee, September.

1965   Martin Glaberman, "Be His Payment High or Low," *The American Working Class of the Sixties,* Detroit: Bewick, 1966, 1975. Originally published in *International Socialism,* #21, Summer 1965 and *Liberated Guardian,* June 3, 1970. [Available from: Bewick Editions, address below.]

1967   W. Jerome and A. Buick, "Soviet State Capitalism? The History of an Idea," *Survey* 62, January, pp. 58–71.

_____   Guy Debord, *Society of the Spectacle,* Detroit: Black & Red, 1983. Originally Guy Debord, *La Société du Spectacle,* Paris: Ed. Buchet–Chastel, 1967.

_____   Raya Dunayevskaya, *State Capitalism and Marx's Humanism, or Philosophy and Revolution,* Detroit: News & Letters. [Address below.]

_____   C.L.R. James, "Peasants and Workers," in C.L.R. James, *Spheres of Existence,* pp. 191–220. Originally written in 1967 and published in *Radical America,* November 1971.

_____   C.L.R. James, "Black Power," in *Spheres of Existence,* pp. 221–236. Originally written in August 1967.

1969   George Rawick, "Working Class Self-Activity," *Radical America,* Vol. 3, #2, March–April 1969, pp. 23–31.

_____   Dario Fo, *Mistero Buffo,* (English translation by Ed Emery) London: Methuen, 1988. (Originally copyrighted by Dario Fo in 1969).

_____   "Battle in Corso Traiano," in Big Flame, *Italy: New Tactics and Organization,* July 1971 pp. 21–28. Originally in *La Classe,* #10, July, 1969.

_____   "Organizing at Fiat," in *Italy: New Tactics and Organization,* pp. 7–19. Originally in *La Classe,* #13-14, August 1969.

_____   A. Sofri, "Organizing for Workers' Power," *Rising Free* Reprint 3, 1973, pp. 1–12. Translated from *Les Temps Modernes,* Oct. 1969, #279, pp. 435–445.

1970   "The Line Delegates," in *Italy: New Tactics and Organization,* pp. 31–35. Originally *Lotta Continua,* #4, Feb. 14, 1970.

_____   News & Letters (National Editorial Board), *American Civilization on Trial: Black Masses as Vanguard,* A News & Letters Pamphlet, Detroit: News & Letters, August. [Address below.]

_____   Offord Road Collective, "Proposal for a Marxist-Leninist Study /Intervention Group on British Capitalism and Class Struggles," typescript, London, December 1970. [Available from the Texas Archives, address below.]

_____   C.L.R. James, "The Atlantic Slave Trade," in *The Future in the Present,* pp. 235–264. Originally published in *Amistad,* #I, 1970.

1971   Offord Road Collective, "Notes on the Present Phase of Class Struggle in Britain, and Implications for Work by the Study Group on Britain," typescript, London, Feb. 5. [Available from the Texas Archives, address below.]

_____   Big Flame, *Italy: New Tactics and Organization,* July.

_____   J.M. / C.M.[probably John Merrington & Christian Marazzi], "Notes of Strategic Analysis of Class Struggle: Class Composition/Recomposition," (typescript) London, July. [Available from the Texas Archives, address below.]

_____   Offord Road Collective, "The Network of Struggles in Italy (Alquati)," London. [Available from the Texas Archives, address below.]

1972   Guido Baldi [Silvia Federici and Mario Montano], "Theses on Mass Worker and Social Capital," *Radical America,* Vol. 6, No. 3, May–June, pp. 3–21.

_____   Raya Dunayevskaya, *For the Record: The Johnson–Forest Tendency, or The Theory of State-Capitalism, 1941–51; its vicissitudes and ramifications,* News & Letters, July. [Address below.]

—— Bruno Ramirez, "Review of *Operaie e Stato*," *Telos*, #13, Fall, pp. 140–147.

—— Matin Glaberman, "Unions vs. Workers in the Seventies: The Rise of Militancy in the Auto Industry," in Martin Glaberman, *The Working Class and Social Change: Four Essays on the Working Class*, Toronto: New Hogtown Press, 1975. pp. 20-27. First appeared in *Society*, November–December 1972. [Available from: Bewick Editions]

—— Guiliana Pompei, "Wages for Housework," in Montréal Power of Women Collective, "What is Wages for Housework?" January, 1975. (Originally 1972.)

—— George Rawick, *From Sundown to Sunup: The Making of the Black Community*, Greenwood: Westport.

—— Gilles Deleuze and Félix Guatarri, *Anti–Oedipus: Capitalism and Schizophrenia*, Minneapolis: University of Minnesota Press, 1983. Originally: Gilles Deleuze and Félix Guatarri, *Anti–L'Oedipe*, Paris: Éditions de Minuit, 1972.

—— News & Letters, *Black, Brown and Red: the Movement for Freedom Among Black, Chicano, Latino and Indian*, Detroit: News & Letters Committees. [Address below.]

1973 Gisela Bock, "Italian Analysis of Class Struggle and the State," *Kapitalistate*, #1, May, pp. 121–122.

—— Suzie Fleming, *The Family Allowance Under Attack*, London, June.

—— Selma James, "Women, the Unions and Work, or ....What is Not To Be Done," *Radical America*, 7, nos. 4-5, July–October, pp. 51–72.

—— Martin Glaberman, "The American Working Class in Historical Perspective," in *The Working Class and Social Change*, pp. 35–41. First appeared in *Radical America*, Vol 7, No. 6, November–December 1973. [Available from: Bewick Editions, address below.]

—— Power of Women Collective (London), "The Perspective of Wages for Housework," in Montréal Power of Women Collective, "What is Wages for Housework? typescript, January 1975, pp. 10–11. Originally 1973.

—— Félix Guattari, "Molecular Revolution and Class Struggle," in Félix Guattari, *The Molecular Revolution: Psychiatry and Politics*, Penguin, 1984, pp. 253–261. Félix Guattari, *La Révolution Moleculaire*, 1977. Originally written 1973.

1974 Martin Glaberman, "Review of *False Promises*," in *The Working Class and Social Change: Four Essays on the Working Class*, pp. 28–34. First appeared in *Liberation*, February 1974. [Available from Bewick Editions, address below.]

—— Power of Women Collective, *Power of Women*, Vol. 1, #2, July/August 1974.

—— Martin Glaberman, "Marxist Views of the Working Class," in *The Working Class and Social Change*, pp. 3–19. Originally written in September, 1974. [Available from Bewick Editions, address below.]

—— John Zerzan, "Organized Labor Versus 'The Revolt Against Work'," *Telos*, #21, Autumn, pp. 194–206. Reprinted in: John Zerzan, *Creation and Its Enemies: "The Revolt Against Work,"* Rochester: Mutualist Books, 1977.

—— Rising Free, *Take Over the City*, Rising Free Pamphlet, 1974(?)

—— Modern Times, "The Social Factory," *Falling Wall Review*, #5, Bristol.

—— Nicole Cox and Silvia Federici, *Counterplanning from the Kitchen: Wages for Housework, A Perspective on Capital and the Left*, 1975. Written 1974.

—— Modern Times Collective (Cleveland), "The Social Factory," *The Activist*, #36,

Vol. 15, #1–2, Spring 1975, pp. 38-41. Also in *Falling Wall Review, #5,* Bristol, England, 1974.

Silvia Federici, *Wages Against Housework,* pamphlet, April, 1985. Written 1974. Reprinted in Ellen Malos (ed.), *The Politics of Housework,* Allison & Busby, London 1980.

1975   Silvia Federici, "When Wages for Housework Becomes a Perspective," in Montréal Power of Women Collective, "What is Wages for Housework?" typescript, January, pp. 12–18. [Available from the Texas Archives, address below.]

Power of Women Collective, *Power of Women,* Vol. 1, #3, January.

Montréal Power of Women Collective, "What is Wages for Housework?" typescript, January 1975. [Available from the Texas Archives, address below.]

Suzie Fleming, "All Women are Housewives," *The Activist,* Vol. 15, #1–2, Spring, pp. 10–20.

Wages for Housework Collective (Windsor), "Portrait of a Canadian Housewife," *The Activist,* Vol. 15, #1–2, Spring, pp. 10-20.

Wages for Housework Collective (Toronto), "Wages for Housework: Questions and Answers," *The Activist,* Vol. 15, #1–2, Spring, pp. 21–24.

Wages Due Collective, "Fucking is Work," *The Activist,* Vol. 15, #1–2, Spring, pp. 25–26.

Sylvia Gentile and Betsy Lewis, "History of Our Collective (Oberlin, Ohio)," *The Activist,* Vol. 15, #1–2, Spring, pp. 34–37.

Silvia Federici and Selma James, "Notes on the Leninist Party," (typescript) New York. [Available from the Texas Archives, address below.]

Wendy Edmond and Suzie Fleming (eds.) *All Work and No Pay: Women, Housework and the Wages Due,* Bristol: Falling Wall Press.

Mario Montano, "Notes on the International Crisis, " *Zerowork* #1, December, pp. 33–60. [Available from the Texas Archives, address below.]

Peter Linebaugh & B. Ramirez, "Crisis in the Auto Sector, " *Zerowork* #1, December, pp. 61–85. [Available from Texas Archives, address below.]

Peter Taylor, " 'The Sons of Bitches Just Won't Work:' Postal Workers Against the State," *Zerowork* #1, December, pp. 86–113. [Available from Texas Archives, below.]

William Cleaver, "Wild Cats in the Appalachian Coal fields," *Zerowork* #1, December, pp. 114–127. [Available from the Texas Archives, address below.]

George Caffentzis, "Throwing Away the Ladder: Universities in the Crisis," *Zerowork* #1, pp. 128-142. [Available from Texas Archives, address below.]

Bruno Ramirez, "Working Class Struggle Against the Crisis: Self-Reduction Struggles in Italy," *Zerowork* #1, pp. 143–150. [Available from Texas Archives, below.]

Peter Linebaugh, "The Tyburn Riot Against the Surgeons," in Douglas Hay et al., *Albion's Fatal Tree: Crime and Society in Eighteenth Century England,* New York: Pantheon, pp. 65–117.

Selma James, *Sex, Race, and Class,* Bristol: Falling Wall Press. [Available from Wages for Housework, address below.]

Martin Glaberman, *The Working Class and Social Change: Four Essays on the Working Class,* Toronto: New Hogtown Press. [Available from: Bewick Ed., address below.]

1976   Wendy Schuman, "Brooklyn Women Seek Wages for Housework," *The New York Times*, January 11.

—   Big Flame, "Workers' Struggles and the Development of Ford in Britain," *Bulletin of the Conference of Socialist Economists*, Vol. VI (#13) March.

—   Harry Cleaver, "The Internationalization of Capital and the Mode of Production in Agriculture," *Economic and Political Weekly*, March 27, pp. A2–A16.

—   Tim Grant, "Student as Worker: Wages for Homework," *The Sheaf*, March 26, 1976, pp. 4–5.

—   Peter Linebaugh, "Karl Marx, the Theft of Wood and Working Class Composition," *Crime and Social Justice*, Fall–Winter 1976, pp. 5–16.

—   Wages for Housework Collective (Los Angeles), *Wages for Housework Newsletter*, Vol. 1, #3, November.

—   Christian Marazzi (with John Merrington and Mike Sohenscher), "Money in the World Crisis: The New Basis of Capitalist Power," typescript, December.

—   Struggle Against Work Collective (Toronto), "The Perspective of the Working Class Struggle in the 1970s: Suggested Readings," 1976 (?).

—   Red Notes, *A Battle for Power — the Motor Industry Crisis in Britain 1975-76*, London: Red Notes.

—   Angela Terrano, Marie Dignon and Mary Holmes, *Working Women for Freedom*, Detroit: News & Letters. [Address below.]

—   M. Franki and J. Hillstrom, *America's First Unfinished Revolution: The Untold Story of the True Creators of Independence — the Workers, Yeomanry, Blacks and Women*, Detroit: News & Letters. [Address below.]

—   The Wages for Students Students, *Wages for Students*, Amherst.

—   Income Without Work Committee, *We Want Everything: An Introduction to the Income Without Work Committee*, Brooklyn.

—   George Caffentzis, "Not URPE but Machiavelli," typescript, 1976(?).

—   Larry Cox, "If We're So Powerful, Why Aren't We Free? White Men, The Total Wage and the Struggle Against Work," typescript, 1976 (?).

—   Silvia Federici & Mariarosa Dalla Costa, "Crisis and Revolution," 1976(?).

1977   Harry Cleaver, "Malaria, The Politics of Public Health and the International Crisis," *Review of Radical Political Economics*, Spring, pp. 81–103.

—   News & Letters, *On the 100th Anniversary of the First General Strike in the US*, News & Letters, June. [Address below.]

—   Peter Bell, "Zerowork: The Historical Background to the Theoretical Perspective," Notes on a Conversation with John Merrington, typescript, October 20.

—   Cornelius Castoriadis, "From Bolshevism to the Bureaucracy," *Our Generation*, 12, #2, Fall, pp. 43–54.

—   *Zerowork* #2 (New York). [Available from Texas Archives, address below.]

—   Zerowork Collective, "Introduction," *Zerowork* #2, pp. 1–6.

—   Harry Cleaver, "Food, Famine and International Crisis," *Zerowork* #2, pp. 7–70.

—   Philip Mattera, "National Liberation, Socialism and The Struggle Against Work: The Case of Vietnam," *Zerowork* #2 , pp. 71–90.

—   Christian Marazzi, "Money in the World Crisis: The New Basis of Capitalist Power," *Zerowork* #2, pp. 91–111.

—   Donna Demac & Philip Mattera, "Developing and Underdeveloping New York: The 'Fiscal Crisis' and the Imposition of Austerity," *Zerowork* #2, pp. 113–139.

—   Bruce Allen *Poland 1976: State Capitalism in Crisis*, (pamphlet) Edmonton:

Black Cat Press, 1979. Written in June.)

____ Andre Liebich, "Socialism ou Barbarie, a Radical Critique of Bureaucracy," *Our Generation*, 12, #2, Fall, pp. 55–62.

____ "Italy: Documents of Struggle," *Ripening of Time*, #12.

____ "The Other Side," *Ripening of Time*, #13.

____ Peter F. Bell, "Marxist Theory, Class Struggle and the Crisis of Capitalism," in Jesse Schwartz (ed.), *The Subtle Anatomy of Capitalism*, Santa Monica: Goodyear, pp. 170–194.

____ Red Notes, *The Class Struggle in Portugal: Chronology and Texts of 1976*, London: Red Notes.

____ Peter Linebaugh, "The Ordinary of Newgate and His Account," in J.S. Cockburn (ed), *Crime in England 1550–1800*, Princeton: Princeton University Press, pp. 246–269.

____ Raya Dunayevskaya, *New Essays*, Detroit: News & Letters. [Address below.]

____ Red Notes, *A Songbook*, London: Red Notes, 1977 (?).

____ John Zerzan, "Creation and Its Enemies: The Revolt Against Work," Rochester: Mutualist Books.

1978 Raya Dunayevskaya, *Marx's Capital and Today's Global Crisis*, Detroit: News & Letters, January. [Address below.]

____ Red Notes, *Fighting Layoffs at Ford*, London: Red Notes.

____ Lou Turner, and John Alan, *Frantz Fanon, Soweto and American Black Thought*, Detroit: News & Letters, June. [Address below.]

____ Peter Bell, "Cycles of Class Struggle in Thailand," *Journal of Contemporary Asia*, Vol. 8, #1, pp. 51–79.

____ Housewive's Initiative & Women's Action Group, *Taking What's Ours: Everywoman's Guide to Welfare and Student Aid*, Toronto.

____ Red Notes, *Italy 1977–78: Living with an Earthquake*, London: Red Notes.

____ Bruno Ramirez, *When Workers Fight: The Politics of Industrial Relations in the Progressive Era, 1898-1916*, Westport: Greenwood Press.

1979 Guy Debord, "Preface To The Fourth Italian Edition," *The Society of the Spectacle*, London: Chronos Publications, October. (Written in January.)

____ Thomas Sheehan, "Italy: Behind the Ski Mask," *New York Review of Books*, August 16, pp. 20–26.

____ Diana Johnstone, "Autonomous Left," *In These Times*, Sept. 5–11, pp. 10–11.

____ Harry Cleaver, *Reading Capital Politically*, Austin: University of Texas Press.

____ "Class Autonomy: A Chronology" (in Italy) in *Working Class Autonomy and the Crisis*, pp. vii–x.

____ CARI [Committee Against Repression in Italy], *Bulletin* #1.

____ Midnight Notes Collective, "Strange Victories: The Anti-Nuclear Movement in the U.S. and Europe," *Midnight Notes*, Vol. I, #1. [Address below.]

____ Raya Dunayevskaya, *Outline of Marx's "Capital Volume One,"* News & Letters. [Address below.]

1980 Harry Cleaver, "Technology as Political Weaponry," in Robert S. Anderson, et al., *Science, Politics and the Agricultural Revolution in Asia*, American Association for the Advancement of Science, Boulder: Westview Press, pp. 261–276. Originally written January.

___ Martin Glaberman, "To the Editors," [Re: Sheehan article on Negri in *NYRB*, August 16, 1979] *New York Review of Books*, April 17, p. 46.

___ Phil Mattera, "Small is not Beautiful: Decentralized Production and the Underground Economy in Italy," *Radical America*, Vol. 14, #5, Sept.-Oct., pp. 67–76.

___ Devon Peña, "Las Maquiladores: Mexican Women and Class Struggle in the Border Industries," *Aztlan: International Journal of Chicano Studies Research*, Vol. 11, #2, Fall, pp. 159-229.

___ Martin Glaberman, *Wartime Strikes: The Struggle Against the No-Strike Pledge in the UAW During W.W.II*, Detroit: Bewick Editions. [Address below.]

___ C.L.R. James, *Spheres of Existence: Selected Writings*, Westport: Lawrence Hill & Co.

___ Midnight Notes, *The Work/Energy Crisis and the Apocalypse*, Jamaica Plain, Mass. [Address below.]

___ Ellen Malos (ed.), *The Politics of Housework*, London: Allison & Busby.

___ Midnight Notes, "No Future Notes: The Work/Energy Crisis and the Anti-Nuclear Movement," *Midnight Notes*, Vol. I, #2 [Address below.]

___ Ronnie J. Phillips, "Global Austerity: The Evolution of the International Monetary System and World Capitalist Development, 1945–1978," Ph.D. Dissertation, University of Texas at Austin.

___ Eddi Cherki and Michel Wieviorka, "Autoreduction Movements in Turin," *Autonomia: Post-Political Politics*, Semiotext(e), New York, pp. 72-78.

___ Félix Guattari, "The Proliferation of Margins," *Autonomia: Post Political Politics*, Semiotext(e), New York, pp. 108-111. [Address below.]

___ Paul Virilio, "Popular Defense and Popular Assault," *Autonomia: Post Political Politics*, Semiotext(e), New York, pp. 266-272. [Address below.].

___ Silvia Federici, "Restructuring of Social Reproduction in the U. S. in the 70's," Paper presented at German Marshall Fund conference on "Economic Policies of Female Labor in Italy and the United States," Rome, Italy, December 9-11.

___ Raya Dunayevskaya, "Hegel's Absolute as New Beginning," in W.E. Steinkraus and K.L.Schmitz, *Art and Logic in Hegel's Philosophy*, Humanities Press. Also available as reprint from News and Letters.

___ Sojourner Truth Organization, *Workplace Papers*, Chicago.

___ Gilles Deleuze and Félix Guattari, "Rhizome," in G. Deleuze and F. Guattari, *A Thousand Plateaus: Capitalism and Schizophrenia*, Mineapolis: Univ. of Minnesota Press, pp. 3–25, 518–521. (Published in French in 1980.) Also available in *On the Line*, New York: Semiotext(e), 1983, [Address below.]

1981 J.-P. Faye, F. Guattari, G. Deleuze, P. Halbwachs, C. Benetti, "Appeal for the Formation of an International Commission to Inquire about the Italian Judiciary Situation and the Situation in Italian Jails," Translated from French, January.

___ John Fraser, "The Inner Contradictions of Marxism and Political Violence: The Case of the Italian Left," *Social Research*, Vol. 48, #1, Spring, pp. 21–44.

___ Peter Linebaugh, "Suppose C.L.R. James had Met E.P.Thompson in 1792..." typescript, March. Published in *Urgent Tasks*, #12, Summer, pp. 108–110.

___ Devon Peña, "Maquiladores: A Select Annotated Bibliography and Critical Commentary on the United States-Mexico Border Industry Program," *Human Resources Bibliography Series*, #7–81. Austin: Center for the Study of Human Resources, June.

___ Paul Buhle, "Marxism in the USA," *Urgent Tasks*, #12, Summer, pp. 28–38.

___ George Rawick, "Personal Notes," *Urgent Tasks*, #12, Summer, pp. 118–121.

Robert Hill, "In England, 1932–1938," *Urgent Tasks,* #12, Summer, pp. 19–27.

Walter Rodney, "African Revolution," *Urgent Tasks,* #12, Summer, pp. 5–13.

Ferrucio Gambino, "Only Connect," *Urgent Tasks,* #12, Summer, pp. 95–96.

Paul Lawrence Berman, "Facing Reality," *Urgent Tasks,* #12, Summer, 105–107.

Dan Georgakis, "Young Detroit Radicals: 1955–1965," *Urgent Tasks,* #12, Summer, pp. 89–94.

Ferruccio Gambino, "Spaces for Marxism in Italy," *URPE Newsletter,* Vol. 13, #6, November–December, pp. 8-11.

Harry Cleaver, "Special Preface to the Mexican Edition" of *Reading Capital Politically.* Written in 1981; appeared in *Una Lectura Política del "El Capital,"* Mexico: Fondo de Cultura Economica, 1985, pp. 29-55.

Midnight Notes, "Space Notes," *Midnight Notes,* Vol. II, #2. [Address below.]

Peter Linebaugh, "All the Atlantic Mountains Shook," *Labour / Le Travailleur,* #10, Autumn, pp. 87–121. Written 1981.

Joseph Ricciardi, "Class Struggle, Classical Economists and Factory Acts: Towards a 'Reformulation'," *Research in Political Economy,* Vol. 4, pp. 81-100.

Martin Glaberman, " 'Let the Capitalists fight the Car Wars,': U.S. Auto Workers Visit Japan," *AMPO: Japan–Asia Quaterly Review,* Vol. 13, #1.

Claire Sterling, "The Ishutin Solution," in C. Sterling, *The Terror Network,* 1981, pp. 202–227, 328–333.

C.L.R. James, *80th Birthday Lectures,* London: Race Today. (Lectures originally given 6th, 9th and 12th January 1981.)

C.L.R. James, *Walter Rodney and the Question of Power,* London: Race Today. (Pamphlet.) (Originally a speech given on January 30, 1981 at Walter Rodney memorial symposium.) [Available from *Race Today,* address below.]

1982   Philip Mattera, "Euroterrorism and Eurocommunism," *Socialist Review,* #61 (12:1), January–February, pp. 121–133.

New Haven Collective, "Poland, Dec. 13: Murder on the Orient Express," *URPE Newsletter,* Vol. 14, #1, Jan / Feb, pp. 3–9.

Wages for Housework, *International Campaign Journal,* Spring.

Riot Not to Work Collective, *We Want to Riot, Not to Work: The 1981 Brixton Uprisings,* London, April, 1982. [Available from: PDC, Bldg K, Albion Yard, 17a Balfe St., London, N1]

Estevan T. Flores, "Post-Bracero Undocumented Mexican Immigration to the U.S. and Political Recomposition," Ph.D. Dissertation, Univ. of Texas, May.

Peter Linebaugh, "Crime and Industrialization: 18th Century Britain," Paper for the XII Congress of the International Political Science Assoc., Brazil, August.

Kevin Anderson, "Rubel's Marxology versus Marx's Marxism," December.

Committee Against Repression in Italy (CARI), *The Italian Inquisition.*

Midnight Notes, "Computer State Notes," *Midnight Notes,* Vol. III, #1.

Raya Dunayevskaya, "Marx's and Luxemburg's Theories of Accumulation of Capital, its Crises and its Inevitable Downfall," in *Rosa Luxemburg, Women's Liberation and Marx's Philosophy of Revolution,* pp. 31–50.

Devon Peña, "Invisible World of Work: US Factories on Mexico's Northern Border," A series of six articles prepared for publication in *The Laredo News.*

Peter F. Bell and Harry Cleaver, "Marx's Crisis Theory as a Theory of Class Struggle," in *Research in Political Economy,* Vol. 5, pp. 189–261.

Michael Ryan, *Marxism and Deconstruction,* Baltimore: Johns Hopkins UP.

1983   Harry Cleaver, "Notes on the Present Stage of the Crisis," Paper for Sojourner Truth Organization Conference, January.

———   Harry Cleaver, "Karl Marx: Economist or Revolutionary?" in Suzanne W. Helburn and David F. Bramhall (eds.), *Marx, Schumpeter & Keynes: A Centenary Celebration of Dissent*, Armonk: M. E. Sharpe, pp. 121-146. Written 1983.

———   Midnight Notes, "Posthumous Notes," *Midnight Notes*, #6. [Address below.]

———   Estevan T. Flores, "Chicanos and Sociological Research: 1970-1980," in Isidro D. Ortiz (ed.), *Chicanos and the Social Sciences: A Decade of Research and Development (1970-1980)*, Santa Barbara: Center for Chicano Studies, pp. 19–45.

———   Gilles Deleuze and Félix Guattari, "Rhizomes," in G. Deleuze and F. Guattari, *On the Line*, Foreign Agent Series, New York: Semiotext(e), pp. 1–55.

———   CARI, *Dossier on Torture and Prison Conditions in Italy: 1979-83*.

1984   Andy Philips, *The Coal Miners General Strike of 1949–50 and the Birth of Marxist-Humanism in the United States*, Detroit: News & Letters, June.

———   Devon Peña, "Immigration and Social Work," *Aztlan*, 15:2, Fall.

———   Midnight Notes, "Lemming Notes," *Midnight Notes* #7, [Address below.]

1985   Solomon Izielen Agbon, "Class Struggle and Economic Development in Nigeria: 1900-1980," Ph.D. Dissertation, Univ. of Texas, Austin, Texas, May.

———   Bruno Ramirez, "In Search of a Lost Culture,"*VisaVersa*, #1, May/June, p. 20.

———   Gustavo Esteva, "Cease Aid, Stop Development: An Answer to Hunger," Aug.

———   Ron Brokmeyer, "The Fetish of High Tech: Marx's Mathematical Manuscripts vs. 'Computer Consciousness'," News and Letters, September, pp. 1-14.

———   Yann Moulier-Boutang, "Resistance to the Political Representation of Alien Populations: The European Paradox," *International Migration Review*, Vol. XIX, #3, Fall, pp. 485-492.

———   Harry Cleaver, "Development or Autonomy," Paper presented to a Conference in México City on México al Fino del Siglo XXI, November.

———   Joseph Ricciardi, "Essays on the Role of Money and Finance in Economic Development," Ph.D. Dissertation, University of Texas.

———   Ann Lucas de Rouffignac, *The Contemporary Peasantry in Mexico: A Class Analysis*, Praeger, New York.

———   Philip Mattera, *Off the Books*, New York: St. Martin's Press and London: Pluto.

———   Don Parson, "Plan and Counterplan: Notes on Moving Beyond the Crisis in Planning Theory," *Contemporary Crises*, #9, pp. 55-74.

———   P.M., *Bolo Bolo*, New York: Semiotext(e). [Address below).]

———   Midnight Notes, "Outlaw Notes," *Midnight Notes*, #8. [Address below.]

———   Raya Dunayevskaya, "Dialectics of Revolution: American Roots and Marx's World Humanist Concepts," *News & Letters*, April, pp. 5, 7-8. A slightly different version appears as the introduction to the fourth edition of her *Marxism and Freedom*, New York: Columbia University Press, 1988, pp. 1-12.

1986   Paul Buhle, *C.L.R. James His Life and Work*, London: Allison & Busby.

———   Harry Cleaver, "The Use of an Earthquake,"*Visa Versa* December/January 1987, pp. 33-35. (Written 1986.) Reprinted in *Midnight Notes* #9, 1989 (Boston) and *Commonsense* #9, 1989 (Scotland).

———   Devon Peña, "Between the Lines: A New Perspective on the Industrial Sociology of Women in Transnational Labor Process," in Teresa Cordova, et al., (eds.), *Chicana Voices: Intersections of Class, Race and Gender.* Austin: Center for Mexican American Studies and University of Texas Press, April.

—— Peter Linebaugh, "In the Flight Path of Perry Anderson," *History Workshop,* #21, Spring, pp. 141-146.

—— Ricardo D. Salvatore, "Labor Control and Discrimination: The Contratista System in Mendoza, Argentina, 1880-1920," *Agricultural History,* Vol. 60, #3, Summer 1986, pp. 52-80.

—— James H. Johnson, "Worker-State Conflict in Revolutionary Nicaragua: A Marxist Critique," M.A. Thesis, University of Texas at Austin, December.

—— Estevan T. Flores, "The Mexican-Origin People in the United States and Marxist Thought in Chicano Studies," in B. Ollman and E. Vernoff (eds.), *The Left Academy: Marxist Scholarship on American Campuses,* Vol. III, New York: Praeger, pp. 103-137.

1987 Ricardo Salvatore, "Class Struggle and International Trade: Rio de la Plata's Commerce and the Atlantic Proletariat, 1790-1850," Ph.D. Dissertation, University of Texas at Austin.

—— Vivienne Bennett, "Urban Water Services and Social Conflict: The Water Crisis in Monterrey, Mexico, 1973-1985," Ph.D. Dissertation, Univ. of Texas.

—— Captain Nemo, "Thoughts on the Machine: A Pamphlet," English translation of German edition, Zurich, March.

1988 Gustavo Esteva, "Tradifas, or the End of Marginality," (typescript) May 1988.

—— Midnight Notes, "The Paper is not Blank: The Paperworkers Strike of Jay, Maine," Jay, Maine, September.

—— Raya Dunayevskaya, "The Letter of May 12, 1953" and "The Letter of May 20, 1953," (on Hegel's Absolutes) with an introduction by the Resident Editorial Board, News & Letters, November, pp. 5-9.

—— Martin Glaberman, "Shop Floor Struggles of American Workers," paper delivered to the Conference on Workers' Self-Activity, St. Louis, November 11.

—— Raya Dunayevskaya, "A Post-World War II View of Marx's Humanism: 1843-83, Marxist Humanism in the 1950s and '80s," *Praxis International,* Vol. 8, #3, pp. 360-371.

—— Paul Buhle, *C.L.R. James: The Artist as Revolutionary,* New York: Verso.

1989 George Caffentzis, *Clipped Coins, Abused Words, and Civil Government: John Locke's Philosophy of Money,* New York: Autonomedia. [Address below.]

—— Harry Cleaver, "Comments on Dunayevskaya's 1953 letters on Hegel's Absolutes," *News & Letters,* Vol. 34, #3, April 1989, p. 9.

—— Martin Glaberman, "Workers Versus Unions in the Coal Industry," [reply to Herbert Hill] *International Journal of Politics, Culture and Society,* Vol. 2, #3, Spring.

—— Raya Dunayevskaya, *The Philosophic Moment of Marxist–Humanism.* Chicago, News and Letters. [Address below.]

Journals and Newspapers

American Owl (American — defunct)
Autonomia: ettimanale Politico Comunista (Italian — current)
Autonomie (German — ?)
Autonomie Ouvrière (French — defunct)
Babylone (French — current)
Camarades: Revue Militante dans L'Autonomie (French — defunct)
Combat Pour L'Autonomie Ouvrère (French — defunct)
CONTROinformazione (Italian — defunct)
Cultural Correspondence (American — defunct)
Desvios (Brazilian — ?)
Jamais Contentes!!, Journal de Femmes Autonomes (French — defunct)
Metropoli (Italian — defunct)
Midnight Notes (American — current)
Le Operaie della Casa (Italian — ?)
Primo Maggio (Italian — current)
Quaderni Rossi (Italian — defunct)
Quaderni del Territorio (Italian — ?)
ROSSO (Italian — defunct)
Semiotext(e) (American — current)
I VOLSCI: Mensile dell' autonomia operaia romana (Italian — defunct)
Wages for Housework Campaign Bulletin (International — ?)
Wildcat (German — current)
Zerowork (American — defunct)

For Further Reference

Autonomedia / Semiotext(e), P.O. Box 568, Brooklyn, New York 11211-0568.
Bewick Editions, P.O. Box 14140, Detroit, Michigan, 48214.
The Raya Dunayevskaya Collection, Archives of Labor and Urban Affairs, Wayne State University, Detroit, Michigan, 48202. A guide to the collection is available from News & Letters, 59 East Van Buren St., Room 707, Chicago, Illinois, 60605.
The Martin & Jessie Glaberman Collection, Archives of Labor and Urban Affairs, Wayne State University, Detroit, Michigan, 48202. A guide to the collection is available from the Wayne State Archives.
Midnight Notes, POB 204, Jamaica Plain, Massachusetts 02130
The *Red Notes* Italian Archives, BP 15, 2a St. Paul's Road, London, England N1. A listing of archival holdings is available.
Race Today, 165 Railton Road (Brixton) London, England SE2 0LU.
Semiotext(e), 522 Philosophy Hall, Columbia University, New York, New York 10027
Texas Archives of Autonomist Marxism, c/o Harry Cleaver & Conrad Herold, Department of Economics, University of Texas, Austin, Texas, 78712. A listing of the collection is available, there are regular supplements, and Archive materials otherwise unavailable can be obtained at costs of reproduction and mailing.
Wages for Housework Campaign, P.O.Box 14512, San Francisco, CA 94114.

Index

Abstinence, Marx's critique of, 72

Abstract labor, 10, 130, 133, 183

Alienation, 34

Althusser, Louis, vii, xiv, 154

Antagonism: 4, 9, 10, 12–14, 18, 23, 77, 194; of the categories of capital, 54; determines movement of capital, 73; of labor and capital, 67–68; logic of, xxi, 31, 166, 175; as motor of development, 54; and money, 26

Armed struggle, 198, 200

Asor Rosa, Alberto, ix

Automation, 204

Autonomia: vii, ix, xii, xxviii, xxxii, xxxiii, xxxviii; vocabulary of, xi-xiii

Autonomous committees, ix

Autonomy: as destabilization, 214; as destructuration, 214; of wage labor, 68; of the political, 200, 205, 219; as refusal of economic development, 214; rigidity of, 186 (See also *Autonomia*)

Autoreduction, 212

Avanguardia Operaio, ix

Bastiat, 53–54, 55

Bianchini, Guido, viii

Bologna, Sergio, viii, ix, xxviii, 2, 18, 25

Bravo, Luciano Ferrari, viii

Brigada Rosa, (See Red Brigades)

Cacciari, Massimo, viii

Capital: and capitalists, 75–76, 110; in general, 120; limits to development of, 80–81; moved by class struggle, 116; as process, 66; as social capital, 114; as subject, 76, 123; as totality of labor and life, 122; as working class use value, 148, 207

Capital (Das): xix, xxvii, 9, 42, 120, 121, 122, 131, 132–133, 174, 187, 188; "Afterword", 12; and the *Grundrisse,* 5–9, 15–19, 27; Stalinist reading of, 16; Volume III, 137

Capital-logic, xxxiii, 132

Carey, 53–54, 55

Catastrophe, 2, 9, 72, 152, 158, 174, 196; and revolution, 98–99

Catastrophism, xv, 101–102, 143, 167

Circulation: xxiv; antagonism of, 34–35; of capital, 112; and collective class-subject, 106; and crisis, 94; as fabric of exploitation, 105; and reproduction, 213; produces socialization of capital, 114; and productive capital, 142, 177; small-scale, 134–139, 178; and theory of surplus value, 105; theory of introduces class struggle, 133

Civil society, 205, 207; CPI theory of, 211; subsumed by state, 213

Civil war, 203–204, 210

Class composition: 9, 11, 14, 111, 125, 136, 178–179, 202; as communist composition, 186; the displacement of, 180

Class hatred, 9, 18, 23

Class interest, xxvi

Class Politics, 219–220

Classe Operaia, ix, xxviii

Codetermination, 208

Coin, 119

Collective administration, 209

Collective capitalist, 77

Collective worker, 77, 146

Command, the material of money, 61

Commodity form, 10, 39

Communism: xxv, xxxvii, 2, 9 148, 149–150, 198; as abolition of work,